ISRAEL'S OCCUPATION

ISRAEL'S OCCUPATION

Neve Gordon

University of California Press   Berkeley   Los Angeles   London

University of California Press, one of the most distinguished
university presses in the United States, enriches lives around the
world by advancing scholarship in the humanities, social sciences,
and natural sciences. Its activities are supported by the UC Press
Foundation and by philanthropic contributions from individuals
and institutions. For more information, visit www.ucpress.edu.

University of California Press
Berkeley and Los Angeles, California

University of California Press, Ltd.
London, England

Library of Congress Cataloging-in-Publication Data

Gordon, Neve, 1965 –.
   Israel's Occupation / Neve Gordon.
      p.   cm.
   Includes bibliographical references and index.
   ISBN 978–0-520–25530–2 (cloth : alk. paper)
   ISBN 978–0-520–25531–9 (pbk. : alk. paper)
   1. Arab-Israeli conflict — Occupied territories.
2. Jews — Colonization — Government policy — West Bank.
3. Jews — Colonization — Government policy — Gaza Strip.
4. Israel — Politics and government — 1993 –.   5. West
Bank — Politics and government.   6. Gaza Strip — Politics and
government.   7. Palestinian Arabs — Politics and government.
8. Military occupation — Social aspects — West Bank.
9. Military occupation — Social aspects — Gaza Strip.
10. Arab-Israeli conflict.   I. Title.

DS119.7.G646   2008
956.9405′4 — dc22   2007052239

Manufactured in the United States of America
17   16   15   14   13   12   11   10   09
10   9   8   7   6   5   4   3

This book is printed on Natures Book, which contains 50%
post-consumer waste and meets the minimum requirements
of ANSI/NISO Z39.48 – 1992 (R 1997) (*Permanence of Paper*).

For my parents, Rachella and Haim

CONTENTS

ILLUSTRATIONS

TABLES

ABBREVIATIONS

DFLP   Democratic Front for the Liberation of Palestine
GSS   General Security Services
HRW   Human Rights Watch
IL   Israeli lira (old currency)
MO   military order
NGO   nongovernmental organization
OT   Occupied Territories
PA   Palestinian Authority
PFLP   Popular Front for the Liberation of Palestine
PLO   Palestinian Liberation Organization
PNF   Palestinian National Front
UNRWA   United Nations Relief and Work Agency

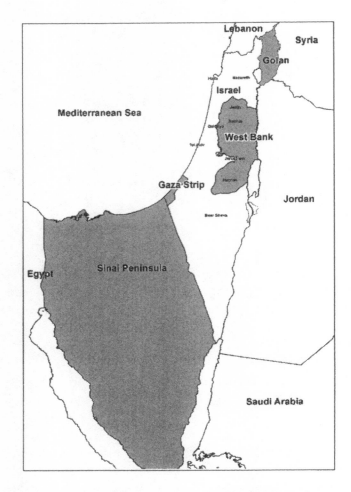

Map 1. Areas occupied by Israel during the 1967 War. Source: Peace
Now.

ACKNOWLEDGMENTS

This book could not have been written without the insights and support of numerous people. Yinon Cohen, Ariel Handel, Niels Hooper, Adi Ophir, Catherine Rottenberg, and Eyal Weizman read the whole manuscript and offered useful comments, as did the anonymous reviewers from the University of California Press. Lynne Alvarez, Efrat Ben-Ze'ev, Nitza Berkovitch, Robert Blecher, Wendy Brown, Roane Carey, Hillel Cohen, Dani Filc, Shira Robinson, James Ron, Gina Rucavado, Jacinda Swanson, and Yuval Yonay read different chapters, and their insightful suggestions helped me reshape my ideas as I revised the book. Yehezkel Lien from B'Tselem was an invaluable resource as I was writing, Hagit Ofran from Peace Now helped prepare the maps, and my research assistants, Dan Gurfinkel, Ohad Ivri, and Erela Portugaly, gathered useful material.

The idea for the book emerged as a result of my participation in the "Humanitarian Action in Catastrophe" group at Van Leer Institute in Jerusalem, where Tal Arbel, Sari Hanafi, Ariel Handel, Michal Givoni, Shir Hever, Ruthie Ginsburg, Adi Ophir, and several others underscored the urgent need to theorize Israel's occupation and helped me to formulate some of my thoughts about the operation of power in the West Bank and Gaza Strip. Conversations with Gadi Al Gazi, Yigal Bronner, Fred Dallmayr, Salomka Dunievitz, Irit Eshet, Farid Ghanem, Haim Gordon, Rivca Gordon, Ruchama Marton, Yoram Meital, Ann Pettifer, Uri

Rosenwaks, Amnon Sadovsky, Peter Walshe, Oren Yiftachel, as well as many of those mentioned above, forced me to think critically about the occupation. Others have simply been there over the years, supporting me and my work. Among them are Muhammad Abu Humus, Amnon Agmi, Barak Atzmon, Mordechai Gordon, Nitsan Gordon, Galila Spharim, Tal Yagil, Niza Yanay, Ariel Van Straten, and Gil Winraob. Members of the Department of Politics and Government at Ben-Gurion University have always stood by me, even in times of fierce attacks, and I would like to use this venue to express my deep gratitude to Lauren Basson, Dani Filc, Fred Lazin, Becky Kook, David Newman, Sharon Pardo, Renee Poznanski, Ahmad Sa'di, and Haim Yacobi, as well as to Nurit Klein and Anat Segal.

I began writing the book in 2004 during a sabbatical at the University of California, Berkeley, where Nezar AlSayyad from the Center for Middle Eastern Studies and Eric Stover from the Human Rights Center welcomed me and provided me with the necessary resources to write. I also want to take this opportunity to thank Wendy Brown and Judith Butler for making Berkeley a home away from home, and to express my gratitude to Beshara Doumani and Salim Tamari, who wittingly or unwittingly helped me gain a better perspective about the occupation's history. The Herzog Center for Middle East Studies at Ben-Gurion University provided me with the necessary resources to complete the work once I returned to Israel.

Finally, this book would not have been written without Catherine, Ariel, and Aviv, the three most important people in my life.

It took me a moment before I understood why my story about a few relatively inconsequential incidents, which occurred years ago at my high school, had such an effect on the undergraduates taking my course in the fall semester of 2006. One of the anecdotes was about my classmates who lived in the Jewish settlements located in the northern tip of the Sinai Peninsula. It was 1981, and the following year they would be forced to leave their homes as part of Israel's peace agreement with Egypt, but at the time, I told my students, the evacuation did not seem imminent, at least not in the minds of many teenagers for whom each year stretches without end. A particular issue that did occupy us, I continued, was learning to drive. I described to my students how my friends from the farming communities located in the Sinai and the small town of Yamit took their lessons in the Palestinian town of Rafah and were among the first to pass their driving tests.

My students found this story incomprehensible. They simply could not imagine Israeli teenagers taking driving lessons in the middle of Rafah, which, in their minds, is no more than a terrorist nest riddled with tunnels used to smuggle weapons from Egypt—weapons that are subsequently used against Israeli targets. The average age difference between me and my students is only 15 years, but our perspectives are radically different. Most of my students have never talked with Palestinians from the Occupied Territories (OT), except perhaps as soldiers during their military service.

Their acquaintance with Palestinians is consequently limited to three-minute news bites that almost always report on Palestinian attacks on Israeli targets or Israeli military assaults on Palestinian towns.

When I was a high school student, by contrast, I frequently hitched a ride back from school with Palestinian taxis on their way from Gaza to Beer-Sheva. Within the current context of the Israeli-Palestinian conflict, this act is unfathomable. No taxis from the OT are allowed to enter Israel, and even if they had somehow managed to obtain an entry permit, Israeli Jews would be afraid to use them. Palestinians, who not so long ago were an integral part of the Israeli landscape, primarily as low-wage laborers who built houses, cleaned streets, and worked in agriculture, have literally disappeared. If in 1981 most Israelis and Palestinians could travel freely between the OT and Israel (the pre-1967 borders) and, in many respects, felt safe doing so, currently Palestinians are locked up in the Gaza Strip, and Israelis are not permitted to enter the region. Palestinians from the West Bank are also confined to their villages and towns; however, within this region, Jews, and particularly Jewish settlers, are allowed to come and go as they please.

The students' reaction to my teenage experiences brought to the fore a crucial issue that is often overlooked: namely, that Israel's occupation has dramatically changed over the past four decades. Yet, the obviousness of this observation does not, in any way, suggest that one can easily explain the causes leading to the transformation. What, one might ask, distinguishes the occupation of the late 1960s, 1970s, and 1980s from the current occupation?

REPERTOIRES OF VIOLENCE

While the changes in the OT have manifested themselves in all areas of life, they are particularly conspicuous when counting bodies (see table 1). During the six-year period between 2001 and 2007, Israel has, on average, killed more Palestinians per year than it killed during the first twenty years of occupation. Moreover, since the eruption of the second intifada, Israelis have killed almost twice as many Palestinians as they killed in the preceding thirty-four years. How can one make sense of the increasing violence Israel has used to uphold the occupation of the West Bank and Gaza Strip, and why did the Israeli military government radically alter the forms of control it deployed to manage the Palestinian residents of the OT?

Those who help manufacture public opinion within Israel claim that the

TABLE I   Number of Palestinians killed since 1967

Years	Palestinians Killed	Annual Average
June 1967–December 1987	650	32
December 1987–September 2000	1,491	106
September 2000–December 2006	4,046	674
Total	6,187	

SOURCES: The numbers in this table are taken from several sources. B'Tselem, The Israeli Information Center for Human Rights in the Occupied Territories has documented the number of Palestinians killed since the eruption of the first intifada in December 1987. The number of Palestinians killed during the first two decades of the occupation was gathered from different sources. According to the Palestinian Organization of Families of the Deceased, an estimated four hundred Gazans were killed during the first twenty years of occupation (*Ha'aretz*, August 23, 2005). David Ronen claims that 87 Palestinians were killed in the West Bank from the end of the war until December 1967; see his *The Year of the Shabak* (Tel-Aviv: Ministry of Defence, 1990), 57, in Hebrew. Meron Benvenisti notes that between 1968 and 1983, 92 Palestinians were killed in the West Bank; see *The West Bank Data Project, 1986 Report: Demographic, Economic, Legal, Social, and Political Developments in the West Bank* (Washington, DC: American Enterprise Institute for Public Policy Research, 1986), 63. In 1986 and 1987 another 30 were killed; see Meron Benvenisti, *The West Bank Data Project, 1987 Report: Demographic, Economic, Legal, Social, and Political Developments in the West Bank* (Washington, DC: American Enterprise Institute for Public Policy Research, 1987), 42. Al-Haq notes that in 1984, 11 Palestinians were killed. See Al-Haq's *Response to the Chapter on Israel and the Occupied Territories in the U.S.'s State Department*, Al-Haq, "Country Reports on Human Rights Practices for 1984" (Ramallah: Al-Haq, 1985), 5. Thus, the total number is 620, while there is missing data for the year 1985 in the West Bank.

dramatic increase in Palestinian deaths is due to the fact that the Palestinians have changed the methods of violence they employ against Israel, and that Israel, in turn, has had to begin using more violent means to defend itself. And indeed, the number of Israelis killed has dramatically increased over the years. During the thirteen-year period between December 1987 and September 2000, 422 Israeli were killed by Palestinians, but during the six-year period from the eruption of the second intifada until the end of 2006, 1,019 Israelis were killed.[1] Palestinians, however, might invert this argument, claiming that they have altered their methods of resistance in response to Israel's use of more lethal violence. Even though the steady increase in deaths is striking and no doubt an important factor that must be reflected upon, such explanations are symptomatic and do little to reveal the root causes underlying the processes leading to the substantial increase in fatalities. They are not very helpful for those interested in making sense of what has been going on in the West Bank and Gaza Strip because they are merely an effect of other significant changes that have taken place over the years.

Also worth noting is that the number of Palestinians who have been killed is relatively small in comparison with those killed during other military occupations. During the military occupation of Iraq by the United States, for example, on average more civilians have been killed per day than were killed during a whole year in the West Bank and Gaza Strip between the years 1967 and 1987. Moreover, the United Nations reports that during the four-month period of May through August 2006, 12,417 Iraqi civilians were killed, many more than the number of Palestinians killed during four decades of Israeli military rule.[2] The civilian death tolls in Chechnya, East Timor, and other areas that have been under military occupation tend to resemble the death toll in Iraq and, in certain instances, are much higher.[3]

What is common to these places is that they are part of what Derek Gregory has called the "colonial present," which is characterized, among other things, by two cartographic performances.[4] The first is a performance of sovereignty through which the ruptured spaces of Afghanistan, Iraq, and the Occupied Territories (after Oslo) are simulated as coherent states. Even though none of these entities is in fact a real state, sovereignty has to be conjured to render the categories of political action meaningful. The second is a performance of territory through which fluid networks like Al-Qaeda are fixed into a bounded space that can then be legitimately bombed and occupied. Indeed, the artificial ascription of a fixed and well-delineated space to Al-Qaeda and other similar networks justifies the subsequent bombing and military seizing of space. Thus, while Gregory tries to outline the features common to the colonial present, my objective is to focus on the differences between contemporary colonial regimes and the changes they undergo over time. In this book, I concentrate on the changes in the West Bank and Gaza Strip.

It is, I believe, important to try to understand why, in comparison with other military occupations, a relatively small number of Palestinians have been killed, particularly during the first thirty-four years of occupation. The basic assumption in this book is that there is an inverse correlation between sheer violence, which is used primarily to suppress resistance and to create endemic uncertainty and insecurity, and forms of control that aim to normalize military occupations by harnessing and directing the energies of the inhabitants toward activities that coincide with the occupier's interests. Thus, the increase in the number of Palestinians killed is a sign that Israel's efforts to normalize the occupation have failed.

Showing that there was indeed a change in the way Israel has controlled the OT does not, however, explain what propelled this shift. Hence, over and above the historical portrayal of Israel's occupation, the aim of this book is to uncover the causes leading to the transformations that have taken place in West Bank and Gaza Strip. The book's central thesis is that certain elements in the occupation's structure, rather than the decisions made by a particular politician or military officer, altered the forms of control. For many years, I maintain, the occupation operated according to the colonization principle, by which I mean the attempt to administer the lives of the people and normalize the colonization, while exploiting the territory's resources (in this case land, water, and labor). Over time, a series of structural contradictions undermined this principle and gave way in the mid-1990s to another guiding principle, namely, the separation principle. By *separation* I mean the abandonment of efforts to administer the lives of the colonized population (except for the people living in the seam zones or going through checkpoints), while insisting on the continued exploitation of nonhuman resources (land and water). The lack of interest in or indifference to the lives of the colonized population that is characteristic of the separation principle accounts for the recent surge in lethal violence. Thus, by underscoring the structural dimension of Israel's military rule, I hope to explain why for many years Israel's occupation was much less violent than other military occupations and why it has radically changed. However, before I turn to the introduction, which outlines the book's major arguments, two crucial points about the book's historical and spatial framework need to be stressed.

As is well known, the conflict between Israelis and Palestinians commenced much before 1967 and has, to a large extent, been shaped by the struggles that began toward the end of the nineteenth century. These struggles reached their peak in the 1948 War, which Jewish Israelis refer to as the War of Independence and which Palestinians call the Nakbah, or "catastrophe." I firmly believe that one cannot understand the current disputes informing the Israeli-Palestinian conflict without taking into account the ethnic cleansing that took place during and after the 1948 War.[5] So long as decision makers continue to relate to the conflict as if it can be resolved by addressing the wrongs committed in 1967 while ignoring 1948 and the Palestinian refugee problem, there will be no lasting political solution in the region. I accentuate this point to underscore that my decision to concentrate on 1967 and its aftermath does not intend—in any way—to suggest that the Israeli-Palestinian conflict can be reduced to the military occupation of the West Bank, Gaza Strip, and East Jerusalem. Many of my liberal allies in Israel, including some who are prominent members of the peace camp, are still unwilling to face up to this long history. I decided, nonetheless, to concentrate on the post-1967 period because I am interested in interrogating how the Israeli military occupation has operated rather than examining the root causes of and possible solutions to the conflict.

By concentrating on the West Bank and Gaza Strip, *Israel's Occupation* also makes a spatial distinction that is analytically very useful for the purposes of this book, but at the same time helps obscure the de facto connection that has been established between the West Bank and Israel.[6] Israel has been ambivalent about emphasizing either the de jure distinction or the de facto bond between the regions, because in each case an acute contradiction emerges. Imagine, for example, the minister of housing or the secretary of state living permanently outside the United States. This might sound absurd, but if one takes the de jure distinction between Israel and the OT seriously and ignores the de facto connection between the regions, this is exactly the situation in Israel. Several Israeli legislators and government ministers live in the OT and therefore do not reside within the internationally recognized borders of the country that they were elected to lead and represent. Along similar lines, the Jewish settlers who comprise about 7 percent of the Israeli citizenry live permanently "abroad"; they vote and pay taxes and for all practical purposes are extraterritorial citizens who, like diplomats, carry the Israeli law on their backs. In order to resolve these paradoxes one might stress the de facto connection between the regions, but then the inaccuracy of describing Israel as the only democracy in the Middle East would be exposed. The de jure distinction helps eclipse the fact that for the past four decades about 30 percent of the people living within the territory controlled by the Israeli government are not citizens, cannot vote, and are denied the most basic rights.

While an analysis based on the de facto situation provides, in many respects, a more accurate depiction of reality, my decision to treat the territories that Israel occupied in 1967 as a separate unit, even though such an interrogation helps mask certain historical and spatial truths, was determined by the book's primary objective. I am interested in trying to understand how Israel's military occupation ticks. The goal is to uncover the daily practices through which the Palestinian inhabitants within the OT have been managed, and to explain why Israel's mechanisms of control were altered over the years. In this way, I not only wish to unravel some of the major processes leading to the terminal shifts in Israel's occupation, but also to underscore the structural causes leading to the escalation of violence as well the dangerous implications of Israel's insistence on continuing to control Palestinian land. Readers who are uninterested in my theoretical argument can skip the introduction and go directly to the first chapter, where I begin the historical portrayal by outlining the infrastructure of control.

INTRODUCTION

Of Dowries and Brides

> When I asked Eshkol: "What are we going to do with a
> million Arabs?" he said: "I get it. You want the dowry,
> but you don't like the bride!"
>
> *Exchange between* LEVI ESHKOL *and* GOLDA MEIR
> *during a Mapai Party meeting September 1967*

On June 8, 1967, just a few hours after the Israeli military captured Jerusalem's Temple Mount, Harem al Sharif, Defense Minister Moshe Dayan visited the site. Noticing that troops had hung an Israeli flag on the cap of the Al-Aqsa shrine, Dayan asked one of the soldiers to remove it, adding that displaying the Israeli national symbol for all to see was an unnecessarily provocative act.[1] Those who visited the Occupied Territories (OT) in the 1980s and 1990s no doubt noticed Israeli flags fluttering over almost every building Israel occupied as well as above every Jewish settlement. Moreover, most military jeeps and armored vehicles had flags attached to one of their antennas as they patrolled Palestinian villages, towns, and cities. Ariel Sharon's highly publicized visit to the Al-Aqsa compound in September 2000—an act deemed by many to be intentionally provocative and that served as the trigger for the second intifada—could be considered the final step in a process that has ultimately undone Dayan's strategic legacy of trying to normalize the occupation by concealing Israel's presence. "Don't rule them," he once said, "let them lead their own lives."[2]

Another significant change that has transpired over the years involves the Israeli government's relationship to trees, the symbol of life. If in 1968 Israel helped Palestinians in the Gaza Strip plant some 618,000 trees and provided farmers with improved varieties of seeds for vegetables and field crops, during the first three years of the second intifada Israel destroyed more than

10 percent of Gaza's agricultural land and uprooted more than 226,000 trees.[3] The appearance and proliferation of the flag, on the one hand, and the razing of trees, on the other, signify a fundamental transformation in Israel's attempts to control the occupied Palestinian inhabitants and point to a profound modification in the modes of power employed in the territories. It appears as if Israel decided to alter its methods of upholding the occupation, replacing a politics of life, which aimed to secure the existence and livelihood of the Palestinian inhabitants, with a politics of death.

Military documents, newspaper articles, and a series of reports indeed indicate that the occupation in the late 1960s and 1970s was very different from the occupation in the 1980s and 1990s; the 1980s and 1990s, in turn, witnessed an occupation quite different from the one of the past several years. What spurred Israel to change—so dramatically—the way it manages the Palestinian population? How did Israel administer the Palestinian inhabitants during the occupation's first years? Why did it modify the methods it employed to manage the lives of the residents? And what is the relationship between the changing forms of control and the changes taking place in the political arena? The fact that I could not find satisfactory answers to these questions is due, I believe, to the kind of scholarly investigation that has thus far dominated the field.

Nearly all of the commentators who have written about the occupation have chosen one of three focal points: (1) the different diplomatic and peace initiatives between Israelis and Palestinians as well as the effects of international and global processes on the occupation (such as the 1973, 1982, 2006 wars, the revolution in Iran, the 1987 Amman Summit, the two Gulf Wars, and the demise of the Soviet Union);[4] (2) Israel's different policies toward the occupied Palestinians and Jewish settlers as well as the impact its political institutions have had on the occupation;[5] or (3) Palestinian resistance—most notably the two Palestinian uprisings.[6] While these studies are crucial for understanding certain features of the occupation, many of them portray Israel's military rule as static, as if the occupation had remained stable for thirty or forty years. Scholars who do discuss the changes that have come to pass in the OT attribute them to Israel's policy choices, Palestinian resistance, or global processes.

Although such explanations are certainly helpful, some of them depict the Israeli state as a free agent issuing policies unhindered by contingencies or portray Palestinian resistance as if it were led by people who stand in some free zone and whose beliefs and actions have not been shaped by the occupation and Israel's controlling apparatuses. Taking into account Timothy Mitchell's criticism of such statist approaches, in the following pages I claim that many of the changes in the West Bank and Gaza Strip were and continue to be an outcome of the daily practices characterizing life under occupation.[7] Even though the Israeli state appears to be a free actor from which a series of policies originates, a closer investigation reveals that its policies and, more particularly, the modification of its policies over the years have been shaped by the different mechanisms of control operating in the OT. The same is true of the policy choices of resistance groups like Fatah, Hamas, and the Popular Front for the Liberation of Palestine and other nonstate actors, such as the United Nations Relief and Work Agency and the Red Cross. More specifically, I maintain that the interactions, excesses, and contradictions produced by the means of control that have been applied in the OT help explain the dramatic changes that have taken place over the years in the West Bank and Gaza Strip and why we are currently witnessing a macabre politics characterized by an increasing number of deaths.

By *means of control* I do not only mean the coercive mechanisms used to prohibit, exclude, and repress people, but rather the entire array of institutions, legal devices, bureaucratic apparatuses, social practices, and physical edifices that operate both on the individual and the population in order to produce new modes of behavior, habits, interests, tastes, and aspirations. Whereas some of the civil institutions, like the education and medical systems, operate as controlling apparatuses in their own right, frequently attempting to further the project of normalization, they are simultaneously sites through which a variety of other minute controlling practices are introduced and circulated. The purpose and function of controlling mechanisms are often determined by the context, so that at times certain practices harness and direct human beings in ways that expand the possibilities available to them, while in other instances the same practices are deployed to dramatically limit possibilities.[8] Moreover, as the controlling mechanisms circumscribe and influence people's behavior, these same mechanisms not only presuppose but also help produce the resistance of the people they are employed to manage.

In the following pages, I accordingly aim to complicate and problematize the pervasive misreading of Israel's means of control as the straightforward effects of its policy choices and Palestinian resistance. Far from simply determining which mechanisms of control would be deployed, the policies and resistance have themselves been shaped by the interactions, excesses, and contradictions within and among the apparatuses and practices of control. In order to substantiate this claim, I offer a historical overview of the occupation that draws attention to the way in which the Palestinian inhabitants have been managed. By doing this I hope to expose how Israel's means of control have actually helped to mold the Israeli-Palestinian conflict. Thus, *Israel's Occupation* fills a lacuna in the existing literature not only because it offers an overview of the occupation—something, surprisingly, that has not yet been done—but also because it is the first attempt to make sense of Israel's policies in the West Bank and Gaza Strip by means of a detailed analysis of the controlling apparatuses and practices.[9] Finally, an interrogation of this kind is advantageous because it helps us see beyond the smoke screen of political proclamations and statements and sheds new light on the way power, people, and place have been shaped in this bitter, ongoing conflict.

BACKGROUND

Perhaps the most significant consequence of the June 1967 War was that it reignited the Palestinian problem.[10] For the first time since the 1948 War, one sovereign power ruled all of Mandatory Palestine (the area administered by the British Mandate from 1920 until 1948), and thus "the two peoples, one land" problem returned to the fore.[11] In addition to the West Bank, Gaza Strip, and East Jerusalem, which had been part of Palestine under British rule, the Israeli military captured the Golan Heights and Sinai Peninsula. Even before the war had ended, Israel began setting up military administrations in the territories it had occupied. Yet the Levi Eshkol government treated the captured regions differently, suggesting that from the outset Israel had distinct intentions regarding each area.[12]

The West Bank, Gaza Strip, and Sinai Peninsula were placed under a military government, and, to facilitate the administration of these regions, Israel reimposed the Ottoman, British Mandatory, Egyptian, and Jordanian laws that had been in place prior to the war, while adding an array of military orders published by military commanders. There was no intention of incorporating the residents of these areas into Israel (the internationally recognized pre-1967 borders). East Jerusalem as well as an additional 64 square kilometers surrounding the city—which had belonged to twenty-eight Palestinian villages in the West Bank—were annexed on June 27, just over two weeks after the war ended, and Israel extended its own laws to this entire area. For the price of annexing this territory, East Jerusalemites were partially integrated into Israeli society.[13] The Golan Heights was defined as ~Syria~ occupied territory (the region was only annexed in 1981), but in sharp contrast to the West Bank, Gaza Strip, and Sinai Peninsula, from the very beginning Israeli law was applied in this region by means of decrees published by the military commander.[14] During the war, most of the Golan's residents either fled or were expelled, thus rendering about one hundred thousand inhabitants refugees. Despite the resistance of the sixty-five hundred residents who remained, they were subsequently made Israeli citizens.[15]

Because Israel treated each region and its inhabitants differently, this book concentrates on the West Bank and Gaza Strip, the areas where most of the Palestinians who were occupied in 1967 reside.[16] Israel was, from the beginning, unwilling to withdraw from these two regions and hoped to integrate the land or at least parts of it into its own territory at some future date. This desire can be traced back to two strains of political thought: militaristic and messianic. From a militaristic perspective, the newly secured territories were seen as necessary for defending Israel's borders against external ~1)~ attacks, while the water reservoirs in the West Bank were considered a vital security resource because of Israel's scant water supplies. From a messianic ~2)~ perspective, the captured regions were seen as part of the biblical land of Israel and therefore as belonging to the Jews. These strains of thought often converged to create a united front.[17] For example, immediately after Israel's independence, the right-wing political parties, the religious Zionists, and part of Labor all agreed that the 1949 armistice borders should be considered temporary, and that in the future Israel should try to expand its territories; for some this desire was informed by a militaristic vision, for others by a messianic one, and for still others by both.

The problem was that the land captured in 1967 had a considerable number of people living on it. If in 1948 Israel led a campaign that today would be termed ethnic cleansing—whereby approximately seven hundred and fifty thousand Palestinians (out of a population of nine hundred thousand in the region that became Israel) either were forcefully expelled or fled across international borders—in 1967 Israel only "cleansed" two West Bank areas of their Palestinian inhabitants: the Jordan Valley (excluding Jericho) and the Latrun enclave.[18] The Jordan Valley was partially cleansed because Israel wanted to secure the border with Jordan. The Latrun enclave was depopulated of

Palestinians because the Israeli military did not want any Palestinian villages to be in a position to threaten the highway leading to Jerusalem.[19] All in all, between two hundred thousand and two hundred and fifty thousand people, more than 30 percent of the West Bank's inhabitants, fled to Jordan during the war and its direct aftermath, and only about seventeen thousand were ultimately allowed to return.[20] However, an estimated one million Palestinians remained in the Gaza Strip and West Bank, and Israel quickly realized that it had to install a system of internal governance within these two regions.

The unwillingness to offer the Palestinian inhabitants of the West Bank and Gaza Strip citizenship has been informed by the militaristic and messianic ideologies mentioned above and involves demographic concerns. The different Israeli governments have always contended that Israel is the homeland for the Jews and therefore Jews must retain a clear majority within its territory. After all, Israel is a Jewish state. If Israeli citizenship had been granted to the occupied Palestinians, within a couple of decades the country's Jewish population would no longer have been the majority.[21] Thus, from the very beginning, Israel governed the territories by making a clear distinction between the land it had occupied and the people who inhabited it, or as Levi Eshkol told Golda Meir in the epigraph to this chapter, between the dowry and the bride.[22]

A series of mechanisms were thus developed to expropriate the occupied land without fully annexing it,[23] while numerous apparatuses and practices were introduced to regulate and manage the lives of the Palestinians without integrating them into Israeli society. The ongoing attempt to separate the occupied land and its inhabitants, which is in fact an effort to incorporate the West Bank and Gaza Strip into Israel's territory without integrating the Palestinian population into Israeli society, reflects Moshe Dayan's "functional compromise," which was formulated in opposition to Labor Minister Yigal Allon's territorial compromise.[24] Allon's compromise advocated the redrawing of state borders in order to gain "maximum security and maximum territory for Israel with a minimum number of Arabs," while Dayan was in no hurry to make any territorial concessions and instead proposed granting the Palestinians some form of self-rule. Israel's unwillingness to incorporate the occupied Palestinians and the distinction it made between the inhabitants and their land swiftly became the overarching logic informing the occupation, a logic that has been only slightly altered over the years, while many aspects of Israel's military rule have changed dramatically.

Israel's control focused on two principal sites: the occupiers and the occupied. The first site, the one I do not discuss in this book but which is analyzed in Ian Lustick's *Unsettled States, Disputed Lands,* is the Jewish population living inside Israel proper.[25] A historical examination of this site reveals an array of controlling devices that have aimed to naturalize and render the occupation invisible, concealing the political violence and exploitation that have upheld it. On the one hand, the morality and the temporary nature of the occupation were incessantly reiterated, while, on the other hand, a series of apparatuses and practices attempted to alter the citizenry's conception of its borders by erasing the Green Line (the internationally recognized, pre-1967 border based on the 1949 Armistice Agreements). The overall objective was to weaken internal resistance to the occupation, and since rhetoric does not always have to avoid contradiction, the occupation was presented as simultaneously temporary, moral, *and* nonexistent.

In the effort to obfuscate the occupation and incorporate the captured territories into Israel, numerous erasure practices were introduced within Israel. Less than six months after the war, on December 17, the Israeli government began referring to the West Bank as Judea and Samaria, thus drawing a connection between the state of Israel and the biblical land of Israel.[26] Gradually, the Green Line was erased from all atlases, maps, and textbooks published by the Israeli government, making it nearly impossible for Israeli school children to learn that Israel's recognized international borders actually pass along the line of the 1949 Armistice Agreements.[27] Not unlike the Palestinian maps that depict all of Mandatory Palestine as Palestine, Israeli maps depict all of Mandatory Palestine as Israel, leading many school children to believe that the recognized borders are south of Rafah and pass through the Jordan valley.[28]

To reify the erasure of borders, Israel also connected the physical infrastructure between its territory and the regions it had captured. It linked the transport and communication networks of the West Bank and Gaza to Israel proper, making it easy for the increasing number of Jewish settlers and Palestinian laborers to reach Tel-Aviv and Jerusalem.[29] Rapidly, almost all of the obstacles characterizing an international border were removed. Any Israeli could drive to the West Bank or Gaza as if he or she were going to visit an adjacent district. Several Israeli field schools were opened in the

West Bank, and the Israeli public regularly hiked and picnicked throughout this region. Thousands of shoppers went on weekend excursions to buy cheap produce in the territories. Most of the customs, tariffs, and barriers that typify the exchange of commodities across international borders did not exist. Moreover, at a certain point the distinction between government expenditures within Israel proper and expenditures in the OT was expunged from the annual budget, in effect transforming the entire area from the Jordan Valley to the Mediterranean Sea into one economic unit. Along the same lines, Jewish settlers who moved to the West Bank and Gaza Strip were subjected to Israeli law rather than to the law of the land in which they actually resided. This act served, among other things, to erase the Green Line in their own minds as well as in the minds of the citizens within Israel. These and several other efforts bore their intended fruit, and for many years the OT became indistinguishable from the state from the point of view of most Jews.[30]

At the same time, Israel's actions in the OT were presented as moral. The resources Israel allocated to improve the Palestinian inhabitants' living conditions in the OT were continuously highlighted and publicized, and investments in health care, education, social services, and religious affairs was underscored. The Jewish population was constantly reminded that enormous sums were being spent on laying water and electricity lines, paving roads, and expanding transport and communication lines, and that favorable conditions were being created for industrial development, while agriculture was being "advanced and modernized beyond recognition."[31] Thus, Israel portrayed itself as bringing progress to the uncivilized Palestinians, while emphasizing both the "purity of arms" of its military and the temporariness of the occupation. The Palestinians, or so the line went, were the ones preventing Israel's withdrawal from the OT because they continued to demand all of Mandatory Palestine.

While this perception was altered in many respects after the eruption of the first intifada in 1987 and the signing of the Oslo Peace Accords in 1993,[32] it was, ironically, the second intifada (2000) — which left thousands of Palestinians and Israelis dead — that managed to reintroduce the difference between Israel and the OT. Today, for most Israelis, a conceptual border does exist between the two entities, especially given Israel's dismantlement of the settlements in the Gaza Strip and the redeployment of its forces, and the fact that hardly any Jews other than the settlers travel to the West Bank.

Yet, currently the West Bank's border does not run along the internationally recognized Green Line. Instead, the separation barrier, which Israel is constructing deep inside Palestinian territory, is conceived by the majority of Israelis as their country's border.

SETTING UP THE MEANS OF CONTROL IN THE OCCUPIED TERRITORIES

This book focuses on the second site toward which the means of control were directed: the Palestinian population under occupation. Following the cessation of hostilities, a variety of surveillance mechanisms were rapidly set up, monitoring every aspect of Palestinian life.[33] Televisions, refrigerators, ~~supplies~~ and gas stoves were counted, as were the livestock, orchards, and tractors. ~~counted~~ Letters sent to and from the different regions were checked, registered, and examined. School textbooks, novels, movies, newspapers, and political leaflets were inspected and frequently censored. There were detailed inventories of Palestinian workshops for furniture, soap, textiles, olive products, and sweets. Even eating habits were scrutinized, as was the nutritional value of the Palestinian food basket.

Israel also assumed control over all major resources, such as water and electricity, and took over the welfare, health care, judiciary, and educational systems — the most prominent institutions through which modern societies are managed. During the occupation's first two decades, these institutions were used to normalize the occupation and to shape Palestinian behavior by modifying daily practices, both on the level of the individual and the population at large. In the health field, practices were introduced to encourage women to give birth at hospitals (a means of decreasing infant mortality rates and monitoring population growth) and to promote vaccinations (in order to decrease the incidence of contagious and noncontagious diseases). Palestinian teachers were sent to seminars in Jerusalem, where they were instructed in methods of "correct" teaching. A series of vocational schools were established to prepare Palestinians who wished to join the Israeli workforce, and model plots were created to train farmers. Many of these controlling devices aimed to increase the economic productivity of the Palestinian inhabitants and to secure the well-being of the population.

Simultaneously, juridical forms of control were adopted to restrict freedom of movement and association, and to forbid all types of political activ-

OT : occupied territories

ity. An intricate permit regime was introduced requiring licenses to build houses, open businesses, sell produce, practice law and medicine, or work in the public sector. Military decrees even regulated access to grazing grounds for sheep, the use of donkey carts to transfer goods, the kinds of vegetables and fruits one could plant, and the picking of wildflowers in deserted fields, while criminal sanctions were imposed for breaches and violations. In addition to all these forms of control, there was the sword, which shaped daily practices through the threat and execution of a series of coercive sanctions, ranging from house demolitions and deportations to curfews and arrests. An analysis of the way Palestinian society was managed suggests both that the different forms of control operated simultaneously and that all spheres of life were meddled with and acted upon.[34]

The relative swiftness with which the different mechanisms of control were put in place was not coincidental; rather, it was a result of historical circumstances. First, prior to the 1967 War the West Bank had been annexed to Jordan, and the Gaza Strip had been under Egyptian administrative rule. Israel simply reactivated certain institutions and practices that had been employed previously by the two neighboring countries. Second, several years *before* the war erupted, Israel had begun preparing contingency plans for the military administration of the West Bank and Gaza Strip on the "occasion" that these territories fell into Israeli hands.[35] In the early 1960s, the military carried out seminars simulating problems that could arise if an Israeli military government were to be installed in these territories. Moreover, a comprehensive manual, which included instructions and guidelines for setting up the legal and administrative apparatuses of a military government, had been prepared in advance and was distributed to the troops before the war ended.[36] Some of the plans—and the logic informing them—facilitated the establishment of an elaborate administrative apparatus within the territories once the two regions had actually been occupied by Israel. Finally, the military learned from its experience of managing the Palestinian population within Israel as well as from the brief period of Gaza's occupation in 1956 and early 1957.[37] While several apparatuses and practices used during the internal military government (1948–66) were reproduced in the OT, the dissimilar political and social circumstances of the two regions as well as Israel's different objectives meant that the model created inside Israel would serve more often as a prototype for comparison rather than for emulation. Indeed, as we will see, the forms of management adopted in the West Bank and Gaza Strip were often very different from the ones used inside Israel proper.

The introduction of different controlling apparatuses in the OT was, after all, to be expected, if only because all modern societies, regardless of whether they are democratic or authoritarian, are managed through the application of numerous mechanisms and practices that operate both on the individual and the population at large. To be sure, the actual controlling apparatuses employed differ dramatically from place to place, and they both shape and are shaped by, among other things, the regime type and the makeup of the population toward which they are directed (citizens, migrant minorities, refugees, occupied inhabitants, etc.). They take on numerous forms, coercive and noncoercive, legalistic and extralegalistic, overt and covert.

Interestingly, though, my examination of Israel's forms of control reveals that most of the coercive measures used in the West Bank and Gaza Strip during the first years of the occupation were still in use four decades later. The military, in other words, imposed curfews, deported leaders, demolished homes, carried out arrests, tortured detainees, and restricted movement both immediately after the 1967 War and in the wake of the new millennium.[38] The fact that the vast majority of these practices are still used today, while very few new ones have been introduced in the intervening years, is worth stressing.[39] This suggests that the dramatic transformation that has occurred in the OT (in terms of the way Israel controls the region) is not attributable to a radical modification of the means of control (i.e., the replacement of old forms of control with new ones), but is, I maintain, the result of a shift in emphasis of the modes of power informing the different controlling apparatuses and practices.

MODES OF POWER

My claim, then, is that the different controlling apparatuses and practices that have been employed in the OT have been informed by the three fundamental modes of power—disciplinary, bio-, and sovereign—which Michel Foucault describes, and that it is the shifting emphasis on one or the other modes of power, rather than the introduction of new forms of control, that helps explain the extensive transformation in Israel's occupation.

During the occupation's first years, Israel emphasized disciplinary power and biopower. Disciplinary power is continuous and spread out, operating

1) on the minutest parts of daily interactions in order to produce and disseminate an array of norms and social practices. Discipline operates from below as it attempts to impose homogeneity on the inhabitants both in thought and comportment, thus striving to render people docile. But, at the same time, the forms of control informed by this mode of power endeavor to individualize the inhabitants by making it possible to detect differences among the members of society and to determine each person's abilities and specialties as well as abnormal activities.[40] Think about exams given to children at school. They produce a certain type of homogeneity by ensuring that everyone studies the same material, and they also allow teachers to differentiate and arrange students according to abilities, class rank, and so forth. Even though discipline aims to engender normalization through the regimentation of daily life, frequently by increasing the inhabitants' productivity in terms of economic utility while diminishing their political astuteness, it is important to emphasize that disciplinary forms of control are often incoherent.[41] For instance, while Israel encouraged Palestinian farmers to grow certain crops during a given period, during later years it limited the export of these crops outside the OT, a fact that hurt the farmers' income and thus created a fair amount of bitterness. Thus disciplines, as Mitchell indicates and as I demonstrate in this book, can counteract one another, break down, or overreach; they create spaces for maneuver and resistance and can be turned to counter-hegemonic purposes.[42]

2) Biopower deals with the *population* (as opposed to the individual) as a political problem. It does not oppose the deployment of disciplinary power, but integrates and modifies it, operating on a different scale while applying a series of distinct instruments. It too is continuous and spread out, but if discipline seeks to administer the individual subject, biopower manages the individual only insofar as he or she is a member of a population. Biopower deploys an array of institutions that coordinate and regulate medical care, welfare services, the economy, and so forth, while configuring and circumscribing the political sphere and normalizing knowledge. In order to administer the population, biopower uses statistical devices and scientific methods as well as mechanisms of surveillance. It measures and intervenes in a set of processes relating to mortality rate, longevity, the fertility of the population, hygiene, vaccinations, prevalent illnesses in a population, birth rates, unemployment rates, and the distribution of labor in terms of age, gender, and sectors of occupation, per capita income, and so on.[43] Israel's

effort to increase the rate of births in Palestinian hospitals is an instance of this kind of power.

Like those of disciplinary power, the mechanisms used by biopower are designed to maximize and extract forces from individual subjects, but they do not work at the level of the individual. Instead of disciplining the individual, biopower regularizes the population.[44] The objectives of the different forms of control deployed in the OT and informed by both disciplinary power and biopower were, however, different from what they are elsewhere in the world. In most countries, discipline and biopower regulate people through processes of incorporation into the state, constituting them as citizens. Because there was never an intention of fully integrating the Palestinian inhabitants and making them part of the Israeli citizenry, discipline was never employed to incorporate the Palestinian inhabitants into Israeli society; rather, it was used to constitute them as subjects of the occupying power. This, as we will see, is crucial, and it is one of the reasons the forms of control employed to manage the Palestinian population within Israel proper were so different from those used in the OT.

During the first years following the war, biopower, like disciplinary forms of control, was emphasized and used to normalize the occupation by boosting the economy and producing prosperity in the West Bank and Gaza, and a great deal of energy was invested in reshaping the collective identity of the population and suppressing Palestinian nationalism. Concurrently, though, Israel never refrained from utilizing the more traditional mode of sovereign power, by which I mean the imposition of a legal system and the employment of the state's police and military to either enforce the rule of law or to suspend it. This kind of power is exercised through juridical and executive arms of the state; it tends to operate from the top down, and it is often intermittent, appearing only when the law has been breached by members of society or when it has been suspended by the sovereign.[45] In our case this has meant the introduction and implementation of a legal apparatus that views all forms of Palestinian resistance as terror and that employs Israeli security forces to ensure that all "terrorism" is suppressed. Simultaneously, the same legal system has become a mechanism of dispossession, through which Israel has expropriated Palestinian land and property.

Proclamation Two, published by the military commander and enacted on June 7, 1967, the day in which the military government was established, is a paradigmatic example of this kind of power. It declares that "all powers of government, legislation, appointment and administration in relation to the Region and its inhabitants shall henceforth vest in me alone and shall be exercised by me or by such other person appointed by me or to act on my behalf."[46] This proclamation goes on to state that the military commander has the power to enact any law, cancel or suspend an existing law, or make legislative changes, thus underscoring the fact that Israel would use sovereign power not only to pass and enforce laws, but also to withdraw and suspend them.[47] Following the consolidation of Israel's rule, sovereign power was for a while de-emphasized, so that for more than a decade most of the controlling apparatuses and practices were informed by disciplinary power and biopower.

All three modes of power, it is important to stress, tend to operate concurrently and are part and parcel of the modern form of governing. Governing in this sense does not only denote institutions and practices that can be traced back to the state, but refers to any apparatus, practice, or action that aims to "shape the conduct of conduct;"[48] it concerns not only practices of governmental, religious, financial, and other institutions, but also ways through which each individual governs him or herself.[49] Governing the West Bank and Gaza Strip has entailed regulating and managing its economic, medical, educational, and political institutions as well as the inclinations, identity, and comportment of each inhabitant. A primary objective of this modern form of governing is security, but not merely in the narrow sense of deploying military, police, and secret services. Security in its broad sense includes the management of the economy as well as the health, education, and social welfare of the population. It thus encompasses those institutions and practices concerned with defending and maintaining the demographic, economic, and social processes that regulate the population.[50]

My claim is that even though the three modes of power tend to be simultaneously deployed, the specific form of governing is shaped by their particular configuration. One form of governing might emphasize disciplinary and bio modes of power and put relatively little emphasis on sovereign power, while another form of governing may accentuate bio and sovereign modes of power and pay less attention to discipline.[51] The particularity of each configuration determines how individuals and the population are managed, while no configuration is fixed, so that certain processes modify the relation and emphasis among the different modes of power and consequently change the way society is governed and controlled.[52]

The changing configuration of these modes of power had two primary effects: qualitative and quantitative. From a qualitative perspective, the Israeli case exemplifies that a change in the emphasis on one or another mode of power does not necessarily lead to the replacement of the controlling apparatuses and practices that are used to govern the inhabitants; rather it alters the way they operate. So, for example, if a school was initially used to transmit certain knowledge to children in an attempt to normalize the occupation, but children resisted this knowledge and on their way back from school threw stones at the military government offices, the military could decide to shut down the school. In this way, the school would be transformed from an institution whose role was to encourage the internalization of certain norms and a field of knowledge to an instrument of collective punishment.[53] The Palestinian inhabitants were, in other words, frequently punished when they did not embrace the norms Israel established, and the same form of control that was used to encourage the appropriation of the norm could easily be turned into an instrument of punishment. From a quantitative perspective, although almost all of the existing forms of control were employed from the beginning of the occupation, some were used more often when a sovereign mode of power was emphasized, others when biopower was prominent, and still others when a disciplinary mode was accentuated.

EXCESSES AND CONTRADICTIONS

My argument, though, is not only that the shifting emphasis on one mode of power rather than another helps account for the changing nature of the occupation, but also that the interactions, excesses, and contradictions within and among the controlling practices and apparatuses modified the configuration of the modes of power. This is where I diverge most radically from the statist approach. A genealogy of Israel's forms of control and an analysis of how they interacted suggest that the excesses and contradictions engendered by the controlling apparatuses helped shift the emphasis among the modes of power and shape Israel's policy choices and Palestinian resistance. This is the book's central claim.

By excesses I mean effects that are not part of the initial objective of the means of control. A curfew restricts and confines the population, but also produces antagonism; the establishment of a Jewish settlement on a hilltop is used to confiscate land, partition space, and monitor the Palestinian villages below, but also underscores that the occupation is not temporary. By 1987, Israel had managed to confiscate about 40 percent of the land in the West Bank and Gaza Strip; it had also established 125 settlements dispersed throughout these two regions that were home to some sixty thousand settlers.[54] How did this affect the Palestinian inhabitants who, on the one hand, witnessed the expropriation of their land and the movement of thousands of Jewish citizens from Israel into the West Bank and Gaza, and, on the other hand, were told that the occupation would soon end?

In addition, the interactions among the controlling apparatuses and practices have produced two different types of contradictions. One type is created within the controlling apparatus itself. Perhaps the most apparent internal contradiction is the one created by the settlement project. By confiscating more and more land and transferring hundreds of thousands of Jews to the OT, the settlement project rendered the one-state solution, in which Jews do *not* have a majority between the Jordan Valley and the Mediterranean Sea, increasingly probable. Another type of contradiction emerges in the interaction among different forms of control. During the 1970s, Israel, for example, allowed the Palestinians to open several universities as a way of normalizing the occupation. Within a relatively short period, these universities produced a fairly large professional class made up of college graduates. Yet, due to a series of restrictions and constraints imposed on the Palestinian economy, the industry and service sector could not be developed, and the employment opportunities open to professional Palestinians within the OT were very limited. Consequently, many of the graduates could not find jobs that reflected or made use of their skills. The lack of jobs created a fair amount of bitterness among the graduates, who, according to Ze'ev Schiff and Ehud Ya'ari, were a major oppositional force by the time the first intifada erupted.[55]

Such excesses and contradictions helped shape the political arena and created distinct modalities of control.[56] They triggered Palestinian resistance, which, in turn, helped form Israel's policy choices. This suggests that the forms of control themselves have had a major impact on the local political processes and on the changing character of the occupation. To better understand the occupation, it is therefore crucial to examine the means of control, uncovering how they engendered their own modifications and how they helped define the occupation's diverse and changing structure.[57] Thus, in the following pages I aim to offer a genealogy of the controlling apparatuses and practices that stimulated political change, whether by shaping Israel's policy choices or by molding Palestinian resistance; and although I hardly touch upon the international realm, I would venture to say that the means of control have even had their effect on global processes.

It is important to emphasize that even though my focus is on the different forms of control and the modes of power informing their usage, I do not want to suggest that one should ignore or dismiss the agency of political actors. Indeed, any attempt to portray both Israelis and Palestinians as objects rather than subjects of history would be misleading. Israelis are responsible for creating and maintaining the occupation as well as its consequences, while Palestinians are responsible for their resistance and its effects. And yet the very interests and desires of Israelis and Palestinians, as well as their comportment, are constituted, at least in part, by a multiplicity of controlling apparatuses. Thus, even though certain forms of control generate excesses and contradictions and in this way force Israeli policymakers to alter the methods used to manage the population, these policymakers have a number of possibilities from which they can choose. The choice of one possibility over another, however, is also shaped in specific ways by the controlling practices themselves. [58]

A GENEALOGY OF CONTROL

What does the phrase *genealogy of control* actually mean? In the present book, I use it to denote a history that traces the institutions, mechanisms, apparatuses, and, more generally, the means of control used to manage the population by shaping people's daily practices. It refers to a certain kind of history from below, which includes an analysis of the power relations informing the forms of control as well as the effects they have produced. In the OT the controlling apparatuses have manifested themselves in legal regulations and permits, military procedures and practices, spatial divisions and architectural edifices, as well as bureaucratic edicts and normative fiats dictating forms of correct conduct in homes, schools, medical centers, workshops, agricultural fields, and so forth. A single book does not suffice to create an inventory of these apparatuses, considering that the military orders issued over the years in the West Bank and Gaza Strip alone fill thousands of pages and deal with anything and everything, from business transactions involving land or property and the installation of water pumps to the planting of citrus trees and the structure of the governing body. Each one of these orders can be analyzed in depth so as to uncover both the processes that led to its creation as well as the effects that it generated. Why, for example, did Israel prevent Palestinians from installing water pumps? Which practices did the military introduce to enforce this regulation, and how did the lack of water pumps affect the inhabitants' daily lives?

Instead of offering a meticulous interrogation of a single controlling apparatus, as some commentators have done,[59] *Israel's Occupation* provides a bird's-eye view of the means of control so as to explain the changes that have taken place over the past four decades in the West Bank and Gaza Strip. It uses the information published by a variety of Israeli governmental institutions (ranging from the Civil Administration and the Ministry of Agriculture to the Bank of Israel and the Central Bureau of Statistics), scholarly studies that have examined different aspects of the occupation, as well as reports published by human rights and development NGOs, the World Bank, and several United Nations agencies that have monitored the OT over the years. Although most of the reports and studies that I examine seldom refer to their objects of study as controlling apparatuses, they actually describe in great detail the mechanisms deployed to manage the lives of residents in the occupied regions. They thus provide the information needed to outline and clarify precisely how the different forms of control operated, how they interacted with each other, and how they produced certain effects.

Even though the following pages do not always advance chronologically, in order to trace the means of control that Israel employed, I divide the occupation into five periods: the military government (1967–1980), civil administration (1981–1987), the first intifada (1988–93), the Oslo years (1994–2000), and the second intifada (2001–present). These periods are, to be sure, organically linked and overlap to a considerable extent, while some of them can be divided into subperiods. Although they coincide with political events and therefore appear to endorse a statist approach, a careful examination reveals that each period is distinguished by a particular emphasis on one or another mode of power and the concurrent accentuation of distinct forms of control. The underlying claim, then, is that the policies and resistance that characterize each period were actually shaped by the controlling apparatuses and practices that were employed, their excesses, and their contradictions.

For those more acquainted with the occupation today, the most striking feature of the first period is the large number of practices introduced to improve the population's standard of living and increase individual prosperity. Palestinian farmers were given fertilizers and pesticides for their agricultural crops, and Israel distributed vaccines against diseases that could compromise livestock. These controlling practices were not informed by altruism, but by a desire to normalize the occupation, and they were balanced against other practices aimed primarily at undermining Palestinian attempts to create a self-sufficient and independent economy and to establish a national movement.

Along with numerous forms of control informed by disciplinary power and biopower, sovereign modes of power were also employed. The external borders of both the West Bank and Gaza Strip were sealed, and Israeli security forces crushed internal resistance. The military imposed curfews, deported leaders, demolished homes, carried out arrests, restricted movement, and shut down schools and businesses.[60] In later years, particularly after 1971, however, the use of such coercive measures was not as prevalent. Overall, a politics of life informed the administration and management of the Palestinian residents during the occupation's first period. And when a politics of life reigns, both a disciplinary power that is concerned with the production and maintenance of "correct behavior" and a biopower concerned with the population's welfare are emphasized. During the second intifada a series of controlling apparatuses were employed to kill thousands of Palestinians, destroy the infrastructure of their existence, and thus engender grinding poverty, but in the occupation's first years numerous practices were put in place to do away with unemployment, to help save the livestock, and to assist farmers in increasing their production.[61]

The move from a military government to a civil administration (1981) was, ironically, a move from a system that had been operated by both Israeli civil institutions and security forces to a system dependent solely on the military and other security forces. On the one hand, the creation of the civil administration symbolized Israel's admission that the occupation was not temporary and underscored its desire to continue normalizing and perpetuating it. On the other hand, it represented Israel's recognition that the methods it had hitherto employed to normalize the occupation and suppress the nationalist drive were not working. This period is characterized by an emphasis on sovereign power, but at this point it was still directed primarily against the Palestinian leadership inside the OT rather than the Palestinian masses.

The eruption of the first intifada in December 1987 was a clear reaction to the excesses of Israel's means of control as well as to a series of contradictions engendered by the interaction among different controlling practices and apparatuses. Most prominent among these were the discrepancies between Israel's insistence that the Palestinians manage themselves through some kind of self-rule and its ongoing efforts to repress all manifestations of Palestinian nationalism. In addition, the economic subjugation of the territories as well as the continuing confiscation of land did not fit well with the mechanisms that aimed to secure the population's livelihood. The "iron fist" policy, which was implemented in reaction to the mass unrest and which emphasized sovereign power through the deployment of a large number of troops and the incursion of armored vehicles into Palestinian cities, towns, and villages, was, paradoxically, a sign of the failure of existing forms of control. Indeed, the daily skirmishes with the Israeli military should be considered as a crisis of control, an indication that Israel was losing ground, since power is tolerable only insofar as it manages to hide part of itself; and the intifada made the occupying power and the means of control it deployed visible for all to see. Gradually, it became apparent to Israel that it would have to continue deploying troops in order to sustain the occupation and would be unable to normalize the occupation using the same strategies it had used in the past.

The ingenious idea, as several commentators have noted, was to *out-source* the responsibility for the population.[62] This is where the Palestinian Authority (PA) enters the picture. Instead of conceiving it as an autonomous body with an external existence that in some way transcends the occupation, one can tenably claim that the PA is a product of the occupation, and, more precisely, the controlling apparatuses that failed to uphold the occupation. It is an effect produced by a series of legal-bureaucratic mechanisms, the reorganization of the economy, and the repartitioning of space. Less than a year after Rabin and Arafat signed the Oslo Accords (September 1993), all of the civil institutions, including education, health, and welfare were passed from Israel to the hands of the fledgling authority. Without renouncing its sovereign authority over the two regions, Israel transferred responsibility for the occupied inhabitants and in this way dramatically reduced the occupation's political and economic cost, while continuing to hold on to most of the territory.

Not unlike the first Palestinian uprising, the second intifada, which erupted in September 2000, was an effect of the excesses and contradictions informing the controlling apparatuses used during the Oslo years. However, as it redeployed troops in the West Bank and Gaza and disabled the PA, Israel did not reinstate any disciplinary forms of control and refused to reassume the role of managing the population's lives. Instead, Israel emphasized a series of controlling practices informed by a type of sovereign power, which have functioned less through the instatement of the law and more through the law's suspension. Israel now operates primarily by destroying the most vital social securities and by reducing members of Palestinian society to what Georgio Agamben has called *homo sacer,* people whose lives can be taken with impunity.[63] This helps explain, for example, Israel's widespread use of extrajudicial executions and the use of Palestinians as human shields. These extralegal actions stand in sharp contrast to the approach Israel adopted during the first intifada, which was in many ways characterized by a proliferation of trials and legal interventions.[64] Thus, if up until September 2000 Israel controlled the occupied inhabitants primarily through the application of the law—including, to be sure, the enforcement of draconian laws that legalized both the incarceration and torture of thousands of political prisoners and permitted deportations, house demolitions, extended curfews, and other forms of collective punishment—perhaps the most striking characteristic of the second intifada is the extensive suspension of the law. In the first intifada any suspension of the law was still considered an exception to the rule; in the second one it became the norm.

The culminating effect of the second uprising has been devastating for Palestinians in the West Bank and Gaza Strip. A large percentage of Palestinians are now dependent on aid offered by international humanitarian organizations and Islamic charities, and this aid alone ensures that the ongoing crisis does not develop into a full-blown catastrophe. So if in 1994 the PA replaced Israel as the authority responsible for disciplining the inhabitants and guaranteeing their welfare, following the eruption of the second intifada, charity organizations have taken over many of the responsibilities for sustaining Palestinian life. Thus, in the first two decades Israel attempted to manage the population by sustaining some form of security, while currently it controls the occupied inhabitants by producing endemic insecurity.

This thumbnail sketch serves to suggest that a genealogy of control can help explain how and why the occupation has changed over the years. While the book aims to advance in chronological order, the chapters are actually organized around specific themes. The first chapter is different from all the rest since it lays out the infrastructure of control: namely, the legal mechanisms, institutions, and surveillance devices that enabled the different controlling apparatuses and practices to operate. It is interesting to note that even though the occupation has dramatically changed over the years, most of the components making up the infrastructure of control have undergone only cosmetic modifications. In the second chapter I show that during the first decade following the 1967 War Israel emphasized both disciplinary and bio modes of power in order to normalize the occupation. The third chapter examines economic forms of control, showing how they rapidly began producing excesses and contradictions that empowered the Palestinian nationalist movement. Using the Palestinian municipalities as a case study, the fourth chapter focuses on the attempt to manage the occupied residents through forms of control that aimed to erase national identification. It also discusses Israel's ultimate inability to suppress Palestinian nationalism and some of the strategies it adopted to deal with this failure. The fifth chapter analyzes spatial control, suggesting that settlements, bypass roads, and the Jewish settlers should be thought of as civilian controlling mechanisms. The excesses and contradictions engendered by the controlling apparatuses discussed in chapters 3, 4, and 5 help explain the eruption of the first Palestinian uprising and the subsequent emphasis on sovereign power, which is described in chapter 6. This chapter analyzes the crisis of control in the West Bank and Gaza Strip, arguing that the ineffectiveness of apparatuses and practices informed by sovereign power helped produce the Oslo agreements. Chapter 7 reads the different Oslo agreements, which the two parties signed over a period of six years, not as part of a peace process or a withdrawal of power, but rather as texts that outline the reorganization of Israeli power in the OT. It then goes on to analyze the changes on the ground, showing how the Oslo accords precipitated the second intifada. The last chapter analyzes the means of control that have been employed during the second intifada and maintains that Israel has lost all interest in the Palestinian population as an object of control. In the epilogue I briefly discuss what might lie ahead.

Chapter 1 | THE INFRASTRUCTURE OF CONTROL

> Organizational norms and working procedures in the
> territories were formulated a short while after the end
> of the fighting. The major elements took shape that first
> month; the many and frequent changes instituted since
> then have mostly been of marginal importance.
>
> SHLOMO GAZIT,
> *first coordinator of government activities*
> *in the administered territories*

The landscapes and populations of the two regions Israel occupied in 1967
were quite different. The West Bank, which had been under Jordanian
rule, is about seventy miles long and thirty miles wide, an area the size of
Delaware. It is an arable, mountainous region that spreads from north to
south and is circumscribed on the east by a barren plateau and on the west by
the 1949 armistice agreement border known as the Green Line. Following
the war, close to six hundred thousand Palestinians were living in 12 urban
centers and about 527 rural communities, including 19 refugee camps.
About 70 percent of the population lived off agriculture in rural villages,
while the remaining 30 percent were concentrated in the urban centers and
refugee camps; 18 percent of the inhabitants were refugees.[1] By contrast, the
Gaza Strip, which had been under Egyptian rule, is a flat, narrow, and arid
region that extends some twenty miles along the Mediterranean coast and
totals 135 square miles. In 1967, 385,000 Palestinians lived in the Strip in 23
communities: 4 cities, 8 refugee camps, and 11 villages. About 70 percent of
the inhabitants were refugees who had either fled to or had been expelled
to the region during the 1948 War. Approximately 45 percent of the Gaza
Strip's population lived in the cities, 15 percent in villages, and the remaining
40 percent lived in the crowded refugee camps that had been set up by the
United Nations.[2]

Even before the 1967 War ended, Israel had adopted a series of strategies to govern the population living within these two regions. It began overseeing many of the administrative institutions that had been utilized by the Jordanians and Egyptians, using, for example, the already-existing Palestinian municipalities and mayors to help govern urban residents, and the village *muhktars* to manage those living in the rural areas. Simultaneously, however, Israel introduced some crucial changes—the modification of the legal system being perhaps the most significant. Obviously, Israel also deployed its own military to enforce law and order and immediately set up a bureaucracy that was charged with running all of the civil institutions. In addition, Israel's General Secret Services (GSS) dramatically expanded its operations in the territories, as it was given the task of undermining all Palestinian insurgency. These and a few other key institutions and practices, like the permit regime and surveillance apparatuses, served as the basic mechanisms by and through which the inhabitants were managed for years to come. By serving as the infrastructure of control, they also functioned as the vehicles through which all of the other controlling apparatuses operated.

It is important to add here that the infrastructure of control as well as the different apparatuses and practices that have emerged from the infrastructure have been governed by a number of modalities of control. By *modality of control* I mean an underlying principal that informs the way the forms of control have operated in the OT. Unlike the three modes of power mentioned in the introduction, which inform power relations in an array of political contexts and in different countries, the modalities of control characterize Israel's occupation and do not necessarily exist in other places. A modality of control, in other words, is the logic that shapes the operation of numerous controlling practices within a specific historical and geographical context.[3]

Two modalities are worth mentioning at the outset—temporariness and arbitrariness—since both have facilitated the management of the Palestinian population throughout Israel's military rule. The use of the provisional term *occupation* in order to describe the political status of the West Bank and Gaza Strip, as opposed, for instance, to *colonization,* is a prominent example of the temporary modality of control.[4] As we will see, numerous administrative arrangements, legal orders, and policies were constantly modified to conceal the permanent nature of Israel's control. Israel continuously imposed temporary curfews and closures, set up temporary checkpoints and roadblocks, and continuously issued and revoked permits, thus trying to create the illusion that entrenched practices were provisional. Along similar lines, the suspended status of Palestinian refugees within the West Bank and Gaza Strip, not unlike the temporary status of the Jewish settlements and by-pass roads, was deployed to elide the occupation's permanent nature and to facilitate the management of both Palestinians and Israelis. Temporariness was, in other words, used to prevent opposition and to thwart Palestinian resistance. Even when the lie concerning the provisional nature of certain practices was exposed, the temporary logic was immediately redeployed in new spheres and in new ways. Following Oslo, for example, temporary outposts have replaced Jewish settlements, since the latter are no longer conceived as transitory.

Many controlling apparatuses and practices were also informed by an arbitrary logic that concealed the consistent nature of Israel's military rule. Throughout the occupation, not a single plan about the number of Jewish settlements to be built or where they were to be located was ever approved by the Israeli government, rendering the settlements enterprise "arbitrary," that is, something that is much more difficult to classify and oppose.[5] A structural arbitrariness informed the very operation of the permit regime, which was part and parcel of the colossal juridical-bureaucratic apparatus that upheld the occupation.[6] Numerous rights like freedom of movement were transformed into privileges that were handed out in the form of a permit that could be revoked at any moment for an array of known and unknown reasons. The total absence of transparency in the way decisions were reached regarding permits ranging from family reunification to opening businesses and traveling abroad helped produce a form of uncertainty that was used to manage the population in different ways. The lack of plans and clear procedures alongside the absence of clear and transparent regulations forced the Palestinians to constantly second-guess what the Israeli authorities considered correct behavior, while even those who became docile were often denied permits for no apparent reason.

My claim then is that one cannot really understand how the occupation ticked without examining, even if very briefly, the major systems and institutions that enabled all the other forms of control to work, as well as the underlying principles that informed their effective operation.[7] Thus, before turning to describe the historical development of Israel's occupation and the different ways the inhabitants were managed, I outline in this chapter the infrastructure of control.

On June 5, 1967, the day the fighting erupted, the military advocate general, Colonel Meir Shamgar, issued a letter reminding the military's commanding officers of the principles of international law as well as the operative measures allowed during armed conflict.[8] Immediately following the war, however, this same Shamgar advised Israel to rethink its position vis-à-vis international law. Together with a number of other officials, he formulated a policy that rejected the applicability of the 1949 Fourth Geneva Convention — the most important humanitarian law pertaining to the occupation of conquered territories and their civilian population — to the OT. Shamgar's rationale was that the West Bank and Gaza Strip should *not* be considered occupied territories because the two regions had been seized by Jordan and Egypt during the 1948 War and thus had never been an integral part of a sovereign state. Consequently, he maintained that the West Bank and Gaza Strip should be considered "disputed" rather than occupied areas; they were, he claimed, *sui generis.*[9]

Shamgar's focus on the status of the land (regarding it as *sui generis*) rather than the population (with national rights to self-determination) was, as Lisa Hajjar cogently observes, a strategic legal maneuver to separate the land from its inhabitants.[10] Shamgar further advised the government to abide by the Geneva Convention on a de facto rather than de jure basis by respecting its humanitarian provisions, but he never specified when these provisions should actually be respected.[11] Thus, although the land was not subjected to the Geneva Convention, its Palestinian inhabitants were, but their rights remained ambiguously and, one could add, arbitrarily defined. In this way, Israel hoped to continue a process that actually began in 1948, whereby it ignored the Palestinian national right to statehood.[12] Although the international community has overwhelmingly rejected this interpretation and has regarded the West Bank and Gaza Strip as occupied territories, Israel adopted Shamgar's construal of the Geneva Convention and over the years has firmly maintained this position.

Shamgar also insisted that the Eshkol government accept the 1907 Hague Convention, which stipulates that the occupying power should recognize the laws that were in force before the occupation.[13] By June 7, 1967, the military commander had already issued Proclamation Two, a declaration dealing with the governance and legal arrangements in the territories. The laws existing in the territories prior to the occupation were declared valid provided they did not contradict any legislation issued by the military commander.[14] Accordingly, a complex legal system was put in place composed of Ottoman, British Mandatory (particularly the emergency regulations of 1945), Jordanian, and Egyptian law (depending on the region), and Israeli military orders. Military orders are decrees issued by the military commander that immediately become law for all Palestinians living in the area.[15]

Over the years, the military commanders have used their legislative powers extensively, issuing more than 2,500 orders, which have dealt with a wide range of topics: from military, judiciary, and fiscal matters to administrative affairs, including education, welfare, health, and even the status of Jewish settlements.[16] The orders codified Israel's control of the OT far beyond the concern for security of its military forces. Already in 1967 one finds orders that reveal how Israel's concerns far exceeded those of a temporary occupying power, as formally understood by international law.[17] For example, alongside orders concerning the restriction of movement and the imposition of curfews, one finds orders regarding the use of public parks, currency exchange rates, duties on tobacco and alcoholic beverages, postal laws, and the transportation of agricultural products. The implementation of this complex and comprehensive legal system has not only enabled Israel to enact any law it wishes, but also to change or cancel local laws that were in place prior to the occupation. Those parts of the Jordanian or Egyptian law that advanced Israel's political objectives were maintained, while other parts that hindered these objectives were altered or annulled.[18] Not unlike its interpretation of the Fourth Geneva Convention, Israel opted for a partial adoption of the pertinent clauses of the Hague Convention, ones that corresponded to its needs.[19]

Israel's idiosyncratic interpretation of international humanitarian law has had an immense impact on the occupation. Its ingenuity lies, on the one hand, in its effective distinction between the people and the land, and, on the other hand, in the fact that it does not reject the law outright but embraces a selective approach toward the law. Shamgar seems to have recognized that even as Israel suspended significant elements of international law and bestowed on the military commander the authority to cancel and enact domestic laws according to immediate political objectives, it was also crucial to espouse a "rule of law" approach. Adopting laws that had existed before the occupation while making room for the enactment of military orders that could cancel these laws actually enabled Israel to argue that the rule of law reigned in the West Bank and Gaza Strip. In this way, Israel managed to deflect criticism of despotic rule for many years.

To strengthen the conception of "enlightened rule" Israel established a whole institutional apparatus, which consisted of military courts and, after 1989, courts of appeal; it appointed military judges and prosecutors, and even employed translators who were responsible for ensuring that Palestinian defendants understood the court proceedings.[20] The creation of judiciary institutions was crucial, since, as Raja Shehadeh has convincingly observed, Israel aspired to project an image of itself as a community committed to and ruled by principles of justice.[21] Indeed, the complex legal system and institutions Israel established served, in many important ways, to sanction the legality, legitimacy, and morality of the occupation.

Yet, the conception of the law as an instrument that protects the individual from the sovereign — which can be traced all the way back to the Magna Carta (1215) and, more recently, to the French Declaration of the Rights of Man and Citizen and post–World War II international law — was totally foreign to the legal system Israel set up in the OT. It is therefore no coincidence that this system was never applied to the Jewish settlers who moved into the West Bank and Gaza Strip. These settlers, as well as residents of Israel who traveled to the territories, were subjected to Israeli civilian law, which was granted an extraterritorial status. By transforming Jewish citizens into turtles of sorts, i.e. creatures that are entitled to "personal jurisdiction" (i.e., laws that follow people), Israel managed to create a situation whereby two ethnic groups sharing the same space have actually been subjected to radically different legal systems.[22]

Without establishing this comprehensive legal system, Israel could never have effectively administered the occupied regions. The law served as the foundation for almost all of the other controlling apparatuses and practices and in many ways shaped their operations. The legal system established the institutional framework of and for the occupation, determined the military government's mandate, and defined the powers of the military commander as well as the responsibilities of the different civil institutions. Yet the legal system itself, once established, also became a means of control in its own right. It established rules and disseminated a substantive and procedural legal discourse. This apparatus produced a series of norms, which the inhabitants were simultaneously encouraged and compelled to emulate, and was used to authorize and legalize administrative detention, house demolitions, land confiscation, and other daily forms of control.[23]

The legal system was also informed by the temporary and arbitrary modalities of control. The fact that the military commander had the authority to issue decrees according to what he considered to be Israel's interests and needs not only enabled him to cancel existing laws and introduce new ones, but also ended up rendering many of the legal arrangements both temporary and arbitrary. New decrees were constantly issued, revising and annulling older ones. The temporary nature of the decrees always left open the possibility that they could be altered for the better or for the worse — the way they would be modified supposedly depended on the inhabitants' behavior, thus helping to shape Palestinian comportment.[24]

Simultaneously, the adoption of several legal frameworks enabled Israel to exploit the gaps and contradictions engendered by their interaction, and to use both the laws and the exceptions that the gaps and contradictions made possible in order to control the inhabitants. The legal system's structure also left a tremendous range of issues at the discretion of the military commander and even at the discretion of officers who were in charge of subregions within the OT or of specific fields like health care and education. The lack of procedural transparency rendered the criteria for obtaining a referral to a hospital in Israel, receiving a permit to build a store, or approval of family reunification unclear. The arbitrariness created both by the lack of transparency and the gaps among the different legal frameworks was used to secure the services of certain individuals and to manage the population through the production of endemic uncertainty.

THE MILITARY FORCES AND ADMINISTRATIVE BUREAUCRACY

Two days after the war erupted, Israel used the newly established legal system to set up a military government so that it, in turn, could actively administer the population in the West Bank and Gaza Strip (and Sinai Peninsula). With the issuing of Proclamation Two, the military commander became both the legislator and the executive authority in the region. There were actually two military governments, one in the West Bank and the other in the Gaza Strip, and both were manned by military personnel (both conscripted and reserve), whose responsibilities were divided between two branches: security and civil. The officers in both branches had to report to the regional military governor.

The security branch, made up of Israeli military forces, was responsible for maintaining law and order in the territories and for guaranteeing the safety of Israel's citizenry. It established military bases in the OT, deployed troops who were in charge of policing both regions, and, when deemed necessary, punished Palestinian residents by imposing curfews, closing schools, demolishing houses, and deporting leaders.[25]

The civil branch was divided into two sub-branches: the economic and service departments (see appendix 1). The former oversaw industry, commerce, agriculture, labor, and financial activities in the OT. The service department dealt with education, welfare, health care, postal matters, and so on, and, together with the economic department, it was used as the scaffolding for almost all the apparatuses that aimed to normalize the occupation. These two branches served as the infrastructure for an intricate network of controlling practices that were rapidly deployed. While the people who ran these branches and who served as the heads of the different civil institutions were Israelis who worked for the military government, thousands of Palestinians — school principals and teachers, social workers, doctors and nurses, policemen and postal clerks, as well as bureaucrats — constituting well over 90 percent of the military government's employees, and ran the daily operation of the different civil institutions. Thus, most residents' day-to-day contact with the civil institutions entailed encounters with other Palestinians rather than Israelis.

Whereas the military government served as the executive branch in the OT, the Israeli cabinet was in charge of introducing policies.[26] A Ministerial Committee for the Affairs of the Administered Territories and two inter-ministerial committees dealing with practical political, economic, and security issues met regularly for more than a decade to determine policy.[27] Because the interministerial committees had a hands-on approach, and since the coordinator of activities in the territories reported to the minister of defense rather than to the military's chief of staff, during the first years of occupation some form of separation between the civil and security branches existed. It is precisely this separation that differentiates the first period of occupation from the ones following it, when the interministerial committees no longer functioned and the coordinator of activities in the territories was asked to report directly to the chief of staff.[28]

In addition to the military government's security and civil branches, the GSS, also known by its Hebrew acronyms Shabak or Shin Bet, played a central role in the OT, rapidly becoming the most influential Israeli authority in the West Bank and Gaza Strip.[29] According to one officer, after the 1967 War the GSS began "to set the pace, methods and timing [in the OT]. The big change was that we were no longer just collecting intelligence. We went operational in our own right."[30] And, indeed, the security services had a major impact on the Palestinian inhabitants, shaping, as it were, a significant part of their daily lives. The GSS influenced decisions about if, when, and where to impose curfews, who to arrest, who to deport, and which houses would be demolished. It was involved in the hiring and firing of principals and teachers as well as doctors and clerks, and decided when to open or shut down schools, universities, and charitable organizations. The military government required the GSS's approval before allowing a resident to travel abroad, giving out licenses to open a business, or providing a permit to establish a medical clinic. Swiftly it became the king of the land, operating like the mythological Indian character Ravana, the ten-headed king who has twenty hands.

Paradoxically, the GSS worked as a legal specter. Until the so-called Shabak Law was passed in 2002, not one Israeli law dealt specifically with the GSS, and, as Avigdor Feldman has pointed out, the organization had little more legal authority than a parking lot attendant; it had no authority to conduct searches, to carry out arrests, or to launch an independent investigation.[31] The secret organization's existence, actions, and power were, consequently, the result of unwritten agreements between it and other state authorities.[32] While at times it used the legal system Israel created in the OT, unlike all of the other organizations and institutions Israel established, the GSS existed and commonly operated outside the law. The GSS was, accordingly, an omnipresent exception, operating through the suspension of the law rather than its implementation and enforcement. As we will see toward the end of the book, following the eruption of the second intifada the suspension of the law became part of the norm for the military as well.

Feldman stresses that the GSS's ambiguous status both within Israeli legal space and within the occupied one is actually the key for understanding its vast powers. The GSS benefited from its extralegal status in two intricately connected ways. On the one hand, because it had no legal authority, it became a "body snatcher" of sorts. It used the military, police, prison services, and even the attorney general's office to carry out tasks for it. In Feldman's words, the GSS penetrated and assumed control of these state bodies like a parasite that supports itself by "feeding on the powers of the institutions in whose gut it has settled." On the other hand, its extralegal status allowed it to maintain an invisible existence, and its invisibility enabled it to perpetrate numerous illegal activities, not the least of which was torture.[33] Thus, Israel not only set up a dual legal system in the OT, one for Jews and the other for Palestinians, but the legal system that was used by the military and civil bureaucracies to manage the Palestinians was itself also regularly ignored by the GSS, which operated extralegally without oversight. The Palestinians were continuously managed through the simultaneous application and suspension of a legal system. The new Shabak Law has changed some of this, since it purports to regulate the GSS's legal status, defining how the head of the organization is elected as well as the organization's role and authority. The GSS can now legally carry out searches and interrogate suspects, yet the law's wording is vague and formulated in such a way that the secret organization actually continues to maintain its vast powers.[34]

THE HIGH COURT OF JUSTICE

The role played by the Israeli Supreme Court, which acts as a High Court of Justice responsible for reviewing the policies and actions of government institutions, has surely been very different from the one played by the systems and institutions just described.[35] The Court did not serve as a channel through which the means of control directly operated, and, unlike the other institutions, it was never physically present in the territories; I therefore consider it an auxiliary element. It existed before the 1967 War and, in contrast to the GSS, it did not change its structure or receive more operating funds following the war so that it could attend to issues directly relating to the occupation. Nonetheless, one cannot understand Israel's occupation without taking into account the crucial role performed by the High Court. By lending its symbolic capital to the military occupation, it legitimized the deployment of many of the controlling apparatuses and practices.[36]

Since Israel never applied its own legal system to the population in the

West Bank and Gaza Strip, it was not obvious that the Court's authority would extend to the Palestinian inhabitants. Nonetheless, following a petition filed by a Palestinian from the West Bank two weeks after the war, the High Court decided that it did have jurisdiction over the areas and people Israel had occupied and in this way set a precedent in international practice. Israeli sociologist Baruch Kimmerling points out that by hearing cases brought by inhabitants of the OT, the Court "not only bestowed on the occupation an enlightened face and a kind of legitimacy anchored in the modern concept of 'law and order' but committed a 'judicial annexation' of the territories producing an image of 'legality.'"[37]

Over the years, Israel's highest tribunal has been asked to review literally thousands of petitions dealing primarily with the legality of coercive measures employed in the territories, such as house demolitions, extended curfews, harsh restrictions of movement, administrative detention, deportations, torture, and extrajudicial executions, and it has almost always concluded that the military commander exercised his powers in conformity with international humanitarian law without exceeding his authority. In his book *The Occupation of Justice,* David Kretzmer reveals that in almost all of its judgments relating to the OT, "especially those dealing with questions of principle, the Court has decided in favor of the authorities, often on the basis of dubious legal arguments."[38] Thus, the High Court fulfilled four important functions that are relevant to us here. First, it carried out a judicial annexation of the territories. Second, it rationalized Israel's interpretation of international humanitarian law and its applicability to the territories, giving credence to Shamgar's initial construal. Third, through its rulings, it sanctioned and legitimated many forms of control that Israel has deployed in the territories, most notably the coercive ones. Finally, as the major authority on issues of justice within Israel, it helped produce the "morality" of the occupation.

THE PERMIT REGIME

The permit regime and the networks of surveillance also deserve to be considered as part of the infrastructure of control. As with other forms of control, Israel began introducing an elaborate permit regime in the West Bank and Gaza Strip before the armed conflict had ended.[39] This regime was created by a complex fabric of military orders and included licenses, such as car registration and driving licenses, as well as permits for engaging in certain financial activities like registering a business or exporting and importing goods. Building homes or any other kind of edifice also required permits. Permits also had to be obtained for less obvious reasons, such as traveling abroad for medical treatment or in order to study; live outside the village, town, or city where one was registered; or grow certain kinds of fruits and vegetables. The procurement of a permit often entailed a long process that included filling out forms, paying fees, and frequently being interviewed (i.e., a recruitment attempt) by a GSS officer.[40]

The permit regime managed to transform the most basic rights—ranging from the right to livelihood, shelter, and health to the right to freedom of movement, speech, and association—into privileges that could be taken away at any moment without the revocation being considered a violation. The temporary and arbitrary nature of many permits served the two modalities of control mentioned above. The regime can be characterized by its ubiquitous nature, creating a grid that extended across every part of Palestinian society. Indeed, during the past four decades it has continued to expand and has constantly colonized new domains. While it has functioned through restrictions, prohibitions, and exclusions, it has also aimed to shape the comportment of both Palestinian individuals and the population in general through the dissemination of a series of norms that, if approximated, seemingly increase the probability of receiving the desired permit. For instance, if one does not participate in protests or any other kind of political activity, one has a higher chance of receiving an entry permit into Israel.

All social relations, including the way people relate to their fellow citizens, their occupiers, and to the surrounding environment, as well as the way they govern themselves have been shaped by the permit regime. In order to illustrate just how deeply the regime has permeated the occupation, how it was used both to constrain and harness the inhabitants' energies, I briefly review some of the permits issued during the occupation's first decade, dividing them into three categories according to the predominant field they strove to regulate: livelihood, space, and knowledge. While each permit can be analyzed on its own in order to show how it controlled a specific sphere, by noting examples of several permits from each category I hope to provide a glimpse of how the permit *regime* operated to shape practically every aspect of Palestinian life.

Many of the military orders published during the first years dealt with work and commerce. By June 18, 1967, a week after the war, Israel had issued a military order that made it illegal to conduct business transactions involving land or property without a permit. On the same day, it published an order notifying all Palestinians possessing foreign currency that they would either need to exchange it or acquire a permit. Violations of this regulation could result in five years of imprisonment or a 1,500 Jordanian dinar fine. All merchants who wanted to import or export goods had to obtain a permit, while banks and credit institutions were not allowed to operate without permission. Residents needed permits to work in the public sector, whereas those who were not official residents of the two regions had to obtain permits to work in any sector.[41]

Other permits relating to livelihood involved basic resources. The military commander was given full control over all water resources, and any person or entity wishing to install a water device (such as a pump, irrigation equipment, etc.) had to obtain a permit. Along similar lines, it was forbidden to carry out any kind of electricity work or connect a generator without a permit. It was even prohibited to "harm nature," although the authorities did preserve "the right to permit people to pick flowers or tamper with nature in the course of research studies." Reclamation of one's own land, if it involved bulldozing a piece of property in order to remove rocks, boulders, or any other obstructive material to make it cultivable was forbidden unless the farmer obtained a permit from the military authority. Military orders rendered it illegal to plant new citrus trees, replace old nonproductive ones, or plant fruit trees without permission.[42] The military commander also prohibited the transport of any plant, animal produce, and commodity in or out of the OT without a permit. All forms of transportation for the transfer of goods needed a license, including donkey carts. Farmers needed permits to obtain and operate tractors, and permits were required for grazing livestock in certain areas.[43]

Permits Relating to Palestinian Space

In order to monitor the inhabitants, in March 1968 Israel also began issuing identity cards to every male over the age of sixteen, registering the residents as wards of the military.[44] The cards had to be carried at all times, thus allowing the military to keep track of the movements of individuals. Although the restrictions on movement during the first years were not nearly as harsh as in later years, movement both within the OT and to and from the two regions was always limited. A cursory examination of the military orders from the first decade reveals that entire areas, such as the Jordan Valley, were declared closed zones, and anyone wishing to enter or exit them required a permit. Whoever entered closed areas without a permit or remained in such areas after their permit expired was regarded as an "infiltrator." In some areas that were otherwise open to Palestinians, those who wished to travel within them had to follow specific routes and enter during specific hours. In addition, it was prohibited to transfer or change one's place of residence either permanently or temporarily without a permit; and if one wished to visit friends in another city for more than forty-eight hours, one had to obtain a permit.[45] It is interesting to note here that during the first two decades, movement restrictions in the OT were not as strict as they had been for Palestinian citizens living inside Israel proper during the military government (1948–1966). Moreover, many of the permits relating to movement were not enforced during the first years, even though Israel's ability to monitor, regulate, and restrict movement served as one of its most prominent and effective forms of control. This is not surprising, given that almost every aspect of daily life is dependent on the ability to move within space.

Permits Relating to Knowledge

The permit regime was also employed to control the fields of knowledge accessible to the occupied population and indeed to help Israel create new knowledge; this occurred primarily through censorship and the regulation and dissemination of information. This part of the regime was based on the 1945 British Emergency Regulations (part 8, articles 86–101). Article 88, for example, states that "the censor may by order prohibit the importation or expropriation or the printing or publishing of any publication . . . which in his opinion, would be or [is] likely to be or become, prejudicial for the defense of Palestine or to the public safety or to public order." Clause two of the same article states that "any person who contravenes any order under this regulation and the proprietor and editor of the publication, in relation to which the contravention occurs, and any person . . . who has in his possession or his control or in premises of which he is the occupier, any publication prohibited under this regulation or who posts, delivers, or receives any such prohibition, shall be guilty of an offense against these regulations."[46]

Military order 50 from July 1967 reiterated these regulations, forbidding the distribution or publication of newspapers without the permission of the military authorities. The order defines "newspapers" as including "any pamphlet containing news, information, events, occurrences, or explanations relating to news items, stories, or any other item of public interest." Those newspapers that did receive authorization were subjected to strict censorship, while the permit itself had to be renewed every three months.[47] News articles describing events taking place in the West Bank and Gaza frequently had the details expunged. Articles reporting on curfews, strikes, protests, and Israeli seizure of land and water were typically reduced to a single paragraph simply pointing out that an event took place.[48] The ultimate goal was to create a regime of truth that did not threaten Israeli military rule and that would actually help normalize the occupation. So, for example, the Israeli communist paper *Al-Itihad* was outlawed in the OT, while simultaneously an Arabic paper published by the governing Mapai Party was distributed in the West Bank. When Israel realized that hardly any Palestinian bothered to purchase the latter paper, it increased its Arabic radio news programs and added a few other programs in an effort to reach some of the inhabitants.[49]

Printing, publishing, or distributing political leaflets and articles as well as pictures, posters, flags, and artwork with "political significance" without obtaining a permit from the military commander was also strictly prohibited.[50] The word *printing* is defined in the military order as "lithography, typing on a type writer, copying, photographing or any other manner of representation or of communicating expressions, numbers, symbols, pictures, maps, painting, decorations, or any other similar material." As Virgil Falloon points out, the term *publishing* denotes a wide array of practices, thus allowing the authorities to convict a librarian from Ramallah for "publishing" illegal material after he had purchased what he thought was a permitted publication and made it available to the larger public.[51] Falloon underscores that the military order's key concept, "political significance," is left undefined, and shows that the censor considered "political significance" to be "any suggestion that West Bank inhabitants are suffering under occupation, any talk of love and loyalty to the homeland, or any representation of national aspirations." Common examples of illicit "political content" have included pictorial representations of Israeli soldiers assaulting Palestinian civilians, schools surrounded by barbed wire, and the use of the colors of the

Palestinian flag together—red, green, black, and white. The employment of words like *homeland, return,* or *PLO* in the newspapers were also declared illegal.[52]

As I show in the following chapter, one of the sites in which Israel attempted to control knowledge was the education system. School textbooks were censored, as were hundreds of other books, including classical poetry, plays, and novels.[53] In addition, it was forbidden to protest or associate in groups. Any group of ten or more people who wished to meet in order to discuss issues concerning or related to politics broadly defined had to acquire a permit from the military commander. Finally, all attempts to influence public opinion in a way "detrimental to public order" were rendered illegal. These examples illustrate how the permit regime attempted to manage the population by repressing certain fields of knowledge that were circulating in the public sphere while concomitantly introducing and disseminating others.

Permits and Control

Even this cursory overview suggests that the permit regime infiltrated almost every aspect of Palestinian society, creating an intricate web through which the population was managed. Indeed, revealing the way the permit regime spread across the entire social terrain and the way it shaped the minutest daily practices sheds light on the vast resources and energy put into administering the occupied inhabitants, both on the level of the population as well as on the level of the individual Palestinian. The permit regime functioned simultaneously as the scaffolding for many other forms of control and thus as part of the infrastructure of control, as well as a controlling apparatus in its own right.

As a controlling apparatus, permits obviously function as restrictive fiats, producing and enforcing prohibited zones. But the permit regime was never informed solely by a sovereign mode of power, which uses the regulations in a negative way, through the imposition of restrictions and exclusions. Just as importantly, the permit regime has always operated in the service of disciplinary and bio modes of power, since it has created and promulgated norms of "correct" behavior and thus has helped shape the interests and comportment of the inhabitants in a productive way. The permits determined which crops could be planted, how they could be transported, and where they could be sold, all of which helped shape the behavior and habits of the Palestinian farmer as well as form the Palestinian economy as a whole. Moreover, by determining who would be allowed to move freely, conduct business transactions, obtain a job, or acquire university training, it helped certain people improve or maintain their position on the social ladder, thereby influencing the economic and political hierarchy of Palestinian society within the territories.[54]

As part of the infrastructure of control, the permit regime was instrumental in shaping the Palestinian economy, space, politics, and civilian life. It helped constrain the development of an independent Palestinian industry and agriculture, and it restricted Palestinian construction. It operated in complex ways to ensure that the Palestinian workforce would consist mostly of unskilled labor. It enabled Israeli officials to determine the curriculum in schools and thus helped promote a certain history while suppressing another history. It determined the licensed medical fields that could be practiced in the OT and the whereabouts of hospitals and clinics. Yet, again it is important to reiterate that the regime shaped not only the economy and the civil infrastructure, but the comportment of Palestinian inhabitants as well. It also enabled the GSS to recruit thousands of collaborators, who not only relayed information to their operators, but also fragmented Palestinian society.

On a different level of analysis, the permit regime was informed by the modalities of control mentioned above. First, the regime itself helped generate, reproduce, and exploit the gaps and fissures among the different legal frameworks, and in this way helped transform the law into an instrument of control devoid of any force to protect the rights of the Palestinian inhabitants. Second, in addition to facilitating the production of a colossal bureaucratic apparatus, the ever-changing character of the regime and the lack of transparency relating to how it operated helped engender the ostensibly temporary and arbitrary character of the occupation. It was instrumental in introducing an uncertain, even aleatory, dimension that was utilized, in turn, to manage the Palestinian population through the constant play of security and insecurity. Israel, for example, issued permits that secured jobs for tens of thousands of Palestinians, and in this way helped secure the livelihood of hundreds of thousands of people. Yet the fact that their livelihood depended on a permit that could be revoked produced a profound sense of insecurity, which during certain periods was merely a hovering threat and during other periods became a reality. Finally, the permit regime also served to define the contours of the surveillance apparatuses, determining, as it were, which domains needed to be monitored in order to assess whether the inhabitants were following the rules of "correct" behavior. At the same time, though, the efficient operation of the permit regime relied on the ubiquitous surveillance of Palestinian society, since without the ability to monitor the population, the regime was in many respects useless.

SURVEILLANCE

Considering that almost all forms of control depend for their successful operation on the collection and analysis of data pertaining to the population, it is not surprising that within months of the occupation almost every aspect of Palestinian life was surveyed, examined, and registered. The seemingly endless number of tables, charts, and figures published by the military government, Israel's Central Bureau of Statistics, and the Bank of Israel's Research Department, as well as different government ministries reveals the extent to which the population was monitored and provides a sense of the vast amount of resources Israel invested in ensuring that nothing escaped its observation. Indeed, what comes across very prominently in the reports published during the first years following the war is both the swiftness with which the surveillance apparatus was set up and the degree of surveillance and scrutiny to which the population was subjected.

In order to ensure the efficient working of Israeli control, information from several different fields — ranging from population characteristics, employment, and public health to education, infrastructure, and bureaucracy — was aggregated. Data was collected about the number of Palestinians Israel had to manage and how they were distributed across space in terms of regions, urban versus rural habitation, as well as refugee versus permanent residents. Population surveys attempted to ascertain the exact distribution of gender, age, and religion among Palestinian workers in the different sectors of occupation. The military authorities examined the infant mortality rate, the population's growth rate, poverty levels, per capita income, and the size and makeup of the labor force in terms of age, gender, and field of occupation. The scale and type of industry in the territories was also surveyed, as was the amount of arable land and the kinds of crops planted; even the cattle and poultry were counted. Satellite and aerial images were used to monitor the construction of homes, public buildings, and private businesses.

Each cluster of data dealt with specific issues. Several tables and charts appearing in early reports underscore Israel's effort to survey the population's lifestyle. The Bank of Israel's Research Department documented, for instance, a series of social indicators, such as the number of households with electricity, private kitchens, toilets, bathrooms, and the number of people per room. It monitored furniture and household maintenance, keeping track of the per-household percentage of gas-cookers, electric refrigerators, television sets, telephones, sewing machines, and private cars. Israel was accordingly able to track the changing rate of private consumption, the energy and nutritional value of the food basket, and the proportion of household expenditure allocated to services like health, education, transportation, and entertainment.[55] Such surveillance is common among modern states, since the knowledge it produces is necessary for the efficient management of the population. But the rapid establishment of such an extensive surveillance apparatus and the huge expenditure that it no doubt incurred raises the question of whether Israel ever had the intention of withdrawing from the OT or conceived the occupation as temporary. Moreover, this massive investment soon became, as James Ron has observed, a double-edged sword, since by inscribing Palestinian lives and assets into Israel's bureaucratic registries, those entities were transformed into objects of state responsibility.[56] The fact that in the late 1990s Israel ceased to monitor most of the practices it had so carefully inspected during the occupation's first three decades accordingly suggests that it no longer considered itself responsible for the lives of the Palestinian inhabitants.

Several other domains were also constantly monitored, such as the forms of communication among Palestinians. One finds tables enumerating the amount and destination of phone calls made during the calendar year 1969–1970 (90,298 inside the Gaza Strip; 13,554 from the Strip to the West Bank; 66,899 from the Strip to Israel; and 666 from the Strip to other countries); the amount of incoming and outgoing letters sent to and by Palestinians (254,624 and 232,046 respectively); the amount of incoming and outgoing Red Cross dispatches (147,506 and 134,383 respectively); the number of stamps sold (45,000); and the amount of incoming and outgoing parcels, telegrams, and cables (2,297 and 2,343 respectively).[57] Such tables intimate how quickly Israel managed to set up mechanisms that could monitor the different forms of association among the occupied inhabitants. As the years passed, these mechanisms were constantly updated and expanded in order to deepen the degree of surveillance and to keep up with the development of new communication technologies.

While most forms of surveillance operate through their invisibility (like keeping track of the communication among Palestinians, the use of land, and the movement of individuals), some actually function through their perpetual visibility. Particularly salient among these are buildings. Israel seems to have been aware of this and early on relocated some of its military training bases to the OT.[58] The mere existence of the military bases within close proximity to Palestinian villages and towns helped create the impression that the inhabitants were constantly being observed. The Israeli military was accordingly not only used as a mechanism that enforced law and order through coercive measures, but also as a panoptical tower of sorts, imposing a compulsory visibility on the population. As we will see in chapter 5, the Jewish settlements built on hilltops overlooking Palestinian villages aimed to achieve a similar end. The idea was to use military bases, settlements, and bypass roads in order to strengthen Israel's control over the population.[59]

Palestinian Collaborators as Part of the Surveillance Technology

The seemingly endless amount of data gathered and the construction of buildings could not, however, ensure the perpetual visibility of the Palestinian inhabitants. To further enhance its surveillance of the population, Israel began recruiting a massive number of collaborators.[60] It did not discriminate among Palestinians and enlisted both adults and children, the rich and the poor, urban professionals and rural farmers.[61] There were two main methods used to enlist collaborators. One operated through the permit regime. The permits, as mentioned, transformed many rights into privileges that were bestowed according to the discretion of the occupying authorities. Frequently, a person requesting a permit had to go through the GSS offices and was interviewed by one of the officers. A positive response to a request for a permit, ranging from access to medical treatment and family unification to building a home or opening a business, was at times conditional upon the applicant's willingness to collaborate.[62] Without the permit regime it would have been extremely difficult to recruit so many collaborators. The second recruitment method involved Palestinians suspected, accused, or convicted of security or criminal offenses. Often they were recruited by promising to withdraw charges, lighten sentences, or improve their imprisonment conditions.[63] "The theory was that if a sufficiently large number of people were approached, some, simply by the law of statistical averages, would likely turn out to be useful sources."[64] Before long, thousands of collaborators were operating in the OT.[65]

Formally, collaborators have had five principal roles: (1) to infiltrate into the ranks of different organizations and institutions, newspaper staff, political groups, and so on, so as to relay information to Israeli authorities about the organization and the whereabouts of its leaders; (2) to extract confessions from political prisoners and to intimidate them; (3) to recruit new Palestinian agents; (4) to help Israel gain control of Palestinian land; and (5) to carry out paramilitary activities such as capturing wanted suspects and at times even killing them.[66] They are, accordingly, part of an apparatus that enforces (by, for example, carrying out arrests) and suspends (by carrying out extrajudicial executions) the law.

On a deeper and informal level, though, the collaborators have assumed a few other roles. They have been used as a surveillance apparatus that monitors Palestinian society at large. As opposed to a military base or a Jewish settlement, which is like a panoptic tower whose gaze is centralized and visible, the collaborators are much more efficient, since they are dispersed throughout society, for the most part invisible, and operate from the bottom up. The uncertainty regarding the collaborator's identity renders the surveillance apparatus omnipresent and therefore much more efficient. Almost anyone, anywhere, at anytime could potentially be a collaborator.

This suggests, in turn, that collaborators serve two additional roles that are probably more consequential than their more formal roles. They function as a means of control that encourages "correct" conduct. The mere possibility that someone could be a collaborator—and practically anyone can be a collaborator—becomes an extremely effective tool for encouraging people to act and even think in a certain way. From a slightly different perspective, the extensive employment of collaborators has helped to create new social hierarchies, since some of the incentives offered to collaborators by their operators have allowed them to climb the social ladder, while harsh restrictions are frequently imposed on those who refuse to cooperate. Simultaneously, collaborators also facilitate the fragmentation of society, undermining the basic trust needed to create alliances, promote solidarity, and spur political resistance. By destroying trust, they also individualize and depoliticize society.[67]

Surveillance and Control

Not unlike the permit regime, the surveillance apparatus that Israel set up served both as part of the infrastructure of control as well as a form of control in its own right. The efficient operation of almost all the controlling apparatuses or practices deployed to manage the Palestinian population depended on the ongoing collection of data. If, for example, Israel wanted to increase agricultural productivity in the OT, it first needed to determine the amount of arable and cultivated land and the kinds of crops being planted. Subsequently, it would have to determine whether the introduction of new kinds of crops and improved seeds as well as the training it offered farmers had helped achieve its intended objectives. Thus, without the ongoing surveillance of Palestinian society, Israel could not test the efficiency of the measures it introduced. Along similar lines, ongoing surveillance was necessary for monitoring Palestinian behavior so as to keep track of transgressive activities, ranging from building "illegal" homes and planting prohibited crops to joining an underground political cell.[68] In these and several other ways surveillance operated as part of the infrastructure of control.

As a form of control in its own right, surveillance encourages each individual to govern him or herself. The notion that someone is always monitoring one's behavior and activities propels forms of self-governing.[69] The gaze emanating from the military government, civil institutions, Palestinian collaborators, and Jewish settlers often penetrates the individual, encouraging him or her to act in accordance with some of the existing rules, codes, and mores set by the occupying authorities—yet, at times, it also encourages subversive acts.

MOVING BEYOND THE CARROT AND THE STICK

The swiftness with which Israel set up the infrastructure of control is worth reemphasizing. Within days of the war's end, the basic rationale informing the complex legal system was established, and the High Court of Justice accepted the role of supreme arbitrator between the occupied inhabitants and the military commander. Just a few weeks later, the civil bureaucracies were operating, and the military and GSS were policing and managing the population. Moreover, the permit regime was created, and many of the surveillance apparatuses were installed within months. One cannot understand Israel's occupation without taking into account this infrastructure of control, since its different components have informed every aspect of Palestinian life from the inception of the occupation until this day.

The legal system, civil and security institutions, permit regime, and surveillance apparatuses continued to develop until the mid-1990s, but the changes introduced were relatively minor. Since all forms of control both depend on and are shaped by the infrastructure of control, the fact that the infrastructural modifications were not substantial helps explain why the means of control did not change dramatically over the years. The significant changes taking place in the West Bank and Gaza Strip over the past four decades are thus a result of the way the means of control were used; their function, as mentioned earlier, was adjusted according to the modes of power that were emphasized during each period. In other words, the way the Palestinian population was managed changed dramatically not so much because the occupying power introduced new forms of control, but primarily because the emphasis on the modes of power shifted. And the alteration in the modes of power was propelled by the excesses and contradictions produced by the controlling apparatuses and practices.

In the following chapters I trace some of the excesses and contradictions that helped modify the modes of power, showing how they shaped both Palestinian resistance and Israel's policy choices. But before turning to analyze the historical developments in the West Bank and Gaza Strip, it is important to underscore the inadequacy of the pervasive "carrot and stick" metaphor, which has been repeatedly invoked by commentators of all stripes in order to explain how the Palestinian inhabitants were administered.[70] This metaphor was introduced by Dayan immediately after the war to intimate that Israel could and would manage the Palestinian population in the OT through appeasement and pacification on the one hand, and coercive punitive measures on the other. The pervasive invocation of the metaphor is unfortunate, since it both reinscribes the statist approach which understands the state to be a free agent that determines policies according to the whims of its leaders and assumes a very limited conception of power. It therefore fails to capture the vast majority of controlling apparatuses and practices deployed in the West Bank and Gaza Strip and ends up concealing rather than revealing most of the methods employed to manage the occupied population. It also obscures or fails to account for many of the reasons why the occupation has changed so dramatically over the years.

Shlomo Gazit, the first coordinator of government activities in the administered territories, who wrote a book about the occupation called *The Carrot and the Stick*, maintains that Israel did not really have a premeditated philosophy regarding how it wanted to govern the population. Thus, in stark contrast to the statist approach that informs the carrot and stick metaphor, he claims that many of the policies were actually shaped from below.[71] Dayan and several other people certainly implemented policies based on their strategic intuition, and the interministerial government committee met every other week to determine policy, but their decisions were shaped by concrete local political, social, and economic developments that arose from the ground. The overall strategy of control in the OT, in other words, did not exist before the occupation or come into being out of nowhere once the territories were captured; rather, it was partially molded by the interactions among the different forms of control that were adopted on the local and regional level in order to manage the population.

The metaphor's major inadequacy, however, results from the fact that it assumes a space, indeed a fairly large space, devoid of all power relations. Israel, according to this metaphor, enabled Palestinians to live their lives without interference so long as they behaved well. The carrot and the stick were used only when Israel wanted to either encourage or discourage the Palestinians from acting in certain ways. Power, according to the metaphor, is reduced to visible acts of intervention. In reality, however, the grid of controlling apparatuses and practices employed to manage the population was so widespread that it saturated every aspect of Palestinian life, leaving no space untouched. All facets of daily life within the territories were continuously meddled with, acted upon, and shaped, often in order to produce and channel the energy of the inhabitants in directions that Israel considered conducive to its own interests. Israel's attempt to increase hospital deliveries, its distribution of improved seeds for agricultural crops, and its vaccination of livestock are not considered forms of control or effects of power according to the metaphor of the carrot and the stick.

In sum, this metaphor presupposes that most daily practices are uncontaminated by power and therefore considers only the most visible, intermittent interventions as the workings of power, thus ignoring the apparatuses that ceaselessly operate on the minutest parts of daily life in order to produce and disseminate an array of norms and social practices. Referring back to the distinction discussed in the introduction among the three modes of power, the carrot and stick metaphor recognizes only sovereign power. Considering that most forms of social control cannot really be captured by this conception of power, the carrot and stick metaphor has actually served to cover up the more subtle means by which the Palestinians were managed and controlled.

Chapter 2 | "THE INVISIBLE OCCUPATION"

> One might say, in principle, that the aims of the Military
> Government were that an Arab resident of the area might
> be born in the hospital, receive his birth certificate, grow
> up and receive his education, be married and raise his
> children and grandchildren to a ripe old age — all this
> without the help of an Israeli government employee or
> clerk, and without even setting eyes on him.
>
> SHLOMO GAZIT,
> *Coordinator of Government Activities*
> *in the Administered Territories, 1970*

Immediately following the 1967 War, the head of Israel's GSS, Yosef
Harmelin, submitted a proposal to Defense Minister Moshe Dayan elabo-
rating on how he thought the population in the West Bank and Gaza Strip
should be governed. Harmelin suggested that the same framework that had
been used to manage the Palestinians inside Israel during the period of the
internal military government (1948–1966) should be adopted in the West
Bank and Gaza Strip.[1] Dayan disagreed, maintaining that given the very
different social and political situations of the Palestinians inside Israel after
1948 and the newly occupied inhabitants, the form of military government
established inside Israel should not be emulated.

A relatively small percentage of Palestinians had remained in what became
Israel after 1948. The vast majority of leaders and intelligentsia had fled the
urban centers, leaving them practically empty, while the inhabitants who
did not leave were mostly rural dwellers who were not organized under a
unified political umbrella. This, alongside the fact that not long after the
war Israel decided to offer these Palestinians citizenship and incorporate
them, at least partially, into the Israeli demos, shaped the forms of control
adopted by the internal military government. In the OT, by contrast, most
of the inhabitants were not displaced during the 1967 War; both the urban
and rural leadership had, to a large extent, stayed put, and Israel had no
intention of integrating these Palestinians into its own citizenry. From

Israel's perspective then, these social and political differences called for a different form of government, and Dayan decided to adopt a more open and less interventionist policy than the one that had been used to manage the Palestinians inside Israel.[2] Israel's intention, according to military reports published after the war, was to implement "a policy of normalization" through the encouragement of self-rule, which would "allow the population of the areas to carry on their life and activities just as they had been used to until the 5th of June 1967."[3] Or, as Dayan once put it, the goal was to make the "occupation invisible."[4]

To accomplish this objective, Israel set up the infrastructure of control discussed in the previous chapter. It also preserved most of the civil institutions that had existed in the OT before the war and continued to employ the vast majority of civil servants who had held public office.[5] "Don't set up an Israeli administration," Dayan is quoted as saying to his subordinates. "Use the existing Jordanian administrative apparatus. Don't make the same mistake that the Americans made in Vietnam."[6] Israel accordingly extended the tenure of most of the Palestinian mayors and councilmen and recognized the village *mukhtars* as the local representatives of the occupied inhabitants, thus bestowing both administrative and political powers on them. By retaining the civil servants and local representatives, Israel wished to convey a sense of continuity, while simultaneously hoping that a relatively strong *local* political presence would undermine Palestinian efforts to create a *national* leadership in the territories.[7]

In order to reduce some of its responsibility for the local inhabitants, undercut the emergence of a Palestinian nationalist movement, and normalize the occupation, Israel also established an informal power-sharing agreement with Jordan.[8] It preserved the Jordanian dinar as one of the legal tenders, permitted Jordan to maintain some of its prewar functions, and allowed the Hashemite regime to continue paying the salaries of civil servants, teachers, health professionals, and bureaucrats who were employed in government institutions. While Jordan used the salaries as well as other arrangements to prolong its authority in the territories, Israel not only benefited financially but also administratively from this undeclared pact. Moreover, the power-sharing agreement, as Meron Benvenisti points out, was also compatible with Israel's attempt to distinguish between the Palestinian population and its land, since Jordan's readiness to help Israel manage the population was not premised on an Israeli promise to refrain from confiscating land.[9]

In the days following the armed conflict, Israel also adopted a three-pronged policy: "Non-presence; Non-interference; Open Bridges."[10] This proclaimed policy, however, has to be taken with a grain of salt. First, the notions of nonpresence and noninterference invoked by the authorities who formulated the policy were very limited and referred only to visibly coercive measures, while altogether ignoring the forms of control that aimed to shape the daily practices of Palestinians in noncoercive ways. Second, a wide gap existed between Israel's declarations and its actual practices on the ground. The military was frequently present, and both the security and bureaucratic apparatuses constantly interfered in the lives of the occupied inhabitants. Moreover, the bridges between the West Bank and Jordan were not always open—and surely not to everyone—and often they were only open in one direction.[11] Yet, in comparison to the methods used to manage the Palestinians inside Israel during the eighteen years of military government and the restrictions imposed in later years in the West Bank and Gaza Strip, the forms of intervention adopted after the 1967 War were much less overt.

It is fair to say that the defining feature characterizing the occupation's first period (1967–80) and part of the second (1981–87) was Israel's attempt to stabilize its rule in the territories by emphasizing disciplinary and bio modes of power. To be sure, Israel employed coercive measures against the population in the West Bank and Gaza Strip, particularly during the first four years of the occupation. But by the end of 1971, after Israel had succeeded in crushing the armed resistance in Gaza, the application of brute force was dramatically reduced. Thus, even though sovereign power has always been present, there was during the first decade a clear—if not altogether even—shift of emphasis from sovereign power and coercive measures to disciplinary and bio modes of power. The logic, so it seems, was to render the occupied inhabitants docile not so much by the deployment of military forces as by raising their standard of living and transforming the population's lifestyle.

Indeed, the general mood in the OT during the first two decades was very different than it is today. For several years, the Israeli military government published annual reports entitled "Accountability" (Din VeHeshbon), suggesting that Israel both considered itself responsible for the population and felt a need to provide an account of the social and economic developments taking place in the regions that it had captured.[12] Two central points stand out in these reports. First, Israel adopted the colonial discourse of the civilizing mission and portrayed itself as bringing progress to the uncivilized Palestinians. The underlying claim in these reports can be summed up in the following way: Due to our interventions, the Palestinian economy, industry, education, health care, and civilian infrastructure have significantly developed. As we will see in later chapters, the notion that Israel was responsible for the occupied inhabitants changed over the years. Second, the immense amount of data presented in such reports, which provide detailed information about life in the OT, aims to create the impression that the occupation is transparent, that the occupying power is telling everything and has nothing to hide.

Concentrating on three sites, this chapter illustrates how Israel consolidated its military rule in the OT by increasing the inhabitants' economic productivity while diminishing their political capabilities. I begin by briefly describing the coercive measures Israel employed to crush all oppositional forces and then discuss some of the changes introduced in the education system in order to suppress both national identification and political aspirations. Finally, I describe how, alongside its efforts to quell the population's desire for emancipation, Israel encouraged economic practices that promoted Palestinian prosperity and, in this manner, hoped to normalize the occupation.

COERCIVE MEASURES AND THE LOGIC OF RESTRAINT

Despite the initial shock at Israel's swift success in capturing the West Bank and Gaza Strip, within less than a month the Palestinian inhabitants began mobilizing against the occupying power, organizing strikes and demonstrations. Israel's response was to issue military orders categorizing all forms of resistance as insurgency—including protests and political meetings, raising flags or other national symbols, publishing or distributing articles or pictures with political connotations, and even singing or listening to nationalist songs—and deployed security forces to suppress opposition.[13] It was clear to both sides that the first months were crucial, and each camp aspired to shape the rules of the game. Interestingly, fewer than one hundred Palestinians were killed in the West Bank in the first six months after the cessation of hostilities, a relatively small number, particularly when compared to periods of consolidation of other military occupations.[14]

Like most coercive measures, the ones used by the Israeli military were centralized, visible, operated from the top-down, and utilized the complex legal system Israel had installed. A brief overview of the coercive methods employed right after the war reveals that many if not most of them continue to be operative today. It is important to underscore, though, that during the first period, and particularly after 1971, the coercive methods were only intermittently enforced, and, when they were employed, they were implemented with less intensity.[15]

One of the first measures Israel adopted in order to suppress opposition was the removal of all leaders and activists who showed any signs of uncompromising opposition to the occupation. Already in July 1967, four Palestinian leaders who protested Israel's annexation of East Jerusalem had been deported to other parts of the country for a period of several months. By September of that year, however, the Israeli military commander decided that this form of punishment was inadequate and issued a *permanent* deportation order against Abdel Hamid a-Sayegh, the chief Kadi of the West Bank's Muslim population. And when Nadim Al-Zaro, the mayor of Ramallah, was suspected of supporting acts of resistance, he too was deported, not only because there was not enough evidence to convict him, but also because the military commander was afraid that his administrative arrest might provoke further protests.[16] Rapidly, deportations became ubiquitous.[17] By the end of 1971, Israel had deported 1,009 Palestinians from the West Bank and Gaza Strip.[18] While these deportations depended on the suspension of international humanitarian law, they were carried out in accordance with local law, specifically the British Mandatory's 1945 Emergency Regulations.[19] The military government continued using deportations in the following years but much less frequently.[20]

Along with the deportations, Israel also used administrative detentions (i.e., incarceration without trial) to separate leaders from their communities. In 1970, 1,261 Palestinians were held in administrative detention. In 1971, the number dropped to 445, and between 1973 and 1977 only about 40 people per year were held in this way.[21] The deportation and detention of leaders and activists were no doubt crucial for hindering widespread mobilization, but they did not manage to contain the Palestinian emancipatory drive. In September 1967, the occupied inhabitants launched a widespread school strike in the West Bank; teachers did not show up for work, children took to the streets to protest the occupation, and many shopkeepers did not open their stores.[22] In response, Israel enforced severe police-style measures, ranging from nightly curfews and other restrictions of movement to cutting off telephone lines, detaining leaders, and increasing the harassment of the population. This, in many ways, became Israel's modus operandi when dealing with Palestinian resistance. The message was clear: any act of resistance would result in a disproportionate response, which would make the population suffer to such a degree that resistance would appear pointless.[23]

Following commercial strikes that lasted several hours or entire days, the military government would shut down dozens of shops "until further notice." When West Bankers tried to emulate Martin Luther King's transportation strike, the security forces completely immobilized the local fleet of buses. In addition, punitive measures were introduced that were unrelated to any acts carried out by the residents. Pharmacies and restaurants were closed on the pretext of public welfare or sanitation. "Searching for terrorists" became an excuse for blocking off agricultural fields during harvest.[24] Moreover, any sign of opposition led to arrests, at times mass arrests, while Israeli security forces routinely tortured the political suspects it detained and demolished the homes of Palestinians who were suspected of being part of the resistance movement.[25] Even though these measures may appear uncannily familiar to those who have followed Israel's activities in the OT during later years, it is important to stress once again that they were not nearly as intense or frequent during the occupation's first two decades. Their purpose, though, was the same: to repress the inhabitants' political aspirations and undermine their ability to bring about political change.

In the Gaza Strip, Palestinian opposition to Israeli rule was in many ways different from the acts of civil disobedience staged in the West Bank, assuming a more violent character.[26] In 1971, General Ariel Sharon, the head of the southern command, was asked to suppress armed resistance in the Strip's refugee camps. Fatah and PFLP cadres had been using the camps as bases from which they carried out military operations against the occupying forces, as well as terror attacks against Israeli civilians and Palestinians suspected of collaboration. In order to uncover and crush the insurgency, a fence was erected, which surrounded parts of the region, as Israeli troops, the GSS, and Palestinian collaborators combed the area with a list of wanted men. The families of these men were also rounded up, and approximately twelve thousand inhabitants were sent to the remote Abu Zneima detention center on the coast of the Sinai Peninsula. An estimated two thousand houses were demolished in refugee camps like Shati and Jabalya in order to make it easier for the military to patrol the camps. These demolitions displaced, again, more than fifteen thousand refugees.[27] Simultaneously, curfews were imposed on the camps, adult males were randomly stopped and searched, and several Palestinians were shot and killed for failing to halt for routine searches.[28] After the armed resistance was crushed, however, Israel changed the repertoires of violence it employed in the Strip and used measures similar to those utilized in the West Bank.[29]

One of the most telling figures relating to this period and the one following it (1981–87) is that during the first twenty years of occupation no more than 650 Palestinians were killed by the Israeli military in the West Bank and Gaza Strip.[30] This relatively small number stands out not only when compared to the thousands of civilians killed annually in other military occupations, such as East Timor, Afghanistan, and Iraq, but also when considering the number of Palestinians killed by the Israeli military in later years. In 2002, for example, 989 Palestinians were killed by Israeli security forces, many more than the 650 people killed during the first two decades of the occupation. This suggests that during the early years, death or even the threat of death, which serves as the paradigmatic manifestation of forms of control operating under the sway of sovereign power, was not nearly as prevalent as it could have been.

The particular way Israel exercised force in the OT reveals yet another modality of control, not mentioned in the previous chapter, which informs the deployment of coercive measures and can be referred to as the logic of restraint. "Restraint," as Eyal Weizman cogently observes, "is what allows for the possibility of further escalation."[31] That is, in the OT force has continuously been exercised through the maintenance of gaps between, on the one hand, the destruction the military can potentially inflict when it applies its full destructive capacity or, alternatively, the level of lethal violence it can potentially deploy, and, on the other hand, the actual destruction it inflicts and the actual repertoires of violence it employs. The actual force Israel has exercised in the OT has, in other words, always been less, often much less, than the force that it could have potentially employed. It is important to stress that in order to become a modality of control, the logic of restraint—that is, the gap between actual and potential violence—must be discernable. Regardless of how lethal Israel's military attacks are, the Palestinian population must recognize that potentially they can become more deadly and brutal. This guarantees that violence, both when it is and is not deployed, remains an ever-lurking threat and, as such, a modality of control that can be exploited in order to facilitate the population's management.

While the gap between the possible and actual deployment of violence has been sustained throughout the occupation, as a rule all visible Palestinian opposition was confronted with visibly coercive measures, even though invisible measures were always employed as well. In general, the more visible the resistance, the more visible and destructive the coercive measures used to suppress it, and the more Israel used destructive coercive measures, the less emphasis it put on forms of control informed by disciplinary and bio modes of power. This suggests that resistance actually unmasks the occupation, since it exposes the occupier's fangs for all to see. This process, in turn, weakens the occupier since power's success is in proportion to its ability to hide its own mechanisms.[32] Dayan seemed to have realized this, and, as mentioned, his announced goal was to make the occupation invisible. While Israeli troops did not hesitate to employ harsh coercive measures, there was a concerted attempt during this period, and especially post-1971, to emphasize the role of the military government's civil branches. Thus, within the first decade one can identify a shift from an initial emphasis on sovereign power to its de-emphasis, alongside a concurrent, ongoing accentuation of disciplinary and bio modes of power. Israel, it is clear, tried to rule the Palestinians through a politics of life. The idea, as the passage cited at the beginning of this chapter states, was to create a situation whereby the inhabitants could carry on with their lives "without the help of an *Israeli* government employee or clerk."

EDUCATION

Israel used the various civil institutions to accomplish this objective. The educational system complimented the coercive measures in the sense that it too was used to suppress opposition and, more precisely, Palestinian national resistance. This is not surprising, given that modern educational systems are expected to engender and reinforce a national identity. In Mandatory Palestine, for example, the salience of nationalist indoctrination in the

Palestinian educational system was noted by the Peel Commission Report of 1937, which claimed that teachers had turned the government schools into "seminaries of Arab nationalism." According to Rashid Khalidi, the system fostered a specifically Palestinian national consciousness, even though the teaching of history, normally the most potent and effective entry point for nationalist ideas, was closely monitored by the British to prevent the spread of such "subversive" thinking.[33]

Israel was well aware of the educational system's potential impact and used its authority to alter the curricula in order to repress all forms of identification with Palestinian nationalism. However, unlike coercive measures that operate mostly through restrictions and repression, the practices of control employed in the educational system operated through the repression and subjugation of certain knowledge and the simultaneous creation and dissemination of alternative knowledge, employing, as it were, all three modes of power to accomplish this task.

Prior to Israel's occupation, the Jordanians and Egyptians administered the educational systems in the West Bank and Gaza Strip respectively, determining their curriculum. The West Bank schools had used Jordanian textbooks, while those in Gaza had used Egyptian ones, and although these textbooks could be characterized as having been culturally relevant to the local population, the Jordanians and Egyptians did not encourage Palestinian national identity; thus, there was hardly any reference in the textbooks to Palestinian history.[34]

Israeli authorities took over the educational system immediately after the war, establishing an office for educational affairs in each region that was manned by military personnel. The Israeli officers in charge were directly responsible for the management and pedagogical supervision of the governmental educational system. The system was highly centralized and left all administrative and decision-making powers, including decisions to build or expand schools and the hiring and firing of teachers, entirely in the hands of the officers in the educational affairs office. These officers also provided licenses for all of the nongovernmental educational institutions and oversaw the finances and curricula of private schools as well as the pedagogy of the United Nations Relief and Work Agency schools, which provided services to all the refugees.[35]

Examining the way Israel consolidated its control over the educational system during the occupation's first six months helps reveal how this civil institution was deployed to manage the Palestinian residents. As opposed to the military government inside Israel, which, for several years, employed Jewish teachers of Iraqi descent to teach the Palestinian citizenry, in the West Bank and Gaza Strip almost all teachers, principals, and administrative staff who had been employed by the Jordanians and Egyptians before the war continued teaching. In this way, Israel hoped to weaken the sense that the 1967 War constituted a dramatic break. It was also the easiest and most convenient solution, considering that it would have been practically impossible to replace all of the teachers and still open the schools in September.

Problems emerged, though, when officials from the Ministry of Education began inspecting the Jordanian and Egyptian teaching material, since several textbooks had anti-Israeli and anti-Jewish passages.[36] In a seventh-grade textbook, for example, the children were asked to respond to the following assignment: "Israel was born in order to die. Prove this statement." In a ninth-grade textbook the students were told that "the European Jews were annihilated because of their corruption, wretchedness and deception."[37] And while most books did not really mention Palestinians, one textbook in the West Bank had a chapter about Palestinian history. The officials from the Ministry of Education, who were apparently unaware of Dayan's non-interventionist policy and modeled their response on the 1948–66 military government within Israel, proposed introducing totally new texts in the OT, using the ones that had been written for the Arab schools within Israel.[38] These texts adopted the Zionist historical narrative, erasing, for example, all traces of the Palestinian Nakbah (the 1948 catastrophe that led to the displacement of the vast majority of Palestinians), in an attempt to integrate the Palestinians living inside Israel into dominant Jewish society. The efforts to disqualify the existing textbooks and introduce new ones created an uproar in the West Bank and East Jerusalem, and the inhabitants threatened to launch a general strike at the beginning of the 1967–68 school year.

After a few weeks of pressure, the military took the reigns from the Ministry of Education and partially conceded to the demands of the Palestinian leadership, announcing that Israeli textbooks would only be used in the government schools located in annexed East Jerusalem and not in the West Bank and Gaza Strip.[39] The distinction Israel made between East Jerusalem and the two other regions suggests that from the very beginning

Israel had no intention of integrating the Palestinians residing in the West Bank and Gaza Strip, while it did intend to incorporate the inhabitants of East Jerusalem. This solution, however, did not satisfy the Palestinian leaders, who rejected the distinction Israel made between the West Bank and East Jerusalem as well as the decision to replace about half the textbooks that had been used in the West Bank.[40]

At the beginning of September 1967 a general school strike was launched. The Israeli authorities once again examined the Palestinian textbooks and this time decided to disqualify only two out of the 120 and to erase passages in an additional 20 books. About one hundred textbooks were found entirely acceptable.[41] Since this move did not solve the problem of East Jerusalem, the Palestinians continued with the strike. Israel, in turn, began a punitive campaign, focusing on Nablus, which was the strike's primary instigator. After a few weeks of harsh measures, including nightly curfews, barring the use of public transportation, cutting off the telephone system, detaining leaders, and increasing the level of harassment and searches, Israel managed to break the strike.[42]

The strikers succeeded in preserving almost all of the Jordanian and Egyptian textbooks in the West Bank and Gaza (but not in East Jerusalem), but these textbooks did not seriously threaten the Israeli authorities since they did not touch upon issues relating to Palestinian national identity or to their nation-building aspirations. The strike did nothing to alter Military Order 101, issued in August 1967, which specified that the military censor must approve all reading materials, books, and periodicals. It did not change the fact that any reference to Palestinian nationalism and identity was systematically erased.[43] The Israeli authorities continued to subject schoolbooks brought in from Egypt and Jordan each year to strict censorship. Words, paragraphs, and entire chapters were erased and, at times, whole books were disqualified for discussing Palestinian roots, cultural heritage, or national identity.[44] The censorship applied not only to history and geography books, but also to literature and poetry. Over the years, more than 1,700 titles were banned, including such books as Christopher Marlow's *The Jew of Malta* and Shakespeare's *Merchant of Venice* (presumably for the way they depict Jews), as well as books by Israeli political leader Yigal Allon and *Ha'aretz* correspondent Ze'ev Schiff.[45]

Through censorship Israel strove to create a specific field of knowledge, which Benedict Anderson has called an "imagined community." In his study of Indonesia, Anderson shows that nothing nurtured the bondage among the different peoples more than the colonial school system. "[T]he government schools formed a colossal, highly rationalized, tightly centralized hierarchy, structurally analogous to the state bureaucracy itself. Uniform textbooks, standardized diplomas and teaching certificates, a strictly regulated gradation of age-groups, classes and instructional materials, in themselves created a self-contained, coherent universe of experience."[46] Israel, to be sure, recognized the importance of producing a form of knowledge that creates an artificial unity among disparate peoples when it put together its own textbooks for the diverse immigrant Jewish population and for the Palestinians who remained in the region that became Israel after the 1948 War. In sharp contrast to the textbooks used inside Israel proper and those used in the colonial educational systems, however, in the newly occupied territories Israel strove to undermine national unity by censoring all mention of a common Palestinian past.

Directives were introduced to ensure that teachers would not teach their students extracurricular material for fear that they might adopt a historical narrative depicting a shared Palestinian past, intertwined with heroic tales of victory as well as stories of loss and defeat. It is well known that narratives of the "nation" have the capacity to transform an otherwise heterogeneous population into a homogenous one. A shared past postulates a collective destiny, which helps, in turn, to assure the cohesion of the population. Conversely, preventing the appearance of such a past helps promote fragmentation and division within society and consequently attenuates attempts to form a coherent opposition. Since the nation is always constituted through territory (e.g., blood and soil), the attempt to erase the nation is also an attempt to undermine the connection between the people and their land and the right of the people to self-determination. One could also say that, wittingly or unwittingly, the massive censorship enterprise aimed to facilitate the expropriation of land.

Israel's efforts to monitor and control the Palestinian curriculum should, however, be distinguished from what Paulo Freire has called "cultural invasion." By denying the Palestinians the right to teach and learn about their own national identity, Israel indeed attempted to produce the "cultural inauthenticity of those who are invaded." Freire was also correct when he noted that the more the invaded people "mimic the invaders, the more stable the position of the latter becomes," but the occupied Palestinians (as opposed to those living inside Israel proper) were *not* encouraged to mimic Israelis. Israel did not strive to transform the Palestinian schools into places that would compel and encourage the occupied population to see reality from the perspective of the invaders, as it had done in the Arab educational system inside Israel, since it did not intend to incorporate the Palestinians into the Israeli demos.[47]

Israel's unwillingness to incorporate the occupied Palestinians, on the one hand, and the distinction it made between the inhabitants and their land, on the other, created a *sui generis* objective which was, as mentioned, different from the objectives it had with respect to the Palestinians inside Israel and the objectives of the colonists of old. In the latter cases, students were taught to mimic the invaders, while in the OT students were neither encouraged to identify with or as Israelis, nor were they permitted to identify as Palestinians. Rather, Israel wanted them to identify as Arabs. Shabtai Teveth recounts that the Israeli military allowed students to protest so long as they cheered for Nasser (namely, pan-Arabism), but when the students publicly identified with the Palestinian nationalist group Fatah, the military clamped down on the demonstrators. Even more telling, the censor instructed all the editors of newspapers distributed in the OT to use the word *Arab* rather than *Palestinian* when referring to Palestinians. Along similar lines, Israel censored the lyrical play *The Returners,* which consists of a dialogue between an Arab and Palestinian, where the latter expresses his aspiration for Palestinian liberation and revenge.[48] The objective, from Israel's perspective, was to weaken the Palestinians' claim to nationhood and strengthen their connection with other Arab countries. It accordingly promoted a mythic pan-Arab past that only vaguely includes the Palestinians and erases Palestinian particularity and Palestinian claims. This approach fits well with the pervasive Israeli view at the time, which strove to collapse all Arab countries into one homogeneous unit. There are twenty-two Arab states, Israelis often argued, but only one Jewish state.

Censorship of textbooks was not enough, however. Although Palestinian district directors were the ones who nominated new staff, the new recruits had to be approved by the Israeli security authorities. Once hired, teachers did not immediately become civil servants but were required to pass a probationary period. Probationary periods are, according to Said Assaf, common features of teacher recruitment practices in other countries where the interlude is used to provide further classroom-based training and to allow for professional assessment of new teachers before final appointment. Yet the purpose of implementing a probationary period in this case was for the GSS to approve or refuse appointments.[49] Thus, the forms of control that operated on the teachers in the West Bank and Gaza were different from the ones operating on teachers in Western liberal democracies. Whereas in liberal democracies teachers must conform to certain professional norms, in the OT they were also expected to repress any expression relating to Palestinian national aspirations. Israel forbade Palestinian teachers from engaging in political activity, from joining a political party, or even from expressing support for one. Participation in strikes or sit-ins was prohibited, as was writing articles for the press without prior approval.[50] In 1982, for example, more than one hundred teachers were fired because they were either politically active or were unwilling to bow down to the Civil Administration's demands.[51] In the classroom, as mentioned, teachers were not allowed to use any supplementary material to enhance the curriculum, which was narrowly defined to mean the preapproved textbook material.

Israel also strove to control all of the teacher-training programs. In many cases, teachers and principals were instructed to attend courses at the Hebrew University in Jerusalem, but they were never allowed to take similar courses at local universities. Even on the rare occasions when teachers found the resources to study outside the country, an exit permit was not easy to obtain.[52] The goal was to root out anyone who might stir the children against Israeli rule, while dissuading those who intended to seek a post in the public educational system (or any other public institution) at some future point from taking part in any political activities in the present — since those who did would most likely not be hired.

While Israel did not succeed in preventing the emergence of Palestinian nationalism in schools, the forms of control it adopted made it practically impossible to create a unified and homogeneous historical narrative, the kind of narrative that is needed during processes of nation-building. The total absence of a formal curriculum that taught Palestinian history no doubt contributed to the continuing fragmentation of Palestinian society. And yet, Israel failed to normalize the situation, which is, in many respects, the litmus test for determining the success of controlling apparatuses operating in the service of disciplinary and bio modes of power. It could not expel national politics from the classroom, not least because the attempt to control the curriculum, how it was taught, and who would teach it, actually accentuated the relevance of politics to education and helped sensitize the student population to many of the issues Israel was attempting to repress.[53] Israel's attempt to implement an alternative regime of truth in order to prevent the revitalization of a Palestinian national identity ultimately failed, though, because schools are not islands cut off from daily reality, but are firmly connected to the sociopolitical environment in which they exist. The idea that Palestine was an occupied land that needed to be liberated continuously infiltrated into the educational system. From the nursery rhymes taught in kindergartens all the way to the classes offered in the universities, Palestinian children and students were constantly exposed to a highly politicized reality that managed to penetrate despite the censor's efforts and was very different from the official reality Israel strove to create.[54]

Israel's conspicuous efforts to impose a regime of truth within the educational system encountered the most vigorous opposition immediately after the war, since resistance frequently surfaces when the means of control are set up, when they are seen as a break from the past and are therefore visible. After the initial struggle, the emphasis on sovereign power slowly receded (even though it was always present, particularly in relation to the hiring and firing of teachers), and Israel began emphasizing the two other modes of power. It was only in the early 1980s, when Palestinian children regularly demonstrated against the occupation, that sovereign power reemerged to the fore, and Israel began shutting down schools and universities.

PROMOTING PROSPERITY

The coercive measures adopted after the war as well as some forms of control used in the educational system continued to play a role in managing the Palestinian population for years to come. The one feature that stands out as almost completely unique when comparing the occupation's first decade with those that followed is Israel's attempt to manage the Palestinian population through the promotion of prosperity. A series of practices were introduced to increase the economic utility of the Palestinian inhabitants, both as a way of harnessing the energies of Palestinian society to advance Israel's economic interests, but also as a way of raising the standard of living in the OT. The hope was that prosperity would help repress the inhabitants' political aspirations, prevent social unrest in the OT, and help normalize the occupation. Unlike the coercive measures and even certain forms of control employed in the educational system, most of Israel's efforts to promote prosperity were carried out by forms of control that operated in the service of disciplinary and bio modes of power.

According to a 1970 military report, the "Six-Day War erased the 'Green Line' that used to separate Israel from the areas now administered and it is quite unavoidable and natural that these areas now depend on Israel in all economic matters and services. . . . The only way to avoid a potential outburst of social forces is to strive continuously for the improvement of the standard of living and the services of this underprivileged society."[55] Given these assumptions, it is not altogether surprising that already in the midst of the war Israel provided services to Palestinian farmers in order to save crops and to prevent the death of livestock. And when the fighting subsided, Israel established a series of programs whose goals were to improve economic productivity. Consider, for a moment, a telling passage taken from a 1969 military report.

> In the course of a veterinary action all cattle herds, about 30,000 heads, were marked, and immunization shots against mouth and hoof disease administered. The cattle is examined for tuberculosis, and sick cows are purchased by the Military Government for slaughtering without loss to the farmer. The entire poultry stock—about half a million heads—received shots against the New Castle disease. There has been a radical decline in the mortality of poultry as a result of these injections to a very small number this year in comparison with a 60% loss in the past. Thousands of dogs were destroyed to prevent the spread of rabies.[56]

This passage exposes that Israel immediately put to use up-to-date forms of surveillance, monitoring the number of cattle and poultry and keeping track of diseases to which the livestock had been subjected and how many had died due to infection. To be sure, it had a vested interest in monitoring and preventing any epidemic from developing, since viruses and diseases do not stop at the Green Line. But it also had an interest in increasing the economic utility of the Palestinian farmers; the introduction of an immunization program had a huge impact on the mortality rate of livestock and substantially raised the productivity of Palestinian farmers. Moreover, Israel's policy of purchasing sick cows from the farmers suggests that it was also genuinely concerned with guaranteeing the livelihood of the local population. In the same report quoted above, one reads that

> the area of tobacco cultivation has been increased from 1,500 dunams to 8,000 dunams, the area of pulses from 20,000 dunams to 40,000 dunams, and the area cultivated with sesame likewise from 20,000 dunams to 40,000.... As a result of agricultural instruction, improved varieties of seeds for vegetables and field crop were introduced.... Approximately 400 model plots, scattered all over the area under review, were cultivated in collaboration with local farmers. About 80 "field days" were held. During the first year the field days were attended by 12,000 farmers, and during the second their number went up to 18,000 persons.... In the course of a campaign of pest control, the whole area of citrus groves was sprayed with pesticides against the Mediterranean fly, and several thousands of dunams planted with olive trees were likewise sprayed against olive flies.[57]

Passages like these highlight the dramatic difference between the occupation in the late 1960s and the occupation today. Israel not only implemented a vaccination program for livestock, but also increased some of the cultivated areas and introduced improved varieties of seeds for vegetables and field crops. It planted hundreds of thousands of trees and created model plots where Palestinian farmers could be trained in the use of modern equipment and technology.[58] The Central Bureau of Statistics conducted a survey of thirty thousand farms in about 50 percent of West Bank villages, examining the utilization of farm areas, including the age of orchards, which vegetables were grown, and the yield rate per plot size.[59] Since most of the population, particularly in the West Bank, was dependent on farming, Israel was interested in increasing the yields. In an early study conducted by the Israeli Agriculture Ministry, one finds tables enumerating the annual increase of the monetary value of production according to agricultural sector, the growth of produce yields, and the amounts spent on raw materials, including the amount of pesticides bought and the cost of buying young chickens.[60]

Up until 1976, Israel also offered the occupied inhabitants development loans to purchase tractors, agricultural equipment, and machinery.[61] Not surprisingly, between 1968 and 1972 the agricultural productivity in the territories increased annually by 16 percent. From 1973 to 1976 the growth stabilized, and between 1977 and 1980 it increased annually by 11 percent.[62] What comes across most forcefully when examining such programs is not only the stark contrast in which they stand vis-à-vis actions carried out by Israel in later years, but also Israel's emphasis on one of the features characterizing a politics of life, which Foucault has called modern "pastoral power." This power does not aim to assure individual salvation in the next world, but is oriented toward the population's salvation in this world by ensuring its health, well-being, and security.[63] For instance, less than three years after the war, the Gaza Strip was connected to the Israeli electrical grid, so that in Gaza City alone twenty-four thousand homes had electricity as compared to five thousand before the war.[64] While in later years Israel would shut down the electricity to punish the population (see chapter 8), transforming the grid into a controlling apparatus in the service of sovereign power, in the first period it was used to alter the lifestyle and increase the economic utility of the inhabitants as well as to erase the border between the Gaza Strip and Israel.

As part of its strategy to manage the population through a politics of life, Israel used the Bank of Israel research department and the Central Bureau of Statistics to continuously scrutinize and analyze the Palestinian labor force. One finds tables depicting the age and gender of laborers, the number of workers according to their occupation and the sector in which they were employed, and the number of local businesses, as well as their size and location.[65] One also encounters ongoing discussions within military documents and the protocols of the interministerial committee concerning strategies for reducing the unemployment rate, which was considered by the military government to be a potential cause for social unrest and opposition.

Vocational courses and New Deal–style relief work were introduced both in Gaza and the West Bank. Whereas during the nineteen-year period that the two regions were under Jordanian and Egyptian rule only one vocational training program was opened in each region, by 1980 Israel had established a total of twenty-six vocational training programs in a number of fields, including carpentry, draftsmanship, metal-working, welding, and sewing.[66] Along similar lines, the inter-ministerial committee decided to invest IL 7.5 million in Gaza's development while also providing Palestinian investors low-interest-rate loans, with even better rates than the ones offered to Israelis. Between 1967 and 1969 approximately one hundred workshops were established in the region, and several thousand workers were employed.[67]

While all these efforts helped produce prosperity, the incorporation of Palestinian laborers into the Israeli workforce had the greatest impact on the population's standard of living. It was, according to the Bank of Israel, "the chief factor behind the vigorous development [in the OT] of the early years."[68] The swiftness of this incorporation is worth noting. In 1968, just one year after the war, 6 percent of the Palestinian labor force had found jobs in Israel. By 1974, 69,400 Palestinians worked in Israel, making up one-third of the workforce.[69] The Palestinians who worked in Israel earned anywhere from 10 to 100 percent more than they would have if they worked in the territories, depending on their occupations. As a result, the average daily wages of all employees from the West Bank rose by 35 percent in the period 1970–74 and by 13 percent during the period 1974–79. In the Gaza Strip, wages rose by 50 and 18.4 percent, respectively.[70]

The income of Palestinians who worked inside Israel added considerable and badly needed resources to the West Bank and Gaza Strip. Accordingly, the OT experienced rapid economic growth. Between 1968 and 1972 GNP increased annually by 16 and 20 percent in the West Bank and Gaza Strip, respectively. During these years there was an 8 to 9 percent annual increase in the Palestinian labor force due to the incorporation of laborers into the Israeli workforce, while the estimated annual population growth was about 2 percent. Consequently, the official unemployment rate dropped from 11 to 1 percent in the West Bank and from 17 to 2 percent in the Gaza Strip. From 1973 to 1980 the economic growth continued—albeit at a slower but nonetheless very impressive rate—with a 9 and 6 percent annual increase of GNP in the West Bank and Gaza Strip, respectively.[71]

The change in Palestinian lifestyle becomes apparent in reports published by the Bank of Israel, which also monitored the standard of living in both regions, showing that parallel to the swift economic growth there was a rapid increase in private consumption: an annual average rate of 13 percent in the West Bank and 15 percent in Gaza.[72] If in 1968 per capita private consumption expenditure in the West Bank was IL 517 and IL 222 in Gaza, by 1974 it had risen to IL 1,033 in the West Bank and IL 474 in the Gaza Strip (in 1986 prices).[73] In the West Bank, for instance, the proportion of households with gas cookers increased from 23.9 to 75.3 percent between 1972 and 1981, while in the Gaza Strip it increased from 6.5 to 70.9 percent. There was similar increase in the proportion of households with electric refrigerators and television sets, and about a 20 percent increase in the

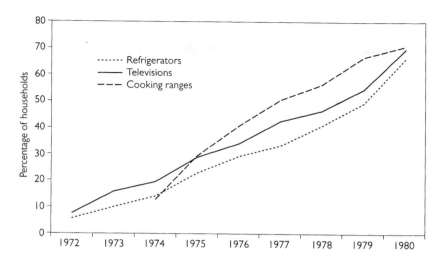

Figure 1. Percentage of Gaza Strip households with selected appliances, 1972–81. Central Bureau of Statistics, *National Accountability,* 172. For cooking ranges, there is data missing for the first two years.

number of private kitchens and toilets (see figure 1).[74] "The fast increase in per capita private consumption (especially in the first half of the decade [1970s]) and the high share of food in total household consumption," the bank reported, "are well reflected in the continuous improvement in nutritional standards."[75] Thus, not only was there an increase in the population's consumption of commodities, but there was also a change for the better in the Palestinian food basket.

A public relations report about the vocational training programs Israel had set up states that the occupied residents were able to carve out a new way of life for themselves and their families. "Not only has their standard of living risen beyond recognition, but, far more important, past attitudes and previously accepted standards have undergone basic changes. Economic conceptions and, perhaps even more significant, social reaction and habits have undergone profound transformation, and entirely new outlooks have emerged."[76] Several Palestinians who took part in the training programs are cited in the report in order to corroborate this claim. A Palestinian woman from Tul-Karem maintains that "Arab girls are not ashamed to go out to work. The young woman in the West Bank is free today, she has begun to make great progress—she trains for a brighter future and looks ahead with confidence and self assurance." Another woman from Beita says that learning a profession is "no longer a shameful thing for an Arab girl. It does not conflict with happiness in marriage." And a locksmith from Assirah conveys a message to his Palestinian brethren: "If you are unable to complete your education, learn a vocation and come back to serve your native village, which needs your help to develop."[77]

The testimonies of these Palestinians no doubt reflect the attitudes of Israeli officials as much as they reflect the views of those interviewed. The report clearly reveals that changing the norms, habits, and comportment of the Palestinians was considered crucial for increasing the population's economic utility. The emphasis on disciplinary power and biopower seemed to be producing the results Israel had desired—docile but economically useful subjects. Israel, accordingly, did not need to deploy many troops in the OT, and for a while it even seemed that the moderately tranquil state of affairs could continue for years because of the partial economic integration of the OT. The rapid economic growth and the change in consumption habits *did* succeed in transforming the inhabitants' lifestyle and daily practices, and while there were localized confrontations with the Israeli military throughout the first period, the degree of resistance to Israel's occupation was relatively low. According to one Fatah leader who was imprisoned in the late 1960s, the possibility of working in Israel and earning a relatively high salary undermined their efforts to recruit cadres to the resistance.[78]

Ultimately, though, Israel's efforts to create, in Geoffrey Aronson's words, "an economic foundation for Palestinian participation in the status quo," did not produce normalization.[79] The notion that by raising the standard of living Israel could, in some way, suppress the Palestinian aspirations for self-determination rapidly turned out to be little more than a fantasy. Ironically, it was the racist leader of the Jewish Defense League, Rabbi Meir Kahane, who clearly exposed Israel's myopic stance when he rhetorically pondered, "What kind of Jew believes that he can buy the national pride of an Arab [sic] at the price of a toilet with running water?"[80] But there was also something else going on. As the forms of control informed by disciplinary and bio power increased Palestinian prosperity, other controlling apparatuses operating in the service of sovereign power were also put to use in order to hinder the development of an independent Palestinian economy. Because the economic growth was so impressive, it took a while before these apparatuses began undoing the effects of the prosperity that had been created. Yet, as we will see in the following three chapters, the interactions among different controlling apparatuses and practices, not least those used in the economic field, rapidly produced a series of contradictions that engendered widespread resistance to Israeli military rule.

Chapter 3 | OF HORSES AND RIDERS

The Six-Day War abolished to all intents and purposes
the "green line" that in the past demarcated the Israeli
sector from the administered territories. Naturally and
unavoidably, these areas are becoming dependent upon
Israel for all their economic and service needs.

SHLOMO GAZIT,
*Coordinator of Government Activities
in the Administered Territories, 1971*

Israel's attempts to create prosperity in the West Bank and Gaza Strip
and to normalize the occupation were simultaneously marked by a series
of constraints and restrictions that hindered the development of an independent Palestinian economy. Military orders were constantly issued in
order to hamper local economic expansion and to transform the Palestinian
economy into a captive market for Israeli producers.[1] Complex tax and
custom laws, restrictive marketing arrangements, and a slew of bewildering
decrees and regulations were, in the words of Ze'ev Schiff and Ehud Ya'ari,
used as weapons to hold the territories hostage to the Israeli economy. As far
as the Palestinian inhabitants could see, the symbiosis between Palestinians
and Israelis was, in the words of these two commentators, more accurately
described as "the relationship between a horse and its rider."[2]

Sara Roy corroborates this claim in her extensive analysis of the Gaza
Strip's economy. Israel, she shows, undermined the two primary conditions
needed for development: the progressive expansion of a productive capacity,
which would allow for capital accumulation, and the formation of vital
and sustainable political and economic alliances between the dependent
economy and other economies, as well as with the international financial
system.[3] Thus, Roy's analysis reveals that alongside Israel's efforts to boost
prosperity in the OT through the emphasis on disciplinary and bio modes
of power, controlling apparatuses informed by sovereign power were also

extensively deployed to subject the Palestinian economy to Israel's own economic interests and needs. The remarkable economic growth, the dramatic rise in the standard of living, and the individual prosperity experienced for more than a decade in the OT served to conceal the communal stagnation that Israel was creating in the economic field and managed, for several years, to suspend the devastating effects of Israel's restrictive policies.[4] Put differently, for a number of years the effects of the means of control informed by disciplinary and bio modes of power overshadowed the restrictive policies operating in the service of sovereign power.

As a way of beginning to explain some of the changes that have transpired in the OT, in this chapter I examine more closely the economic field. The assumption is that the policies in the economic field not only aimed to satisfy Israel's economic interests, which is the way they are usually presented by economists, but that they also served a crucial role in the administration of the OT. For example, in the previous chapter I claimed that Israel encouraged the economic productivity of the Palestinian inhabitants while repressing their political aspirations. Here I show that by hindering the development of an independent Palestinian economy based on industry and sophisticated agriculture, Israel encouraged the Palestinian inhabitants to become unskilled laborers, and thus directed the economic utility of the Palestinians in a very specific way. The different forms of control that were utilized in the economic field produced excesses and contradictions that ultimately spurred Palestinian resistance and helped shape Israel's policy choices.

CONTROLLING THE ECONOMY

Economists of different stripes tend to agree that had the Israeli government decided to maintain the economic separation of the West Bank and Gaza Strip from Israel proper, as was the case before 1967, there would have been a rapid deterioration of economic life and a sharp drop in the standard of living in the OT. These kinds of economic consequences were unacceptable to both the Israeli government and the military because they would have likely engendered social upheaval.[5] Accordingly, during the occupation's first two decades, the occupied economy was integrated into Israel proper; this integration was never meant to be complete, whereby the two economies would eventually become a single unit (i.e., the total erasure of the

Green Line), and was, in fact, used to render the Palestinian inhabitants economically and socially dependent on Israel. What comes across very clearly when examining the economic field is that no part of Palestinian economic life was left untouched.

control over monetary flow

The military introduced numerous regulations and restrictions that specifically aimed to shape the occupied economy according to the requirements of Israel's interests. One of the first actions taken after the war was the closure of the Arab financial and monetary institutions, including all of the banks, while bestowing authority over all monetary matters upon the Bank of Israel.[6] The Israeli currency became the legal tender (along with the Jordanian dinar), and Israeli foreign exchange controls were enforced in the two regions. These actions had profound effects on real savings and on investments in physical capital and growth, and ultimately led to distorted financial development.[7]

We saw in the previous chapter that around the same time that Israel took over all the financial institutions and imposed monetary regulations, it helped Palestinians plant thousands of fruit trees, offered growers improved seeds for vegetables, and trained farmers in modern technologies. I did not mention, however, that it also began controlling the types of fruits and vegetables that could be planted and distributed, and introduced an array of planning regulations that determined where crops could and mostly could not be planted. Although constraints on planting are common in other countries, the objectives of those imposed in the OT were to create dependency, to undermine development and competition, and to facilitate the confiscation of land. Israel limited the reclamation of lands in order to make them arable. It also restricted the population's access to land and water, seizing no less than 40 percent of the land by 1987 and appropriating the major water resources.[8] Simultaneously, it rendered the planting of new citrus trees, replacing old nonproductive ones, or planting other fruit trees without permission illegal, and acquiring permits for such actions frequently took five years or more. Of the fruits and vegetables that the Palestinian farmers were permitted to grow, many types could not be legally marketed in Israel, a measure designed to protect Israeli producers. The Israeli farmers, by contrast, had unlimited access to the markets in the OT and managed to provide some products at prices with which their Palestinian counterparts could not compete, leading to a reduction in the variety of produce grown in the territories.[9] The fact that the access was unlimited in only one direction also created an absurd situation whereby the prices of certain products were higher in the OT than they were in Israel.

In the industrial sector the strategy was similar to the one used in agriculture. Initially, Israel offered some support for industry because the military authorities were concerned that unemployment could destabilize the OT. In the late 1960s and early 1970s small loans were given to existing factories so that they could expand and retool. By 1980, however, the development budget in the territories amounted to zero.[10] The absence of intermediary financial institutions, development banks, and credit sources of various kinds hindered industrial development. Simultaneously, Israel introduced a series of constraints to obstruct the development of capital-intensive industry. Government assistance in the form of tax breaks, export subsidies, subsidized credit, and surety bonds was not extended to the Palestinians.[11] External trade was strictly controlled by numerous military orders, and complicated certification procedures separated the territories from neighboring Arab countries. Israel also imposed restrictions on the type and amount of raw materials that could be imported into the OT. Palestinians rapidly became dependent on Israeli firms for electricity, fuel, gas, and communications. The same was true for basic commodities such as flour, rice, and sugar.[12]

Israel also required licenses for all industrial activities and used the licenses to restructure industries in line with Israel's needs while suppressing all competition. So, while textile factories offering services to Israeli producers were given licenses, fruit-processing factories were denied permits because they could potentially compete with Israeli producers. In other words, creating labor-intensive subsidiaries and outsourcing labor-intensive work to Palestinian workshops was Israel's major source of industrial investment in the Palestinian economy. In this way, Palestinian industry was integrated with Israel's industry and became totally dependent on Israeli demand, which, in effect, transformed the industrial base in the OT into a de facto free zone, operating, in Sara Roy's words, for the benefit of Israeli producers.[13]

In addition, Israel issued numerous military orders pertaining to company registration, trademarks, and trade names, and determined the conditions of trade, and the kind and amount of taxes, customs, and duties to be paid. It levied a series of taxes on Palestinian manufacturers, who ended up paying between 35 and 40 percent more taxes than Israeli manufacturers.[14] One should keep in mind that a large percentage of these taxes was not reinvested in the territories but transferred directly to Israel's coffers. Up until 1993 Israel imposed a one-way system of tariffs and duties on the importation of goods, so that there were no tariffs or other regulations on merchandise leaving Israel to the OT. According to some estimates, such policies deprived the OT of significant customs revenue, estimated to be somewhere between $118 and $176 million in 1986 alone.[15] According to other estimates, the loss of revenue due to the commercial and monetary integration averaged 13 percent (or one-eighth) of Palestinian GNP over the period 1970–87. The total revenue loss would range between a low estimate of $6 billion to a high estimate of $11 billion (in 1990 prices).[16] Theoretically, this money could have been invested in the creation of an independent industry.

Israel also hindered the development of a Palestinian economy in several other ways. In stark contrast to the British mandatory power, which had performed or permitted private parties to carry out a series of development projects—Haifa's seaport, the Lydda (today Ben-Gurion) airport, and a series of railway lines—that played a crucial role in the future economic growth of Palestine, and later Israel, the military government not only refrained from investing its own funds in the civil infrastructure needed for the economic development of the OT, but also prevented others from doing so.[17] All in all, these and several other restrictions created structural constraints on the industrialization process. Such constraints help explain why the industrial sector's contribution to the West Bank's GDP actually fell from 9 percent in 1968 to 8.2 percent in 1975 and 6.5 percent in 1980.[18] By 1989 the industrial sector's share in the OT's GDP ranked among the lowest in the world, with 7 percent in the West Bank and 12 percent in the Gaza Strip.[19] The average industrial complex in the Strip employed only five people, and by 1991 the total revenue from industry in Gaza was less than 1 percent of what it was in Israel.[20] It is therefore no surprise that as the years passed, the economic dependency deepened, and the Palestinian trade deficit with Israel grew. In 1968 the deficit was $11.4 million, and by 1987 it had grown to $237.3 million, comprising 93 percent of the total deficit for that year (in 1993 prices).[21]

What is amazing and at times confusing is that despite all of these constraints and restrictions, during the first decade of the occupation the Palestinians experienced impressive economic growth, and the standard of living in the OT, which is measured by food consumption levels, housing density, household items, and health standards, definitely improved. We now know that it was the Palestinian laborers' remittances coming from Israel and the Gulf States and not domestic resources that served to satisfy consumption demand.[22] Roy points out that the reorientation of the Palestinian workforce to labor-intensive work in Israel as well as work in the Gulf States created a situation whereby the OT's income was disproportionate to the region's productive capabilities. As a result, such production-linked indicators as GNP are inappropriate measures for evaluating the strength and efficiency of the OT's economy, because they are largely based on transferred resources.[23] This was reflected in the gap between GDP and GNP (GNP equals GDP plus the net factor payments from Palestinian laborers who commuted to Israel or worked abroad), which was among the highest in the world, so that the 1985 GDP represented only 68 percent of the GNP.[24] Israel's decision to allow the free movement of unorganized labor across the borders served, in other words, as a dominant factor in the erosion of the productive capacity of the West Bank and Gaza Strip. Thus, even though the Palestinian economy experienced impressive growth, the actual resource base of the economy was steadily eroding, as local investment and development remained stagnant.[25]

Roy shows that most of the regulations and constraints operated through processes of integration and externalization. She highlights five major acts of commission and omission that were adopted by the occupying authorities: (1) the reorientation of the labor force away from domestic agriculture and industry and its integration into the Israeli workforce; (2) the reshaping of local agriculture toward export production and reliance on Israeli inputs; (3) the realignment of industry according to Israel's needs through subcontracting and trade; (4) the redirection of trade to Israel; and (5) restriction of the development of a viable institutional infrastructure capable of stimulating development and supporting structural reform. In this way, Roy concludes, local resources were transferred to Israel, and the OT's own productive capacity was diminished.[26] The dire effects of Israel's controlling apparatuses in the economic field were not felt during the first years of occupation because the integration of the labor force into the Israeli economy as well as several other interventions like planting thousands of trees and introducing improved seeds and new agricultural technologies managed to compensate for the structural ramifications of the integration and externalization processes.[27]

What comes across forcefully when examining the different forms of control operating in the economic field is that from the beginning they were not only utilized to subject the occupied economy to Israel's economic interests, but were also used as central instruments for managing the Palestinian population. At a certain point, though, the means of control informed by sovereign power began undoing the controlling apparatuses and practices that operated in the service of disciplinary and bio modes of power, thus rendering the exploitative character of the occupation visible. A brief description of Israel's relation to the Palestinian worker, a key site of control, reveals how the different forms of control began producing excesses and contradictions.

PALESTINIAN LABOR

The integration of Palestinian laborers into the Israeli workforce was not an obvious choice. It entailed putting an end to a Zionist policy (which had been under pressure for many years) of refusing to use "native"—namely, Palestinian—labor. This long-standing policy had distinguished the Zionist enterprise from colonial experiences, for it had flouted the profit principle in employment—Jewish labor was more expensive than Palestinian—in order to advance national objectives aimed at attracting and keeping Jewish immigrants who were used to a European standard of living and levels of consumption. Jewish laborers, in other words, were hired and paid a decent wage in order to attract them to and keep them in Israel.[28] By 1967, however, Israel's national goals had changed, and integration of Palestinian labor into the Israeli economy was considered a priority. The war had helped set the Israeli economy back on track after two years of recession, and a new situation evolved whereby Israel needed cheap, unskilled labor to fill in shortages.[29] Joost Hiltermann clearly describes the economic changes leading to the integration of Palestinian laborers:

> With the influx of international capital in the aftermath of the war
> (especially United States economic and military aid, which increased
> dramatically), investments were redirected toward services and industry,
> revitalizing these sectors, especially the armaments industry. These changes
> were accompanied by a continuing drop in Jewish participation in the wage
> labor force, by a low rate of Jewish immigration to Israel, and by a strong
> pull for Jewish labor emanating from those industries either designated

as strategic (thus excluding non-Jews) or requiring a high level of technical competence. At the same time, other high-growth sectors such as food processing, textiles, tourism and—most important—construction were faced with an increasing shortage of unskilled labor. A major result, therefore, of the post-1967 boom was the new and high demand for a cheap, mobile, unskilled, and unorganized labor force. This Israel found in the population of the newly occupied West Bank and Gaza Strip.[30]

The Palestinian laborers who commuted to Israel commanded much lower wages than their Israeli counterparts, particularly in the early years. In mid-1971, Israeli workers earned six times more than Palestinians from the West Bank and eight times more than those who commuted from the Gaza Strip.[31] Yet, the significant point is that Israel's internal economic needs following the war coincided with its strategic approach to managing the occupied population, particularly its determination to ensure the livelihood of the Palestinian residents and to raise their standard of living. The Palestinian economy had been severely hurt as a result of the war, and Israel was adamant about preventing the transformation of the economic crisis into a political one.[32] Indeed, it understood that economic growth would most likely help attain political stability and normalization.

During the early years one accordingly encounters ongoing discussions concerning strategies of reducing the unemployment rate. But even as Israel considered the creation of jobs vital for managing the population, it imposed constraints that hindered the possibility of creating a sound economic base that could absorb workers in the OT. Thus, unemployment was curbed primarily through the incorporation of laborers into Israel. As we will see, after the eruption of the first intifada, Israel began introducing policies that produced massive unemployment and used this unemployment as a form of control. The reduction of unemployment rates during one phase and their intensification during another underscores how during different periods the same means of control was used to accomplish different political goals. But to this I return later. Here it is important to stress that in order to decrease unemployment during the years following the war Israel allowed free movement of Palestinian labor across its borders, established vocational training programs, and created New Deal–style public work projects. While all of these initiatives can be analyzed from a strictly economic point of view, they can and should also be considered as forms of control that were adopted to manage the occupied population.

NEW DEAL PROJECTS

New Deal–style public work projects, or "relief work," as the Israeli military authorities called them, were used primarily right after the war and were eventually terminated once the occupied economy had stabilized (though they were renewed briefly during the first intifada). During the occupation's first nine months Israel had spent almost IL 8 million on such projects in the West Bank in order to reduce unemployment.[33] While in 1968, 44 percent of the Palestinians who were hired through the Israeli Ministry of Labor's employment offices were offered relief work inside the West Bank, by 1971 only 1 percent of Palestinians were assigned work in the OT.[34]

One of the public work projects, which the government implemented in 1968, is worth mentioning because it exposes the multifaceted dimensions of Israel's job-creation policy. This project was the construction of a "security road" along the west bank of the Dead Sea, connecting the Israeli kibbutz Ein Gedi with a newly established Jewish settlement called Kalya and the Jericho-Jerusalem road. Minister of Labor Yigal Allon initiated the project as a way of advancing the Allon Plan, which aimed to redraw Israel's borders by annexing about one-third of the West Bank, from the mountain range to the Jordan Valley, as well as a large portion of the Gaza Strip. According to his plan, the more densely populated parts of the OT were to become demilitarized regions of a single Jordanian-Palestinian entity.[35] The security road project, which employed hundreds of Palestinians for several months, was part and parcel of this annexation plan.

Allon's road project reveals how the employment of Palestinians in relief work was used to accomplish numerous objectives simultaneously. In this case, as in several other public work projects, Israel wanted to ensure the inhabitants' livelihood in order to prevent despair and thus avert the possibility of social upheaval. But as it created jobs to improve the financial circumstances of Palestinians, Israel used the laborers to advance so-called security projects (at about the same time Palestinians began building Jewish settlements), which were inimical to Palestinian interests because their ultimate objective was the annexation of Palestinian land. Finally, the road work was meant to serve as an impetus for Gazans to leave the region in which they resided and relocate to the West Bank. The Israeli military had hired only Palestinians from the Gaza Strip for this particular West Bank project, hoping that the "prolonged sojourn in the vicinity of Jericho would induce some of them to take up residence in the West Bank."[36] This latter objective is particularly interesting since it highlights how Israel's strategic thinking and the methods it uses have changed over the years. Today, Israel would prefer to transfer Palestinians from the West Bank to the Gaza Strip, and instead of encouraging the residents to relocate by offering them employment opportunities in the other region (disciplinary power), it uses military decrees to deport them (sovereign power).

The public work projects lasted for a very short period, since the incorporation of laborers into the Israeli workforce both solved the unemployment problem and was actually advantageous to Israel's economy. In other words, the efficiency of incorporating laborers rendered relief work unnecessary, thus suggesting that the success of one controlling practice determined the policy decision to cancel another. During the first intifada, as the borders between the OT and Israel proper were first sealed, the Civil Administration reintroduced relief work, once again creating short-term public service jobs for some of those who had lost their jobs in Israel. These projects, like the ones implemented twenty years earlier, aimed to alleviate some of the excesses of the economic crisis—this time the one produced by the uprising and the restrictions of movement. However, Israel's investment in public works in the late 1980s and early 1990s was very limited when compared to the investment immediately after the war, and its objectives were different. In the second instance, it was implemented to ensure that people did not go hungry and was not part of a strategy that aimed to produce normalization by propelling prosperity or raising the standard of living. During the second intifada, when the economic situation in the OT was much worse than it had ever been, Israel did not even consider introducing relief-work projects. This, as we will see, sheds some light on how Israel's approach changed during the four decades of military rule.

VOCATIONAL COURSES

During the nineteen years that the West Bank and Gaza Strip were under Jordanian and Egyptian rule, only one vocational training program was opened in each region.[37] By contrast, within a decade Israel had established a total of twenty-six vocational training programs in several fields, includ-ing carpentry, draftsmanship, metal-working, welding, and sewing. [38] The Palestinians who participated in training programs were given a small salary. Salaries in courses like construction, for which there was an acute need of laborers inside Israel, were somewhat higher and thus served as a pull factor. Not surprisingly, of the 1,260 Palestinians who had completed courses in 1969, 700 had studied construction. Military authorities frankly admitted that the vocational schools were designed to cater to Israel's market needs, and were not set up to help develop an independent Palestinian economy. [39] At least during the first years, all of the graduates were absorbed by the Israeli labor market. [40]

While the vocational programs functioned as training schools that served the interests of Israeli employers, they also were useful for harnessing the energies of Palestinians and directing these energies toward increasing their economic utility. This entailed the participants' induction into a series of normative fiats relating to "correct" behavior at the workplace, which included complete abstinence from any kind of political activity. It also entailed the introduction of regulatory ideals that at times were in opposi-tion to traditional norms, like the notion that woman should seek work in the public sphere. [41] Thus, the vocational schools aimed to manage the occu-pied inhabitants by developing their economic capabilities, encouraging correct conduct, suppressing national aspirations, and raising the standard of living—all of which were intended to enhance Israel's normalization project.

THE INCORPORATION OF PALESTINIAN
LABORERS INTO THE ISRAELI WORKFORCE

The overall impact of the relief-work projects and vocational training pro-grams was, however, not great and certainly pales when compared to the incorporation of Palestinians into the Israeli workforce. By the early 1970s Israel had opened at least twenty employment offices in the West Bank in order to recruit workers who would satisfy Israel's growing needs. [42] The meager wages paid to the Palestinian laborers who commuted to Israel were still much higher than the wages they could have earned in the OT, and therefore their integration injected capital into the OT, producing rapid economic growth while dramatically raising the standard of living. Since well over 30 percent of the OT's GNP was generated from these laborers' income, their absorption into the Israeli economy also reflected the level of Palestinian dependency on Israel.

If in 1970 the total Palestinian workforce amounted to 173,300 people, of whom 20,600 worked in Israel (11.8 percent), on the eve of the first intifada (1987) the Palestinian workforce was 277,700, of which 108,900 were employed in Israel (39.2 percent).[43] These figures are widely regarded as understated because they only take into account those who found work through formal channels and do not include unregistered workers. The number of unregistered workers fluctuated over the years and has been estimated to be an additional 40–70 percent of the total number of workers just cited as entering Israel.[44]

Registered workers were recruited through state agencies, such as the Ministry of Labor and Social Welfare and the Civil Administration. These workers received pay slips, paid the required deductions, and received a limited amount of social benefits. They were also relatively better protected from arbitrary detention, fines, and violence by security forces than were unregistered workers. By contrast, unregistered workers were recruited directly by Israeli employers, and while they usually received a higher net wage than registered workers since their employers did not deduct social benefits, their jobs were often seasonal, and they were more likely to be exposed to violence, degradation, imprisonment, and fines.[45] Even if one does not take into account the unregistered workers, the phenomenon whereby almost 40 percent of the workforce is employed outside the local market has no parallel in the world. In order to outline some of the ways by which the incorporation of the Palestinian laborers helped the occupying power manage and control the population during the first two periods (1967–87) and how it produced a series of excesses and contradictions, one can differentiate among three levels of analysis: the individual, the regional, and the national.

The Individual Level

As the figures cited above suggest, a large percentage of Palestinian laborers rapidly became dependent on Israeli employers for their sources of revenue and indeed for their livelihood. Surveys conducted indicate that their incorporation into the Israeli workforce had a dramatic impact on private consumption in the OT (a 100 percent increase in seven years), which attests, in turn, that the standard of living and lifestyles also rapidly changed.[46] The integration of the Palestinian laborers into the Israeli workforce was, however, always partial. Not only were they paid lower salaries, but the Palestinian workers were not permitted to join any of the existing unions within Israel and were not allowed to form their own unions for laborers who worked inside Israel.[47] The truncated economic integration and the consequent perpetual job insecurity reflected the fact that Palestinians were not integrated politically and therefore could not enjoy the rights and status of Israeli workers.[48] Their incorporation was, as Michael Mann suggests in a different context, "without legitimization."[49]

The lack of legitimization and the absence of job security can be conceptualized as another manifestation of the temporary and arbitrary modalities of control that Israel deployed in the OT. Not unlike the notion concerning the temporary nature of the occupation or the temporary and arbitrary facet of the legal system, the temporary nature of the labor market helped shape Palestinian behavior. The Palestinian workers were defenseless when confronting the whims of their employers, and they were much more vulnerable when market forces underwent a change for the worse. When the Israeli economy experienced a crisis, as it did in the mid-1980s, the effects were felt immediately in the OT, since the Palestinian laborer had no job security and was therefore often the first to get laid off. Accordingly, in times of economic crisis Palestinians had to be even more careful. This meant that in addition to emulating codes of comportment relating to correct work conduct, like diligence, punctuality, and obedience, which were expected of all workers, the Palestinian laborers also had to follow a series of codes relating to correct political conduct, not least of which was the suppression of national aspirations. Put differently, in exchange for their partial economic incorporation, the Palestinians had to contain their political desires. This form of control is less conscious and functions primarily in a productive way by disseminating norms aimed at structuring both the conduct and the possible field of action of the Palestinian individual.

One should keep in mind that during the first two decades of occupation, the borders between the OT and Israel were, generally speaking, open except for short periods during the 1971 military campaign in Gaza and the 1973 October war, and almost any Palestinian who wanted to could look for work in Israel; work permits were granted more or less automatically and were used for monitoring and taxation purposes only.[50] This suggests that the employer-employee relationship was considered sufficient for producing the correct conduct of the Palestinian laborers, and indicates that a disciplinary mode of power was the primary form of control. After the eruption of the first intifada in December 1987, Israel's long-standing policy of allowing Palestinian laborers free access across the pre-1967 borders was modified, and a working-permit regime aimed at monitoring and restricting their entry was introduced. The permit regime reflects a shift in the configuration of power and the primacy of controlling methods informed by sovereign and bio modes of power. By limiting the number of Palestinians who were allowed to pass the Green Line, the Israeli government hoped to prevent the entrance of Palestinians who sought to attack its citizenry, to appease the majority of the Jewish inhabitants who did not want the Palestinians to enter Israel, and to collectively punish the Palestinian population so that it, in turn, would oppose the resistance movement.

Work was consequently transformed from an individual right to a privilege, something that could be taken away if one did not conform to the requirements of correct conduct. After 1987, the employer was no longer the sole arbiter of correct conduct, since the GSS, Civil Administration, police, and military regularly intervened in order to determine who could and who could not go to work. Their power was more extensive than the employer's because they could ban the laborer from entering Israel, whereas the employer could only fire the laborer, who could then search for another job. With the introduction of the working-permit regime, Palestinian laborers had to watch how they behaved and what they said more closely—and not only at the workplace, but during every moment of the day, even at home. Those who participated in a protest, distributed leaflets, or belonged to a political party could lose their permits and thus their livelihood. (For an analysis of this permit regime see chapter 7.)

From a slightly different perspective, the demands of the Israeli market, which were predominantly oriented towards unskilled menial labor in construction, industry, agriculture, and services, did not encourage Palestinians to broaden their professional skills or to acquire higher education. The Israeli demand for unskilled laborers not only influenced the individual workers, but also had long-term detrimental effects on the Palestinian economy because the pull factor of unskilled labor helped maintain the underdeveloped economic conditions in the OT and hindered the process of professionalization.

Simultaneously, however, Israel adopted a "liberal policy" that provided the occupied inhabitants with permits to open universities.[51] Within a relatively short period of time several universities were opened, rapidly producing a fairly large professional class made up of college graduates. The problem was that the employment opportunities open to professional Palestinians were very limited, and many of the graduates could not find jobs that reflected their skills. Not only was the labor market in Israel hiring only unskilled laborers, but, as illustrated above, Israel also hindered practically all Palestinian attempts to establish an independent industrial sector and an up-to-date service sector. Consequently, most professionals had to look for employment overseas, frequently in the Gulf States.[52] The lack of professional jobs created a fair amount of bitterness among the unemployed and underemployed graduates, who totaled about fifteen thousand at the outbreak of the first intifada, and they were instrumental in helping consolidate the resistance to Israeli rule.[53] Put differently, the restriction of integration to unskilled laborers alongside the constraints and restrictions imposed on developing a local economy based on industry and services ended up contradicting the liberal policy of opening universities.

This is but one contradiction arising from what I term the *partial* integration of Palestinian laborers into the Israeli workforce. The fact that the integration was only partial ended up generating widespread resentment among Palestinians, which stimulated opposition to Israeli rule, spurring, in turn, a series of modifications in Israel's policy within the OT. This becomes obvious in chapter 6, which deals with the first intifada. The same forms of control that helped produce normalization during the first few years engendered contradictions during later periods and thus helped spur changes in Israel's policies.

The Regional Level: West Bank

The incorporation of laborers into Israel had a different impact in the West Bank and Gaza Strip due to the social makeup of the laborers coming from each region. Most of the laborers from the West Bank came from rural villages, which are still home to 70 percent of this region's population, while the majority of Gaza workers came from refugee camps. The physical proximity of the two regions to the work centers allowed the laborers to commute and therefore to continue their relationship with their home environment.[54] The increasing number of young Palestinians who worked in Israel as well as the above-average salaries earned by these laborers altered the social stratification within the West Bank's rural areas and had numerous consequences relating to the management of the population.

According to Joel Migdal, the incorporation of the workers created two major social cleavages in the West Bank, which were characterized by generational and income gaps, and which ultimately weakened the traditional village leadership.[55] Those who worked in Israel became economically independent and were demanding a say in local politics. So while the Palestinian laborers became dependent on Israel for their livelihood, a fact that was used by Israel to expand its control over them, the process of incorporation simultaneously weakened the control of the traditional elites over these workers and, by extension, also weakened Israel's control over them because one of the ways Israel controlled the population was through these elites.[56] In other words, Israel's attempt to control the population by providing benefits to the traditional elite failed, not least because the incorporation of young men into the Israeli workforce empowered many workers who were looking for ways of translating their economic achievements into political power. Hence, the integration of workers, which had been used as a way to manage the population, helped undo another means of control, namely, the use of traditional elites to administer the area.

The growing number of Palestinians entering Israel to find work also resulted in a substantial drop in the number of laborers who remained in the territories to cultivate Palestinian land. In 1970, 42,500 Palestinians worked in agriculture in the West Bank; by 1980 that number had dropped by about 30 percent, with only 28,900 agriculture workers.[57] Migdal's fieldwork in the early 1970s suggests that in certain areas farmers were cultivating only 20 percent of the land that had previously been plowed and sowed.[58] According to a report published by the Israeli Communist Party, in 1969 238,000 dunams of agricultural lands were left untilled, while in 1970 the figure had grown to 354,000 dunams. The report explains that since laborers and even owners of small farms earned more money by working in Israel, agricultural land was not cultivated.[59]

A prominent West Bank economist corroborates these findings. In a 1977 interview he notes that "it no longer pays to attend to one's olive trees or rocky piece of land. The farmer chooses the more sensible course of action: to seek work elsewhere. West Bank farmers have increasingly fallowed their land and totally neglected the maintenance of their terraces."[60] The failure to cultivate more land was aggravated both by the fixed water quotas set in the early 1970s, which were not changed for over a decade, and by the fact that Palestinian farmers were paying four times as much for the water as Israeli farmers.[61] Thus, it is not totally surprising that in 1984 less land was cultivated than in 1968, although the population had increased by some 30 percent.[62] This, however, did not lead to reduced production. Until 1982 productivity actually increased due to changes in cultivation methods, increased machinization, improvement of agricultural technology, and the replacement of some low-value crops with high-value cash crops. Only after 1982 does the share of agriculture in the West Bank GDP show a continuous decline as a result of decreased productivity.

An analysis of the labor movement in the West Bank reveals how during the occupation's first years some controlling practices complemented each other and thus served two primary objectives: managing the inhabitants without integrating them into Israeli society and seizing Palestinian land. I have already underscored that the incorporation of laborers into the Israeli market served the latter's economic interests by providing the local markets with cheap laborers and also improved the Palestinian inhabitants' standard of living, thus helping to normalize the occupation and suppress resistance.[63] Most analysts fail to acknowledge, however, that the incorporation of Palestinian laborers from the West Bank's rural areas vacated agricultural land, making it more susceptible to confiscation. This claim gains credence particularly when one takes into account that from 1980 onward the leading legal mechanism Israel used to expropriate land was an Ottoman law that allows the sovereign to appropriate property that had not been farmed for three consecutive years.[64] This example underscores how forms of control that were ostensibly utilized to increase the economic utility of the Palestinian residents also assisted material confiscations. Although bureaucratic legal mechanisms were the predominant tools employed to advance Israel's expropriation project, the legal mechanisms were supported by the effects of several seemingly unrelated practices. In other words, Israel's management of the population facilitated the expropriation of land and, as I show in chapter 5, seizure of land also helped manage the occupied population.

It was only during the first years, however, that forms of control informed by disciplinary and bio modes of power complemented the mechanisms employed to expropriate the land. Later, such controls began producing a series of contradictions. One condensed example relating to the agrarian character of the West Bank will have to suffice here. As mentioned, for twenty years Palestinian laborers were encouraged to find work in Israel. Yet, other than the incorporation of laborers into the Israeli workforce and Israel's support of Palestinian workers' emigration to other countries, Israel actually increased Palestinian dependency on the land by not allowing them to develop a self-sufficient industry. Simultaneously, though, Israel seized large quantities of land and severely limited the water resources available for agriculture.[65] It is not surprising, therefore, that the amount of cultivated land actually decreased over the years.[66] The constraints on establishing a self-sufficient industry and the mechanisms used to appropriate land did not, so to speak, clash until the late 1980s when Israel introduced the entry-permit regime that imposed harsh restrictions on the movement of Palestinian laborers who wished to enter Israel. At this point numerous forms of control that had been producing seemingly unrelated effects began creating serious excesses and contradictions and engendered significant social unrest.

The Regional Level: Gaza Strip

The incorporation of Palestinian laborers into Israel served an additional objective in the Gaza Strip, where, according to a 1981 census, the total population was 470,535, of whom 278,708 were refugees.[67] The majority of Gazans seeking jobs in Israel were refugees. It is crucial to keep in mind that following the 1967 War, Palestinian armed resistance was concentrated in the Gaza Strip and originated in the refugee camps, from which most of the armed cadres came. The camps' inhabitants not only lived in extreme poverty but also in what had become the place with the highest population density in the world. Israel realized that the inhumane living conditions — the absence of running water, a sewage system, and electricity, alongside overcrowded living quarters — rendered the camps perfect breeding grounds for resistance. Therefore, it hoped that the integration of Gaza's laborers would change the living conditions in the camps and thus undermine some of the forces that encouraged opposition to Israeli rule.

In 1973, Dayan proposed moving the refugees out of the camps in order to create "normal life in new towns, in apartments with water in the faucets, education and services for the children."[68] Israel, Eyal Weizman suggests, intended to stimulate a process of forced *embourgoisement* in order to produce certain sentiments among the refugees and a sense that they had something concrete to lose.[69] In this way it hoped to reduce their motivation to support active resistance. It also wished to sidestep the refugee problem. "As long as the refugees remain in their camps," Dayan explained, "their children will say they come from Jaffa or Haifa; if they move out of the camps, the hope is that they will feel an attachment to their new land."[70] The Palestinians, to be sure, were well aware of Israel's intentions, and the unwillingness of most people to leave the camps and relocate to apartment buildings became a form of resistance. Nonetheless, the relative prosperity that was created through the integration of many refugees into the Israeli workforce, alongside Sharon's 1971 military campaign in the camps, did help weaken the resistance for a short period of time.

This strategy of controlling the refugee population stands in stark contrast to the one Israel adopted in later years. If in the 1970s and early 1980s Israel tried to normalize the refugee problem by drawing the camp's residents into the Israeli proletariat, following the outbreak of the first intifada, Israel started restricting the movement of refugees into Israel.[71] After the eruption of the second intifada, it periodically stopped the water and electricity supply to several refugee camps and destroyed much of the scant infrastructure that had been built in the camps over the years. Thus, while in the first two decades Israel sought to manage the refugees by raising their standard of living, later it tried to control them through a politics of dearth and repression.

The National Level

On the national level, the swift incorporation of laborers into the Israeli workforce was the leading factor in reducing the unemployment rate and increasing the economic utility of the occupied population. It was also the leading cause for the boost in the standard of living in the OT, particularly among the rural sectors in the West Bank and the refugees in the Gaza Strip. The partial integration of laborers helped prevent social upheaval and contributed to Israel's attempt to undermine Palestinian resistance, undercutting, as it were, some of the criticisms voiced by the emerging nationalist camp. However, as the years passed, the integration of Palestinian laborers into Israel produced a series of effects that Israel had neither planned nor wished for, some of which actually helped consolidate Palestinian resistance. In the next chapter we will see that another means Israel used to manage the Palestinian population was the production and reinforcement of fragmentation. Yet here we can already note that the increasing exploitation of Palestinian workers and the ongoing indignities that they had to undergo created bitterness and antagonism, while the lack of local economic development became a structural force that diminished class differences in the OT and facilitated the creation of national alliances.

The fact that Palestinians from different segments of society, and not just the lower classes, were integrated into the Israeli workforce, and that all the workers were treated with equal contempt, helped alter social stratification within Palestinian society. The work experience inside Israel alongside the realities of their daily lives in the OT produced a common sense among workers that they were being exploited and were destined, according to the existing economic system, to remain at the bottom of Israel's economic ladder.[72] It precipitated the transformation of the village class structure in the West Bank, producing class homogeneity among different clans and among those who owned land and those who did not.[73] Along similar lines, the incorporation of laborers into Israel blurred the distinction between the refugees and the indigenous residents in the Gaza Strip. Economic actors who otherwise were in conflict with one another, such as landowners and laborers, were, at least partially, united due to Israel's economic policies. The nationalists realized this, and in the early 1970s the Palestinian trade unions in the West Bank decided to freeze the class struggle and to engage in a national alliance of classes with the Palestinian managerial sector in order to create the requisite environment for collective struggle against the common enemy.[74] But to achieve this objective was not easy, and, as we will see, a number of other social processes had to develop before cross-class alliances could be formed.

In a similar fashion, one of the effects of incorporating Palestinians into the Israeli workforce and relegating them to menial jobs without benefits and security was the emphasis rather than the erasure of the Green Line. Even though Israel wanted to erase the internationally recognized border in order to integrate the captured land into its own territory, the labor market guaranteed that the Green Line was never totally expunged. The ongoing exploitation and humiliation of the Palestinian workers produced an "us" versus "them" perception between the employees and their employers, between the OT and Israel.[75] This suggests that, although the partial incorporation of laborers into Israel helped blur one kind of border, their exploitation accentuated others.

From a slightly different perspective, for many years the integration of unskilled laborers into the Israeli workforce complemented the constraints Israel imposed on the creation of an independent Palestinian industry. The lack of jobs inside the OT was compensated by the employment opportunities inside Israel, and one might surmise that Israel intentionally obstructed the development of an independent Palestinian industry in order to guarantee the regular supply of cheap labor.[76] But once Israel began restricting the movement of Palestinian laborers, not allowing many workers to enter Israel, a contradiction emerged between the two forms of control, since many of the Palestinians who could no longer enter Israel found it impossible to find a job in the OT.

INFRASTRUCTURAL EFFECTS

The excesses and contradictions just mentioned were produced, for the most part, by the incorporation of the Palestinian laborers into the Israeli workforce, which, as I have claimed, can also be conceived of as a form of control operating in the service of disciplinary and biopower. Another site where these excesses manifested themselves was in the physical infrastructure of the OT. If one were to jump for a moment to the early 1990s, a quarter of a century after the occupation began, one would be amazed at the stark contrast between the civil infrastructures in the OT and within Israel. Whereas the roads, sewage, water network, electricity, educational, and health care systems in the West Bank and Gaza Strip resembled those of a Third World country, just across the Green Line and in the adjacent Jewish settlements the infrastructure was not very different from that in Western industrialized countries.

On the eve of the Oslo agreements (1993), right before responsibility for the infrastructure was transferred from Israeli hands to the Palestinian Authority, 5 percent of Gaza's residents and about 26 percent of the rural inhabitants in the West Bank did not have access to running water. Less than 10 percent of the West Bank's rural population had access to piped sewage networks, and just 50 percent had access to garbage collection. In Gaza, 38 percent of the population did not have access to a sewage system, and while almost the entire population had access to some form of garbage collection, the service was usually inadequate, and heaps of garbage lay in the streets. Only 69 percent of the West Bank's rural population had twenty-four-hour access to electricity, while as much as 39 percent of the rural communities received electricity from generators rather than a grid.[77] Even though almost all of the inhabitants in Gaza are connected to an electricity grid, the power often appeared in concentrated bursts for several hours and then stopped. In 1991, each resident in the Strip received on average 400 kilowatt hours of electricity, while each Israeli received an average of 3,500 kilowatt hours.[78] More than two and a half decades after Israel occupied the Palestinian territories, only 9 percent of the West Bank's rural population had twenty-four-hour access to electricity, piped water, garbage disposal services, and piped sewage networks—services that were considered basic within Israel even before 1967.[79] These figures reveal once again that the individual prosperity characterizing the occupation's first years had nothing to do with communal prosperity and development.

The decrepit infrastructure in the OT generated deep alienation. Many of the laborers from rural villages in the West Bank or refugee camps in the Gaza Strip left a house in the morning that had no electricity, running water, or sewage, and worked all day in an environment where these utilities were taken for granted. The dilapidated infrastructure also served to highlight the distinction Israel made between the Palestinians and their land, since Israel did invest in infrastructure within the OT, but only insofar as the infrastructure served the Jewish settlers. Unlike other political contexts where such stark disparities also exist, the distinction between the haves and have nots was based on national identity rather than on class. The disparities no doubt reminded the Palestinians that they were an occupied people and that the situation was not normal. Hence, the lack of investment in infrastructure served to underscore their status as oppressed people.

While the inadequate infrastructure in the villages, towns, and refugee camps was an effect of the retarded economy, the lack of investment in infrastructure also further hindered the development of the economy. This is apparent when examining the educational system, a crucial field that serves as the infrastructure for the development of a vibrant and independent economy. A cursory examination of classroom density, for instance, reveals the dire straits of the educational infrastructure. Instead of building new classrooms to address the population's growing needs, Israel imposed a double-shift teaching day, so that some students studied from the early morning hours until noon, and others studied in the afternoon. Even with the double shifts, on the eve of the first intifada, Gaza had an average of 43.6

elementary students, 44 junior high students, and 37.1 high school students per classroom. Fifty percent of Gaza and West Bank students dropped out by the time they reached ninth grade, the majority dropping out between the ages thirteen and sixteen. In fact, student dropouts constituted 40 percent of all Palestinian laborers in Israel in 1986.[80] This situation had detrimental ramifications for the development of a Palestinian economy.

While some economic forms of control spurred growth in order to normalize the occupation and contain social unrest, other forms of control—or even the same ones—produced infrastructural effects that redrew the Green Line and underscored the difference between the occupied Palestinian inhabitants and their Israeli occupiers. The deepening disparity between the Palestinian and Israeli infrastructure, which was a direct product of the regulations and constraints imposed on the Palestinian economy, had a series of effects, many of which helped engender unity among the Palestinian population and opposition to Israeli rule, and, in turn, a change in Israel's policy choices.

Even though the economic field was only rarely intentionally used as a weapon of social repression to collectively punish the Palestinian population during the first twenty years of occupation—as it was in subsequent years—the economic dependency on Israel and the disparity between Palestinians and Israelis began stimulating opposition to Israeli rule many years before the first intifada erupted. The opposition was engendered by the personal experience of the exploited worker, the lack of opportunities within the OT, the absence of basic infrastructure, and the structural effects that changed the stratification of Palestinian society and produced conditions that enabled the creation of cross-class alliances. All of these stimulated national sentiments, an issue to which we now turn.

Chapter 4 | IDENTIFICATION TROUBLE

The climate of normalcy has been carefully nurtured
by the Israeli administration, which has aimed, as any
responsible administration should, at encouraging
solutions to practical problems and making further
advances possible. The administration has stressed local
participation and control at every level, often to a greater
degree than the previous Jordanian and Egyptian rulers.

BINYAMIN BEN ELIEZER,
*Coordinator of Government Activities
in Judea, Samaria, and the Gaza District, 1983*

In 1981, Menahem Milson, a professor from Hebrew University and a government advisor on Arab affairs, was chosen to be the first head of the newly
established Civil Administration in the West Bank.[1] Before taking on this
role, Milson argued that a more interventionist approach was needed in
order to "free the [Palestinian] population from the grip of the PLO."[2] As a
historian, he was most likely aware that nationalist movements, particularly
in the context of an occupation, could easily become a potent political force.
National identification has the power to override other forms of identification and in this way to unite and facilitate the mobilization of an otherwise
disparate population. In addition, being a member of a recognized nation,
particularly after World War II, guaranteed a series of rights, beginning
with the right to self-determination. In Algeria and India, for example,
the struggle for self-determination was intricately tied to and informed by
the colonized inhabitants' identification as Algerians and Indians and the
emergence of national movements.

Although scholars disagree about when exactly Palestinian national identity evolved—whether it already existed with the demise of the Ottoman
Empire, whether it was formed as a result of the interaction with the Zionist
movement, or whether it emerged only after the British mandate was in
place—they tend to concur that by the mid-1920s and 1930s it had became
a central form of identification among the Arab inhabitants of Palestine.[3]

As Rashid Khalidi points out, the growth of the educational system in Palestine between the two world wars and the attendant spread of nationalist concepts by and through this system greatly facilitated the politicization of the countryside, becoming a conveyer belt for nationalist ideas and, thus, empowering the national movement.[4] All this changed, however, following the 1948 War, which prompted a process of de-Palestinization. The name "Palestine" disappeared geographically and politically, and the Palestinian people were scattered throughout numerous countries, including Egypt, Jordan, Lebanon, and Syria, with a minority remaining within the territory that had become Israel.[5] Khalidi confirms that, after 1948, the Palestinians, as independent actors and indeed as a people, seemed to have vanished from the political map.[6]

The Palestinians living in the West Bank found themselves under Jordanian rule. They were offered Jordanian citizenship, and their absorption into the Hashemite regime also served to encourage them to identify as Jordanians. Although most of the population continued to identify as Palestinians, this form of identification did not threaten the Hashemite kingdom since Israel rather than Jordan was considered to be the obstacle for achieving self-determination. Indeed, in the months leading up to the 1967 War, several Israeli decision makers expressed their hesitation about occupying the West Bank because they realized that such a move would strengthen Palestinian national identity and threaten Israel's efforts to erase the Palestinian question.[7] During the same period (1948–67), Egypt controlled the Gaza Strip, but, unlike their brethren in the West Bank, the Palestinians living in this region were not offered Egyptian citizenship and were not encouraged to identify as Egyptians; instead, they were urged to identify as part of the pan-Arab movement or as Palestinians whose national rights had been usurped by the Zionist state.[8]

The total defeat of the Arab armies in 1967 and the loss of credibility for Arab regimes in the eyes of many Palestinians, as well as the geographical unity of Mandatory Palestine under Israeli rule, helped pave the way for the re-emergence of Palestinian national identity. For its part, Israel decided not to absorb the population living in the two captured regions into its own society because it feared that such a move would undermine the Jewish character of the state. It therefore did not encourage the Palestinians to identify with Israel or as Israelis. Simultaneously, though, it did not allow the occupied inhabitants to identify as Palestinians with national aspirations and rights, since this form of identification entailed, among other things, a relationship with and a claim to a certain piece of land, the same land Israel wanted to keep for itself. All expressions or manifestations of Palestinian nationalism were accordingly prohibited, punished, and suppressed. We have already seen in chapters 1 and 2 that all Palestinian national symbols were outlawed, Palestinian history was banned and erased, and any attempt to produce a national narrative that could unite and help mobilize Palestinian society was censored. It therefore took several years before a new leadership could begin forming a national movement out of the Palestinian montage created in 1948.[9]

While Israel repressed Palestinian national identity, it encouraged alternative forms of identification that created divisions within Palestinian society, which, in turn, facilitated the military government's attempt to manage the population. Israel did not invent or introduce new kinds of identification in the OT, but tried to strengthen some of the existing ones in order to counter the re-emergence of a national movement. Identification with the *hamula,* the extended family or clan, was accordingly encouraged. Israel granted the authority to reinforce traditional institutions and forms of identification to the heads of the *hamula.*[10] It also encouraged religious identification, providing support for religious institutions and leaders in order both to accentuate differences between Muslim and Christian Palestinians, thus creating friction between the religious devotees, and to offset the nationalist movement, which was predominantly secular.[11] Indeed, for many years, Israeli officers maintained that the rise of Muslim fundamentalism in the OT could neutralize the PLO. Israel consequently allowed the Muslim Brotherhood to take over the *waqf* (religious trust), which controls about 10 percent of the real estate in the Gaza Strip and a considerable amount of property in the West Bank, and employs hundreds of workers. Between 1967 and 1987 the number of mosques in the Gaza Strip more than doubled, from 77 to 160, and in the West Bank new ones were being built at a rate of 40 per year.[12] Finally, Israel also encouraged identification with the local geographical space that the Palestinians occupied and in this way hoped to set the rural inhabitants against the urban residents or the indigenous population against the refugees.

While Israel tended to encourage only those forms of identification that helped split Palestinian society, it did not discourage identification with Arabness. Ostensibly, the category "Arab" encompasses and supersedes nationality and can become a unifying form of identification. From Israel's perspective, its role, however, was not to produce Palestinian unity but rather to connect Palestinians with non-Palestinian Arabs, particularly Jordanians, but also Egyptians, Syrians, Iraqis, and Lebanese, and in this way to undermine Palestinian nationalism, which laid claim to Palestine and to numerous rights—of which self-determination was the most prominent. This is another reason why Israel did not obstruct Jordan's efforts to recover its influence in the OT and to maintain its political presence in the West Bank and Gaza Strip following the 1967 War.[13]

Despite Israel's ongoing effort to undermine the nationalistic drive, Palestinian national identification slowly but consistently strengthened following the 1967 War. Not unlike Zionism, which, as some scholars claim, precipitated the appearance and development of Palestinian national identity at the turn of the twentieth century, Israel's occupation of the West Bank and Gaza Strip helped generate the reemergence of Palestinian nationalism. In this chapter, I argue that many of the controlling apparatuses employed to manage the inhabitants affected the Palestinian population as a whole, thus highlighting the similarities among the residents of the two regions rather than their differences. So while Israel deployed several controlling practices to repress Palestinian nationalism and to encourage other forms of identification, the contradictions and excesses of its controlling apparatuses actually reinforced the sense of a shared predicament, which strengthened national identification. In hindsight, it is not surprising that Israel failed to suppress the rise of national identity. But in order to better understand how Palestinian nationalism reemerged and how it, in turn, led Israel to emphasize sovereign power and de-emphasize disciplinary and biopower, it is useful to look back, if only briefly, at one of the sites where the struggle over national identification manifested itself most forcefully: the municipal elections in the West Bank.

MUNICIPALITIES AS APPARATUSES OF CONTROL

As I mentioned in the second chapter, following the war Israel allowed the municipal leaders in the West Bank to remain in office, hoping that they would assist the military government in administering the population. During Jordanian rule, the mayors were not expected to represent or express the political aspirations or identity of the population, but to perform the role of intermediaries between the population living within their jurisdiction and the central authorities in Amman; in exchange, they obtained rewards for themselves and their associates. The municipal leaders had attained their position either through their prominent economic status or through the general social status enjoyed by their families. The Jordanian government, for its part, entrusted the leadership to one family or a group of families within a circumscribed area, thus reducing the influence wielded by any leader beyond his immediate locality. This, Issa Al-Shuaibi points out, was the background that helped shape Israel's attitude towards local leadership in the OT.[14]

The military government preserved this structure of local leadership, reinforcing the authority of the village *mukhtars* in the rural areas and the municipal councils and the members of the chambers of commerce in the urban centers. Not surprisingly, it is precisely these institutions that persevered, while other administrative institutions from the Jordanian era were dismantled following the occupation. Al-Shuaibi concludes, "It can thus be said that Israel maintained the inherited local leadership and carefully delineated the limits of the socio-economic role it was to play. For members of it to go further and engage in political activity usually meant expulsion to Jordan."[15] The idea was to ensure that the Palestinian leadership would limit itself to local issues and not try to articulate national demands. Moshe Dayan was clear about this matter when he declared that the West Bank would "not have a central Arab authority above the municipal level" until its status was determined.[16]

Thus, the municipalities were effectively the only political bodies in the territories that were allowed to operate; they rapidly became the one recognized link between the military government and the inhabitants in all matters relating to daily life, and since their official role was to represent and assist the local residents, they also served as an institution through which Israel managed the population. The mayors and municipal councils were certified just after the war by the military government and, within one year, Israel was able to report that all of the towns had provided municipal services in a satisfactory fashion.[17] This was crucial because Israel regarded the municipal system as one of the major instruments for achieving normalization.[18]

Concurrently, though, a series of military orders limiting the authority of the municipalities was issued.[19] These orders authorized the military commander to appoint and dismiss mayors and council members, thus guaranteeing Israeli control over the local leadership and effectively curbing the authority bestowed upon them by the 1934 Municipal Corporation Ordinance enacted under the British Mandate. According to the ordinance, the municipalities were responsible for, among other things, planning, zoning, granting building permits, water and electricity usage and allocation, public health institutions, and more. All of these responsibilities were transferred to the military government. Under Israeli rule, the functions of the municipalities were restricted to collecting garbage, maintaining and improving the town's infrastructure, including roads and sewage, and at times building new schools and classrooms, markets, and medical clinics.[20]

Swiftly, it became both common and expected that the mayor would serve as a mediator between the residents and the military government. In the words of one Israeli colonel who served in the military government in the early 1970s, "The mayor became an authoritative power to whom all began to turn for advice and favors."[21] During the early years, many of the permit applications relating to a variety of issues — ranging from building to traveling permits — were submitted to the municipality, which, in turn, passed the request on to the military government with its recommendations. Mayors frequently asked the military government to lighten the sentences of political prisoners, they helped families file requests for reunification with members who had fled to Jordan in 1967, and they appealed on behalf of those who were deported.[22]

Such activities suggest that, despite the extensive curtailment of their responsibilities, the municipalities still assumed a crucial role within the occupation's civil bureaucracy and assisted Israel in managing the population. They also served as a buffer between the population and the occupying power and in this way helped conceal the workings of the latter. Indeed, the municipalities were probably the single most important institution Israel utilized in order to advance its announced goal of creating a situation whereby the occupied inhabitants could go through life "without setting eyes" on an Israeli government employee. In this chapter, however, I am less interested in exposing exactly how the municipalities served as an apparatus of control and more interested in understanding how they became a site where one of the central contradictions informing the occupation played itself out. Although the contradiction only became evident in the 1976 West Bank elections, in order to make sense of these elections, one has to go back to the first municipal elections, which took place in 1972.[23] But before we do this, let us first briefly look at the municipalities in the Gaza Strip, if only to get a sense of some of the similarities and differences between the two regions.

THE GAZA STRIP'S MUNICIPALITIES

In the Gaza Strip the situation was very different from the one in the West Bank, since Israel implemented a policy of appointments rather than elections in the region's four municipalities: Gaza City, Rafah, Dir el-Balah, and Khan Younis.[24] In 1970, Israel dismissed Ragheb Al-Alami, who had served as the mayor of Gaza during Egyptian rule, after he contested Israel's decision to connect the Gaza Strip to Israel's electricity grid. For a while, an Israeli officer replaced him, but in 1971 Rashad Shawa, a leading citrus merchant and landowner, was appointed mayor of Gaza. Shawa selected a municipal council from Gaza's elites and initially played a role similar to the one played by the Jordanian appointed mayors in the West Bank. He supported the Hashemite proposal of creating a "United Arab Kingdom"—a federation between the Gaza Strip, the West Bank, and Jordan. In this way he created close ties with the latter, which enabled him, in turn, to serve as an intermediary between Jordan and Israel.

The Gaza municipality helped the military government manage the local population not only by taking on various municipal responsibilities, but also by assuming responsibility for the dispensation of such things as exit permits, which allowed inhabitants to leave the region and came to be known as the "Shawa passports." During his first year in office, Shawa survived a number of assassination attempts carried out by PLO members. In 1972, after ongoing pressure from the PLO to resign and a confrontation with the military government over the Israeli decision to connect the al-Shati refugee camp to the Gaza municipality in an attempt to elide the refugee problem, he decided to quit.[25] In 1973, the military government tried to form local legislative committees in the Strip's towns and refugee camps. But after one committee head was assassinated and others were threatened, the remaining members resigned.[26] From 1973 until 1975, when Shawa was reappointed mayor, the military government took on all municipal responsibilities in Gaza City. This was not an unusual situation in the region, since all the other major towns were managed by military officers.

Thus, in contrast to the West Bank, where the municipalities were run by local Palestinian leaders who had been elected by the population or at least part of it, in the Gaza Strip the municipalities were run by Israeli officers or by Palestinians chosen by them. The municipalities had no control over procedures relating to economic development (e.g., zoning, planning, licensing), infrastructural resources critical to economic development (e.g., water, electricity, transportation), or finance, all of which were controlled by the head of the military government.[27]

THE 1972 MUNICIPAL ELECTIONS

Even though Israel was certainly not the first country to stage democratic elections in an occupied context, it was the first power to reintroduce this practice in a postcolonial age. The goal was to transfer a limited amount of authority to the Palestinian people and thus to legitimize the occupation while continuing to control the resources—in this case, low-wage labor, land and water. Paradoxically, both Jordan and the PLO called on the West Bank inhabitants to boycott the elections. Jordan had nominated the existing mayors—who for the most part remained loyal to the Hashemite regime—and was afraid that a change of personnel would threaten its influence. The PLO leadership believed that the emergence of any local leadership in the OT would be detrimental to its long-term goals, since it could undermine the cohesiveness of the Palestinian problem, creating two separate problems: "One for the Palestinians living under occupation and the other for those who were refugees and in exile."[28] Consequently, during the first years after the war, Jordan and even the PLO had a vested interest in ensuring that the mayors not be replaced, precisely because the existing ones generally refrained from political activity and limited their business to municipal affairs.

Israel, on the other hand, had a lot to gain by staging elections. According to Shlomo Gazit, the first coordinator of government activities in the administered territories, it was important to hold elections in the West Bank for three reasons: (1) elections were considered an "expression of normalization and a successful return to routine life in the West Bank"; (2) "the move was an Israeli challenge to Jordan and the PLO, both of which opposed the elections"; and (3) "the elections could considerably strengthen the mandate of the municipal councils and their leaders," granting them legitimacy and thus allowing them "to cooperate with the military administration more closely."[29]

Using a 1955 Jordanian law, Israel held elections in two stages, on March 28 in the northern West Bank and on May 2 in the southern part. Altogether, council members for twenty-one municipalities were elected, while in two additional towns—Hebron and Salfit—an agreed list of representatives was settled on in advance.[30] The population did not vote for political parties or individuals with a political platform, but for the representatives of leading *hamulas*. Only 5 percent of the inhabitants could take part in the elections because a Jordanian law restricted the vote to men who owned property, were over 21, and had paid their property taxes.[31] About 85 percent of those who had a right to vote participated, and the traditional elite won the majority of the vote, which from Israel's standpoint was a victory. The elected officials were not only considered tractable allies, but since their power was based on traditional social divisions, Israel was sure that they would not hurry to bridge these divisions.[32]

As Ian Lustick shows in his analysis of the methods of control used vis-à-vis the Palestinian citizens within Israel, so long as the traditional social structure of society was still very strong—as it was in the territories at this point—the state could manage the population through the cooptation of the *hamula* notables. The type of political arrangements offered to the patriarchic leaders on the local level by the Israeli regime conformed to long-standing traditions concerning power relations between the population, local elites, and the central government. Lustick reveals how the cooptation of the elites was achieved by means of a careful distribution of favors, privileges, and special dispensations. "These 'side payments,'" he writes, "were made not only to secure the loyalty and services of individual patriarchs, *qadis* (religious judges), sheiks, or notables, but also as part of a general effort to strengthen the traditional social structural forms which made cooptation such a convenient, inexpensive, and effective technique of gaining access to the Arab population."[33]

Israel adopted similar strategies in the OT, favoring the traditional landed families over the new group of urban traders. At least in Israel's eyes, the 1972 West Bank elections helped provide the elected officials with some form of legitimacy, which allowed them to cooperate with the military government. The elections, as Dayan noted, had invested the "nominees with political authority by which, one way or another, they can speak for the Arab public who elected them."[34] In the context of our discussion, it is important to emphasize that the contradictions relating to Palestinian nationalism had not yet manifested themselves and that during these elections other more traditional types of identity actually took precedent over national identification. Accordingly, the elections themselves reinforced the divisions within Palestinian society and thus helped undermine, if only for a short while, the nationalistic drive.

THE REEMERGENCE OF PALESTINIAN NATIONALISM

At the time of the 1972 elections, the PLO was still extremely weak, having been crushed by the Jordanian military in September 1970.[35] By 1973, however, the mood in the OT had changed, and Palestinian nationalism was rapidly gaining ground among the population. There were several factors leading to this change, including the strengthening of local nationalists and the rise of the PLO abroad. Following Israel's assassination of three PLO leaders in Beirut a year after the elections (April 1973), demonstrations with a nationalist overtone erupted in the West Bank. The military government was shocked by the anti-Israeli sentiments expressed in these demonstrations, since it had assumed that the population had become reconciled to the "benign occupation."[36] A few months later, the Palestinian National Front (PNF) was established. The fledgling organization regarded itself as the PLO's arm within the OT and aimed, in the words of two of its leaders, to organize mass struggle in the West Bank and Gaza Strip. Its activities included armed resistance, and the mobilization of labor unions, student federations, and women's associations to strike and protest against the occupying power.[37]

The 1973 October war also contributed to the rise of Palestinian nationalism because it helped undermine the notion that Israel was invincible and thus encouraged a resurgence of nationalist protests. At around the same time, the Israeli newspaper *Ma'ariv* conducted a survey in the West Bank, which suggested that popular support for the PLO was rapidly growing and that a large percentage of the population was in favor of establishing a Palestinian state. The Israeli daily claimed that the ideological changes were "extensive and alarming."[38] The PLO gained further recognition when in 1974 it was declared the sole legitimate representative of the Palestinian people at the Arab summit conference in Rabat, recognition that was only strengthened a couple of months later when Yasser Arafat was given the opportunity to address the United Nations General Assembly.[39] Although Israel had managed to prevent the infiltration of PLO *fedayeen* (literally, people who are willing to sacrifice themselves) into the region, it could not prevent the penetration of the organization's ideology into the West Bank and Gaza Strip. The PLO's success in spreading its ideology was also due to the fact that no solution had been found for the Palestinian refugees, whose very existence had become, in Ibrahim Dakkak's words, Israel's Achilles heel. Simply put, the failure of Palestinian refugees to assimilate in Arab countries or even to agree to a permanent solution within the OT was extremely beneficial to the Palestinian national movement, which promised the refugees some kind of future remedy for their plight.[40]

But the rise of Palestinian nationalism in the OT was not only the result of processes taking place on the international level or the outcome of the work of individuals or social movements promoting it within the territories. Several controlling practices also precipitated the reemergence of the national movement, not least of which were the excesses resulting from the confiscation of land and the changes in social stratification following from the incorporation of Palestinian laborers into the Israeli workforce. By 1976 no less than 20 percent of the land in the West Bank had been expropriated and a similar amount in the Gaza Strip, and Israel had already built twenty-seven Jewish settlements in the two regions.[41] Israel took land from everyone, making no distinctions between wealthy landowners and subsistence cultivators.[42] In the West Bank alone, 70 percent of the population lived in rural areas and depended on the land for their livelihood, and many of these people were either hurt directly by the confiscations or knew people who were hurt. The confiscation of land and the establishment of settlements created the sense of a shared predicament among different social groups, helping to unify an otherwise divided population.

While the land confiscations had a cohering effect that helped undermine Israel's efforts to reinforce the traditional stratifications within Palestinian society, the incorporation of Palestinian laborers into the Israeli workforce, as we have already seen, also altered the social stratification in the OT and played a crucial role in weakening the influence of the traditional elites by securing the financial independence of a large portion of the labor force.[43] It is also important to keep in mind that these laborers were in daily contact with Israeli society and culture, which was highly invested in a hyperactive nationalist ideology, and they began using national discourse to challenge the traditional village leadership.[44] In short, although the land confiscations and incorporation of Palestinian laborers into Israel's workforce were used by the occupying power to manage the population, they simultaneously created favorable conditions for the emergence of a national consciousness and thus helped unify the disparate elements of Palestinian society while weakening the traditional leadership.

THE 1976 MUNICIPAL ELECTIONS

Israel hoped to use the 1976 elections as a means of undermining the PLO, which had gained considerable ground in the OT during the four-year interval. Although the Israeli intelligence services were aware that new elections might lead to undesirable results, Defense Minister Shimon Peres decided to carry out the elections as planned. He met with notables and existing mayors in order to advance a "self-administration plan" that would expand the authority of the local town councils, bestowing upon them more responsibility for administering daily life in the West Bank.[45] Peres also realized that a decision *not* to conduct the elections as scheduled (according to Jordanian law elections were to be called every four years) would be seen as a deliberate act of intervention and would thus hamper Israel's efforts to normalize the occupation.[46] He hoped that the traditional elite would maintain its standing and could be used as a counter force to the PLO.[47] But while Israel attempted to use the 1976 elections in the OT to block the influence of PLO elements, the major factions within the PLO considered the elections to be an opportunity for assuming control of the municipal councils.

Before the elections, Israel amended the Jordanian law, extending the franchise to women and to every resident who paid municipal sewage taxes; the number of eligible voters thus almost tripled. Israel mistakenly thought that by extending the vote in this way it would weaken the PLO. It did not, however, lower the voting age from twenty-one to eighteen for fear that such a change would increase the number of young "extremist voters" and therefore "threaten the stability of the area."[48] The elections were held on April 12 in twenty-two out of twenty-five West Bank towns.[49] The venture proved counterproductive despite Israel's intervention in the elections.[50] Of the 205 newly elected council members, three-quarters were neophytes, many of them nationalists. The mayors of the northern and southern capitals of the West Bank—Ma'azouz Al-Masri from Nablus and Muhammad Al-Jabari from Hebron—were ousted along with the councilmen who supported them. A similar takeover occurred in towns like Al-Bireh, Birzeit, Beit Jalla, and Jericho. People who had cooperated with the Israeli authorities had been replaced by nationalists, some of whom had served time in Israeli prisons.[51]

According to Moshe Ma'oz, a professor of Middle East Studies at Hebrew University who later served as advisor to Defense Minister Ezer Weizman, "The elections results came as a shocking surprise and a bitter disappointment to the Israeli Military Government in the West Bank, as well as to the policy makers in the cabinet." They demonstrated that most of the West Bank's population "had developed strong nationalist feelings under Israeli rule; that they supported the PLO as their sole legitimate leader; that they rejected Jordan's policies regarding the West Bank . . . and that they opposed Israeli occupation and its 1975 self-administration plan."[52] Instead of helping to promote Peres's self-rule program, the elections bore witness to the population's profound solidarity with the PLO. Indeed, according to Ma'oz, the amount of *hamula* infighting among council members in the different municipalities dramatically decreased after the 1976 elections.[53] Just as importantly, the 1976 elections represented the beginning of the de-Jordanization process. Jordanian influence was in decline, and the Hashemite regime could no longer play a significant role in managing the occupied population.

THE MUNICIPALITIES AS A SITE OF RESISTANCE

It did not take long before an increase in Palestinian opposition to the occupation became noticeable.[54] Within weeks of the elections the Palestinians began staging a series of protests and demonstrations against land expropriation and the establishment of Jewish settlements. During a May 15 demonstration commemorating the Palestinian 1948 Nakbah (catastrophe), Lina Nabulsi, a teenage girl from Nablus was killed by Israeli soldiers, and a teenage boy, Mahmud al-Kurd, was killed in East Jerusalem. In response, the recently elected mayors led a series of protests and demonstrations and, in this way, established themselves as national leaders and representatives of the West Bank community. When asked by the military government to restore order and peace, they first demanded the withdrawal of Israeli troops from the towns, the abolition of the curfews, and the release of detained demonstrators. Their conditions were partly met, which only served to reinforce their status in society.[55]

The new mayors also began working together. They met regularly and coordinated their political positions and goals, using the PNF as their institutional base.[56] They created welfare institutions and special committees to address the harsh conditions in which political prisoners were held. They strategized about how to confront the establishment of new Jewish settlements and how to address the closure of schools and universities. By the late 1970s one notices the intensification of Palestinian opposition, precipitated in part by the Likud victory in Israel and the Israeli-Egyptian peace agreement, which proposed the creation of a Palestinian autonomy rather than the establishment of an independent state.[57] The National Guidance Committee was established in 1978 to confront these developments by facilitating the emergence of a more cohesive national political community. Even Rashad Shawa, who had been reappointed as Gaza's mayor a few years earlier, joined the committee, shifting his political alliances to the PLO. After adopting the Fatah party line, he rejected President Anwar Sadat's "Gaza First" initiative as well as Prime Minister Menachem Begin's autonomy plan.[58]

Hence a site that had been used to manage the population and to normalize the occupation was transformed into a major site of resistance. In order to deal with the increasingly unyielding civilian population in the OT, Israel decided to break the Palestinian leadership. In October 1979 it outlawed the PNF, while in November it briefly imprisoned mayor Bassam Shak'a of Nablus. Six months later, on May 2, 1980, Israel deported the mayors of Hebron and Halhul and the Qadi of Hebron. In June of that year a settler terrorist group planted bombs in the cars of several West Bank mayors, and the mayors of Nablus and Ramallah were critically maimed. At around the same time, the military government prohibited the distribution of the East Jerusalem newspapers *Al-Fajr* and *Al-Shaab* in the West Bank because of their nationalist overtones.[59] Despite these and other efforts, Palestinian opposition to Israeli rule did not stop. Moshe Dayan himself, the architect of Israel's "non-intervention policies," acknowledged that "now more than ever before, there is a general and mass opposition to Israel, to the presence of Israel, and to its policy" in the OT.[60]

In 1981, Israel decided to transform the governing body in the OT, replacing the military government with the Civil Administration. Commentators tend to link this move to two developments. On the one hand, the creation of the Civil Administration has been understood as a unilateral attempt to implement Prime Minister Menachem Begin's autonomy plan.[61] Begin, the leader of the right-wing Likud party, had adopted a plan that in many respects resembled Dayan's functional compromise.[62] Like his predecessors, Begin distinguished between the Palestinians and their land, offering the inhabitants a limited form of self-rule within the OT. The Civil Administration was to begin executing the autonomy plan, transforming what had been regarded as a temporary occupation into a permanent one. On the other hand, the establishment of the Civil Administration has also been considered a manifestation of Ariel Sharon's "iron fist" policy. Sharon had been appointed defense minister a mere three months before the Civil Administration was created, and he intended to use the new governing body to tighten the belt of control in the OT. Ironically, the new scheme was presented as a separation of the civil from the military administration.

These two explanations are not mutually exclusive and certainly appear to be accurate. However, they completely ignore the effects of Israel's controlling apparatuses. Even though Begin and Sharon seem to have been the originators of the new governing body, using it in order to advance certain policies, their decisions can actually be conceived of as effects of the contradictions and excesses discussed in the previous chapter as well as the next one. These contradictions helped trigger oppositional forces within the West Bank and Gaza Strip that the existing controlling practices could not contain, and the Civil Administration was an Israeli attempt to alter some of the methods of control in order to make them more effective.

One of the modifications that preceded the establishment of the Civil Administration was a change in the chain of command. The coordinator of government activities in the territories—the person in charge of civil affairs in the West Bank and Gaza Strip—was instructed to report to the chief of staff instead of reporting directly to the minister of defense as he had done in the past.[63] In this way all powers were consolidated within the military. A few months later, military order 947 was issued, legally constituting the Civil Administration.[64] Unlike most of the orders preceding this one, MO

947 did not merely affect a specific area of life in the OT or alter a specific law; rather, it created a new governing body, which was — ostensibly — supposed to transfer more power to the local inhabitants. It would, after all, seem logical that with the creation of the *Civil* Administration, civil affairs would be separated from the military. Yet, this was not the case.

All of the civil branches were, from this point on, managed by the Civil Administration and did not have to report to the military commanders, and the heads of the Civil Administration were given the authority to appoint staff officers and Palestinian workers in each region. In reality, however, the Civil Administration was subordinate to the Israeli military and GSS. This was true not only regarding appointments, but also in all matters relating to licenses and permits; the Civil Administration could either grant or withhold a license, but the GSS made the decisions behind the scene or at the very least had the authority to trump all decisions made by the administration's staff. Legislative powers to set policies continued to be held by the military, while the Civil Administration became a front for dispensing patronage selectively among the occupied population.[65] So although the creation of the Civil Administration was presented as the withdrawal of the military government and the establishment of an autonomous body responsible for the civil affairs among the occupied population, it was actually used to further integrate the military government within Palestinian society and to transfer all powers to the military. The new governing body was designed, in other words, to create the impression that Israel was terminating the occupation — without actually granting the Palestinian inhabitants meaningful political authority and without hindering the ongoing confiscation of land or the establishment of new Jewish settlements.[66]

EMPHASIZING SOVEREIGN POWER

Menahem Milson, as mentioned, was appointed to be the first head of the Civil Administration in the West Bank precisely because he supported a more interventionist approach. This amounted to an emphasis on sovereign power so as to advance a two-pronged strategy. Sanctions were imposed on mayors and their municipalities in order to weaken the nationalist movement, and the Village Leagues were created to counter the urban leadership that was promoting a nationalist agenda.[67] Hence, the Civil Administration, which was ostensibly established to promote self-rule, was deployed as an instrument to curtail the limited authority that was still vested in the municipalities, village councils, and chambers of commerce. Simultaneously, Israel also banned the transfer of funds from Arab states, which had passed through a joint PLO-Jordanian committee in Amman, thus dramatically cutting the financial resources available to the leaders and undermining the Jordanian influence that had been a crucial component of Israel's strategy of control until this point.[68] Israel, in other words, focused during this period on undermining the leadership rather than on changing the attitude of the population at large, substituting, in a sense, the symptoms for the cause.

Some of the nationalist mayors decided not to cooperate with the new governing body. On March 12, 1982, the mayor of Al-Bireh, Ibrahim Tawil, was dismissed and his council was dissolved for refusing to meet with Milson. An Israeli military officer was immediately appointed to head the Al-Bireh municipality. A week later, following widespread protests in other West Bank towns, the mayors of Nablus and Ramallah, Bassam Shak'a and Karim Khalaf, were also discharged and replaced by military officers.[69] Ultimately, the Civil Administration dismissed nine West Bank mayors as well as Gaza's mayor Rashad Shawa.[70] That spring, the National Guidance Committee, which aimed to consolidate PLO loyalists in the West Bank and Gaza and had become the leading organ of the Palestinian national leadership after Israel had banned the PNF, was also outlawed.[71] These moves suggest that as long as Palestinian leaders and institutions served as vehicles of articulation for Israel's policies, then Israel vested powers in them. Once they attempted to advance a national agenda, the leaders were dismissed and the institutions shut down.

The dismissal of the mayors marks the end of a six-year period during which Israel turned a blind eye to individuals and organizations that tried, despite ongoing Israeli suppression, to advocate a nationalist cause, albeit in a low-key manner. By mid-1982, most of the major towns in the OT were run by Israeli military officers, while all nationalist efforts to organize opposition had to go underground and operate solely through front groups like educational associations, medical institutions, and charities. Strict censorship was imposed on newspapers published in East Jerusalem (which operate under Israeli law and therefore are not subjected to the military commander), and their distribution to the West Bank and Gaza was prohibited. The military authorities imposed harsh restrictions of movement on the Palestinian leadership, and military decrees were used to dismiss the Palestinian leaders, disband the nationalist institutions, and obstruct the dissemination of information; when the Palestinian inhabitants protested, troops were brought in to clamp down on the demonstrators.[72] Thus, a sovereign mode of power was emphasized in an effort to contain the growing opposition.

Israel also began imposing curfews on the population living in the territories, and put several cities under a partial blockade. Central Region Commander General Ori Or acknowledged that "blocking towns with road blocks was a collective punishment, but riots were also a collective act and people who threw stones now realized that this caused them discomfort."[73] House demolitions were used more extensively than they had been for several years.[74] The intensification of such measures underscores the fact that Israel began emphasizing sovereign power, which, in turn, led to a quantitative change in the coercive forms of control deployed in the OT.

Confrontations between Israel and the occupied Palestinians reached a high point in the spring of 1982.[75] All protests were confronted with extensive force, and scores of schools were shut down for weeks on end, both in order to prevent social unrest and as a means of collective punishment.[76] During 1982 the Israeli military killed an estimated 31 Palestinians and wounded 365 more, most of them at protests, in what was subsequently called the "spring uprising."[77] Although during the first intifada there were periods in which more Palestinians were killed in a single day, such levels of violence had not been seen in the OT since the 1971 excursion into Gaza. Simultaneously, Israel was less prone to restrict punishment to those who carried out the transgressive acts, and began extending it to those around them, using collective punishment more pervasively. The military's response seemed, from Israel's point of view, to be effective because for a short while it managed to contain the population.

It is important to note, though, that the deployment of harsh coercive measures in 1981 and 1982 did not reflect a dramatic change in the means of control used to manage the population. The contradictions and excesses of the controlling apparatuses and practices had helped propel Palestinian resistance, which then spurred Israel to accentuate a sovereign mode of power, but the means of control it used—curfews, house demolitions, arrests, and torture—were similar to the ones it had used until then. Thus, the Civil Administration did not lead to the introduction of new forms of control; it only changed they way they were deployed. The major difference, then, between the first and second period is that during the latter period Israel accentuated sovereign power, which operated more intermittently and was often directed toward the leaders and the people whom Israel believed were the instigators of social unrest, as opposed to a power that is continuous and whose target is society at large.

THE VILLAGE LEAGUES

The only new apparatus of control that Israel introduced during the first twenty years of occupation was the Village Leagues. A few months after the 1976 West Bank municipal elections, the same Milson who later became the head of the West Bank's Civil Administration was appointed to be the advisor on Arab affairs for the military government. Milson believed that Palestinian society in the territories had for centuries functioned according to a traditional system of patronage, whereby local notables acted as intermediaries between their "protégés" and the central authority. He maintained that Israel had not exploited the patronage system to its advantage and had replaced it with "objective administrative rules."[78] Milson thus conveniently ignored the patronage relations that Israel had in fact fostered during the early years of the occupation and focused on the crisis engendered by the 1976 elections.[79] He advocated the creation of the Village Leagues, which were a direct extension of the peasant-based collaborative organization called the Farmers' Party, which the Jewish Agency had set up in the 1920s to counter the nationalist goals of Haj Amin Al-Husseini and his supporters.[80]

The idea was to exploit the urban elite's discrimination against villagers in the allocation of resources and services in order to emulate the pre-state experience. The logic was simple: although 70 percent of the West Bank inhabitants were villagers with special needs and desires, power was concentrated within the 30 percent of the population who were urban residents, whose representatives dominated the Palestinian political realm. Hence, it would be only rational to set the rural population against the urban nationalists by creating an organization that would represent the villagers and serve to counter the nationalist mayors and their followers.[81] In Salim Tamari's words, Milson wanted to "storm the radical towns with the reactionary peasants."[82] On the one hand, this strategy diverged from the efforts to render the involvement of the Israeli authorities in the everyday lives of the residents invisible. On the other hand, it was consistent with Israel's approach since the 1967 War to favor the traditional landed families over the urban traders. From the outset the military authorities banked on the former for support (through patronage, and by offering them truncated leadership roles), which helped push the nouveau rich into the nationalist camp; this helps account for the strong showing of the PLO in the municipal elections of 1976.[83]

The first Village Leagues had already been created in accordance with military order 752 in 1978, three years before the Civil Administration was set up. The military government chose Mustafa Dudin to lead the organization. Dudin had returned in 1975 to his home in Dura, a village in the Hebron District, after having held several posts in the Jordanian government. In the following four years, the organization was extended to five additional districts — Bethlehem, Ramallah, Jenin, Tul-Karem and Nablus — and while each district had its own leader, Dudin was considered the supreme leader. The Leagues received a budget of tens of millions of shekels each year from the Israeli government, not including fees the organization collected from the Palestinian inhabitants for services they offered.[84] For instance, the operation of bus companies in Bani Naim and Hebron was made subject to permission by the Hebron Village League, and villagers had to pay an annual operation tax of 2,500 Jordanian dinars directly to the League.[85]

With the establishment of the Civil Administration, the Leagues' powers were extended in an attempt to reinsert the patronage system that had existed before the rise of the nationalist mayors. They facilitated the process of obtaining traveling permits to Jordan and were given "right of recommendation" regarding family reunification requests (enabling family members from Jordan to return to the West Bank) and the release of political prisoners. They helped determine who would get appointed to an array of public posts, ensuring that people who supported the Leagues would be given a position. At a certain point the Civil Administration required the rural population to obtain the endorsement of the Village Leagues' functionaries before their requests would be considered.[86] The Leagues also served as a conduit through which Israel channeled money for development projects. The idea was to create the impression that the Leagues were the ones that funded the construction of schools and roads and the installation of electric generators. They sold fertilizers — which were given to them by the Israeli military — at a price that undercut market rates. At times League leaders even managed to cancel house demolition orders and provided building permits to local residents.

Simultaneously, the Civil Administration gradually halted development projects for villages that refused to seek aid through the Leagues (e.g., al-Daharia, Surif, Haris) and replaced some of the "noncooperative" village *mukhtars*. It also, as mentioned, banned the activity of the National Guidance Committee and closed universities — which were considered nationalist hotbeds — for extended periods.[87] Thus, many of the responsibilities pertaining to the administration of the population were delegated from the Civil Administration to the Leagues in an attempt to create a new patronage system.[88]

In the early 1980s Israel also provided guns to League members and employed them to help carry out arrests and interrogations. In the spring of 1982, while the military was clamping down on protesters, Israel began providing combat training to the members of the Leagues and helped to create small militias in each district. Thus, the Leagues were not only used to provide an alternative leadership meant to weaken the nationalists, but also as subcontractors of the Israeli military whose role was to police the population and forcefully suppress all forms of opposition. In March 1982, League members arrested a faculty member from Birzeit University; they patrolled the Ramallah region searching and arresting people; scores of villagers from Dir Amar near Hebron were taken from their homes at night and frightened by League militias; and Elias Freij, Bethlehem's mayor, was threatened because he expressed opposition to the Leagues.[89]

Israel initially thought that Jordan would support the Leagues because they were created to undermine the PLO. But since it had dissolved the last important governmental institution that had been supported by the Jordanian regime — the municipalities — and transferred its powers to the Civil Administration, Jordan was not keen to back the newly established leadership.[90] Thus, at around the same time that Israel dismissed the Palestinian mayors, the Hashemite regime publicly characterized the Leagues' members as collaborators and as people who were committing treason. This served as a blow to the Leagues, creating divisions within the puppet organization and spurring the resignation of some members while inhibiting the ability to recruit new ones. Consequently, the Leagues began to wane, and by 1984 Israel realized that this controlling apparatus was failing to produce results and changed its approach toward its constituents, arresting a few prominent members and convicting them for murder and corruption. Israel, nonetheless, continued to provide protection to a small number of League leaders, like Mustafa Dudin and Jamil Al-'Amala, until the eruption of the first intifada.

CONCLUSION

If in the early 1970s Israel used the municipalities in the West Bank to manage the population, by the late 1970s these same municipalities became organs of Palestinian resistance. The change can be traced to the rise of nationalism within the territories and to the replacement of leaders who represented traditional hierarchies (and in this way, reinforced the fragmentation of Palestinian society) with leaders who promoted a national agenda and national unity. There were many factors that precipitated this change, yet my claim is that the excesses and contradictions that resulted from the interactions among the different forms of control were a central force. On the one hand, Israel deployed an array of controlling practices to repress Palestinian national identity, whether by censoring any mention of a Palestinian history in the educational system or by strengthening the traditional elites. On the other hand, other forms of control helped reinforce national identity, such as the incorporation of laborers into the Israeli workforce and the indiscriminate confiscation of land from both the rich and the poor. So although Israel was wary of Palestinian nationalism and tried to suppress it, the means of control ended up empowering it.

Even though the 1976 elections signify a watershed in the OT, it took about five years until Israel changed the governing body in the territories and another six months before it dismissed all of the nationalist mayors. While it is obvious that Israel established the Civil Administration for a number of reasons, by the time the new governing body was founded it had become apparent that in order to contain the oppositional social forces that had been awakened and were rapidly gaining ground, Israel had to change the way it managed the population. Instead of introducing new forms of control, it used the existing ones as vehicles for sovereign rather than disciplinary or bio modes of power. Instead of targeting the population as a whole in an effort to alter the worldview and comportment of the inhabitants, it focused on changing the Palestinian leadership. One could say that Israeli decision makers strove to do away with the resistance movement's head, while failing to invest new energy in taming its recalcitrant body.

Thus, three central changes occurred during the late 1970s and early 1980s. First, Israel began modifying the emphasis on the modes of power, accentuating sovereign power in order to suppress Palestinian opposition. Second, Israel founded the Village Leagues, a proxy of sorts, which were supposed to replace the nationalist leadership. The underlying assumptions that informed the Leagues' creation were simplistic and did not take into account the changes that Palestinian society had undergone following Israel's occupation, particularly the emergence of a new social stratum due to the incorporation of laborers into the Israeli workforce. Finally, Israel established a new governing body in the West Bank and Gaza Strip, banning all political associations and dismissing most of the mayors. Its objective was not only to obstruct the increasing popularity of the PLO by clamping down on its representatives and institutions within the OT, but to prevent the development of institutions that could serve as a basis for an independent Palestinian state. While Israel succeeded in hindering the development of such institutions and in removing many of the Palestinian leaders who advocated a nationalist agenda, the emphasis on sovereign power did not manage to suppress the nationalist spirit that was mounting among the occupied population. And this spirit would continue haunting the occupying power for years to come.

> I told [them]: don't build fences around your settlements.
> If you put up a fence, you put a limit to your expansion. . . .
> We should place the fences around the Palestinians and
> not around our places.
>
> ARIEL SHARON

On June 27, 1967, the day East Jerusalem was annexed, a group of Israeli archaeologists were appointed as the supervisors of the archaeological and historical sites in the West Bank. In a press release issued by the military, these sites were defined as Israel's "national and cultural property."[1] This act, which may appear relatively benign, reveals nonetheless that the ideology of a Greater Israel—namely, that the West Bank and Gaza Strip are part of the biblical land of Israel and should therefore be integrated into the state—informed Israel's policies immediately following the war.[2] Alongside this messianic ideology, a militaristic ideology that considers the West Bank to be a defensive corridor against invasion from the east also gained ground after the fighting had subsided. The spatial significance of the region was emphasized by the proponents of both these ideologies, while the connection between the indigenous inhabitants and their land was conveniently ignored.

By September 1967, Jews had already begun settling in the West Bank, receiving support from the Israeli government as well as the military. Initially only one Jewish settlement was established, but soon a number of military outposts housing civilians were erected, and eventually large swathes of land were confiscated on which new villages, towns, roads, and electricity grids were built, while more and more Jews relocated from Israel to the OT. The developments on the ground stood in stark contrast to

Israel's declarations that in exchange for peace it would withdraw from the land it had captured.

Taking into account the dissonance between the peace discourse and the massive settlement enterprise, whose ultimate objective has been to block the possibility of creating a Palestinian state in the territories Israel occupied in 1967, it is not surprising that Israel's explicit policies vis-à-vis the territories remained vague for many years. Not one Israeli government ever formally adopted the numerous proposed plans to annex the West Bank and Gaza Strip or parts of these regions, including the Allon Plan, the Ra'anan Weitz Plan, the Dayan Plan, the Sharon-Wachman Plan, or the Drobles Plan.[3] Indeed, as one commentator has pointed out, the governments deliberately fostered an "anti-planning" ethos.[4] This vagueness concerning Israel's territorial objectives was both instrumentally convenient and genuine, and can be seen as serving the temporary and arbitrary modalities of control.

Instrumentally, the ambiguity was advantageous because a substantial proportion of the Israeli public and the international community considered the settlement project undesirable, not least because it contravened international law and obstructed the possibility of reaching a peaceful solution in the region.[5] A declaration that Israel intended to annex the two regions or even the issuing of a clear plan regarding how it intended to settle them with Jews would no doubt have triggered international condemnation as well as massive Palestinian resistance, both of which would have undermined the normalization efforts. This was one of the reasons the Israeli government frequently depicted the Jewish settlers as defiant citizens, even as it transferred millions of dollars to support their "recalcitrant" behavior. The appearance of being unable to control the settlers allowed the state—when criticized—to absolve itself of responsibility by attributing the confiscations to illegal initiatives carried out by ideological citizen groups.[6]

Finally, a publicly authorized plan would have undercut the occupation's ostensible temporariness and exposed Israel's territorial aspirations as being permanent. An approved plan would have rendered it easier to resist the settlement project, because the arbitrary process by which settlements were established—namely, the establishment of one settlement here and another there according to political circumstance and opportunity—as well as the lack of information about the construction of settlements created a structural difficulty that served to hinder the mobilization of a forceful opposition. It is, after all, much easier to resist an official plan. Thus, it was politically beneficial to portray the occupation as temporary and the establishment of settlements as arbitrary.

But there was also something authentic about this vagueness. Even though the ideology of a Greater Israel and the notion of the West Bank as a security corridor circulated in the Israeli public arena before the war, it took some time for these ideologies to become dominant within formal political institutions (at least until the second Likud government in 1981). The actual practices on the ground — that is, the legal and bureaucratic mechanisms, the seizure of Palestinian land, the construction of military bases, settlements, and bypass roads, and the transfer of thousands of Jewish citizens to the OT — were all crucial for consolidating and normalizing these ideas. These practices, whose primary goals were, initially, to seize land and later to manage the occupied population, actually helped shape Israel's policy decisions. What may, in other words, have been vague and contested immediately after the war became common sense in later years precisely because of the effects of numerous mechanisms of dispossession that were put into place right after the territories were captured. The daily practices of seizing Palestinian land and property and obstructing Palestinian development created, in other words, a certain dynamic that helped shape Israel's policy choices over the years.

Simultaneously, the same practices that strengthened Israel's hold on the land engendered several excesses and contradictions, which hindered its attempts to normalize the occupation and helped modify policy decisions. What interests us here, however, is that the mechanisms which Israel used in order to appropriate Palestinian land also served as forms of social control. The creation of suburban homes, industrial zones, infrastructure, and roads was designed to bisect Palestinian communities, restrict their development and movement into and out of them, and keep them under constant surveillance, while the settler population was utilized to police the local population "just like plain clothes security personnel."[7]

As means of social control, the Jewish settlements have operated in three major ways: (1) they have restricted Palestinian movement and development; (2) they have been used as tools for surveillance; and (3) they have served as an ethnic policing mechanism. Thus, in this chapter I draw the connection between the seizure of Palestinian land and Israel's attempt to manage the occupied population, showing how the mechanisms that were used to dispossess the Palestinians were also employed to police them. But first I describe the bureaucratic-legal mechanisms used both to appropriate Palestinian land and to hold on to it once it had been confiscated.

APPROPRIATING LAND

In the introduction I compared the confiscation of parts of the West Bank and Gaza Strip with the annexation of East Jerusalem, claiming that the latter was annexed and the former remained occupied territory. The distinction between Jerusalem and these regions is, however, more complicated. The difference is that Israel used its own legal system to annex East Jerusalem, taking over the territory in one fell swoop while offering citizenship or residency to its Palestinian inhabitants. In the West Bank and Gaza Strip, by contrast, it carried out a piecemeal confiscation by employing Ottoman and British Mandatory law, regulations from the Jordanian and Egyptian legal systems, and military orders issued by Israeli commanders. For many years Israel desisted from applying its own laws in the OT—as it had done in East Jerusalem—because it did not want to incorporate the Palestinian inhabitants into the Israeli demos. In other words, the objective of the legal mechanisms employed in the OT has been to confiscate as much land as possible without integrating the population. The outcome has been that many Palestinians have been cut off from their land.

The mechanisms of dispossession were modified over the years, but they were always characterized by a dual movement: bureaucratic-legal mechanisms were used to seize land legally by converting it into state property, and then settlements and bypass roads were built on the land in order to translate the de jure confiscation into a de facto annexation. Often, this process operated in the opposite direction, whereby the de facto confiscation preceded the de jure appropriation, applying, as it were, a pre-state Zionist ploy called "wall and tower" (Homa ve-Migdal). In the 1930s, the Zionist leadership in Palestine took advantage of an Ottoman law that forbid the demolition of a house whose roof had been built, and used this law in order to grab and hold on to land that it considered important. Relatively small groups of Jewish settlers were sent to strategic sites, and within a period of twenty-four hours they would build a settlement comprised of a small number of shacks and a watch tower, all of which were surrounded by a wall—thus the name "wall and tower."[8] The rationale informing this pre-state campaign was plainly articulated in a well-known Zionist slogan: "Where the ploughshare stops, the border starts."[9]

The difference between the pre-state campaign and the one in the OT was that Israel, rather than the British, controlled the region and could shape the legal system according to its interests. Legally, however, the situation in the Gaza Strip was somewhat different from the one in the West Bank. In Gaza, large portions of the land had already been appropriated by the state during Egypt's rule, and Israel did not therefore need to create legal mechanisms to convert private land into state land. While some of this land was set aside for refugee housing projects during both Egyptian and Israeli rule, following the war most of the state lands were used for the construction of Jewish settlements. In the West Bank, by contrast, Israel had to introduce a series of bureaucratic-legal mechanisms in order to convert private land into state property.[9]

By and large, Israel has used seven complementary methods to seize land—(1) declaring land to be absentee property; (2) declaring land to be the property of a hostile state or agent; (3) confiscating land for public needs; (4) declaring land to be part of nature reserves; (5) requisitioning land for military needs; (6) declaring land to be state property; (7) helping Jewish citizens to purchase land on the free market—each method resting on a specific aspect of the legal system.[10] Some of these mechanisms were modified or replaced over time in order to address the changing legal circumstances. From 1967 to 1980 Israel employed the first five methods, and between 1981 and 1987 the first two were replaced by the sixth method, namely, declaring that the land was state property, and the seventh was added. In 1988, Israel began imposing its own civilian laws on land in the OT, but not on the Palestinian residents.

In addition to the bureaucratic-legal mechanisms, six other methods were used both in the West Bank and Gaza Strip to guarantee the de facto confiscation: (1) the construction of military bases; (2) the establishment of Jewish settlements; (3) the establishment of Jewish outposts; (4) the construction of bypass roads; (5) the transfer of Jewish citizenry across the Green Line into the OT; (6) the construction of the separation barrier (only in the West Bank). Except for the separation barrier, whose construction began in 2002 and is continuing deep inside Palestinian territory, all the other methods were adopted immediately after the war.

Even though international humanitarian law obliges the occupying power to protect the occupied inhabitants' property, prohibiting its expropriation, Israel employed several legal mechanisms to seize large parts of the West Bank and Gaza Strip.[11] Most of the land Israel sequestered during the first period was appropriated by declaring it either absentee property or property belonging to a hostile state or agent. Military Order 58, which had already been issued on July 23, 1967, defines "absentee property" as "property whose legal owner, or whoever is granted the power to control it by law, left the area prior to 7 June 1967 or subsequently." The military commander also appointed a custodian who was responsible for overseeing the absentee property, bestowing on him the authority to negotiate contracts, manage, maintain or develop the property, or "dispose of it in whichever way he deem[ed] necessary." A report by Israel's state comptroller shows that during the first few years of the occupation, the Israeli authorities registered approximately four hundred and thirty thousand dunams, or 7.5 percent of the West Bank, as absentee property.[12] While this property is not, legally speaking, annexed to Israel, it is under the authority of the custodian and can no longer be used by Palestinians.

Military Order 59, issued on July 31, 1967, declares that any land or property belonging to a hostile state or to any arbitration body connected with a hostile state becomes state property. On October 23, another military order was issued drawing a connection between property owned by a hostile state and absentee property, so that property belonging to a resident of a hostile state, or to a corporation controlled by people residing in a hostile state automatically becomes absentee property. By 1979, 687,000 dunams—constituting some 13 percent of the West Bank—were confiscated using this military order. The Labor-led governments used some of this land to establish fifteen settlements in the Jordan Valley.[13]

A third method of confiscation was the expropriation of land for public needs. As Eyal Weizman cogently observes, the "use of the term 'public' revealed more than anything else the government's political bias: the public on which expropriations were imposed always comprised Palestinians; the public that enjoyed the fruits of the expropriation was always exclusively composed of Jews."[14] This method was applied in the West Bank alone and used the provisions of a Jordanian law. While the precise amount of land seized by applying this law is difficult to estimate, Israel has used it extensively to seize land for the purpose of constructing the extensive network of bypass roads serving the settlements. These expropriations were upheld by Israel's High Court of Justice, which accepted the state's argument that the roads also met the transportation needs of the Palestinian population, an argument that has proven to be completely spurious.[15]

Military Order 363 (December 1969) imposes severe restrictions on the use of land for agriculture and grazing in areas defined as nature reserves. Even though the declaration of land as a nature reserve was ostensibly designed to protect the environment, it was considered by the authorities to be an integral part of the land-seizure program. While it is unclear how many dunams were confiscated using this method during the first period, by 1985, two hundred and fifty thousand dunams, or 5 percent of the land, had been declared part of nature reserves.[16]

Finally, the fifth method used during the first period was the confiscation of land for military needs. The Hague Regulations allow an occupying power to take *temporary* possession of privately owned land and buildings belonging to the residents of the occupied area in order to house its military forces and administrative units. B'Tselem points out that on the basis of this exception almost forty-seven thousand dunams were confiscated in the West Bank between 1968 and 1979. While the state argued that this land was "required for essential and urgent military needs," several Jewish settlements established during this period were built on land that was expropriated in this manner.[17] When these confiscations were appealed, the state's response was that the settlements were planned for military reasons, and, accordingly, the requisition orders were lawful. The High Court accepted the state's response.[18]

De Facto Confiscation

The Israeli government knew that the frontier—as Golda Meir once put it—is where Jews live and not where a line is drawn on a map.[19] So immediately following the war it began moving military bases into the West Bank and Gaza Strip. While some of these bases were used for training, others were NAHAL outposts. NAHAL is the Hebrew acronym for Noar Halutzi Lohem (Fighting Pioneer Youth) and refers to military brigades that combine active military service with civilian service. Well before the occupation began, the NAHAL introduced a practice whereby it erected military outposts on Israel's frontiers and gradually converted these outposts into civlian agricultural communities. Following the 1967 War, most

NAHAL outposts were built in the territories that had been occupied—the West Bank, Gaza Strip, Golan Heights, and Sinai Peninsula—and in due course many of these were converted into civilian settlements.[20] Three military outposts of this kind were already established in the Jordan Valley in 1968—Argaman, Kalya, and Mehola—and later these outposts, just like several others, became civilian communities. It is important to note that the majority of the soldiers making up the NAHAL brigade were from *kibbutzim* and *moshavim* (communal farms) within Israel and were affiliated with the left-wing youth movements. It is precisely these young secular men and women, most of whom were aligned with the Labor party or parties to the left of labor—and not right-wing Jews who believed in a messianic ideology—who established the majority of settlements during the first period.

Simultaneously, the Labor government allowed religious Jews, whose desires and interests were shaped by the messianic ideology of a Greater Israel, to establish a few settlements. On September 24, 1967, just three months after the occupation began, it approved the establishment of Kfar Etzion, located south of Jerusalem on the road to Hebron.[21] A few months later, a group of religious Jews occupied a building in Hebron's Park Hotel in an attempt to establish a settlement in the midst of the Palestinian city. Although after several weeks the government removed them from the hotel, the settlers were given weapons and allowed to reside in a military compound just outside the city, where they stayed until 1970 when a governmental committee decided to allow them to build the settlement Kiryat Arba on Hebron's outskirts, which is right in the center of the southern part of the West Bank.[22] On August 30, 1973, the *Jerusalem Post* reported that the Housing Ministry would make land available, without restrictions, to public housing companies and private contractors willing to build in Kiryat Arba under a government-assisted housing program, emphasizing that the ministry would set up a loan fund for settlers wishing to build their own houses. The *Post* added that a commercial site that would serve a thousand families was being planned.[23]

Two points need to be emphasized here. First, even though the government presented the religious settlers as contrarians, in practically every single case the two opposing camps ended up cooperating, with the government actually providing assistance to the settlers. Second, from the very beginning settlements were established not only according to military-strategic logic, but also according to a national-religious one. By the mid-1970s a suburban logic was also deployed, and, as I explain below, it was precisely this logic that attracted the masses to move from Israel to the OT.[24]

Many of the religious Israelis who established the early settlements considered Israel's victory in the 1967 War as the "beginning of redemption" and as an opportunity to realize the vision of a Greater Israel. A group of them founded the messianic movement Gush Emunim (Bloc of the Faithful) in 1974. The movement's immediate goal was to force the government to establish as many settlements as possible throughout the West Bank and Gaza Strip.[25] The Sabastia affair, which took place between July 1974 and December 1975, was the movement's first major initiative. Members of Gush Emunim made seven attempts to establish a settlement — without legal authorization — eight miles northwest of Nablus and near the archeological site of Sabastia. The eighth attempt led to a compromise between the activists and Defense Minister Shimon Peres. The settlers were allowed to stay at a military base called Qadum to the west of Nablus, and two years later the base was officially transformed into the settlement of Qedumim. Even though Sabastia is usually portrayed as a watershed — that is, a confrontation between the settlers-to-be and the Israeli government — it was, in many respects, a repeat performance.[26] The members of Gush Emunim were simply following a pattern that had been established in Kfar Etzion and the Park Hotel in Hebron.

The main problem with the narrative, which describes the fledgling settlers' movement as establishing settlements against all odds, is that if the government had really wanted to, it could have prevented the settlers from reaching Sabastia or from establishing Kfar Etzion, and it could have done this without investing much energy and without losing an enormous amount of political credit. In *Lords of the Land,* Idith Zartal and Akiva Eldar show that Labor leaders like Shimon Peres, Yitzhak Rabin, Yigal Allon, and Moshe Dayan were for the most part in favor of the settlement project. Thus, the notion that the Labor government and the settlers belonged to opposing ideological camps is true only if one is interested in tactical differences. The fact is that members of both camps shared principal components of the messianic and militaristic ideologies, and the distance between the different views was not all that great. Sabastia, for instance, was considered by both the government and settlers as "national and cultural property," yet each camp, for its own reasons, wanted to present the interaction as a confrontation between forces holding diametrically opposing views.

All in all, twenty-seven settlements were founded during the occupation's first decade and about fifteen more were underway when the Labor party lost the elections to the Likud in May 1977.[27] I emphasize this number for three reasons. First, it is often assumed that the right-wing Likud government began the settlement project in order to preclude the possibility of withdrawing from the OT. Actually, though, one-fourth of the settlements that currently exist were established within the first decade of the occupation; and if one counts those that were being planned, almost one-third of the settlements existing today were initiated by Labor before it lost the 1977 elections. Second, most of the narratives tend to present the settlement project as an extra-governmental enterprise carried out by the settler movement in direct opposition to government policy. In reality, the different Israeli governments established the vast majority of settlements, and, even those that were ostensibly erected against the government's will by religious Jewish circles ultimately received both a green light from the government and its financial support. Finally, just over half of the settlements built by the Labor government were located in the West Bank's Jordan Valley; the government also established two settlements in Gaza, two in Samaria, one just east of Jerusalem, and six others south of the city in the Gush Etzion and Hebron areas (see map 2 and appendix 2). It does not seem likely that a government intending to withdraw from the territories it had captured would invest such vast resources to build so many civilian settlements and transfer its citizenry to these settlements. Shlomo Gazit, the first coordinator for government activities in the occupied territories, corroborates this claim:

> From the first days of Israeli rule in the West Bank and the Gaza Strip, it was clear the Israeli settlements in the Territories in general, and especially in the densely populated areas, had far-reaching political implications. These settlements were designed to establish a new reality that would influence the future political solution. . . . It was clear that building civilian Israeli settlements was a political statement comparable to the Knesset decision in June 1967 to annex East Jerusalem: the settlements were built in places from which Israel had no intention of withdrawing.[28]

So, although they were presented by politicians and military personnel alike as a means of satisfying security needs during the first decade following

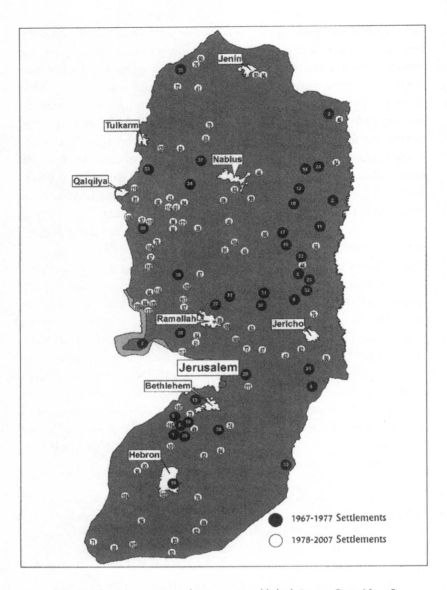

Map 2. West Bank settlements according to year established. Source: Peace Now. See appendix 2 for settlement names and dates of establishment.

the war, the settlements actually served as a de facto element in the confiscation process and can be perceived as a direct continuation of the pre-state
"wall and tower" strategy. But in contrast to the pre-state strategy, whereby
the Jewish settlers carried out clandestine operations in opposition to the
policies of the British authorities, the first settlements in the OT received
authorization from the government and military officials, even though a
clear policy regarding these authorizations did not always exist. Therefore
it is not surprising that by the end of the first period (1980), Israel had seized
more than 20 percent of the West Bank and close to 40 percent of the Gaza
Strip and had built fifty-seven settlements, which comprise half of the
recognized settlements today (see map 2 and appendix 2).[29]

Appropriating Water

During the occupation's first two decades Israel also appropriated the OT's
water resources. Eighty percent of the mountain aquifers, the regions'
largest reservoirs, are located under the West Bank, with the remaining
20 percent under Israel. Realizing the significance of this vital resource,
which currently supplies 40 percent of Israel's agricultural needs and almost
50 percent of its drinking water, Israel began modifying the legal and institutional status of the water rights in the occupied regions after the war.[30] The
changes were made in two main stages, corresponding to the occupation's
first two periods. In August 1967 Israel transferred all decision-making
powers regarding water in the West Bank to the military authorities and
made a similar move in the Gaza Strip in December 1974.[31] The major effect
of this transfer of powers was a severe restriction on drilling new wells to
meet the Palestinian inhabitant's needs, along with the appropriation of
water to meet the needs of Israel's citizenry.[32] During the second stage, many
of the powers held by the occupation authorities, among them the control of
water supply to the urban centers, were transferred to Israel's water commis-
sioner and the Ministry of Agriculture. As a result the West Bank and Gaza
Strip's water resources were integrated with Israel's and were controlled by
a single, centralized system.[33]

The appropriation of Palestinian water is yet another example of Israeli
efforts to exploit the OT's resources and further illustrates how Israel erased
the Green Line every time it was in its interest to do so. But the appropriation of the water is also part of what Eyal Weizman has called Israel's politics
of verticality, namely, Israel's simultaneous attempt to control three spatial

levels—the ground, the air, and even the subterranean level—in order to manage the Palestinian population.[34] Thus, as we will see, the appropriation of water not only served Israeli economic and security needs, but was also used to administer the occupied inhabitants.

The Bureaucratic Legal Mechanisms, 1981–1987

In June 1979, several residents of Rujeib, a village southeast of Nablus, petitioned the High Court of Justice, asking it to nullify a military order that was about to confiscate some five thousand dunams of their land. The land affected by the seizure order was slated for the establishment of a settlement called Elon Moreh. The state's response, as had been customary until this point, was that the settlement was planned for military reasons, and accordingly the requisition orders were lawful. But, in contrast to previous cases, a number of former military generals joined the petitioners, while settlers who intended to live in Elon Moreh joined as respondents to the petition. As B'Tselem points out, what is so interesting and important about this particular case is that both the generals and the settlers challenged the "military needs" argument in their affidavits. The generals claimed that the settlement would not serve Israel's security and might become a liability, while the settlers stressed the "right" Jews had to settle in this land, regardless of so-called military needs. One settler argued that basing the requisition orders on security grounds in their narrow, technical sense rather than their comprehensive sense "can be construed only in one way: the settlement is temporary and replaceable. We reject this frightening conclusion outright. It is also inconsistent with the government's decision regarding our settling on this site." Since affidavits from both sides undermined the argument of military necessity, which had been used until then as the legal justification for expropriation of private lands, the High Court ordered the Israeli military to dismantle the settlement and return the seized land to its owners.

The immediate result of this ruling was the establishment of Elon Moreh on an alternative site. But since it became clear that building a settlement on land appropriated for ideological or other nonmilitary needs would no longer be upheld by the High Court, the government adopted a new method for seizing land.[35] Invoking two articles from the 1907 Hague Regulations—one that requires the occupying power to respect the laws that existed prior to the occupation (article 43) and another that permits an occupying power to manage the properties in the occupied territory and to derive profits from them (article 55) — Israel began applying an Ottoman Land Law from 1858 in order to convert private Palestinian land into state land. According to the Ottoman law, if a landowner fails to farm his or her land for three consecutive years for reasons other than those recognized by the law (e.g., the landowner is drafted into the military), the land is then known as *makhlul,* land which the sovereign may take possession of or transfer to another person. The Ottoman law also stipulates that land that is more than half an hour's walking distance from the person's settlement, or is located at a distance such that the loudest noise made by a person in the closest place of settlement cannot be heard, should remain empty and not be used by any person. Regarding this latter land, the sovereign is responsible for ensuring that no unlawful activities take place on it, and in fact controls it.[36] The acrobatics Israel was willing to perform after the Elon Moreh petition in order to "legally" seize land reveal just how important it was for the government to portray its actions not as the suspension of law but as acts that abide by and follow the rule of law.

Using aerial surveillance and satellite images, the Israeli authorities mapped all of the land that had not been farmed for at least three consecutive years, land that had been farmed for less than ten years (the period of limitation), and land that was, according to the law, too far from the nearest village. Within a number of years, 2.15 million dunams (39 percent) of West Bank land that could potentially be seized using this law were identified. This figure includes land that had already been confiscated using other legal-bureaucratic mechanisms, so that about 1.5 million dunams was actually "new land." By mid-1984, eight hundred thousand dunams of this "new land" (about 14 percent of the West Bank) were seized using the Ottoman law.[37] In sum, the two state branches (judicial and executive) worked side by side to rationalize and legitimize the confiscation of Palestinian land. As the judicial branch restricted the methods of confiscation, the executive branch modified and thus expanded them, receiving a green light from High Court to do so. The effect was the confiscation of much more land than otherwise would have been possible.

An analysis of the Ottoman law also reveals how Israel used the forms of governing it had developed during the first years of occupation in order to gain control of land during the second period. As mentioned in previous chapters, the integration of Palestinian laborers into the Israeli workforce as well as the harsh restrictions Israel imposed on water usage and the production of certain crops facilitated the use of this law. In 1987, eight years after Israel first began employing the Ottoman law to appropriate Palestinian land, 39.2 percent of the Palestinian workforce was employed in Israel, while only 13.8 percent worked in agriculture within the OT, a dramatic drop from the 34.2 percent who worked in agriculture in 1970.[38] These statistics help explain why, despite the more than 40 percent increase in the size of the population, the cultivated land in the West Bank decreased from an estimated 2,435 sq. km. to 1,735 sq. km. between the years 1965 and 1985. In other words, the decrease in cultivated land enabled the confiscation of more land.[39] Since a large percentage of the workforce was earning salaries in Israel, the expropriation of land did not immediately lead to an economic crisis and could initially be implemented with little resistance. This example serves to show how certain forms of control like the integration of laborers into the Israeli workforce and the regulation of water and crops served at a certain stage of the occupation to advance the confiscation of land.

The last method that was employed to seize Palestinian land was private acquisition. The Labor-led governments preferred to limit the confiscation of land to governmental bodies and pre-state Jewish institutions; already in June 1967 the state had issued a military order rendering it illegal to conduct business transactions involving land and property without a permit from the military authorities.[40] Accordingly, until the late 1970s the only nongovernmental body involved in the purchase of land from Palestinian residents was the Jewish Agency's settlement department.[41] This policy was reversed in the 1980s, and private acquisition of Palestinian land began to be encouraged. Jews now purchased land and settled throughout the West Bank, including areas that could not be declared state land.

To help Israeli entrepreneurs, several military orders were issued to amend the Jordanian land laws and facilitate the acquisition process. B'Tselem explains that because Palestinians considered the sale of land to Israeli Jews to be an act of treason, an order was issued to enable such land transactions while postponing registration for many years in order to circumvent the potential dangers created by exposing the identity of the Palestinian seller.[42] Although it is unclear how much land was purchased by Israeli entrepreneurs, this land was bought specifically for real estate projects (i.e., settlements) and was mostly near the Green Line. This is one of many examples of how Israel's civilian population was used to advance the expropriation project. By 1987 Palestinians were restricted to an area that comprised less than 60 percent of the area Israel had occupied in 1967.[43] In the Gaza Strip the land was divided between Jews and Palestinians in such a way that there were, conservatively speaking, 115 Jews per square mile as opposed to 7,905 Palestinians per square mile. Due to the expropriation of land, population density in Gaza was among the highest in the world, and ten times higher than in Israel.[44]

MORE SETTLEMENTS AND BYPASS ROADS

While the land was seized primarily through the employment of mechanisms informed by a sovereign power, the confiscated terrain was controlled through the construction of buildings and the transfer of a civilian population to inhabit it. During the second period, the expansion of the settlement project was much swifter. By 1987, Israel had established 110 settlements in the West Bank and an additional 15 in the Gaza Strip, comprising about 85 percent of all the settlements that existed in 2005, before the withdrawal from Gaza. The estimated amount of money invested in these settlements was more than $8 billion.[45] Thus, during the first twenty years of occupation, Israel had already built most of the settlements, seized over 40 percent of Palestinian land, and had managed to transfer about sixty thousand Jewish citizens to the OT.

The new settlements controlled most of the seashore in the Gaza Strip and were scattered throughout the West Bank, often located on hilltops overlooking a number of Palestinian villages. Few areas were left without some kind of Jewish presence. The settlements had a threefold objective. First, they were part and parcel of the mechanism of dispossession and helped transform the legal confiscation of land into a concrete reality. Second, as I describe below, the settlements and settlers within them served as a civilian apparatus to monitor and police the Palestinian population. Finally, the settlements in the West Bank were part of Israel's defense line against external enemies, deployed in order to help the military guard the border, secure roads, and ensure internal communications.[46]

The establishment of the settlements entailed the construction of access roads. If in the late 1960s and 1970s Israel justified the settlement project by claiming that it served the country's military needs, by the 1980s and 1990s it justified the construction of bypass roads by claiming that they secured the safety of the civilians who lived in the settlements. Moreover, according to the *Settlement Master Plan for 1983–1986* (which was never formally adopted by the government), it was assumed that the construction of roads would motivate Israeli citizens to move to the OT and would enhance the development of the settlement project.[47] Thus, these new roads were not part of an attempt to improve Palestinian infrastructure; they were built to serve and perpetuate the settlements by creating a grid that connected the OT to Israel. These objectives were clearly spelled out in a Ministry of Defense report, which noted that the system of bypass roads being built would meet four key needs: to permit Israelis to travel in the OT without passing through Palestinian population centers; to permit Israelis to travel across the Green Line by the shortest route; to maintain "an internal fabric of life" within the Israeli settlement blocs; and to ensure that Palestinian traffic did not pass through the settlements.[48] To achieve these objectives Israel built a vast network of bypass roads, extending over hundreds of kilometers and criss-crossing both the West Bank and Gaza Strip.[49]

The settlements and bypass roads not only served as physical apparatuses that operated in tandem with the legal-bureaucratic mechanisms in order to secure the confiscation of Palestinian land, but also functioned as part of the apparatuses that were deployed to manage the occupied population through restriction of movement and development, surveillance, and ethnic policing.

THE RESTRICTION OF MOVEMENT AND DEVELOPMENT

The settlement enterprise was used to inhibit Palestinian movement and development. In and of themselves the Jewish settlement's physical edifices only partially restrict the occupied inhabitants' movement and development, since the built-up areas of all of the settlements put together—and not only those that existed in the 1970s and 1980s—comprise less than 2 percent of the West Bank.[50] But the settlements' built-up area is not the only area Palestinians are not allowed to enter. There are the municipal boundaries that currently comprise 6.9 percent of the West Bank. And toward the end of the first period (1980), the military commanders used their authority to incorporate all of the lands that Israel had declared state lands within the regional—as opposed to municipal—boundaries of the settlements and to restrict Palestinian use of this land for agriculture, grazing, and construction. The regional boundaries comprise 35 percent of the West Bank, a figure that does not include the municipal boundaries, indicating that Palestinians were denied access to almost 42 percent of the West Bank.[51]

Map 3 shows that the territory incorporated into the West Bank's six Jewish regional councils and Jewish municipalities separates clusters of Palestinian villages and towns from their urban centers. The entire area incorporated into the regional councils was categorized as "closed for military reasons"; however, entry permission has been granted to Israeli citizens, Jews from anywhere in the world, and anyone who visits Israel as a tourist with a valid entry visa. Only local Palestinian residents require special authorization from the region's military commander to enter the closed areas—an authorization they receive only if they are hired by settlers as cheap laborers. In this way, Israel has succeeded in dramatically diminishing the areas accessible to Palestinian economic and agricultural development.[52]

Examining the map, one also begins to appreciate how even a small percentage of confiscated land can be used to slice the West Bank into several parts. The 0.25 percent of land included within the Ariel settlement's jurisdiction has enabled Israel to control a long corridor (the Trans-Samaria Highway) leading to the settlement. This corridor, as B'Tselem points out, severs the contiguity of the northern West Bank. Similarly, while the area of jurisdiction of Ma'ale Adummim occupies just 0.8 percent of the West Bank, it nonetheless succeeds in slicing the West Bank into two parts that are almost completely separated.[53] "Our control of a region is a function not only of the size of the population which resides within the region, but also of the size of the area in which this population exercises its influence," Gush Emunim explained in 1980.[54]

The aerial photos of the Jewish settlement Beitar Illit exemplify the territorial difference between the built-up area of the settlements and the municipal boundaries. The black lines mark the municipal borders, while the areas covered by a gray shade are Palestinian (the dotted line is the internationally recognized border known as the Green Line). The photo in figure 2 shows that there are two clusters of built-up areas, each one on a separate hill, with an additional cluster still without any houses on it. The lower cluster was built first, but, in order to gain control of the rest of the land allotted to the settlement, another neighborhood was built on the eastern side of the middle cluster and still another is in the process of being built on the

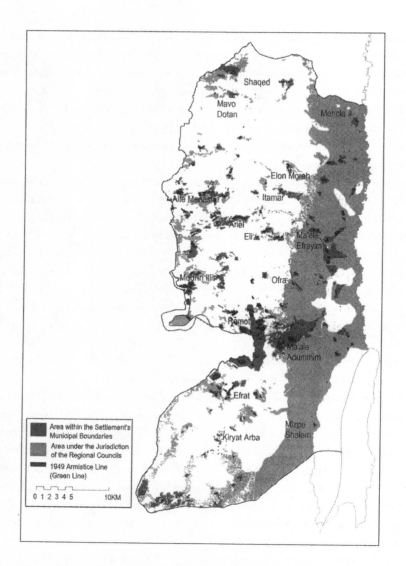

Map 3. Areas controlled by settlements. Source: Yehezkel Lein, *Land Grab: Israel's Settlement Policy in the West Bank* (Jerusalem: B'Tselem, 2002).

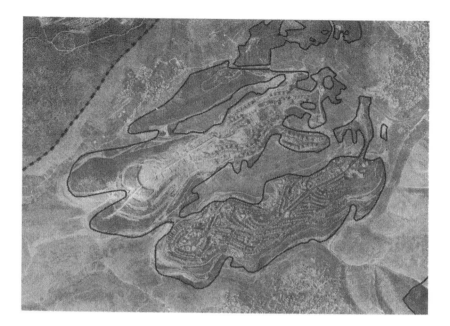

Figure 2. Aerial photo of Beitar Illit, showing municipal boundaries. Source: Peace Now.

western side of that cluster, thus revealing how the settlement's boundaries and planning are used to gain control of as much land as possible. Beitar Illit also overlooks the Palestinian villages Wadi Fuchin from the north, Husan on the east, and Nahalin on the south, demonstrating how Israel establishes settlements very close to Palestinian villages to restrict Palestinian development and to break their communities up into clusters. The lower part of figure 3 (which provides a closer view of Beitar Illit) illustrates how Jewish houses are being built outside the municipal boundaries. It also shows how plots of Palestinian land that the Israeli government could not "legally confiscate" are totally surrounded by the settlement, thus restricting Palestinian farmers' access to their land without actually confiscating it.

The settlements and their municipal and regional boundaries have not been the only mechanisms used for confiscating Palestinian land, surrounding villages and transforming the West Bank into a space made up of small enclaves — zoning restrictions were also put to use. Instead of allowing the Palestinians to extend the areas of their villages and urban centers so that the needs of the growing population could be addressed, the Civil

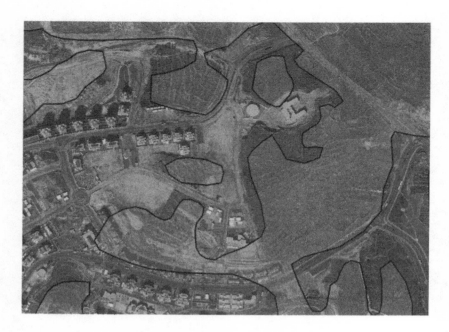

Figure 3. Aerial photo of Beitar Illit: a closer view, showing Jewish houses built outside the municipal boundaries. Source: Peace Now.

Administration adopted the completely outdated village and municipal plans prepared in the 1940s by the British Mandatory powers according to the size of the population at the time. All areas not included in the 1940 plans were designated as "agricultural areas" or "nature reserves" so that nothing could be built on them.[55] In the early 1990s, when the Civil Administration prepared Special Partial Outline Plans for some four hundred villages in the West Bank, aerial photographs were taken of each village, and a schematic line was then added on the photo around the settled area. Construction was prohibited on land outside this line and could legally take place only by the "infill" method, that is, the filling of vacant areas within the demarcated area through high-rise construction and an increase in the population density.[56]

Israel also used roads to circumscribe Palestinian space.[57] While in most places around the world roads are used to connect people, in the OT they have had two additional functions: to seize land and to serve as barriers that separate or circumscribe the Palestinian inhabitants and restrict their movement.[58] The first function enabled Israel to use roads as a way of limiting Palestinian development by confiscating agricultural land and limiting the construction of residences and businesses. The "security" highways are massive in scale, at times 50 meters wide with an additional 100–150 meters of margins on each side, totaling the "width of three to four football fields."[59]

To restrict Palestinian movement, Israel introduced a "forbidden road" regime that limited the inhabitants' access to major traffic arteries in the West Bank, not only to the bypass roads. B'Tselem has classified the roads subjected to this regime under three main categories based on the severity of the restrictions: complete prohibition, partial prohibition, and restricted use. The first category includes 120 kilometers of roads intended for the sole use of Israeli citizens. Some of these roads are labeled by the army as "sterile roads." The second category includes 245 kilometers of roads on which Palestinians may travel if they hold permits issued by the Civil Administration, or if their identity cards indicate that they live in a village that can only be accessed using the road. The third category includes 365 kilometers of roads on which Palestinian vehicles are allowed to travel without a special permit, but access to these roads is frequently blocked by military checkpoints and physical barriers. Thus, during the second intifada, limitations were placed on Palestinian use of approximately 730 kilometers of West Bank roads just by employing a permit regime.[60] The major difference between this road regime and the one institutionalized in South Africa during apartheid is that in the West Bank no legislation was introduced to support this practice, and no official government decision was taken to put such legislation into effect. Indeed, it was never put on paper. The whole regime is based on verbal orders given to security forces.[61]

On the one hand, the forbidden road regime has forced the Palestinian population to use alternate routes, some of which pass through densely populated urban areas, while others involve using unpaved dirt roads running along agricultural fields and mountain valleys. The distance one has to travel using these routes is much greater, as is the time it takes to go from one place to another. Being forced to travel on these alternate roads has affected all aspects of daily life in the West Bank, including the economy and the health and educational systems.[62] On the other hand, such roads are also used as boundaries, checking development and cutting off villages from urban centers, while undermining contiguity in the Palestinian areas of the OT. Taken together, the distribution of settlements, the areas of jurisdiction, the bypass roads, and the permit regime effectively fragment the terrain, thus hindering the establishment of an independent and viable Palestinian state.[63]

SURVEILLANCE

Planning in the OT was almost always subjected to military agendas and was, as Eyal Weizman maintains, the handmaiden of politics and control. The settlements are a case in point. Even though their built-up area comprises less than 2 percent of the land, they were usually built on hilltops and have thus provided three strategic assets: greater tactical strength, protection, and a wider view.[64] The distribution, layout, and architectural design of the settlements were determined by strategic military principles so that the "simple act of domesticity, a single family home shrouded in the cosmetic façade of red tiles and green lawns, conforms to the aims of territorial" and social control.[65]

The settlements' strategic function was integrated into their distribution and topographical location so that they created a "network of observation" that overlooks the main traffic arteries of the West Bank.[66] Weizman and Rafi Segal point out that the desire to maximize the visibility of the occupied space and the Palestinians inhabiting it dictated the mode of design of the settlements, down to the positioning of windows in houses. The two Israeli architects conclude that settlements become, in effect, "optical devices, designed to exercise control through supervision and surveillance."[67]

The settlements are, accordingly, disciplinary artifacts that aim to render the occupied inhabitants visible and docile. They are used to monitor the Palestinians who work in the fields below or travel on the adjacent roads and in this way function as panoptic towers that encourage the inhabitants to adopt certain norms and practices. Not a single settler needs to be in the settlement, since the mere *possibility* that a settler is standing within one of the overarching buildings and watching is often sufficient to ensure that certain restrictions and prohibitions are observed and specific modes of behavior and comportment are followed. The settlements substantiate Foucault's idea that a cleverly designed edifice has the capacity to control people. Ironically, though, the settlements are, in many ways, a more exact model of Foucault's notion of surveillance than the panoptic tower (the example he uses) because their gaze is not centralized; like Foucauldian power they are not located in one identifiable site but are scattered throughout the terrain, supervising the local inhabitants from numerous spots.

The settlers themselves also serve as part of the surveillance apparatus. They are a markedly different group of people than the occupied inhabitants. They dress differently, speak a different language, drive cars that are identifiably different, often carry weapons, and many of them have acquired the reputation of being violent and lawless. While they wear plain clothes, in the eyes of many Palestinians they are no different from the security personnel. Moreover, they are everywhere. In 1980 there were 13,500 settlers in the OT. By 1987 there were about 60,000, on the eve of the Oslo agreements about 100,000, and currently there are 267,000 residing in the West Bank (excluding East Jerusalem).

One should keep in mind that most of the settlers did not move to the OT for ideological reasons. They were simply looking for a suburban home at an affordable price, and the Israeli government handed out economic perks to anyone who was willing to relocate. In 1986, subsidies for housing in the West Bank were almost 50 percent higher than in depressed areas within Israel. All West Bank settlements were eligible for a 7 percent income tax reduction, and all settlement industrial parks were granted the A+ status for industrial development—the highest incentive, which includes a 40 percent grant for the purchase of equipment, low taxation, and subsidized infrastructure.[68] These as well as several other financial benefits offered by the government served as a push factor, to encourage citizens to move from Israel to the OT.

Settlers are constantly traveling both within the OT and to Israel, commuting to work, taking children to school, going shopping, and visiting friends. While these private trips are no doubt part of the settler's daily routine, simply by traveling within the OT the settlers fulfill several functions. They patrol the region, monitor vital strategic sites, and help the state guarantee its control of the occupied inhabitants. Whether a settler moved to the OT for ideological reasons and was interested in dispossessing the Palestinians or whether he or she was encouraged to leave Israel and to relocate to the West Bank and Gaza Strip in order to buy an affordable single-family home is beside the point; in both cases the settlers have been mobilized to serve the purpose of military domination.[69]

In addition to the predominantly noninteractive role of surveillance, the settlers have also been deployed as a coercive form of control that uses violence to police the Palestinian population. While Max Weber claimed that a central feature of the modern state is the successful expropriation of the means of violence from individuals, so that states have a monopoly on the legitimate use of violence, it is important to stress that frequently states license other actors to carry out violence in their stead. Ever since the occupation began, settlers in the West Bank and Gaza Strip have fulfilled this role for the Israeli government. It would, therefore, be a mistake to conceive the Jewish settlers as the originators of a power that seizes land, dispossesses Palestinians, and determines government policy, since the settlers themselves were more an effect of this power and its medium of articulation than its instigator. They are a product of material and ideological forces that informed the pre-state Zionist movement, and they have been utilized by the state as a crucial component of the dispossessing and policing apparatuses. This is not to say that the settlers are not responsible or lack agency. Even while they are an effect of certain forces, they play an instrumental role in consolidating the messianic and militaristic ideological strains in Israel and became a self-perpetuating tool that helps shape government decisions pertaining to the OT.

Major acts of settler violence have included the attempted assassination of three West Bank mayors in 1980; the raid on the Islamic College in Hebron in July 1983, in which three students were killed and many others wounded; and the 1994 massacre in the Cave of the Patriarchs, in which twenty-nine Palestinians were killed during Friday prayer.[70] But these are merely the more visible incidents that received widespread media attention. The accentuation of these acts and the de-emphasis of others have served to create the impression that settler violence is an exception to the rule, carried out by extremists or fanatics, when in fact it is the norm.

Not much was written about the night when residents of Kiryat Arba vandalized dozens of cars in the nearby Palestinian town of Halhul, or when more than a hundred car windows were shattered and some houses damaged in El Bireh. Very little was said about the day six armed settlers entered a Palestinian girls' school, shot in the air, and systematically smashed all the windowpanes and damaged the science laboratories, or about the two hundred settlers who entered the Dheisha refugee camp firing guns and throwing tear gas grenades.[71] Yet, it is precisely these kinds of settler attacks that interest me here, as they have been part of the daily routine in the OT since the 1970s.

The United Nations recorded 772 instances of settler violence in the West Bank during the year 2001 alone, an average of two assaults every day.[72] Such attacks are often carried out with weapons provided by the Israeli military. In 1987 it was estimated that the settler population, around sixty thousand at the time, possessed no fewer than ten thousand firearms of all types as well as other types of military equipment, such as wireless communication devices and armed vehicles.[73] In January 2007 the settlers numbered 267,000, and it is unclear how many weapons they possess.

From the very beginning, Jewish settlements in the OT were granted the status of border communities, authorizing them to receive military weapons for self defense. By law the settlers are compelled to guard their settlements and educational institutions. They are authorized to detain people who refuse to provide identification and to arrest those who try to hide and cannot reasonably explain their behavior.[74] Accordingly, each settlement has an ammunition depot and a state-paid security coordinator who is responsible for organizing the settlement's defense. Adult inhabitants are given semiautomatic rifles and handguns, and the coordinator schedules patrols on the settlement's borders. It is important to remember that all of this is official.

At a certain point, though, Moetzet Yesha (the Council of Jewish Settlements in Judea, Samaria, and Gaza) began to organize militias to guard the small settlements that did not have sufficient manpower. As James Ron points out, during the 1980s these militias extended their operations from the settlement perimeters to fields, access roads, and Palestinian villages. Using the weapons and ammunition given to them by the military, between 1980 and 1984 they attacked Palestinians 384 times, killing 23 and injuring 191.[75] Thus, the official role of securing the settlements was expanded by the settlers, who organized groups of men whose role was to police their Palestinian neighbors. Yesha spokesperson, Yehoshua Mor-Yosef, explained the long-standing rationale for creating these militias: "We act in coordination with the army, if something exceptional happens and the situation worsens, we are also ready to act on our own."[76] Translated into plain English, this means that when the

Israeli military's policing of Palestinians does not meet the standards set by the settlers, they do what they believe is necessary to control the Palestinians.[77]

In the mid-1980s, the militias were incorporated into the Israeli military as "territorial defense auxiliaries." They were given military-issue personnel carriers, weapons, and communications equipment, and were asked to patrol locally, which in practice often meant policing nearby Palestinian villages. At least one of these "auxiliaries" earned a reputation for brutality.[78] In other words, the official role of securing the settlement's borders was expanded by militias to include the policing of Palestinians living in the settlement's vicinity, and these militias were reincorporated into the state apparatus, where they continued their abuse, this time wearing military uniforms. This process underscores one aspect of the close relation between Israel's official law enforcement institutions and the settler population.[79]

In addition to the formal relationship between the settlers and the military, unofficial settler groups and individuals frequently police the Palestinian population. Settlers have set ambushes for Palestinians, hiding near the road and shooting or throwing stones at Palestinian vehicles that pass by. They have fired from their own vehicles at Palestinians walking along the roads. Palestinians have admitted that after several such incidents, they have stopped traveling along the roads where these kinds of attacks have taken place.[80] Settlers have frequently fired at Palestinian shepherds and farmers or beaten them in order to forcefully prevent them from reaching their grazing grounds and agricultural fields, particularly during times of harvest.[81] In the fourteen-year period between 1987 and 2001, 124 Palestinians, among them 23 minors, were killed by Jewish settlers and other Israeli civilians. In addition, the settlers have injured hundreds of Palestinians, burnt mosques, harmed medical teams, attacked journalists, and damaged property in scores of villages.[82] They have stolen Palestinian herds, uprooted thousands of olive trees, and destroyed greenhouses as well as agricultural crops, thus depriving many Palestinians of their source of livelihood. They have entered Palestinian residential areas, shot at houses, damaged property, and committed other acts of vandalism, such as burning cars, breaking windows, and shooting solar heating devices. The objective of many of the attacks is to intimidate and terrorize the Palestinians in order to deter them from resisting acts of dispossession and at times to "persuade" them to abandon their lands and homes.[83]

What is important to emphasize here is that the settlers carry out these acts with impunity. In a survey conducted in 2006, an Israeli human rights group found that only 10 percent of the complaints involving settler violence against Palestinians have made it to the courts, while only 4 percent of the complaints involving settler trespassing and the destruction of olive trees and other property have led to prosecution.[84] According to B'Tselem, an "analysis of the response of the Israeli authorities to settler attacks on Palestinians reveals a blatant disregard for Palestinian lives and property. This disregard is reflected not only in the lack of preparation to handle incidents, the failure to intervene when settlers attack Palestinians, and the incomplete and feeble investigations, but also in the total disregard for the criticism and recommendations of state bodies and officials regarding the law enforcement system."[85] In another report, the Israeli rights organization maintains that the law enforcement system—including the military, the police, the State Attorney's Office, and the judiciary—have treated violent offenses in the OT with "contempt toward Palestinian complaints and leniency toward the offenders. Whereas a Palestinian who kills an Israeli is punished to the full extent of the law, and sometimes his family as well, it is extremely likely that an Israeli who kills a Palestinian will not be punished or will receive only a light sentence."[86] The message that comes across is that settler violence is not only tolerated by the state but is actually sanctioned.

Thus, even though settler violence is often presented as an individual act carried out by extremists, it is actually a state-sanctioned form of control that operates in two distinct ways: (1) settlers are hired as official guardians of the law; and (2) they are given a green light by the different law enforcement bodies to act as hooligans. Often the distinction between the two is not clear, and in both cases the settlers serve as auxiliaries or subcontractors of sorts who help the Israeli security forces police the Palestinian population.

THE ETHNIC DISTINCTION

From the occupation's very beginning, the ethnicity of the individual determined both the legal system to which a person would be subjected as well as whether the letter of the law would be enforced at all. Whereas both the land and its Palestinian inhabitants have been subjected to military rule, the Jewish settlers who took over the expropriated land have been subjected to Israeli civilian law.[87] A mere three weeks after the 1967 War and three months before the first settlement was established, the Knesset enacted a law that ensured the application of a dual legal system in the OT. The law guaranteed that Israeli citizens would not be subject to the military and emergency laws that were used to govern the Palestinians and provided an alternative venue to try Israeli citizens accused of offences in the OT.[88] Thus, from a legal perspective, the citizens who settled in the OT were extra-territorialized, enabling them, among other things, to be tried under the Israeli penal code in civil courts within Israel. Unlike their Palestinian neighbors, they continue to participate in Knesset elections, pay Israeli taxes, receive social security and health insurance, and enjoy all the rights granted by Israel to its citizens even though they do not reside in Israel.[89] For all practical purposes, the extension of Israeli domestic law to the settlers erased the Green Line in both their eyes and in the eyes of many other Israeli citizens.

Although the ethnicity of the individual has determined the legal system to which a person is subjected, it is actually the extralegal privileges that come with being a Jew, and not the vast number of legal rights that settlers, in contrast to Palestinians, enjoy, that allow them to carry out crimes with impunity. The crux of the matter is that the ethnic distinction — Jew versus Palestinian — trumps the legal distinction — criminal versus law-abiding. Case after case documented by human rights organizations such as B'Tselem and Al-Haq reveal that Jews who have committed crimes against Palestinians in the OT are not usually tried (for reasons such as lack of sufficient evidence); and, if they are tried, the large majority are either acquitted or receive very light sentences. Examining 119 cases where Palestinians were killed by Israeli civilians, B'Tselem found that only six Israelis were convicted of murder and only one sentenced to life imprisonment. An additional seven Israelis were convicted of manslaughter, and while one was sentenced to seven and a half years imprisonment for killing a Palestinian child, the rest received much lighter sentences. Some even got off with community service. B'Tselem's findings reveal that a total of 13 Israelis were imprisoned, and only one for life.[90] In this way, the state sends an unequivocal message to the settlers: They can continue terrorizing and policing the Palestinians, and the state will ensure that they are treated with great leniency.

We have already seen how forms of control that were employed to manage the population, such as the incorporation of Palestinian laborers into the Israeli workforce, facilitated the expropriation of land, and how the confiscation of land was utilized for managing the population. The settlements, settlers, bypass roads, and bureaucratic-legal mechanisms were all employed to shape the occupied inhabitants' comportment. Ironically, the different forms of control, which have played a central role not only in managing the population but also in blocking the possibility of creating a Palestinian state in the OT, produced excesses and contradictions that undid Israel's efforts to normalize the occupation, thus fomenting nationalist sentiment among the occupied Palestinians and creating fertile ground for the mobilization of the inhabitants against Israel's rule. This, in turn, led Israel to emphasize a sovereign power and to de-emphasize disciplinary power, thus modifying the way many controlling apparatuses and practices operated, which also coincided with the alteration of policies.

In order to seize the land and manage the population, the settlement project helped consolidate and perpetuate two major distinctions: one between Palestinians and Jews, and a second between the Palestinians and their land. The first distinction was created because the settlers were rendered lords of the land and were used as a form of control that helped the state manage the Palestinian population. Yet, simultaneously the privileged status of the settler emphasized the ethnic distinction between Palestinians and Jews, which served to unite Palestinian society.[91] The settler-owned estates and the violent attacks against Palestinians and their property affected not only the rural class but also the wage laborers, and the widespread hatred of the Jewish settlers helped unravel some of the prominent divisions that fragmented Palestinian society. The ethnic distinction, in other words, strengthened the "us" versus "them" sentiments and helped create the grounds for the first Palestinian intifada.

Along similar lines, one of the effects of the distinction Israel made between the Palestinians and their land was the regulation and, at times, the destruction of the Palestinian infrastructure of existence. After all, people's existence, particularly—but not solely—in a rural context, is dependent on their ability to develop, expand, and cultivate their land and to move freely within the space they occupy, and the settlement enterprise severely restricted the Palestinian capacity to do just that. On the eve of the first intifada, Israel had seized more than 40 percent of the land in the OT, had built 125 settlements and numerous bypass roads, and had transferred about sixty thousand Jewish settlers to the two regions. The settlements and settlers, even more than the military and Civil Administration, rendered the distinction between people and land perpetually visible. As the settlement project exposed, at least to the local inhabitants, the lie concerning the temporariness of the occupation, it also created a new spatial reality for the dispossessed Palestinians, whose living space was dramatically circumscribed. What, in other words, is the point of prosperity if one is dispossessed? Does not dispossession undermine normalization?

But the dispossession and settler violence not only undercut Israel's normalization efforts; the ongoing and rapid expansion of the settlement enterprise underscored that if the enterprise was not stopped, it would, in due course, jeopardize the very possibility of creating a Palestinian state. Since the land was indiscriminately expropriated, the confiscation also helped fuse the interests of rival *hamulas* as well as the poor and the rich, urban and rural, and Muslims and Christians, thus weakening clan, class, regional, and religious fragmentation. By threatening the Palestinian national project, the settlements helped widen and deepen the national awareness among the population. In this sense, the settlement project's excesses actually served to aggravate many of the excesses produced by completely different controlling practices. In other words, as Israel introduced a series of practices to reinforce fragmentation in Palestinian society (e.g., strengthening the traditional elite and censoring the nationalist discourse), it also introduced forms of control that strengthened and empowered the national movement because they helped construct a shared perception of the situation among the population and broke up traditional hierarchies, both of which are among the most basic conditions for collective action.[92]

Chapter 6 | THE INTIFADA

All of the achievements of the past twenty years could not
have come about without the devoted work of the staff,
both civilians and military, of the Civil Administration.
To them we extend our deepest gratitude. I am sure the
population in the areas join me in thanking them.

SHMUEL GOREN,
*Coordinator of Government Activities
in Judea, Samaria, and Gaza District, 1987*

On December 8, 1987, a tank transporter leaving the Gaza Strip crashed
into a line of cars taking Palestinian laborers from Gaza into Israel. Four
workers, three of whom were from the Jabalya refugee camp, were crushed
to death, and seven others were seriously wounded. Rumor rapidly spread
throughout the Gaza Strip that the truck driver was a relative of an Israeli
merchant who had been stabbed to death in downtown Gaza the day before.
The driver, so the rumor intimated, had intentionally crashed into the cars.
That night, thousands of people joined the funeral processions in the overly
crowded refugee camp, and very quickly the memorial marches turned into
massive demonstrations against the occupation. By dawn, most of the alleys
in the refugee camp had been blocked by heavy rocks and piles of garbage.
Two military jeeps, which patrolled the camp in the early morning hours,
were met by hundreds of residents. Curses were followed by stones, and it
took some time before the Israeli soldiers managed to retreat back to the
base. Another patrol, which tried to arrest a Palestinian youth not far away,
was also surrounded by protesters, only this time the soldiers opened fire
at the demonstrators before they withdrew. They wounded two youths and
killed seventeen-year-old Hatem a-Sisi, the first casualty of what in due
course would be known as the intifada.[1]

The intifada spread like wildfire from Jabalya refugee camp to other parts
of the Gaza Strip and West Bank. Every day, thousands of men, women,

and children filled the streets of Palestinian cities, towns, villages, and refugee camps. Access routes were blocked off with big rocks, garbage, and burning tires in an attempt to obstruct the movement of the Israeli military and in this way liberate parts of Palestine from the occupying power. The military's response was swift and decisive; within two weeks eight hundred Palestinians were incarcerated in Ansar prison within the Gaza Strip and an additional four hundred were sent to jails inside Israel.[2] The wholesale arrests did not, however, produce the desired calm, and, as the days passed, the number of Palestinians taking part in the demonstrations grew. Despite the developments on the streets, the Israeli military and political establishments failed to recognize the intifada for what it was, and for the first two months claimed that the demonstrations were part of local outbursts that would soon subside.

There were two central reasons why it took Israel so long to realize that it was facing a popular uprising. On the one hand, the political and military establishments had constructed a colonial fantasy, convincing themselves that the indigenous Palestinians were grateful to the Israeli military government for improving their living conditions. In the book *Judea, Samaria and the Gaza District, 1967–1987,* which was published a few months before the intifada erupted, the Civil Administration used glossy pictures, diagrams, and graphs to describe the great advancements experienced by Palestinians in the OT during two decades of Israeli rule. Indeed, the book presents the Israeli occupation as enlightened, as if Israel was introducing civilization to the natives. Shmuel Goren, the coordinator of government activities in the West Bank and Gaza Strip and the Israeli official most familiar with the OT at the time, seems to have been totally oblivious to the true sentiments of the Palestinian inhabitants. As cited in the epigraph above, he believed that the occupied population was grateful to the employees of the Civil Administration for their achievements during the past twenty years.[3]

On the other hand, the Israeli authorities did not realize they were confronting an uprising because protests and confrontations were not altogether unusual, and therefore did not really entail a break from the past. The large number of cases—approximately five thousand—brought forth annually to the Israeli military courts provides a good indication of the general unrest in the OT during the years preceding the intifada.[4] The occupied population had been clashing with the military on a regular basis since 1982, and while the location and the number of participants in each protest differed, and although there were periods of relative quiet, resistance to Israel's military rule was both manifest and mounting.[5] During the years 1977–1981, the annual rate of Palestinian "disturbances" amounted to 500, but between 1982 and 1987 the annual rate of "disturbances" remained above the 3,000 mark—on average almost 10 every day. In the year leading to the intifada, April 1986 to May 1987, 3,150 protests were documented, of which 1,870 included rock throwing, 600 included the placement of stone roadblocks and burning tires, and 665 incidents involved flag hoisting, leaflet distribution, and slogan painting, all of which were illegal. During the same period (1986–87), there were 65 incidents involving firearms, explosives, or stabbings, and 150 incidents involving Molotov cocktails. Twenty-two Palestinians (seven during demonstrations) were killed, 67 were injured, and almost 3,000 demonstrators were detained, including 1,550 who were accused of terrorism and 109 who were held in administrative detention without trial.[6] There was no particular reason why the December 9 demonstrations in Jabalya triggered the intifada. Palestinian youths had been throwing stones at Israeli soldiers practically every day, and the fact that the intifada broke out on a specific day in Jabalya rather than on another day in Khan Yunis, El-Arub, or Balata was, in many respects, a matter of chance.

The intifada itself, however, was not accidental. The steam had been gathering for a long time, and the deadly car accident followed by the protests in Jabalya merely served as a catalyst, which dramatically intensified the resistance that had been going on for several years. This intensification reflected not only a quantitative change in the number of confrontations with the Israeli military, but a qualitative one as well. A national leadership immediately emerged to coordinate and organize the struggle against Israeli rule, and new oppositional strategies were developed. Palestinian resistance, which had been intermittent and local, became continuous, spreading out geographically throughout the OT and incorporating more and more people. As it turned out, the intifada became the first of many global, mass-based challenges to nondemocratic governing structures.[7] It was also the first struggle for independence that the Palestinians took on by themselves.

In this chapter I briefly discuss the processes leading up to the eruption of the first intifada, claiming that the excesses and contradictions produced by Israel's controlling apparatuses and practices helped spur Palestinian resistance and led Israel, in turn, to alter the modes of power it employed to manage the population. After describing the different forms of Palestinian resistance that developed during the uprising as well as Israel's initial response to them, I go on to show that Israel's attempt to quell the uprising by emphasizing sovereign modes of power failed. Gradually, it became clear that Israel could not manage the population by using forms of control that operated in the service of sovereign power—the political, social, and economic cost was just too high. The Oslo Accords can therefore be considered an effect of Israel's realization that it had to find a new way to manage the lives of the Palestinian inhabitants in order to continue holding on to the occupied land, or at least parts of it.

EXCESSES AND CONTRADICTIONS

The intifada was a result of numerous social processes and events. Commentators such as Ze'ev Schiff and Ehud Ya'ari have argued that Israel's economic policies were the driving force behind the radicalization of the Palestinian public, and that the uprising was an economic outburst caused by unemployment, heavy taxation, and the exploitation of Palestinian laborers inside Israel.[8] Others agree that the December 1987 explosion was caused by economic distress, pent-up despair, and humiliation, which only deepened over the years, but suggest that these sentiments were due to an array of changes in Israeli politics and policies in the OT, which cannot be reduced to the economic field. Ian Lustick notes that one cannot fully understand the intifada without considering how Palestinian humiliation was utilized by the local PLO leadership to ignite and sustain the struggle for Palestinian national liberation, a struggle that was influenced, in part, by grass-roots organizations that had been active in the territories during the preceding decade.[9] Indeed, the PLO's defeat in the 1982 Lebanon war underscored that the struggle had to be political rather than military and that the arena of struggle needed to shift from outside the OT to the West Bank and Gaza Strip. Rashid Khalidi adds that without the nation-building work, organizational foundations, and political experience gained from twenty years of PLO activity, the Palestinians of the West Bank and Gaza would not have had the political maturity or the organizational density to sustain their struggle beyond an initial outburst.[10] While these and other explanations underscore many of the key processes leading to the intifada and are crucial for understanding why it erupted and how it was sustained, they fail to consider how the excesses and contradictions produced by Israel's means of control helped consolidate Palestinian opposition.

Although Israel managed to create a relative calm during the first years following the 1967 War, emphasizing disciplinary and bio modes of power and de-emphasizing sovereign power, it ultimately failed to normalize the occupation. Its unwillingness to incorporate the Palestinians into its own citizenry along with the distinction it made between the occupied inhabitants and their land produced several major contradictions that created wide gaps both within the forms of control and among them. Within these gaps Israel often reasserted itself through the emphasis of sovereign power in order to contain opposition, a move that undid its efforts to normalize the occupation, helped spur opposition, and led the government to alter the way it deployed the forms of control. By the time the intifada erupted, the exploitative and oppressive forces that upheld the occupation were clearly evident to the population in the OT.

This process was described in the preceding chapters through the examination of Israel's deployment of different means of control in four central sites: the political arena, the civilian and geographical spheres, and the economic field. I showed how the apparatuses and practices employed within each site produced their own internal excesses and contradictions, while the interaction among apparatuses deployed within the different sites generated others. This was evident, for example, in the way certain forms of control undid the discourse of temporariness, exposing the occupation's permanent nature. The excesses and contradictions facilitated the awakening of a Palestinian national consciousness, altered the population's social stratification, undermined the claim that the occupation was temporary and would end in the near future, revealed the logic behind the so-called arbitrary processes and decrees, and helped bind together an otherwise fragmented society; they also led Israel to modify its emphasis on the modes of power, slowly increasing its use of sovereign power.

In chapter 2, for example, we saw that by introducing a series of practices that operated in the service of disciplinary and bio modes of power, Israel managed to raise the standard of living in the territories, hoping in this way to normalize the occupation. Chapter 3, however, underscored that despite years of economic growth, Israel introduced a series of constraints and restrictions in the economic field so that the Palestinian farmers would be unable to compete with Israeli producers and so that the Palestinian economy would become dependent on Israel. While the lack of jobs both in industry and agriculture in the OT created a push factor for Palestinian laborers, which helped increase individual prosperity in the short term, the structural weakness of the Palestinian economy produced by the constraints and restrictions that Israel imposed created communal stagnation. Already in the early 1980s the communal economic stagnation began to become apparent, as the Palestinians experienced a 7 percent per capita drop in the value of agricultural products. The industrial and construction sectors also grew at a slower rate than the population, thus pointing to a negative per capita growth. Only the service sector showed a real increase.[11] The economic decline had concrete manifestations. The growth of private consumption in the OT lagged behind Israel's—2.5 percent versus 3.5 percent—constituting a reversal of the situation in the 1970s.[12]

Schiff and Ya'ari add that "every night tens of thousands of laborers who had left their homes before dawn to eke out a living in Israel returned with an ever greater burden of repressed anger against the country that mocked their right to equality and ravaged their dignity."[13] These two Israeli authors were given access to GSS records, which revealed that the common denominator of almost all the detainees during the intifada's first months was their having worked in Israel. When they were asked during interrogation to explain their motives for joining the protests, the detainees responded that they felt they were discriminated against at their workplaces and humiliated. Each prisoner "had his own story to tell, but the gist of their experience was similar: at one time or another they had been subjected to verbal and even physical abuse, cheated out of their wages, set to work under inhuman conditions, and exposed to the sweep of the dragnet that followed every act of terrorism. All complained of the insult and humiliation repeatedly suffered at army roadblocks and checkpoints."[14]

In chapter 3 I showed that the daily indignities and systematic repression experienced by the Palestinian laborers resulted from their *partial* integration into the Israeli workforce. One-tenth of the OT's population and almost 50 percent of the labor force were directly involved in work in Israel, but the number of people with experience in Israel was actually much higher because there was a constant turnover of laborers. It is not surprising then that by 1987 the effects ensuing from this partial integration had helped galvanize a mass base in the OT that opposed Israeli rule. By discriminating against Palestinians collectively as a nation, the economic policies pursued by the Israeli authorities helped make it possible, as Joost Hiltermann points out, for the various social actors in Palestinian society to unite in a common front against the occupation.[15]

In addition to the economic excesses and contradictions that helped sabotage Israel's efforts to normalize the occupation, we saw that the controlling apparatuses and practices deployed in the political, civilian, and geographical spheres produced cross-class solidarities that helped engender unity and broad-based mobilization, all of which strengthened the nationalist drive and undermined Israel's efforts to render the occupation invisible. The growing Palestinian national consciousness and the empowerment of the national movement did not, however, necessarily entail widespread and sustained mobilization, since such mobilization requires institutional support. In the years leading to the intifada, Israel outlawed all Palestinian political organizations and dismissed mayors, while deporting and arresting many of the nationalist leaders; this made it difficult to develop an institutional base that could mobilize the population against the occupying power. Khalidi is certainly correct when he states that without the nation-building work and organizational foundations, the intifada could not have been sustained, but how did the Palestinians manage to create these foundations amid Israeli restrictions and repression?

A single example, relating to Palestinian NGOs, will have to suffice here.[16] The Civil Administration initially permitted the establishment of NGOs — particularly educational and medical organizations — because they helped the Israeli authorities fill in some of the growing gaps between the population's needs and the actual services that the occupying power provided. The different political parties took advantage of this and used NGOs to build hospitals, medical clinics, kindergartens, and other educational and social welfare facilities throughout the OT, thus helping Israel to provide for the inhabitants' basic needs. In this way, the NGOs actually facilitated Israel's efforts to normalize the occupation because they mitigated some of its excesses. Simultaneously, though, some of these NGOs out-administered the Israeli administration, offering better and more reliable services to the population and thus exposing the inadequacy of the Civil Administration. Moreover, they became a central site of resistance, serving both as a model for nonviolent opposition and civil disobedience, as well as an institutional support mechanism for the struggle against the occupation. Thus, even though the political parties had to operate underground, they managed to create trade unions, women's committees, and NGOs that worked together to cement the otherwise fragmented population and to build a vibrant institutional apparatus that could coordinate oppositional activities. When the time came, the networks these organizations had created over the years allowed them to transform local resistance into national resistance.

THE UPRISING

Immediately after the intifada's eruption, a national leadership emerged that was made up of representatives from all of the secular political factions. The role of the leadership, which was called the Unified National Leadership of the Palestinian Uprising in the OT, was to determine the intifada's objectives, outline the strategies for achieving them, and coordinate the activities among the different political parties. The instructions were communicated to the public through a series of communiqués that were clandestinely printed and distributed throughout the West Bank and Gaza, and simultaneously broadcasted through radio stations in Baghdad and Damascus.[17] The role of these communiqués was to unify the resistance, consolidate the values informing it, and determine the population's daily routine. Through the dissemination of political ideas, symbols, and ideologies, the communiqués raised the inhabitants' morale and propagated the struggle's underlying objectives.[18] In every village, town, and refugee camp, local popular committees were established, and they took on the responsibility of ensuring that the instructions were carried out.

Every day, protesters filled the streets, demonstrating against the occupying power; they blocked the major arteries with burning tires and big rocks and threw stones at military patrols. Preservation of law and order in the OT had come to be perceived among the general Palestinian public as serving the interests of an illegitimate government, indicating that violation of the law and disrespect for Israel's authority were considered to be acts of patriotism, loyalty, and heroism. Initially, the strategic objective of the Palestinian organizations was to create "liberated" zones that the Israelis could not enter. Rapidly, though, the leadership realized they did not have the military capability to recapture any of the areas that Israel had occupied in 1967 and decided to focus instead on bringing about the collapse of the Civil Administration. Not only were the Civil Administration workers encouraged to resign (early on, the Palestinian policemen were forced, amid ongoing threats, to quit their jobs), but the public was entreated to stop paying taxes and to defy all Israeli directives. Louai Abdo, one of the leading Fatah members in Nablus during the intifada, describes the objectives of the uprising as an attempt to transform what had been primarily a bureaucratic rule into a military one. The goal was to drive Israel to replace the rule of law, its administrative maneuvers, and its controlling bureaucracies with soldiers and, in this way, to undercut all attempts to present the occupation as normal. Israeli rule, in other words, would apply only where soldiers were present to enforce it.[19] The objective was, in other words, to undo all Israel's efforts to normalize the occupation.

The overall strategy was to move from active attempts to strengthen the *tsumud*—namely, Palestinian steadfastness to the land—to coordinated resistance, characterized by massive civil disobedience, including merchant strikes, boycotting Israeli goods, a tax revolt, and daily protests against the occupying forces. The Palestinians hoped to transform the occupation from a profitable enterprise into a costly project, which would have a high political, economic, and moral price. Communiqué number 19, from June 6, 1988, provides a detailed plan for two weeks of activities and thus reveals some of the principal forms of resistance that were utilized during the intifada. In the communiqué the national leadership calls upon the public to impose a general strike to mark the beginning of the uprising's seventh month. First, the public is entreated to participate in sit-ins, marches, and demonstrations in solidarity with political detainees. The following day was dedicated to storing food, fuel, medical supplies and other essentials. On June 18, an "intensive mass escalation" of the struggle was planned under the slogans of "repatriation, self-determination and a nation state." The call for escalation ends with a message to those who do not comply with the general will, noting that they would be punished. The next day was devoted to a complete boycott of the Civil Administration and an attempt to boost the resignation of its Palestinian employees. Another general strike was to be imposed on June 22, and the population was asked to spend the day working the land as well as destroying and burning the "enemy's" industrial and agricultural property. Finally, Fridays and Sundays were dedicated to prayers for the martyrs alongside tumultuous marches. The communiqué concludes with a general call for further escalation and confrontation, instructing the population to resort "to all methods of popular resistance, including the sacred stones and incendiary Molotov cocktail." "Victory," the writers of the communiqué promise, "is near. Together along the path of liberating land and man."[20]

The Islamist groups put out communiqués similar to those published by the Unified National Leadership, calling on their followers to resist the occupation mostly through forms of civil disobedience.[21] From time to time the Israeli secret services also disseminated fake communiqués in an attempt to sow confusion among the public.[22] Generally, the directives published in all the real communiqués were followed by the public. For a period ranging over five years, not a day passed without protests, strikes, and clashes with the Israeli military. School children threw stones at military patrols, shopkeepers closed their stores, and some towns and villages refused to pay taxes. From time to time, Palestinian militants would attack Israeli targets with Molotov cocktails and automatic weapons, but these kinds of attacks were the exception during the first intifada.

ISRAEL RESPONDS

Despite the seemingly endless number of demonstrations and confrontations, it took several months before Israel acknowledged that it was confronting a well-orchestrated national uprising and not just a series of sporadic protests. From the outset, Israel decided not to meet any of the demands formulated by the national leadership in the OT and tried to quell the uprising and reestablish order by employing more and more force. It emphasized a sovereign mode of power, which led to an exponential growth in certain forms of control that already existed but were not used very often, and altered the function of other forms that had been operating in the service of disciplinary and bio modes of power. Israel, for example, killed more people, tortured more detainees, demolished more houses, implemented more curfews, and simultaneously changed the function of the educational and health systems, transforming them into instruments of collective punishment.

Within a short period the number of troops deployed in the OT was doubled, then tripled, and eventually it increased to five times the size it had been before the intifada.[23] Yitzhak Rabin, who was Israel's defense minister at the time, initiated an "iron fist" policy. Soldiers were given special clubs and permission to use them. The idea was that beatings were not as lethal as live ammunition and therefore would serve as a more appropriate response to the popular demonstrations and protests. Ze'ev Schiff and Ehud Ya'ari describe the ensuing events in the following manner:

> [T]he extent of the injuries caused by the new policy was harrowing. Considering that whole corps of soldiers were engaged in battering away at defenseless civilians, it is hardly surprising that thousands of Palestinians—many of them innocent of any wrongdoing—were badly injured, some to the point of being handicapped. There were countless instances in which young Arabs were dragged behind walls or deserted buildings and systematically beaten all but senseless. The clubs descended on limbs, joints, and ribs until they could be heard to crack—especially as Rabin let slip a "break their bones" remark in a television interview that many soldiers took as a recommendation, if not exactly an order.[24]

Beatings, however, were not the only way Israel dealt with the uprising. By the end of 1992, after five years of intifada, 1,042 Palestinians had been killed, mostly by Israeli security forces, but also by Jewish settlers and other citizens.[25] As the years passed, the military softened its "open fire regulations," allowing soldiers to shoot in situations where they were not experiencing a clear and present danger to their own lives. At a certain point the Israeli military even created a number of undercover death squads that shot to kill Palestinians who were "wanted" by the GSS or who were caught in activities like writing slogans on walls within cities and refugee camps.[26] Notwithstanding the fact that more Palestinians were killed in those five years than in the previous twenty, it is important to emphasize that Israel adopted police-style methods to confront the Palestinian protesters and did not utilize its overwhelming firepower to quell the uprising.

In his groundbreaking book *Frontiers and Ghettos,* James Ron employs these two spatial metaphors to explain why Israel did not employ more violent means to suppress the intifada. He claims that the repertoires of violence are determined by the institutional settings established by the controlling state in a given territory. Ghettos are densely institutionalized areas that are within the legal and bureaucratic sphere of influence of the core state, while frontiers are distinguished from the core state by clear boundaries and are only thinly institutionalized areas. Whereas ghettos are characterized by ethnic policing, mass incarceration, and ongoing harassment, frontiers are more prone to brutal and lawless violence.[27] Employing our terminology, the major difference between ghettos and frontiers is that in frontiers the core state does not really attempt to shape the individual's behavior. By contrast, in ghettos, regardless of the forms of control employed, the occupying power is always interested in controlling the lives of the inhabitants and harnessing their energies so as to shape both the individual's and population's comportment. This, I maintain, was part of Israel's approach until the eruption of the second intifada, thus suggesting that even though Israel modified its forms of control during the first intifada, de-emphasizing disciplinary and bio modes of power while accentuating sovereign power, it was still interested in shaping the behavior of the Palestinian population.

Ron's distinction between ghettos and frontiers only goes so far, since it does not address the fact that within so-called ghettos there can be wide variations in terms of repertoires of violence and forms of control. Simply put, even though the West Bank and Gaza Strip were, according to Ron's parlance, an Israeli ghetto from 1967 until at least 2000, the way Israel controlled the Palestinians in the late 1960s was very different from the way it controlled them in the late 1980s and 1990s. A brief description of some of the more prominent forms of control that Israel deployed during the uprising reveals how the occupation had changed following the intifada's outbreak and the accentuation of sovereign power.

Along with the beatings and killings, Israel introduced a policy of massive incarceration. Between December 9, 1987, and December 9, 1990, about 45,000 indictments against Palestinians were submitted to the military courts, while thousands of Palestinians were arrested and held in jail at any given moment. The rules for holding people for lengthy periods in administrative detention without trial were changed in order to ease the process for the military and GSS.[28] By 1989, about 13,000 Palestinians were imprisoned, 1,794 of whom were held in administrative detention.[29] Israeli prisons were filled not only with people caught during demonstrations, but with anyone who was a known member of one of the Palestinian political factions (Fatah, PFLP, DFLP, Islamic Jihad, etc., except for Hamas, which during the first year was still legal).[30] Not surprisingly, many of the Palestinians who had assumed leadership roles when the intifada erupted were behind bars by the end of its first year. Yet, others quickly took their place, thus undermining Israel's attempt to create a leadership vacuum.

A large percentage of those who were imprisoned underwent torture.

According to B'Tselem, between 1987 and 1994 the GSS interrogated more than twenty-three thousand Palestinians, one out of every hundred people living in the OT. Many of them were tortured. Even Rabin, during his tenure as prime minister, admitted that Israel had tortured some eight thousand detainees prior to mid-1995.[31] The "ticking bomb" scenario was repeatedly cited to justify the use of torture. The logic of this justification is straightforward: the security services assume that there is a "ticking bomb" somewhere, and therefore torture is warranted in order to extract vital information—the immediate procurement of which would help save human lives and prevent serious terrorist attacks in Israel. However, the actual number of Palestinians tortured undermines the logic. Even according to the Israeli security services, during the first intifada there could not possibly have been eight thousand "ticking bombs." This suggests that the torture's major function was not to procure information but to advance other, perhaps more important, objectives.

Examining the use of torture in other historical and geographical contexts proves revealing because it underscores that frequently the major reason behind the use of torture is to silence and control the population rather than extract information. When Galileo proved the motion of the earth, he was declared a heretic by an assembly of cardinals, hauled before the Inquisition and compelled to recant under pain of torture. The Church was determined to stifle any view that threatened its orthodoxy, and, more significantly, its authority. Israel used torture for similar reasons. Yet torture is not only about controlling the individual victim, who is often unable to speak out for the rest of his or her life. The sheer numbers of Palestinians tortured suggest that it was also used to manage the population as a whole. As an imminent threat, torture intimidates groups or individuals who oppose the existing order. It was employed in this way to contain peasants in Mexico, protesters in South Africa under apartheid, members of the Islamic Front in Algeria. When one analyzes the history of torture, where it was practiced and why, it becomes clear that torture is not simply or even predominantly about compelling a person to speak; rather, it is about silence—ensuring that particular activists are broken and popular opposition remains suppressed.[32] This appears to have been the primary reason why Israel opted to torture so many Palestinians.

Nonetheless, wholesale imprisonment and torture did not restrain the uprising, so Israel deployed several other forms of control. It reintroduced its deportation policy, expelling 415 Palestinians for their alleged membership in the Hamas in December 1992, thus bringing the total number of intifada-related deportees to 481. This number, however, is inaccurate. While the Hamas deportation was widely publicized, what is less known is that Israel also deported hundreds of Palestinian women, mostly from Jordan, who had married residents from the West Bank and Gaza Strip and had lived in the territories with their newborn children. The intifada was used as a pretense to deport both women and children who had stayed in the OT without a valid visitor's permit, thus tearing families apart.[33]

Whereas many of the strategies just mentioned can certainly be seen as targeting individuals, they were also used to sow fear among the population as a whole. Israel employed a variety of other controlling practices that did not in any way differentiate among individuals and served as forms of collective punishment. House demolitions targeted the family of a particular individual who had somehow defied Israeli law. Actual proof was not always needed; the mere suspicion that a teenager had torched an empty car in a parking lot could lead to the demolition of his parents' house. During the intifada, Israeli security forces demolished an estimated 447 houses and sealed off 294 others, and these numbers do not include the at least 62 houses that were partially demolished and 118 that were partially sealed.[34] Thousands were left homeless.

The most common form of collective punishment, however, was the restriction of movement. Within the uprising's first year, for example, no less than 1,600 curfews were imposed, so that by late 1988 more than 60 percent of the population had been confined to their homes for extended periods of time. In addition, the military imposed a permanent night curfew from May 1988 to May 1994 in the Gaza Strip—everything was shut down before sunset, and no one was allowed out until the early hours of the morning.[35] Alongside the curfews, Israel introduced two new forms of control during the intifada: the entry-permit regime and the closure. Whereas the entry-permit regime was systematically employed from 1988, the closure was first introduced in 1991.

Although formally Palestinians had always needed a permit to work in Israel, most of those who were actually employed in Israel never filed a request for a permit, and those who did received permits more or less automatically until the eruption of the first intifada. The first major amendment took place in 1988, when Israel introduced green identity cards (the regular ones were either red or orange), which were given to Palestinians who did not have security clearance (people who had been arrested in the past, were known to be active members of a political party, or had a record with the GSS for some other reason). Anyone who possessed a green ID could not leave the West Bank and Gaza Strip. A year later, a magnetic-card regime was introduced for workers entering Israel from the Gaza Strip. This card, which had to be renewed annually, contained coded information about the person's "security background," tax payment, electric and water bills, and so on, and was constantly updated. All Palestinian laborers from the Gaza Strip had to swipe the card through an electronic device at the checkpost each morning, and if any unfavorable data had been entered into the military computer, the worker was denied entry.[36]

The entry-permit regime served both to monitor and limit the access of Palestinians entering Israel as well as to recruit collaborators for the GSS.[37] Every person who wanted a permit had to apply at the Civil Administration offices, and many were interviewed by the GSS during the application process and asked to collaborate in exchange for freedom of movement. This strategy was used mostly in the Gaza Strip, where the GSS exploited the fact that the borders were more difficult to pass and literally thousands of workers had to pass through the checkpoints to enter Israel for their livelihood.[38] Thus, the integration of Palestinian laborers into the Israeli economy and their ensuing dependency on Israel was crucial for the transformation of hundreds if not thousands of residents into collaborators, which became, in turn, a means of control in their own right.

In 1988, the permit regime applied individual mechanisms of differentiation, so that people were denied a permit due to their personal background (e.g., membership in a political party, participation in protests, being a friend of people who actively resisted the occupation, etc.). This kind of differentiation can be seen as an attempt to secure and uphold the correct conduct promulgated by disciplinary forms of control. In other words, work was transformed from a right to a privilege, something that could be revoked at any time if the worker did not conform to certain standards of behavior. Many Palestinians internalized Israel's message and were extremely careful not to participate in any political activities for fear of tarnishing their security records and in this way jeopardizing their family's livelihood.

Toward the end of the intifada, Israel changed the permit regime to include an array of criteria that were social rather than individual and adopted a policy that required the permit's renewal every three months. In addition to individual clearance, restrictions based on profiles of Palestinian terrorists that the GSS created were introduced, so that a worker's age, marital status, and the number of children he or she had determined whether an entry permit would be issued. In addition, quotas according to the needs of the different Israeli economic sectors — like agriculture, construction, and industry — were set, limiting the number of Palestinians who were allowed to enter Israel.[39] Thus, the disciplinary modes of control were de-emphasized, and biopower was accentuated. Overall, the new permit regime reduced the number of Palestinians who could work in Israel, while rendering any attempt to cross the Green Line without a permit illegal. Those who were caught were imprisoned and given hefty fines.

The entry-permit regime became feasible partly due to the fact that a year earlier the Civil Administration began creating a computerized database, which became operational in August 1987. Personal information pertaining to property, real estate, family ties, political attitudes, involvement in political activities, licensing, profession, consumption patterns, taxes, and so forth was entered into the database. According to Civil Administration officials, the computer program enabled them to gain "complete control in real-time of all information on the territories, which ... ensure[d] strategic control and improvement of services." By pressing a key on a computer, Meron Benvenisti observes, any official could "gain access to name-lists of 'positives' and 'hostiles,' and decide on the fate of their applications, from car licensing to water quotas, import permits and travel documents."[40]

During the first Gulf War (August 1990 – February 1991), Israel introduced yet another from of control, one that targets the population as a whole rather than the individual: the hermetic closure. The imposition of a closure entails sealing off all of the borders between the OT and Israel for extended periods and not allowing Palestinians to cross the Green Line. While the closure was only implemented during the first intifada on a number of occasions and was, at the time, the exception to the rule, as we will see in the next chapters it eventually became the norm. It was the first indication that Israel was moving from forms of control that managed both individuals and the population to forms of control that focused solely on the population. In any case, both the permit regime and the closure directly affected every

Palestinian who sought to enter Israel and served as a final break from the policy of open borders that Dayan had implemented right after the 1967 War. Freedom of movement between the OT and Israel was, in other words, replaced by a policy that confined the Palestinians to the West Bank and Gaza Strip. This policy had two direct results. First, it helped redemarcate the Green Line, separating Israel from the areas it had occupied in 1967. Second, it dealt a harsh blow to the Palestinian economy.

In chapter 3 I argued that due to Israeli constraints the Palestinian economy was unable to develop independent productive forces. Even an Israeli committee appointed in 1991 by the Ministry of Defense to determine the economic situation in Gaza noted that "no priority had been given to the promotion of local entrepreneurship and the business sector in the Gaza Strip." The committee admitted that over the years "the authorities [had] discouraged such initiatives whenever they threatened to compete in the Israeli market with existing Israeli firms."[41] The Palestinian economy lacked any viable institutional infrastructure capable of stimulating development and supporting structural reform. It accordingly relied on the wages of Palestinian laborers working in Israel and remittances sent from the Gulf States, and did not have the capacity to absorb new workers. The restriction of movement alongside the inability of the local economy to provide jobs transformed unemployment into a structural effect of the occupation.[42] So if in the late 1960s and early 1970s Israel introduced forms of control that aimed to increase prosperity and decrease unemployment, by the early 1990s Israel's controlling practices were producing an economic crisis as well as high unemployment.

The permit regime and closures that restricted thousands of workers were not only used as a form of collective punishment, however; they were also a divisive controlling mechanism aimed at fragmenting Palestinian society. Israel hoped that many of the Palestinians who were dependent on crossing the Green Line for their livelihood would channel their anger against the Palestinian resistance movement and not only against Israel. In chapter 3, when discussing the forms of control used in the economic sphere, I mentioned how job insecurity was manipulated in order to ensure the worker's "correct conduct." Here it is important to emphasize that from the occupation's very beginning Israel manipulated the laborers' sense of security and insecurity in order to manage the population. The temporary and arbitrary modalities of control allowed Israel to do this.

At the same time, following the eruption of the intifada many of the institutions that had been used to normalize the occupation, like medical and educational institutions, were used to collectively punish the population. Although this was not altogether new, the emphasis of a sovereign mode of power did change the function of many institutions. We saw, for example, that in the 1970s Israel adopted a "liberal policy" that provided the occupied inhabitants with permits to open universities. In the early 1980s it began shutting down specific schools and universities for limited periods. But when the uprising began, it indiscriminately closed down all 1,194 West Bank schools and universities. It seems to have realized that trying to influence the way students and teachers perceive the occupation by monitoring and regulating the curriculum had little if any "positive" effect. The educational institutions had become sites of opposition, and so Israel shut down schools and universities indefinitely, thus preventing approximately three hundred thousand children and eighteen thousand university students from entering their educational institutions. Birzeit University, for instance, was practically closed year round from 1988 to 1992, while all the other universities were also closed for lengthy periods.[43] Israel effectively rendered higher education in the territories illegal. The upshot, though, was that students had plenty of time on their hands and utilized it to confront the occupying power.[44]

Israel used a similar strategy with respect to the health care system. Until the intifada's eruption, many cancer and kidney patients who could not be treated by the OT's underdeveloped health system were referred to medical facilities within Israel, but following the uprising the referral quotas dropped by 65 percent. In 1988, Israeli hospitals admitted 650 patients from the West Bank, almost 1,200 fewer than the year before.[45] Not unlike the educational system, which was transformed from a controlling apparatus that aimed to normalize the occupation into an instrument that collectively punished the population, the health system was used to punish Palestinian society as a whole. Yet, other than the two new forms of control deployed to monitor and restrict movement, all the other controlling apparatuses and practices employed during the intifada had already been employed during the occupation's first two decades. The major difference is that following the uprising's outbreak, Israel de-emphasized disciplinary power and thus altered the way the forms of control operated both quantitatively and qualitatively.

Examining the way Israel modified its relation to the Palestinian individual can help us understand how the forms of management were altered. During the occupation's early years, Israel set up a series of controlling apparatuses and practices that aimed to harness the energy of Palestinians so as to increase the individual's economic utility. We saw that Israel monitored the Palestinian food basket and introduced programs to increase the value of its "nutritional energy." In one study, the Israeli Agriculture Ministry boasts that in 1966 the per capita consumption of a Palestinian amounted to 2,430 calories per day and that due to a series of Israeli interventions by 1973, the per capita consumption had increased to 2,719 calories.[46]

During the first intifada Israel did not lose interest in individual Palestinians, as it did in the second intifada; rather, it modified the forms of control used to shape their behavior. While the population was initially managed by deploying practices aimed at highlighting the individual's economic capabilities, these practices were now eclipsed, and the inhabitants' political energies were repressed with more brutal force. This comes across very clearly when one considers the massive number of people beaten, tortured, and incarcerated. But at the same time, Israel was still interested in molding Palestinian behavior in order to render the population docile.[47] In one of the military regulations describing how a soldier is allowed to beat a Palestinian, it is written that "force is not to be used against sensitive parts of the body [that may] endanger life."[48] Indeed, Israeli decision makers considered every Palestinian death as having detrimental ramifications. Thus, one notices a continuing interest in individual behavior even as Israel slowly abandoned the use of disciplinary power to manage such behavior.

The continued interest in the Palestinian individual is also apparent when one takes into account such practices as the introduction of the entry-permit regime. For the most part, movement was not arrested altogether but put under a very stringent system of regulations. If before the intifada the employer was the major arbiter of correct conduct, from 1988 on the Israeli security forces monitored how each Palestinian behaved, not only at the workplace, but during every moment of the day. Those who were caught participating in a protest, distributing leaflets, or affiliating with a political party lost their permits and thus their livelihood. What the beatings, torture, and permit regime all suggest is that Israel still hoped to influence individuals so that they would abide by the rules of correct conduct. Following the eruption of the second intifada, Israel's approach changed, and it lost all interest in influencing the individual, focusing almost solely on the population as a whole.

THE INTIFADA'S CONSEQUENCES

The emphasis of coercive measures undid many of the disciplinary forms of control that had been functioning until the eve of the intifada. The Palestinian struggle for self-determination helped denaturalize the occupation, if only because Israel had to deploy military forces for an extensive period just in order to keep its administrative apparatus intact. The emphasis on sovereign power through the deployment of a large number of troops and the incursion of tanks and armored vehicles into Palestinian cities, towns, and villages was, paradoxically, a sign that Israeli control was in decline, since power's success "is in proportion to its ability to hide its own mechanisms."[49] Not a day passed without mention in the local and international media of the coercive measures deployed, ranging from deportations, house demolitions, and curfews to beatings, administrative detention, and torture. In many respects, then, the intifada's most significant outcome was its success in undermining the normalcy of the occupation and exposing some of Israel's forms of control for all to see.

The uprising led to the mobilization of the Palestinian masses and their integration into a relatively unified national liberation movement. While the Israeli military continued to control the land, it could not manage the population. Importantly, the intifada also began altering the power relations within the PLO, propelling a shift of some power from the Diaspora to the leadership living in the OT. The external leadership's long-standing failure to cope with the real needs of the people under occupation and to produce a plan capable of halting Israel's de facto annexation of the land enabled the Palestinians inside the territories to develop their own organizational structures and to take on a leadership role. It also pushed the Palestine National Council to formally embrace the two-state solution during its November 1988 meeting in Algiers.

The uprising, however, did not only render the occupation a political liability, it also succeeded in transforming the occupation into a financial burden.[50] In fact, the uprising's economic consequences affected both sides. In the OT, per capita income dropped by 13 percent within two years of intifada, while the situation only worsened during the Gulf War. On the one hand, Israel limited the number of Palestinian workers who were permitted to cross the Green Line. On the other hand, following Yasser Arafat's decision to side with Iraq, Palestinians working in the Gulf States were deported and consequently could not send remittances to their families in the OT, while countries like Kuwait and Saudi Arabia stopped their financial support to the Palestinian people. Ultimately, Palestinians experienced a 30–40 percent decline in their standard of living during these years.[51] For Israel, the intifada transformed the occupation into an economic burden. It had to deploy seven brigades in order to police the population. Simultaneously, there was a sharp decline in foreign investment in and tourism to Israel. Both because the Palestinians lost some of their buying power and because of the economic boycott they imposed, Israel's exports to the territories dropped from $961 million in 1987 to $521 million in 1989.[52] Thus, from a situation whereby it produced great profits, the occupation suddenly became a significant financial burden.

Moreover, the intifada revealed Israel's occupation as a colonial project that was sustained through political violence—a fact that had been obfuscated before the intifada erupted—to the world. The uprising also broadened the struggle that had been defined almost purely in nationalistic terms to one that was also about basic human rights. This change coincided with some of the transformative events taking place in the international arena at the time. The fall of the Berlin Wall, the bloody clampdown on students in Tiananmen Square, the Velvet Revolution, the first free elections in Poland, and the Soviet Union's decision to withdraw from Afghanistan all seemed to point to the dawn of a new era and were usually conceived and portrayed as the collapse or retreat of brutal and oppressive regimes and the triumph of Western liberalism, which represents, at least ostensibly, a culture that values human rights. The Palestinians managed to draw a connection between their struggle and the struggle of some of the liberation movements around the world, thus altering, to some degree, the representation and image of the Palestinian in the international media.[53]

Just as importantly, the large number of soldiers deployed to protect the Jewish settlers changed how the latter were perceived in Israeli society: from an asset to their country's security to a burden. The possible danger of traveling in the West Bank and Gaza Strip kept many citizens away, and despite the state's huge investments in infrastructure and the provision of inexpensive land and houses, for a while fewer Israelis chose to move to the OT. Consequently, as mentioned, the intifada redemarcated the Green Line, which had been erased for many if not most Israelis.[54]

In sum, the uprising managed to unmask and politicize the occupation. The use of punitive measures that had had a powerful impact before the intifada's eruption—such as deportation, torture, house demolition, and curfews—proved largely ineffectual, and it became apparent to Israel that it could no longer count on disciplinary power to produce some sense of normalcy, as it had done in the past.[55] The Palestinian national movement was strong and was not about to collapse, and Israel realized that it would have to continue deploying thousands of soldiers just to sustain its control of the land. All of this underscored the need to change strategies. And this is precisely where Oslo enters the picture.

Chapter 7 | OUTSOURCING THE OCCUPATION

> The PLO had struck a political bargain with the Israeli
> government: In return for recognition and permission to
> return to the occupied territories, the Palestinians would
> police the local population and refrain from insisting that
> Israel cease its settlement activities.
>
> RAJA SHEHADEH

> The great irony of the Oslo accord is that it brought to
> power in Palestine an outside political elite that did not
> lead the revolution — the 1987–93 intifada — but rather
> promised to end it.
>
> GLENN E. ROBINSON

As the years passed, the fact that Israel would be unable to quell the popular uprising began registering among larger segments of the Israeli public. Many Israelis believed that the economic, political, and moral cost of upholding the occupation was too high and that Israel had to modify its policies in the OT. It became clear that the existing forms of control were not producing the desired calm and that another strategy was needed. The ingenious idea was to *outsource* the responsibility for the population to a subcontractor. A Palestinian authority was established to take on the task of managing the occupied inhabitants. In exchange for providing Israel an array of services, Israel offered the new authority some sort of autonomous self-rule. Israel, however, continued to control most of the occupied land.

Employing the term *outsourcing* to describe the Oslo process is helpful because it facilitates the conceptualization of the new way Israel hoped to manage the Palestinian inhabitants.[1] Theoretically, outsourcing should be considered a technique employed by power to conceal its own mechanisms. It is not motivated by power's decision to retreat, but, on the contrary, by its unwavering effort to endure and remain in control. Indeed, power adopts outsourcing in the political or economic realm in order to sustain itself. Thus, the Oslo Accords, which were the direct result of the first intifada, as well as the changing political and economic circumstances in the international realm, signified the *reorganization* of power rather than its withdrawal and should be understood as the continuation of the occupation by other means. After the emphasis on sovereign power failed to produce the desired results, Israel realized that the only way to bring about calm—while continuing to hold on to the land—was by employing a subcontractor that could normalize the situation. As one commentator observed early on, Oslo was a form of "occupation by remote control."[2]

Thus, the historical reading advanced here suggests that the intifada, which was spurred, in part, by the excesses and contradictions informing Israel's forms of control, drove Israel to emphasize a sovereign mode of power and to the modify the ways its controlling apparatuses operated. The Oslo process was, to a large extent, the result of Israel's failure to crush the intifada, and Israel's major goal in the process was to find a way of managing the Palestinian population while continuing to hold on to their land. As Edward Said, Noam Chomsky, and several others pointed out from the outset, Oslo was not an instrument of decolonization but rather a framework that changed the means of Israel's control in order to perpetuate the occupation.[3] It constituted a move from direct military rule over the Palestinians in the OT to a more indirect or neocolonial form of domination.[4] While interpreting events in this way goes against the proclaimed goals of the Oslo process, the interpretation is actually based on the nuts and bolts of the agreements themselves.

To be sure, the use of subcontractors, even in the Israeli-Palestinian context, was not new and can be traced back to the creation of the Palestinian Farmers' Party by the Jewish Agency in the 1920s.[5] As we saw in chapter 2, Israel also opted for an informal power-sharing agreement with Jordan and for many years used the Hashemite monarchy as a subcontractor of sorts. The creation of the Village Leagues in the late 1970s should also be understood as a futile attempt to establish a puppet leadership to counter the urban nationalists. And in 1978, Israel adopted a similar policy in Lebanon and established the South Lebanese Army, which was employed to advance Israeli interests and administer the lives of Lebanese inhabitants.[6] Finally, in the mid-1980s there was another botched attempt to renew the Israeli-Jordanian power-sharing agreement in order to undermine the PLO's rising influence in the West Bank and Gaza Strip. With the eruption of the first intifada, however, this arrangement was also annulled.[7]

After the first intifada, however, the outsourcing technique was reconstructed in a much more refined way. In 1994, Israel's long-standing enemy, Yasser Arafat, was allowed to return to the OT along with his comrades and Palestinian combatants. Following his arrival in Gaza, Arafat did not take orders from the Israeli authorities in the same way as Mustafa Dudin (the head of the Village Leagues) or SLA Commander General Antoine Lahad had. In contrast to the organizations these two men headed, which were considered to be Israeli proxies and enjoyed overt support from the Israeli government, the newly established Palestinian Authority (PA) was perceived to be an autonomous entity—both politically and legally—by local and international parties alike. Indeed, it was frequently depicted, and at times even acted, as Israel's rival and opponent.

The PA's depiction as totally autonomous was advantageous because it managed to obfuscate Israel's connection to the occupation and made it difficult to hold Israel legally, politically, economically, or morally accountable for the violations and repression in the OT. Former Prime Minister Yitzchak Rabin said as much when he explained why Oslo was good for Israel. Palestinian forces, he noted in an interview, will be able to control the population . . . without all the difficulties arising from Supreme Court appeals, human rights organizations like B'Tselem, and all kinds of leftist fathers and mothers.[8] So if prior to the Oslo years Israel could not have denied its obligations as an occupying power, following the Oslo agreements the Israeli government contended that it had transferred all responsibility to the PA and therefore no longer had any obligations towards the Palestinian population. This portrayal of Oslo was widely accepted, so that by and large the Oslo process was understood as the withdrawal of Israeli power and the demise of its controlling apparatuses. The outsourcing strategy, in other words, worked.

The notion that Israel outsourced some of its responsibilities should not be mistaken for a conspiracy theory, nor should it be understood as promoting a statist interpretation of events; rather, it should be read as a structural analysis. Israel's inability to manage the occupied population produced a rupture in the controlling structure, and Oslo is, in many respects, the effect of this rupture and should be conceived as Israel's attempt to seal it. The idea was not simply to give the Palestinians symbols of sovereignty while withholding real sovereignty (Oslo was not an ideological camouflage), but to actually use the Palestinian Authority (PA) as an instrument to manage the inhabitants' daily lives. Oslo, according to this interpretation, was not a process of phased devolution of Israeli rule over the West Bank and Gaza Strip, the transfer of authority to the PA and the implementation of the two-state solution, but the extension of Israeli rule through a subcontractor that was created to manage the population. The PA, however, was never an independent agent that Israel, as it were, hired in order to perform a number of services. Rather, it too is a product of the occupation, and, more precisely, the forms of control that failed to normalize it. The PA is an effect produced by the reorganization of Israeli power, a series of newly constructed legal-bureaucratic mechanisms, the restructuring of the economy, and the repartitioning of space.

The purpose of this chapter is to describe how the reorganization of power was implemented and why it too failed to normalize the occupation. If one reads the eight different Oslo agreements the Israelis and Palestinians signed over the years, not as part of a peace process (i.e., the way they were presented to the public), but rather as texts that depict the modification or replacement of existing forms of control, then the strategy Israel adopted becomes clear.[9] Instead of reaching a settlement regarding the withdrawal of Israeli power, the Oslo agreements actually stipulate how Israel's power would be reorganized and Palestinian space would be restructured. One of the surprising facts is that these changes were never left ambiguous, but were, as I show in the following pages, spelled out in the agreements. The reorganization of power and space, I go on to argue, actually produced a situation in which the PA could not generate economic growth and development, and hindered its ability to introduce new forms of control informed by disciplinary and bio modes of power. This, in turn, undermined the PA and led both to a crisis of legitimacy of the Palestinian governing body and to popular rejection of remote Israeli rule. Palestinian resistance was engendered once again by a series of excesses and contradictions, most of which were produced as a result of the division Israel made between the administration of the population, on the one hand, and the control of space, on the other. Simply put, how can one manage a population without controlling the space it occupies and the resources within this space?

The reorganization of power was carried out in three distinct spheres—the civil institutions, economy, and law enforcement—and was intricately tied to the restructuring of Palestinian space. The overarching logic informing the different agreements is straightforward: transfer all responsibilities (but not all authority) relating to the management of the population to the Palestinians themselves while preserving control of Palestinian space.

According to the 1993 Oslo Declaration of Principles, the Palestinians were to assume responsibility for education, culture, health, social welfare, direct taxation, and tourism. In addition, the PA would establish "a strong police force" in order to ensure law enforcement, while Israel would continue to be responsible for defense "against external threats, as well as the responsibility for overall security of Israelis for the purpose of safeguarding their internal security and public order."[10] The changes on the ground were rapid. By August 1994, the PA had taken upon itself full responsibility for the Palestinian educational system and all health institutions as well as governmental and nongovernmental social welfare organizations and institutions. It also began regulating, licensing, supervising, and developing the tourist industry, and started to collect income tax. From this point in time onward, the salaries of all public servants were paid by the PA; as a result, there was much less direct contact between the occupied inhabitants and the Israeli occupying establishment, whether it was the military or the Civil Administration. Moreover, if the inhabitants were dissatisfied with the services they received, they could file their complaints with the PA, which was now officially in charge.

Full responsibility, however, does not necessarily entail full authority or autonomy. Even though Israel transferred all responsibility over the civil spheres to the PA, it did not give the latter full autonomy to administer them as it wished. In education, for example, Israel continued to have a say about the Palestinian curriculum, and could veto the inclusion of certain topics, particularly in disciplines such as history and geography. The representation of Jerusalem is a case in point. Although Jerusalem is presented in Israeli textbooks as Israel's indivisible and eternal capital, if Palestinians were to depict Jerusalem in a similar manner it would be considered incitement. Along similar lines, many of the acts that Palestinians consider heroic the Israeli government regards as terrorism. Israel has therefore not permitted any mention of these acts in the Palestinian curriculum. Thus, even in the civil institutions that were handed over to the Palestinians, Israel maintained a level of remote control.

In the economic field the Palestinians had even less autonomy. During the first couple of years after the signing of Oslo, there was optimism in the OT, and word on the street had it that the Gaza Strip would be transformed into the Middle East's Singapore: aid would come pouring in, a thriving industry would be established, and the Palestinians would enjoy the fruits of peace. Yet, as we now know, this did not happen. There were several reasons why this fantasy did not materialize. One can gain insight into why the optimism was to be short-lived, however, just by looking at the major economic agreement signed by the two parties. The Paris Protocol on Economic Relations (April 1994) presented the economic relations between Israel and the Palestinians as if these relations were between two equal parties, yet it actually reproduced many of the unequal relations that had existed throughout the occupation. It established a customs union between the two entities based totally on Israeli trade regulations. It ensured Israeli control of labor flows and denied the Palestinians the right to introduce their own currency, all of which imposed severe limitations on the latter's sovereignty.[11] Although the PA did assume responsibility for collecting income tax, it could not choose its own trade regime or adopt trade policies according to Palestinian interests. In effect, the Paris Protocol managed to replicate many of the colonial dynamics that had existed since 1967.

Thus, in contrast to the civil institutions, which were actually handed over to the PA, enabling the new leadership to assume a limited independence, the Paris Protocol guaranteed that Israel would preserve its control in the economic sphere. This, as we will see, has had far-reaching implications, since the economy is one of the primary instruments through which modern societies are managed. Not only does the economy directly regulate the population while inscribing on individuals forms of usefulness, it also serves as the source of revenue for all the civil institutions employed to manage and administer the population, like the health care, educational, and welfare systems. The proper operation of these institutions is, in other words, dependent on the economy's proper performance.

As we will see momentarily, the specificities of the economic agreement alongside the harsh restrictions on movement that were imposed during the Oslo years had dire ramifications. Here it is important to stress that the dilapidated institutional infrastructure that the Palestinians inherited could not stand on its own two feet. Palestinian institutions and the economy had been prevented from developing, and their dependency on Israel had been fostered, and this was how the PA inherited them. In 1993, for example, the Israeli government spent an average of 44 shekels on development for each Palestinian in Gaza compared to an average of 2,100 shekels that it spent on every Israeli in 1991.[12] In the Gaza Strip children were studying in a two-shift system because of the lack of classrooms, and even then the number of pupils-per-classroom was often more than forty. The health system did not have the capacity to provide some of the most basic services, so when responsibilities were transferred from Israel to the Palestinians, there was not one certified oncologist in the Gaza Strip, which was home to eight hundred thousand people. In addition, none of the hospitals in the region had a CT scanner.[13] Anyone who was diagnosed with cancer or needed a CT scan had to be transferred to hospitals outside the Strip. To this day, medical treatments involving pediatric cardiology or neurosurgery, heart bypass, mouth and jaw surgery, and several other surgical procedures, as well as radiology therapy, eye operations, MRI scans, and bone marrow tests cannot be provided in the Gaza Strip.[14] Israel's instant abdication of all responsibility for the history of the occupation along with the Palestinian leadership's willingness to take on responsibility without investing sufficient thought in what such a course would entail sowed the seeds for the next series of contradictions. The way the Oslo process was carried out, in turn, suggests that while Israel helped create the PA as a means of managing the Palestinian inhabitants, it does not seem to have cared whether or not the PA succeeded in carrying out this task.

The Agreement on Preparatory Transfer of Powers and Responsibilities (August 1994) outlined the reorganization of power in two additional spheres: the judicial field and the security forces. Regarding the former, two issues are worth mentioning. First, the agreement specified that the PA could confirm only *secondary* legislation, which had to be consistent with the agreements and existing law, while the procedure for enacting the legislation gave the Israeli authorities an effective veto power. Thus, in reality the PA's legislative power was totally confined. Second, the legal stipulations did not give the PA any authority over Israeli citizens. This was a direct continuation of a pre-Oslo policy, whereby any Israeli civilian, and indeed any non-Palestinian, residing or traveling within the West Bank and Gaza Strip was subjected to Israeli civilian law. The existing situation was simply perpetuated in the agreement. The PA was denied any legal power over Israelis or Jews residing in or traveling through the OT, and this included Israelis entering the areas that according to the agreements were under the PA's jurisdiction. All of this underscores that the agreement ensured the subordinate judicial position of the PA in relation to Israel.

The Preparatory Agreement also announced the creation of a "strong police force," which was to consist of nine thousand policemen whose responsibility was to ensure "public order and internal security within the jurisdiction of the Palestinian Authority." The Palestinians were also given seven thousand light personal weapons, 120 machine guns, forty-five armored vehicles, communication systems, and distinctive uniforms, identification badges, and vehicle markings. The jurisdiction of the police force was, however, limited to the city of Jericho and to the Gaza Strip (excluding 40 percent of the land that was controlled by the Jewish settlers and Israeli military). Israel maintained monopoly over the legitimate use of violence in the OT, since it only gave the PA sole authority to police the Palestinian population in certain areas.

The Israeli-Palestinian Interim Agreement on the West Bank and the Gaza Strip (September 1995), also known as Oslo II, introduced three new issues pertinent to the Palestinian security forces. First, both the job description and makeup of the police were changed. In addition to "maintaining internal security and public order," the police also took on responsibility for "combating terrorism and violence, and preventing incitement to violence." In other words, they were not only responsible for ensuring order within Palestinian society, but also for combating paramilitary groups that threatened Israeli citizens. Second, the structure of the police force was also expanded from four branches to six, thus making it even more difficult to coordinate activities and increasing internal competition among the security apparatuses. Finally, the number of policemen grew from nine thousand to thirty thousand. The West Bank and Gaza Strip were accordingly transformed into zones where the ratio of police to civilians was among the highest in the world: about ten policemen per thousand civilians, three times higher than in most countries where the ratio is about 3.4 policemen per thousand civilians.

The creation of a strong Palestinian police force was crucial not only because it allowed the Israeli military to shed many of its former policing responsibilities, but also because such a force empowered the new governing body, which had taken upon itself a huge amount of civil responsibility with very few of the tools necessary to provide the services it promised to supply. The PA received weak civil institutions, a nonfunctioning economy, and was not allowed to introduce new legislation that could in any way alter the power relations between the new governing body and Israel. Regardless of how the PA itself functioned, the Oslo Accords themselves created the grounds for a crisis of legitimization. The loss of legitimacy in the public's eye led the PA to strengthen its police force even further, this time not so much to advance direct Israeli interests as to repress internal opposition.

RESTRUCTURING PALESTINIAN SPACE

One cannot fully understand the reorganization of power in the OT without considering the way the Oslo Accords restructured Palestinian space. As mentioned, the Oslo Accords preserved Israel's distinction between the Palestinians and their land. So while Israel transferred many of the responsibilities for managing the population to the PA, it retained direct control both over Palestinian space and over what John Torpey has called the "legitimate means of movement."[15] In order to accomplish this goal without being obvious, Israel restructured Palestinian space.

Oslo divided the West Bank into Areas A, B, and C, and designated areas H1 and H2 in Hebron, and Yellow and White Areas in Gaza.[16] Areas A, B, and C determined the distribution of powers in the West Bank by creating internal boundaries (see map 4). These boundaries produced a series of new "insides" and "outsides" within the OT, each one with its own specific laws and regulations. While in all three areas the PA assumed full responsibility for the civil institutions, in Area A, which in 1995 amounted to 3 percent of the West Bank's land and 26 percent of its population, the PA was given full responsibility for maintaining law and order; in Area B, which amounted to 24 percent of the land and 70 percent of the population, the PA was given responsibility for public order, but Israel maintained overriding responsibility for security; and in Area C, which comprised 73 percent of the land and 4 percent of the population, Israel retained full responsibility for security and public order as well as for civil issues relating to territory (planning and zoning, archeology, etc.). Thus, in 1995 the PA was responsible for

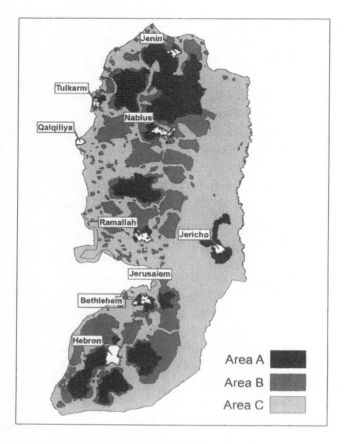

Map 4. Areas A, B, and C of the West Bank. Source: Peace Now.

managing all of the Palestinian inhabitants, but had full control of only 3 percent of the West Bank's land (i.e., the cities Jenin, Nablus, Tulkarem, Qalqiliya, Ramallah, Bethlehem, and Jericho). By 2000, following a series of agreements, the relative distribution of the areas had changed, so that Area A comprised 17.2 percent of the land, Area B 23.8 percent, and Area C 59 percent.[17] Yet area A was divided into 11 separate clusters, Area B was made up of 120 clusters, while the 59 percent that constituted Area C was contiguous.[18] The areas in which the Palestinians had full control were like an archipelago, while the areas controlled by Israel were strategic corridors that interrupted the territorial contiguity of the West Bank.

Israeli anthropologist and political activist Jeff Halper characterizes Oslo's spatial division as a matrix of control, whereby Israel has employed several apparatuses, only a few of which require physical occupation of territory, to control every aspect of Palestinian life in the OT. The matrix, he writes, works like the Japanese game of Go. Instead of defeating your opponent through ongoing confrontations as in chess, in Go you win by immobilizing your opponent, by gaining control of key points of a matrix, so that every time the opponent moves, she or he encounters an obstacle of some kind.[19] Accordingly, Israel created Jewish-only spaces in the form of settlements, industrial parks, and military bases, which were strategically dispersed throughout the OT and connected by a massive network of highways and bypass roads. It also erected road blocks and checkpoints to slice the Gaza Strip into two and at times three or four parts, hindering, when it wished, the legitimate movement of the Palestinian inhabitants from one part to the other. In the West Bank, Israel took advantage of the division of the region into three kinds of areas and the fact that Areas A and B, where the large majority of Palestinians reside, were not contiguous. During certain periods, the West Bank was split into more than two hundred enclaves, making it extremely difficult for the Palestinian residents to travel from one enclave to another.

Israel's control of space allowed it to maintain its monopoly over the legitimate means of movement. This included controlling the movement of the occupied inhabitants who wished to exit the OT as well as those who wished to move from the West Bank to the Gaza Strip (and vice versa), and, through the introduction of the *internal* closure, the movement of Palestinians inside each region was also restricted. In order to maintain its monopoly over the means of movement inside the OT, Israel relied on subtle and not-so-subtle bureaucratic and legal mechanisms that operated primarily through a series of permits and decrees backed by checkpoints, patrols, and the threat of violence.[20] In the midst of the Oslo process Israel built a fence around the Gaza Strip to ensure that all Gazans would be subjected to the closure and permit regime (during those years many workers succeeded in infiltrating into Israel from the West Bank despite closures). Within a relatively short period, a patrol road and a series of fences fifty-four kilometers long closed off the border between the Strip and Israel, leaving only four passageways connecting the two regions (two of which operate in one direction only, from Israel to Gaza) and one more connecting Gaza with Egypt.[21] The Green Line was accordingly converted from a "normally open" border into a "normally closed" one.[22] Only a very small number of Palestinian political leaders and businessmen whom Israel wanted to support and promote received permits to travel during closures.

The partition of space and the reorganization of power were intricately tied. The division of space within the OT not only determined the distribution of certain powers, but also allowed Israel to maintain the distinction between the Palestinian population and their land. For all practical purposes the internal borders dividing areas A, B, and C did not exist with respect to the operation of civil institutions providing health care, education, and welfare, since the PA took on full responsibility for the civil institutions serving the Palestinian population as a whole regardless of where people lived in the OT.[23] Thus, from 1994 onward, the PA relieved Israel of the most difficult aspect of the occupation, while Israel, in turn, kept most of the land and all of the water under its control. The specific organization of space and the transfer of authority over civil institutions to the PA reflects the beginning of a transformation from the principle of colonization to the principle of separation, where the latter does not mean the termination of control but rather its alteration from a system based on managing the lives of the occupied inhabitants to a system that is no longer interested in the lives of the Palestinian residents.

A DEMOCRATIC OCCUPATION

In addition to the reorganization of power and restructuring of space, the Oslo agreements reflect the significance that both parties attributed to the illusion of establishing full Palestinian sovereignty. I say "illusion" because it was clear that the traditional link between sovereign power and the notion of "supreme authority over a given territory" was not part of Oslo's agenda, and the creation of such a link was actually precluded by the agreements themselves. The reorganization of power and the division of the occupied space into small archipelagoes whose external borders were controlled by Israel ensured that the PA would not be sovereign in the sense of having a "monopoly over the legitimate use of violence within a given territory," or a "monopoly over the legitimate means of movement," or, in fact, in any other sense. This is precisely the performance of sovereignty that Derek Gregory discusses; the ruptured space of the OT was simulated as a coherent state.[24]

Even though the West Bank and the Gaza Strip did not become a real state, sovereignty had to be conjured to render the categories of political action meaningful. Moreover, if Israel continued to be conceived as the sovereign power, then people would realize that the occupation had never actually ended. This problem was dealt with in the Interim Agreement (September 1995), which discusses at length the plan for democratic elections in the OT. The important point in the context of our discussion is that the January 1996 elections, whereby the Palestinians chose both a president and legislative council, were also part and parcel of Oslo's controlling apparatuses. One of the elections' roles was to produce the impression that the Palestinians were electing a government that would have the powers to administer the population and that Israeli power was retreating. Their goal, in other words, was to create among Palestinians, Israelis, and outside spectators, a sense that the OT had been freed from foreign rule and that consequently the Palestinians could determine their own destiny. But, as we have seen, on the ground the Oslo agreements created mechanism after mechanism that allowed Israel to preserve its sovereignty, suggesting that the elections served, among other things, to mask Israeli involvement and influence in the OT and to conceal the reorganization of power and space.

THE IMMEDIATE EFFECTS

Initially, the reorganization of power and space produced the desired effects. A general quiet replaced the social unrest in the OT, permitting a sense of normalcy to take over. The nightly curfews in the Gaza Strip ended, children played in the streets, schools and universities were opened, as were coffee shops, restaurants, and new hotels. Many of those who had invested much time in the struggle against the Israeli military turned to securing a stable income for their families. For a while the OT experienced a construction boom, particularly in Gaza and Ramallah, and money was invested in infrastructure, while numerous cooperation projects between Palestinian and Israeli businesses helped produce an atmosphere of peace. And although three thousand Palestinians remained in jails, the majority of the political prisoners were released by 1996.[25]

There was also a sharp decline in the number of Palestinians killed by Israeli security forces (see figure 4). In 1996, for example, 18 Palestinians

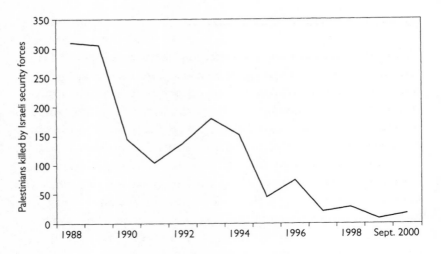

Figure 4. Number of Palestinians killed during first intifada and the Oslo years. Source: B'Tselem.

were killed in the OT in comparison to 155 in 1993. The number of children killed also dropped dramatically. During the three- year period 1994–96, 35 children were killed, while in 1993 alone, 40 children were killed, and in 1989, 78 children were killed.[26] The change in the lives of the Palestinians had quite a bit to do with the redeployment of the Israeli military, which, in turn, reduced the price Israel had to pay for the occupation, both politically and economically.

Oslo, it is important to stress, managed to undo the intifada's most important achievements. If the intifada undermined almost all forms of normalization and exposed the occupation for what it was—that is, military rule upheld through violence and violation—Oslo succeeded in normalizing the occupation once again. Moreover, the creation of the PA led to the disappearance of vigorous popular and civil movements that had been the mainstay of the first intifada. As Reema Hamami and Salim Tamari point out, popular committees, neighborhood committees, mass organizations, and most of the political movements that sustained them began to collapse toward the end of the intifada due to Israeli anti-insurgency methods, and their recovery was preempted by the Oslo agreements and the ostensible state-formation process.[27]

One of the interesting aspects concerning the reorganization of power and the restructuring of space is that it affected the Israeli and Palestinian populations very differently. As Israel redeployed its troops and shed its responsibility for managing the lives of the occupied Palestinians, its economy received a boost. The Israeli tourist industry was revitalized, large investments began pouring in, and new international markets that had been closed due to the conflict gradually opened to Israeli commodities and services. Between 1994 and 2000, per capita GDP rose from $16,076 to $18,363 (see figure 5). It is therefore not surprising that Israeli economists of all stripes constantly praised the Oslo process, underscoring the substantial "dividends" that Israel gained by "investing in peace."[28] Even though the general prosperity was occasionally disturbed by attacks on Israeli targets, particularly in 1995 and 1996 when several suicide bombers exploded themselves on public buses and in shopping malls, killing scores of Israelis and wounding hundreds more, in general the Israeli citizenry considered the Oslo agreements advantageous. Oslo was regarded as the beginning of true peace.

On the other side of the Green Line, Oslo's fruits had a very different taste. The reorganization of power and space had repercussions that totally transformed the regimentation of daily life. Instead of prosperity, the Palestinians experienced poverty, and instead of freedom, they experienced new restrictions — both of which ultimately rendered them weaker and more vulnerable. Some of these effects were a direct consequence of the agreements themselves, while others were a result of the contradictions precipitated by the agreements. In sharp contrast to the optimistic forecasts regarding Oslo's economic benefits as well as the developments taking place within Israel, the Palestinian economy shrank dramatically following the transfer of authority to the PA. Whereas Israel's GNP rapidly rose, in the West Bank and Gaza the per capita GNP fell by 37 percent from the end of 1992 to the end of 1997, while per capita GDP shrank from $1,625 in 1994 to $1,563 in 2000 (see figure 5).[29]

In chapter 3, I described how Israel had prevented the creation of an internal economic base with its own productive capacity, showing how the economic growth experienced by the Palestinians in the OT between 1967

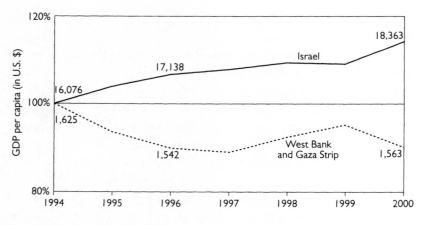

Figure 5. Changes in Israeli and Palestinian per capita GDP during the Oslo years. 1994=100. Source: World Bank data.

and 1980 was a consequence of the remittances sent from Palestinian workers abroad and the salaries of laborers who commuted to Israel. The expectation that the OT would experience economic growth following Oslo was therefore based on the assumption that there would be large investments in infrastructure and industry and that the Palestinians would enjoy freedom of movement for themselves and their goods. It was also assumed that Palestinian laborers would continue to work in Israel and pump money into the OT, while an independent, productive economy would slowly be established. These expectations never materialized.

The backward march had begun even before Oslo. In 1991, as mentioned, many Palestinians working in the Gulf States lost their jobs due to Yasser Arafat's support for Saddam Hussein, a development that further increased the OT's dependency on the laborers who commuted to Israel. In addition, a couple of years earlier the entry-permit regime had been introduced, and during Oslo it was not only preserved but tightened, severely limiting the number of workers who could enter Israel. More importantly, the closure that had begun as a sporadic form of control in 1991 became more frequent and comprehensive over the years, and justified as a legitimate response to terrorist attacks carried out by Palestinian militants who opposed the Oslo Accords.[30] In 1994, the occupied territories were under closure for 43 days; in 1996, the territories were closed off for 104 days; and in 1997, for 87 days.[31] The internal closures had dire results. NGOs estimated that for the duration of each internal closure about two hundred thousand Palestinians (i.e., 80 percent of the labor force) were prevented from reaching their workplaces.[32]

The fact that the Palestinian economy was dependent on laborers who commuted to Israel and that these laborers, in turn, were dependent on the occupying power's readiness to allow them to enter Israel was exploited by Israel during the early 1990s to advance numerous objectives. During Oslo, the restriction of movement, and particularly Israel's control over the flow of Palestinian labor, became its most prominent form of control, overshadowing, as it were, the torture, beatings, and incarceration. Israel used its ability to restrict the flow of laborers to collectively punish the Palestinian public, hoping that such measures would turn the public against the armed resistance; it used its ability to restrict Palestinian movement to pressure the PA to clamp down on Hamas, Islamic Jihad, the PFLP, and other groups that opposed Oslo, as well as to incarcerate people whom Israel characterized as terrorists. It also exploited its capacity to regulate the flow of laborers into Israel as a way of bending the PA's arm during negotiations so that the PA would comply with numerous Israeli demands, like signing the Paris Protocol, which was inimical to Palestinian interests.

The restriction of movement engendered, however, a series of excesses that had far-reaching implications for the Oslo process. For instance, it immediately led to an exponential rise in unemployment. Whereas in 1992 some 30 percent of the Palestinian workforce was employed in Israel, in 1996 that figure had fallen to 7 percent, and the average rate of unemployment in the territories reached 32.6 percent, rising twelvefold from the 3 percent unemployment rate in 1992. During periods of comprehensive closures, unemployment reached a peak of 70 percent in the Gaza Strip and 50 percent in the West Bank, with people from the refugee camps suffering most because the large majority of them depended on work in Israel.[33]

In addition to its direct effect on the workforce, the closure policy also impeded Palestinian exports to Israel and other countries, dealing a death blow to the more lucrative agricultural exports such as flowers and to new — that is, Oslo-made — factories that produced goods intended for European markets. Simply put, the new Palestinian industrialists could not commit themselves to providing the goods on time, and the contracts they had signed with foreign companies and markets were rapidly annulled. The closure policy also created a severance between the Gaza Strip and the West Bank, greatly reducing trade between the two regions and harming Palestinian agriculture and industry by preventing Palestinians from exploiting the relative advantages of each area. Whereas prior to the imposition of the closures approximately 50 percent of goods produced in Gaza were marketed in the West Bank, in 1995 that figure stood at only 8 percent.[34] The entry-permit regime and closures also affected patients who required medical treatment in Israel, and students from Gaza who studied in the West Bank, as well as residents who needed to exit the region for a variety of other reasons.[35]

The economic decline, however, was not only a result of Israel's restriction of Palestinian movement. The Paris Protocol enabled Israel to control the economy in several other ways. For instance, due to the customs union created between Israel and the PA, the Israeli government collected taxes on merchandise destined for Gaza and the West Bank, and only after the tax money went through a "clearance" mechanism was it transferred to the PA. According to the World Bank, these taxes represented up to two-thirds of total Palestinian revenue—a sum amounting to some US$740 million in 2005, or approximately 13 percent of gross disposable income.[36] The continued control of these funds enabled Israel to use them as political leverage. Following a wave of violent attacks in the summer of 1997, the Israeli government decided—in contradiction to the Paris Protocol—to withhold the taxes.[37] The idea was to engender internal pressure by targeting the PA's hundred and fifty thousand workers, whose salaries depended on this money. This included the salaries of the security forces, which employed well over thirty thousand people, as well as the salaries of the workers in the different civil institutions over which the PA had assumed responsibility, including the health, educational, and social welfare systems, the municipalities, and the different government ministries.

The number of public employees is in itself an issue worth emphasizing. The PA employed almost nine times more people than the eighteen thousand Palestinians who worked for the Civil Administration before the transfer of authority in 1993. Even though many of these hundred and fifty thousand workers offered important services, the vast majority of them did not contribute directly to Palestinian productive capacity. More importantly in the context of our discussion, they owed their jobs to the PA, which, like Jordan in the early 1970s, utilized its prerogative to employ people as a way of producing allegiances through patronage, salaries, and prestige. Yet, with the benefits of employing many people also comes the responsibility of paying their salaries. Before Oslo, the Civil Administration was relatively consistent about paying salaries, even during times of strife, knowing that withholding salaries would create more social unrest. After Oslo, the Palestinian public servants no longer worked for the Civil Administration, but Israel continued to control their salaries, albeit in a roundabout way, by controlling the PA's cash flow. The threat of withholding money was often used to pressure the PA to act according to Israeli demands. The fact that Israel controlled the salaries of a hundred and fifty thousand people rather than eighteen thousand gave it more leverage.

The restriction of movement during the Oslo years along with the custom union agreement established in the Paris Protocol led to the deterioration of the Palestinian economy. To be sure, the PA's corruption had a detrimental impact on the economic situation, but its effect was minor when compared to the impact of the restrictions Israel imposed on the OT. The economic deterioration directly affected the occupied population's standard of living, and the consumption of basic products, such as food, clothing, and education, declined dramatically. By the end of 1998, more than 25 percent of the Palestinians in the OT were living under the international $2.10 a day poverty line. In the Gaza Strip, where a significantly larger percentage of the population had worked in Israel, the poverty rate rose from 36 percent at the end of 1995 to 41 percent at the end of 1997.[38] Thus, one of the effects of the harsh restrictions on movement employed during Oslo as well as the economic agreements was the strangulation of the economy, which transformed, in turn, a large percentage of Palestinians into paupers.

ABANDONING THE INDIVIDUAL

It is important to stress that while Israel used both the entry-permit regime and the closures during Oslo, the two forms of control operate differently, and it is not coincidental that the closures ultimately replaced the entry-permit regime as the more prominent form of movement control. While the entry-permit regime impeded the movement of the vast majority of the population, those who did apply for the permit had to measure up to ostensibly neutral, exclusionary demographic criteria (age, marital status, number of children, etc.) as well as criteria that assessed each person's individual comportment and excluded all those who had participated in some form of resistance against Israeli rule or had links to people who were part of the resistance. Those who fell within the parameters of the demographic profile and behaved according to Israel's rules could receive permits, while those who were in any way politically active could not.

The closure, by contrast, did not attempt to manage the individual but was used solely as a mechanism of collective punishment and as leverage for pressuring the population as well as the PA; although it was justified as a measure against Palestinian terrorism, in reality it was not a response to a particular event or threat but a sweeping restriction, largely permanent, and, according to the Israeli rights group B'Tselem, "only marginally affected by the security establishment's assessment of the level of security threats at any given time."[39] It also ignored the permit regime, so that even workers who had received a permit to enter Israel could not cross the checkpoints when the closure was imposed. Quickly, a new situation emerged whereby the number of permits issued did not in any way reflect the number of people who actually entered Israel, since all movement was arrested by the closure. Thus, the closure marks Israel's abandonment of any attempt to discipline Palestinians as individuals. Indeed, the effort to inscribe "usefulness" onto the Palestinian body, which is characteristic of all forms of management in modern societies and was part of the strategy employed by Israel in the OT for many years, was gradually abandoned during Oslo.

This, as I show in the next chapter, prepared the ground for the politics of death Israel adopted during the second intifada. Israel's indifference towards the individual inhabitants is intricately tied to and informed by the way Israel modified its use of the Palestinian economy as a form of control. Undoubtedly, the occupying power was always acutely aware of the impact an economic catastrophe would have on the management of the population. At the beginning of the occupation, Israeli decision makers considered economic deterioration in the OT to be a certain ingredient for social unrest, and accordingly attempted to produce economic prosperity through a series of techniques that aimed to normalize the occupation. Yet, instead of continuing its approach of guaranteeing some kind of livelihood in the OT as it had done in the past, Israel exploited the Palestinian dependency to create an economic crisis, knowing full well that this would engender social unrest. The social unrest, however, was not directed solely toward Israel, as it would have been before Oslo; it was also directed against the new PA, which had assumed responsibility for the population and was therefore, in the public's eyes, also responsible for the sharp decline in the standard of living.

While Israel outsourced responsibility to the PA so that the PA could manage the Palestinian population in Israel's stead, it continued to control Palestinian space and resources. Ultimately, however, the effects of Israel's strategy produced an internal contradiction that helped undermine the PA's legitimacy in the eyes of the Palestinian public.

We saw that Oslo entailed the creation of a strong Palestinian security apparatus. The armed forces' main task was not to guarantee the security of the occupied inhabitants from external attacks or from the occupying power, but to maintain law and order within the West Bank and the Gaza Strip and to protect Israel's citizens from Palestinian militants. Prime Minister Yitzchak Rabin made this blatantly clear when he noted that PA security personnel operated throughout the West Bank with "Israel's knowledge and in cooperation with Israel's security forces to safeguard Israel's security interests."[40] Israel accordingly implemented a policy of "security cooperation" with the PA, working closely with the Palestinian armed forces both directly and through the CIA. The latter provided instruction, training, and a regular supply of security equipment to the Preventative Security organs in both the West Bank and Gaza Strip (headed by Jibril Rajoub and Mohammed Dahlan, respectively) and to the General Intelligence (under the leadership of Amin El Hindi).[41] The security forces shared information and often assisted each other in the daily routine of achieving law and order.

Over the years the Palestinian security forces grew in size, and their numbers soared well above the thirty thousand mark specified in the agreements. Israel did not veto or condemn such developments because the different security apparatuses were, at least ostensibly, serving its interests. As Graham Usher points out, under Oslo the PA's security forces were obligated to "arrest and prosecute" Palestinians "suspected of perpetuating acts of violence and terror" and "cooperate in the exchange of information as well as coordinate policies and activities" with the Israeli security services.[42] Already in 1994, Israeli military officers reported that they had received orders to allow Palestinian security personal to carry weapons in a refugee camp that was under Israeli authority. These officers were told that the Palestinian security services were "friendly forces," and they were directed to allow the armed Palestinians to operate in the camp. Put differently, even in areas where Israel was, according to the official agreements, responsible for security, it permitted Palestinian forces to police the population and to ensure public order.[43] The cooperation between the Israeli and Palestinian security forces was spelled out in the 1998 Wye Memorandum Agreement, which stated that the collaboration between the services was to be informed by the notion of "zero tolerance for terror." The agreement proclaimed that "the Palestinian side will apprehend the specific individuals suspected of perpetrating acts of violence and terror for the purpose of further investigation, and prosecution and punishment of all persons involved in acts of violence and terror."[44] According to B'Tselem, the security provisions made at Wye created a framework allowing for torture, arbitrary arrests, and unfair trials. This, the rights group claims, has resulted in increased human rights violations by different organs of the PA.[45]

Wye institutionalized the pressure exerted by Israel and the United States on the PA to fight Palestinian opposition relentlessly. More than once Israel conditioned the resumption of peace negotiations, the opening of borders, and the implementation of troop redeployment upon proof of concrete actions taken by the PA. These actions included mass and arbitrary detentions, imprisonment without trial, torture, and the denial of the right to due process. So while the international media concentrated on the "revolving door" practice, whereby Palestinian security forces caught residents suspected of assaulting Israeli targets and then released them, the press had very little to say about the fact that Palestinians were tortured by the PA and imprisoned without fair trial. The security forces were mainly criticized by Palestinians from the West Bank and Gaza, who saw no reason to create such a large security apparatus, surely not one whose sole role was to police the population, clamp down on all forms of resistance to the occupation, and abuse the inhabitants' rights.

Simultaneously, the restriction of movement and economic deterioration also helped undermine the PA, because the civil institutions that it now operated could not offer adequate services to the population. Consider, for a moment, the Palestinian health care system. In 1993, right before the transfer of authority to Palestinian hands, the Civil Administration's annual per capita expenditure on health was $33.80. In 1996, due to a large amount of foreign aid, per capita governmental expenditure on health had risen by almost 25 percent to $42.70. Yet, by 2000 it had declined to $30.40, much lower than the expenditure in 1996, and even 10 percent lower than the amount spent when the Civil Administration was still responsible for providing health services.[46] This clearly suggests that the services offered in 2000, the year in which the second intifada erupted, were even poorer than those offered in 1993 by the Civil Administration and intimates that the civil institutions through which modern societies are managed, in this case the health care system, were actually weakened during Oslo. Even though the PA dramatically increased the number of public servants, it did not improve the services it offered Palestinian society.

Moreover, the total per capita health expenditure (governmental and nongovernmental) in 2000 was $121, indicating that governmental expenditure comprised only about 25 percent of the money spent on health. By comparison, in Israel per capita expenditure on health in 2000 was $1,609, of which 70 percent was government-funded.[47] Not only were the funds spent on health care totally inadequate, thus compromising the quality of services offered to the population, but, as opposed to the Israeli health system, the Palestinian one was totally dependent on the nongovernmental sector. This was surely part of the inheritance of the first twenty-seven years of occupation, since during that period the nongovernmental sector was developed by Palestinians in order to fill acute needs that were not being met by the Civil Administration. The situation did not change, however, following Oslo, because, under the auspices of the World Bank, the PA initiated an aggressive policy of rapid privatization.[48] The fact that almost 75 percent of the expenditure on health came from the nongovernmental sector underscores the frailty of government institutions. Thus, one of the consequences of the economic crisis in the OT, which was due mainly to Israel's ongoing control of space and the restriction of movement, was the reduction of the PA's capacity to administer the population through forms of control informed by disciplinary and biopower. As we will see, the absence of a sturdy governmental structure also made it relatively easy for competing forces to take over once the second intifada erupted.

Accordingly, the analysis of how Israel outsourced its forms of control reveals three processes: (1) Israel transferred full responsibility for managing the lives of the occupied inhabitants to the PA; (2) it put to work forms of control that undermined the PA's efforts to fulfill its responsibilities toward the inhabitants; and (3) it armed the PA so that its security forces could preserve law and order by confronting attempts to resist the new political order. This is not to say that the PA was untainted: there is concrete evidence pertaining to the embezzlement of funds, nepotism, mismanagement, and general corruption. However, Israel's unwillingness to take responsibility for the legacy of the occupation, along with the restrictions of movement, the Paris Protocol, and the pressure to privatize basic government services (pressure exerted by the World Bank and other international institutions) all made it practically impossible for the Palestinian leadership to adequately operate the civil institutions needed in order to achieve normalization. A picture of control emerges whereby Israel's subcontractor was drained of any real capacity to operate the civil institutions through which modern societies are administered, while it was simultaneously armed to police the occupied population.

Paradoxically, then, the PA itself, as a governing body, could not provide many basic services to its citizenry, and within a short period it too began emphasizing forms of control informed by sovereign power. The PA's deployment of coercive measures against Palestinian inhabitants alongside looming allegations of corruption led to its de-legitimization. The loss of legitimacy had two important implications: first, it further increased the PA's need or willingness to employ the sword; second, the reduction of its power as an independent political actor rendered it more susceptible to making concessions when negotiating with Israel. In other words, *Israel created the conditions whereby the PA would bow down to its demands, but the very same conditions undermined its ability to manage the population, which had been the original reason for its creation.* As the PA began experiencing a legitimization crisis, it further expanded its security forces both as a way of increasing patronage and in order to protect itself from the frustrated population, all of which augmented the crisis of legitimization and further deepened the contradictions. The general effect of Israel's strategy was that the PA was disempowered. This, in many respects, serves as the backdrop for the second intifada and for the rise of Hamas. And yet a vital part of the puzzle is still missing. In order to better understand why the Palestinians filled the streets in September 2000, one also needs to consider how Oslo affected Israel's settlement project.

SETTLEMENTS, SETTLERS, AND BYPASS ROADS

Along with the processes just described, in the seven-year period leading to the eruption of the second intifada, Israel also fortified its settlement project. It is both ironic and telling that even as the Jewish settlers rejected Oslo, the Oslo years were by far the best years for the settlement enterprise. The Jewish population living in the West Bank increased during Oslo from about a hundred and ten thousand in 1993 to a hundred and ninety-five thousand in 2000. The graph (figure 6) depicts the increase in the number of Jewish settlers in the West Bank during four periods. During the first thirteen years, 12,500 settlers moved to the West Bank. This number was augmented by 45,400 in the seven-year period from 1980 to 1986, and by an additional 53,000 settlers during the following seven years. During Oslo's seven years, the West Bank's settler population grew by 80,700, much more than in any of the previous periods. Together with the population in the Gaza Strip (excluding east Jerusalem), the number reached 195,000.[49] To house the new settlers about twenty thousand apartments were built, almost doubling the number of Jewish housing units that had been built during the first twenty-six years of occupation.[50] In addition, Israel dramatically expanded the network of bypass roads in order to connect these new settlers both to Israel proper and to other settlements. Approximately four hundred kilometers of roads were paved across the West Bank during Oslo.[51] In 1995, the construction of new West Bank roads peaked, constituting more than 20 percent of all road construction in Israel for that year.

It is often said that during Oslo Israel only fortified old settlements and did not build new ones, but this too was not the case. Actually, from late 1992 until 2001, between 71 and 102 new Jewish outposts were established in the West Bank (see map 5).[52] Thus, during the Oslo years, the Israeli government was not only transferring thousands of citizens to the OT, but was also continuously creating new settlements. The outposts are a concrete manifestation of the temporary and arbitrary modalities of control. There is no master plan that determines where they are to be established; they are erected according to local initiatives based on circumstances and opportunity. And while the tents and prefabricated homes serve, as Weizman points out, the needs of immediacy, mobility, and flexibility, since they can be quickly erected under cover of night, these same features also create the impression that the outposts are provisional and random.[53] The "temporary" outposts, which are now dispersed throughout the West Bank, should be understood as a straightforward modification of a previous strategy.

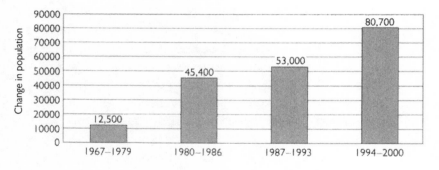

Figure 6. Increase in the number of Jewish settlers in the West Bank during four periods between 1967 and 2000. Source: Yehezkel Lein, *Land Grab: Israel's Settlement Policy in the West Bank* (Jerusalem: B'Tselem, 2002).

In a 2005 report, written for the Israeli government, Talia Sasson describes in great detail how the "illegal outposts" were established with the support of several government agencies, including a number of ministries and the Civil Administration. Even though these settlements were continually presented in the media as if they were the creations of individual settlers who were defying both the rule of law and the wishes of the Israeli government, the report reveals many of the intricate forms of cooperation between government agencies and the settlers, showing that the presentation of the latter as recalcitrant actors who disregard the government and operate against Israeli policy continues to be a fabrication. This suggests, in turn, that as the military redeployed its troops during the Oslo years, the settlers took on an ever-increasing policing role.

The expansion of the settlement project is revealing. On the one hand, it counters the dominant description of the Oslo years. If the basis of the agreements between Israel and the Palestinians was indeed the withdrawal of Israeli sovereignty and the creation of a Palestinian state — or, as some would have it, land for peace — then one would have expected Israel to stop settling more Jews and building new settlements in the OT. Since Oslo was a process based on phases, the ongoing fortification of the settlement project is illogical. On the other hand, if Oslo is not conceived as the withdrawal of Israeli power, but rather as the reorganization of power, then the expansion of the settlement project makes perfect sense.

Map 5. Jewish settlements and outposts. Source: Peace Now.

CONCLUSION

Even though the Oslo process was portrayed as the beginning of the end of the occupation, the preceding analysis underscores that the Oslo framework actually preserved one of the central contradictions informing the occupation: the distinction between the Palestinian inhabitants and their land. The Palestinians were given responsibility for all the modern civil institutions through which populations are managed, administered, and disciplined, while Israel continued to control most of the territory it had occupied in 1967. As we saw, Israel also maintained its monopoly over the legitimate use of violence and the legitimate means of movement in the OT, while granting the PA authority to use violence in order to fulfill the task of securing law and order among the Palestinian population.

The changes on the ground signify two major modifications in Israel's strategy. First, during the Oslo years Israel began moving from direct control to remote control, using the PA as an apparatus to manage the population. As we will see in the following chapter, Israel constantly developed the forms of indirect control, using sophisticated technology both to monitor and strike at Palestinian society.[54] Second, Israel's withdrawal from a politics of life, whereby it considered itself responsible for administering the lives of the occupied inhabitants, to a politics that focuses on the population at large and disregards individual life has had far-reaching implications. It means, among other things, the development of strategies that produce vulnerabilities or crises in order to control the Palestinian population and its leadership.[55] These changes point to a deeper modification, whereby the colonial project in which the Palestinian population is managed and exploited, its land confiscated, and its water expropriated was being replaced by the principle of separation, where control is still crucial, but it no longer entails the economic exploitation of the population and the direct administration of each individual's life. Instead of reconnecting the inhabitants to their land, Oslo engendered further fissures, and instead of empowerment, Oslo came to symbolize a gradual reduction of popular power. Palestinians began to understand that their ability to influence the decisions that most affected them actually diminished during Oslo, as the contradictory effects arising from Israel's forms of control became more and more manifest. Oslo's contradictions, in other words, were the impetus and propelling force underlying the second intifada.

Chapter 8 | THE SEPARATION PRINCIPLE

Us here, them there.

Prime Minister EHUD BARAK

People who do not move in a container of some sort are
difficult to constrain, and the effort to restrict them may
entail turning the area to be controlled itself into a
container.

JOHN TORPEY

In an attempt to affirm Israeli sovereignty over Jerusalem's Temple Mount/ Haram al Sharif, Ariel Sharon strode into the Al-Aqsa compound on September 28, 2000, guarded by an armed entourage. Right after the provocative visit, Palestinian demonstrators hurled stones at Israeli police, who fired back tear gas and rubber-coated metal bullets. Twenty-five policemen and three Palestinians were injured in the confrontations. The next day, demonstrations erupted at the Temple Mount following the Friday prayers; rapidly, they spread to the West Bank and Gaza Strip. Within two days fifteen Palestinians had been killed. Sharon's visit to the Al-Aqsa compound had served as a trigger for the outbreak of the second, much bloodier, intifada.

Six years later, 3,808 Palestinians and 1,010 Israelis have been killed, many of them children.[1] In the West, Yasser Arafat was blamed for instigating the uprising. Many people claimed that the Palestinian president was attempting to gain by force what he had not managed to accomplish by peaceful means at the Camp David negotiations, which had ended just two months earlier (July 25, 2000).[2] While Israel no doubt made an unprecedented offer to the Palestinians at Camp David, it neglected several elements essential to any comprehensive settlement, including the contiguity of the Palestinian state in the West Bank, full sovereignty in Arab parts of East Jerusalem, and a compromise resolution on the right of return of Palestinian refugees.[3]

Arafat rejected the offer, and—according to the narrative concocted by Israel and the Clinton Administration—he decided to send his people to war, and they, like a herd, obediently complied. Such a position not only fails to take into account Camp David's shortcomings, but conveniently disregards the second intifada's structural backdrop and advances a paternalistic interpretation of events. It ignores the inherent contradictions characterizing the Oslo agreements and the effects of Israel's continuing occupation, including the economic crisis in the OT, the establishment of more Jewish settlements, the severe restriction of movement, and daily humiliations. The previous chapter helped uncover some of the central processes leading to the eruption of the second intifada, and suggested that the pent-up anger and despair were directed not only toward Israel, but also toward the Palestinian Authority (PA).

The second popular uprising turned out, however, to be very different from the one that took place during the late 1980s and early 1990s. Simply put, it was much more violent and consequently involved less popular participation. Many commentators placed the blame for the violence on the Palestinians, asserting that Israel made the fatal error of providing the Palestinians with weapons, and the Palestinians made the mistake of using these weapons against Israel. To be sure, during the second intifada the Palestinians used firearms, and suicide bombers increased the level of violence, but the different forms of Palestinian resistance, however ruthless, only partially explain the differences between the two intifadas.

As it turns out, Israel was, to a large extent, responsible for transforming the intifada, which began as a popular uprising into a violent resistance carried out by small groups that often adopted methods of terror. In June 2004, almost four years after the intifada erupted, *Ha'aretz* journalist Akiva Eldar revealed that the top Israeli security echelons had decided to "fan the flames" during the uprising's first weeks. He cites Amos Malka, who was the military general in charge of intelligence at the time, saying that during the intifada's first month, when the uprising was still mostly characterized by nonviolent popular protests, the military fired 1.3 million bullets in the West Bank and Gaza Strip. The idea was to intensify the levels of violence, thinking that this would lead to a swift and decisive military victory and the successful suppression of the rebellion.[4] Israel's armed forces did not, however, manage to contain the uprising, but they did kill more than 270 Palestinians within the uprising's first three months, almost the same amount as those killed during the first intifada's most intensive year of confrontations.[5]

The use of lethal force by the Israeli military should not, however, be considered as an isolated tactic aimed at achieving a particular objective (i.e., quelling the uprising). Rather, Israel's lethal response merely reflects a much wider shift that began taking root during the Oslo years. It underscores that by the turn of the new millennium, Israel had almost totally abandoned forms of control whose goal was to manage the lives of the Palestinian inhabitants residing in the West Bank and Gaza Strip, and was also reluctant to allow the PA to continue administering the occupied population. The difference between Israel's decision to distribute clubs and Rabin's "break their bones" policy from the first intifada and the firing of a million bullets during the second uprising's first month signifies a change in the primary principle informing Israel's occupation, that is, a shift from the principle of colonization to the principle of separation. While I describe these two principles as one following the other, it is crucial to remember that they actually contaminate each other so that there is always a trace of one in the other.

FROM COLONIZATION TO SEPARATION

By "colonization principle" I mean a form of government whereby the colonizer attempts to manage the lives of the colonized inhabitants while exploiting the captured territory's resources (in this case, land, water, and labor).[6] Colonial powers do not conquer for the sake of imposing administrative rule on the indigenous population, but they end up managing the conquered inhabitants in order to facilitate the extraction of resources.

After the 1967 War, Israel assumed responsibility for the Palestinian residents, and tried to normalize the occupation by undertaking the administration of the major civil institutions through which modern societies are managed: education, health care, welfare, and the financial and legal systems. The Palestinian inhabitants were considered to be extremely important objects of management and control, and during the first two decades of occupation Israel attempted to rule the population in primarily nonviolent ways. Simultaneously, it began exploiting the labor force and expropriating Palestinian land and water, the most important natural resources in the region. My claim is that at a certain point during the first intifada, Israel realized that the colonization principle could no longer be used as the basic logic informing its control of the West Bank and Gaza Strip, and began looking for a new principle that would allow it to uphold the occupation. The desire to normalize the occupation and successfully annihilate the Palestinian national movement through a series of disciplinary forms of control that were supported when need be by the sword proved to be unrealistic. It took a few years before a clear policy took shape, but eventually the separation principle was adopted. As opposed to the colonization principle, which was rarely discussed, the separation principle has been talked about incessantly. The paradigmatic sentence describing this principle is "We are here, they are there." The "we" refers to Israelis, and the "they" to Palestinians.

If the colonization principle reflects the logic of the occupation, the separation principle ostensibly offers a solution to the occupation (this is the way it is often conceived in Israeli public discourse). The key word here is *ostensibly*. If truth be told, then the second principle does not aim to solve the occupation, but rather to alter its logic. In other words, "We are here, they are there," does not signify a withdrawal of Israeli power from the OT, but is used to blur the fact that Israel has been reorganizing its power in the territories in order to continue its control over their resources.[7] As I argued in the previous chapter, the Oslo Accords, which were the direct result of the first intifada as well as the changing political and economic circumstances in the international realm, signified the *reorganization* of power rather than its withdrawal, and should be understood as the continuation of the occupation by other means.

The difference then between the colonization and separation principles is that while the first is interested in both the people and their resources, even though it treats them as separate entities, the second is only interested in the resources and does not in any way assume responsibility for the people. Insofar as this is the case, the primary contradiction (i.e., the attempt to separate the people and their land) remains intact under the separation principle, since this principle does not entail severing the link between power and the occupied space, but only modifies the relation between the two as well as the relation between power and the occupied inhabitants.

As the separation principle took over, Israel began to lose all interest in the Palestinians living under occupation (except for those in the seam zones and along borders) and changed the forms of violence it used and the methods of controlling Palestinian space. This entailed a radical de-emphasis of disciplinary power and the accentuation of a particular kind of sovereign power, which in many respects disregards the law. While these changes may appear to be unconnected and arbitrary, an internal logic informed by the principle of separation was governing them.

VIOLENCE

A few weeks after the intifada broke out, Israeli journalist Amira Hass published a chilling interview with an Israeli sniper. "Every day before we go out they define the regulations for opening fire," the sniper told Hass. The regulations "change from place to place," and it was not coincidental that after a Palestinian mob hacked and burned two Israeli reservists to death in Ramallah, "the orders for opening fire were far more lenient than they had been the day before," the sniper said. The sniper's commanders often held back trigger-happy conscripts, particularly after the outpouring of condemnation for the killing of Mohammed al-Dura, a Gazan boy shot dead in his father's arms in front of TV cameras.[8] "You don't shoot at a child who is twelve or younger," he said, while adding that "twelve and up is allowed. He is not a child anymore; he is already after his bar mitzvah."[9]

The sniper's account highlights the change in Israel's open-fire regulations, a change that would be well documented by the Israeli human rights organization B'Tselem a couple of years later.[10] Until the outbreak of the second intifada, the open-fire regulations in the OT were based on Israel's penal code, which indicated that soldiers were allowed to fire live ammunition in only two situations: when they were in real and immediate, life-threatening danger, and during the apprehension of a suspect. To be sure, during the first intifada Israeli soldiers at times fired live ammunition when they were not threatened, but the extent of the phenomenon was restricted, and the number of Palestinians killed in this way was relatively limited.[11] When the second intifada began, the military defined the events in the OT as an "armed conflict short of war," and thus expanded the range of situations in which soldiers are permitted to open fire. The new version of the open-fire regulations has been kept secret, yet B'Tselem suggests that the regulations permit, at least in some instances, the firing of live ammunition even in cases when there is no immediate, life-threatening danger to members of the security forces or civilians. As we will see later in this chapter, the military also granted immunity to virtually every soldier who opened fire, regardless of the circumstances.[12] B'Tselem concludes that the new open-fire policy "has unavoidably resulted in a situation in which shooting at innocent Palestinians has practically become a routine."[13]

But the vague open-fire regulations disclose only one facet of the change in the methods of violence Israel began using after September 2000. Another feature of the change has involved the use of extrajudicial executions. On November 9, six weeks after the intifada's eruption, an Israeli military helicopter hovered over the village of Beit Sahur near Bethlehem as Hussein Abayat, a local Fatah militant, was driving his jeep in the village's main street. Suddenly, the helicopter fired an anti-tank missile at the jeep. The enormous explosion killed Hussein Abayat as well as two other women who were passing by and injured three others. The particular way this extrajudicial execution was carried out marked the beginning of a new strategy. Up until August 2006 the assassination policy has led to the death of 335 Palestinians, more than 200 of whom were children, women, and men who were, according to Israel's own assessment, bystanders.[14] Israel, in other words, has transformed the West Bank and Gaza Strip into the international military complex's lab for aerial assassinations.

Israel created a data bank made up of Palestinians it considers to be terrorists or political leaders of certain organizations; and every time it has had an opportunity to kill someone on the list—and regards the timing as politically advantageous—it has done so. While the assassination policy is, in fact, the continuation of a long-established practice, this was the first time that Israel had officially acknowledged its use of extrajudicial executions.[15] The assassinated Palestinians are killed without trial and without a fair legal process, which presumes innocence until guilt is proven. Rather, they are sentenced to death, with no opportunity to defend themselves or to appeal the sentence.[16] A legal analysis of the assassinations indeed suggests that in most cases Israel did not abide by either international human rights law or humanitarian law.[17] This, in turn, reveals a transformation in Israel's relation to the law following the outbreak of the second intifada, namely, its readiness to openly disregard it.

The assassinations represent another major change in Israel's approach, which one Israeli commentator has referred to as "aerially enforced occupation."[18] While Israel had used airplanes and unmanned drones for reconnaissance missions in the OT many years earlier, the air now became a key arena through which the Palestinian population was controlled. Unmanned balloons, zeppelins, early warning Hawkeye planes, and military satellites were deployed to monitor the population and gather information about it, while Apache helicopters and F-16 fighter jets were converted into conventional weapons of occupation. Until the eruption of the second intifada, the ground was the major sphere in which control was exercised, but following the redeployment of Israeli troops, the air and the underground became prominent spheres of both control and resistance.[19] This is most apparent in the Gaza Strip, where Israel enforces closures by dropping leaflets on villages and refugee camps from airplanes declaring different areas off limits, and then using fighter jets and unmanned armed drones to target whoever tries to enter these areas.[20] One should note that Israel's decision to enforce the occupation through the air—that is, to introduce a new form of control—was, to a large extent, determined by the separation principle, which, in turn, came into being due to the numerous developments on the ground.

In the military operation dubbed Defensive Shield, still other changes in Israel's repertoires of violence became apparent. The massive attack was launched in the West Bank on March 29, 2002, in response to a suicide attack in which a Palestinian blew himself up during a Passover meal in a hotel dining room, killing twenty-eight people. This was the culmination of a bloody month for Israel, perhaps the bloodiest one in the history of modern Israel in terms of civilian deaths, with eighty-one Israelis killed in daily attacks. Call-up notices for twenty thousand reserve soldiers were issued, the largest draft since the 1982 Lebanon War. Tanks rolled into Palestinian cities and towns throughout the West Bank, as population centers were placed under prolonged curfews.[21] In March and April alone, close to five hundred Palestinians were killed. The most lethal raid was the one in the Jenin refugee camp, where for nearly two weeks Israel made use of aerial shelling, tanks, armored bulldozers, and infantry to quell Palestinian resistance. According to Human Rights Watch (HRW), a total of 140 buildings were completely destroyed in the camp and an additional 200 houses sustained major damage. Considering that many of the buildings were multifamily homes, HRW estimates that as many as four thousand residents, representing more than a quarter of the camp's inhabitants, became homeless.[22]

The prolonged blanket curfews in Jenin and several other cities and towns drastically restricted basic movement, entailed the denial of access to medical treatment, and caused a severe shortage of food, water, and medical supplies. While I return to the restriction of movement momentarily, here it is important to stress that during Operation Defensive Shield Israel modified its controlling mechanisms in three key ways. First, Defensive Shield represented a change in the means of violence.[23] Before the operation, Israel primarily used its infantry to police the population; during Defensive Shield both air-force squadrons and tank battalions assumed a central role. Thus, the operation (alongside the extrajudicial executions carried out from the air) denotes a move to more remote and lethal methods of military engagement.

Second, the violence was directed not only toward the Palestinian inhabitants, as it had been in the past, but also against the material means used to administer and manage the population. In Israel's attack on the Ministry of Education, for example, the computer network as well as televisions and file cabinets full of records were destroyed. This same destruction was repeated in office after office, including the Ministry of Civil Affairs, the Palestinian Legislative Council, the Central Bureau of Statistics, the al-Bireh Municipal Library, and so forth. The offices of Palestinian civil society organizations, such as human rights groups, social service and welfare organizations, and radio and television stations received similar treatment.[24]

Third, Israel also targeted the Palestinian infrastructure. Roads, electricity grids, water pipelines, and buildings throughout the West Bank were severely damaged or destroyed during the operation, thus erasing the few signs of the PA's achievements during the Oslo years. According to assessments carried out by the World Bank, Defensive Shield resulted in damages of $361 million to Palestinian infrastructure and institutions.[25] The United Nations' Economic and Social Commission calculated that by May 2002 a total of 385,808 fruit and olive trees had been uprooted, while several wells and agricultural constructions had been destroyed.[26] In addition, Israel destroyed thousands of houses, leaving more than twenty-four thousand people homeless during the first four years of the intifada. This type of violence was unheard of before Oslo, primarily because Israel considered itself responsible for Palestinian infrastructure. Accordingly, it would never have considered wreaking such destruction or undermining civil institutions. But since it was now operating under the logic of the separation principle, it did not hesitate to do so.

Defensive Shield became the paradigm for Israel's new forms of control. The occupying power adopted more intense and remote mechanisms of violence, while discarding and destroying the institutions through which disciplinary forms of control are articulated, exactly those it had transferred to the PA just a few years earlier. Not only was Israel no longer interested in managing the population, it also ensured that the PA would be unable to do so. By attacking the means through which the population is administered, Israel rendered its own subcontractor totally dysfunctional, creating an institutional vacuum, which, as we will see, constituted yet another contradiction.

THE RULE OF LAW

Along with the change in the repertoires of violence and the sites targeted, Israel also altered its relation to the law. If up until September 2000 Israel controlled the occupied inhabitants primarily through the application of the law—including, to be sure, the enforcement of draconian laws that both legalized the incarceration of thousands of political prisoners and permitted deportations, house demolitions, torture, extended curfews and other forms of collective punishment—one of the most striking characteristics of the second intifada is the extensive suspension of the law. In the first thirty-three years of occupation, any suspension of the law was still considered an exception to the rule, even though the law's actual application did not entail any meaningful administration of justice. In the second intifada, the suspension of the law became the norm. One example of this suspension is Israel's pervasive employment of extrajudicial executions. The fact that not one Israeli soldier has been tried for these killings, that no legal inquiry followed the executions, and that they are part of an overt policy suggests that some of the occupied inhabitants have been reduced to what the Italian political philosopher Giorgio Agamben has called *homo sacer*, that is, people who can be killed without it being considered a crime.[27]

Examining the application of law to Israeli soldiers corroborates this claim and helps uncover the character of the change in Israel's relation to the law following the outbreak of the second uprising. During the intifada's first four and a half years, 3,161 Palestinians were killed, 636 of them minors. Moreover, of the 751 Palestinians who were killed in 2004, two-thirds had not participated in any kind of fighting. And yet the military prosecutor opened only 104 investigations concerning unlawful shootings during this period, and, of these, 28 were actually prosecuted and 18 found guilty. One of the soldiers found guilty of killing a 95-year-old Palestinian woman was sentenced to sixty-five days in prison.[28] The first intifada was very different in this respect, since most military offenses were subjected to legal scrutiny. From 1987 to 1990, Israel killed 743 Palestinians—fewer than it killed in 2004 alone—of whom 154 were minors. The military, however, carried out an investigation of every single killing and initiated a total of 1,256 investigations against soldiers who were suspected of breaching the regulations. Although only forty soldiers were prosecuted for unlawful killings, the soldiers' actions were, nonetheless, constantly investigated by the judicial authorities. Thus, if a defining feature of the first intifada was ongoing legal scrutiny, albeit a very superficial and slanted scrutiny, the second intifada can be characterized by the extensive withdrawal of the law.[29] During the first intifada, law was still needed as a form of legitimization; during the second intifada, the law has, in many respects, become redundant.

THE POLITICS OF DEATH

As I pointed out in previous chapters, during the occupation's first two decades, Israel emphasized both disciplinary and bio modes of power and employed numerous forms of control to craft an economically useful Palestinian society, while reducing the inhabitants' political aptitude. Following the outbreak of the first intifada, a sovereign mode of power began to be emphasized over the other modes—most notably through the implementation of the entry-permit regime and the pervasive practice of incarceration, torture, and beatings—in order to repress the population's political aspirations. Even though Israel's treatment of Palestinians was frequently brutal, civilian deaths were considered inimical to Israel's interests, and the military was instructed to avoid killing the occupied inhabitants.[30] The realization that it could no longer discipline the residents eventually led Israel to transfer responsibility for managing the population to the PA. Rapidly, Israel lost interest in the individual Palestinian and emphasized forms of control informed by sovereign and bio modes of power.

Therefore it is not altogether surprising that, with the eruption of the second intifada, Israel adopted a new approach toward the Palestinians, which rendered them, in many respects, expendable. The fact that the average number of Palestinians killed each year during the second intifada has been more than the number of those killed during the first twenty years of occupation is extremely telling. If before the second uprising Israel tried to avoid killing Palestinians, from September 2000 the finger pulling the trigger confronted fewer obstacles. Unlike the soldiers of the first intifada, those in the second were not given clubs, and beatings were not part of the daily routine in the OT. In place of the politics of life that had characterized the OT until the second intifada, a politics of death slowly emerged. The paradigmatic practice of this new politics is the extrajudicial execution, which in contrast to incarcerations or even torture does not intend to shape or alter Palestinian behavior, but to do away with "recalcitrant" individuals.

Another example of the radical shift in Israel's relation to the occupied inhabitants is the adoption of a military protocol that allows soldiers to use Palestinians as human shields. Soldiers have ordered Palestinians to enter buildings to check if they are booby-trapped. They have instructed residents to remove suspicious objects from roads used by the military. They have made civilians stand inside houses where soldiers have set up military positions, so that Palestinians will not fire at the soldiers. And they have forced Palestinians to walk in front of soldiers to shield them from gunfire, while the soldiers hold guns behind their backs and sometimes fire over their shoulders.[31] Although this practice was outlawed by the High Court of Justice in 2005, there have been documented incidents in which soldiers have continued using Palestinians as human shields.[32] Moreover, the practice underscores that Palestinians are conceived by the military as dispensable shields, not unlike the flack jackets that soldiers wear every time they enter the OT.

The far-reaching change in Israel's methods of control becomes even more striking once one compares Israel's approach to the inhabitants during this period with the one it adopted following the 1967 War. For example, in the late 1960s and early 1970s Israel monitored the calorie intake of the Palestinian inhabitants and boasted that during the first seven years of occupation the average calorie intake of the occupied residents had increased from 2,430 (1966) to 2,719 (1973), while the protein intake had increased from 67.1 to 79.4.[33] In 1980, the Bank of Israel proudly noted that the level of Palestinian food consumption was continuing to rise, and the nutritional standards had improved.[34] Thus, during the first period Israel, invested considerable resources in closely monitoring the nutritional value of the

Palestinian food basket in order to ensure that its policies were decreasing Palestinian susceptibility to disease and making inhabitants more useful in economic terms.

By contrast, during the second intifada, Israel has adopted practices that have dramatically decreased the food basket's nutritional value, weakening, as it were, the Palestinian body and reducing its energies. For instance, the World Bank reports that acute malnutrition has affected more than 9 percent of Palestinian children in the territories, and the Food and Agriculture Organization of the United Nations estimated that almost 40 percent of the Palestinians in the OT suffer from food insecurity.[35] Almost half of the children between six and fifty-nine months and women of child-bearing age are anemic due to a lack of iron in their diet. There has been a 58 percent increase in the number of stillbirths due to poor prenatal care, and child mortality increased substantially in 2002 to become the leading cause of death for children under five, and the second leading cause of death overall.[36] Moreover, Israel does not monitor the effects its policies have on the inhabitants, indicating that it no longer considers them as sites that need to be managed.

Ariella Azoulay and Adi Ophir convincingly argue that since the eruption of the second intifada, Israel has held the West Bank and Gaza Strip on the *verge* of catastrophe in order to uphold and preserve the occupation.[37] Both normalcy and full-blown catastrophe would signify the end of the occupation, while the intermediate situation of ongoing crisis serves as a modality of control, whereby the situation can always get better (if you behave) or worse (if you misbehave). The production of a permanent crisis along with Israel's changing relation to the occupied inhabitants reflects a shift from the colonization to the separation principle, whereby there is little if any interest in managing the Palestinian population residing in the OT.

PALESTINIAN SPACE

One cannot fully understand the replacement of the colonization with the separation principle without examining Palestinian space. Historically, the withdrawal of colonial powers from their colonies has entailed the abdication of control over the means of legitimate movement within and from the colonies. Following their withdrawal, the former colony's borders became porous, while movement within the country was no longer monitored and controlled by the colonial power. By contrast, in both the Gaza Strip and West Bank Israel has maintained its control over movement even after its troops have pulled out from certain regions, most notably the Gaza Strip. The withdrawal of troops may have produced the impression that Israel transferred sovereignty to the Palestinians, but in reality it continues to control both the space that the Palestinians occupy and the legitimate means of movement. Ironically, as the Israeli government adopted the separation discourse, it implemented strategies that further contracted Palestinian space. This was accomplished primarily through the imposition of internal and external closures and the construction of the separation barrier.

In some respects, Israel simply continued a strategy it had adopted during the Oslo years; however, its actions and their consequences were more severe. With the outbreak of the second intifada, many West Bank cities, towns, and villages were transformed into restricted military zones, and their residents were held under sustained (often twenty-four-hour) curfew for days on end. On occasion, nearly 900,000 West Bank residents in 74 communities were held under curfew, so that, for example, during the six-and-a-half month period between June 17 and December 31, 2002, 547,000 people in 37 localities were, on average, confined to their homes.[38] Israel also developed a dense network of both fixed and movable military checkpoints, numbering some 140 in the West Bank and 25–30 in the Gaza Strip (see map 6). It also set up literally hundreds of unmanned physical obstacles in the form of concrete blocks, piles of dirt, or trenches, which were used to prevent access to and from towns and villages. During the latter half of 2002, Israel reintroduced permit requirements for internal West Bank movement, so that Palestinians who wanted to travel within the West Bank also had to obtain a permit.[39] Hence, movement was confined to a small space, often no larger than the household or village in which the Palestinian resided. According to the Union of Palestinian Medical Relief Committees, 85 percent of people in the West Bank did not leave their villages during the intifada's first three years due to curfews and closures.[40] The seemingly endless number of physical barriers has not only violated the rights of Palestinians by impeding their access to work, education, and medical facilities, but, on a deeper level, these barriers have distorted basic conceptions of time and space. In the OT there is no longer any way to calculate the time it will take to travel from point A to B, a fact that helps produce widespread uncertainty and disorientation.[41]

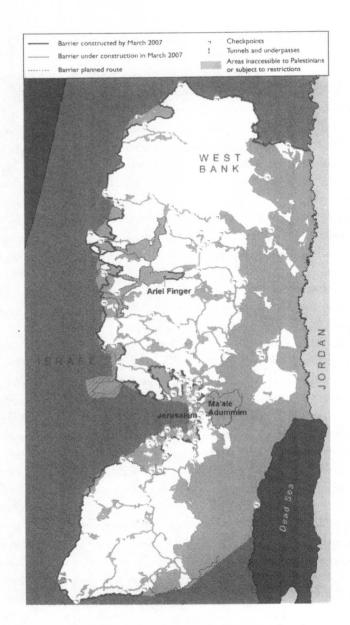

WEST BANK

Ariel Finger

ISRAEL

JORDAN

Jerusalem   Ma'ale Adummim

Dead Sea

Map 6. West Bank separation barriers, checkpoints, and road-blocks. Source: Office for the Coordination of Humanitarian Affairs, Occupied Palestinian Territory.

Along with the internal closure, Israel tightened the external border, dramatically limiting the permits granted to Palestinians wishing to enter or travel through Israel. Following Palestinian attacks on Israeli targets, the Israeli media often reported that the military had imposed a total closure on the OT and a siege on cities in the West Bank. Such routine reports paint a misleading picture, since they depict the severe restrictions on the movement of Palestinians as a response to a particular event or threat. The reality, however, has been altogether different, since the sweeping restrictions have been continuous, as B'Tselem notes, and are only marginally affected by the military's assessment of the level of security threats.[42] The so-called Safe Passage route, designed during Oslo to allow Palestinians to move relatively freely between the West Bank and Gaza, was closed by the Israeli authorities days after the uprising erupted and was never reopened. Along the same lines, Israel restricted passenger and commercial traffic to neighboring countries.[43] Permits were frequently cancelled, and border crossings were often sealed, greatly reducing employment in Israel as well as commercial transactions with or through Israel.

While all of these forms of control were used prior to the outbreak of the second intifada, they were employed with much less intensity and, following the uprising's eruption, the function of some was altered. The transformation of how the border operated as a form of control is a case in point. Instead of a permeable border deployed to monitor and regulate Palestinian movement, the Green Line was converted into an impermeable border vis-à-vis the OT's Palestinian inhabitants (though settlers could always pass through unhindered). According to 1999 figures collected by the Israel Airports Authority, which is responsible for operating the Rafah crossing (the only border through which Palestinians can leave the Gaza Strip in order to travel abroad), approximately fourteen hundred people per day passed through the border.[44] By contrast, the year after Israel withdrew from Gaza, the number of people exiting the region fell to 453 per day, or 32 percent of the 1999 crossings. A similar pattern emerges when one examines the movement of Palestinians from Gaza into Israel. In 2004 a comprehensive closure was imposed for 149 days, more than half the workdays that year. Moreover, if on the eve of the intifada (the third quarter of 2000), an average of 26,500 Palestinians from the Gaza Strip entered Israel daily, during the third quarter of 2004, the number was 1,000 per day—a drop of 96 percent; during the year after the withdrawal from Gaza, on average

723 Palestinian laborers entered Israel each day.[45] Thus, with the adoption of the separation principle, Palestinian space was contracted, and the Green Line that had enabled some form of movement was closed and sealed, thus transforming the OT into a container of sorts.

The crucial point is that with the adoption of the separation principle, Israel loses interest in the lives of the Palestinians and focuses almost solely on the occupied resources. The checkpoints, seam zones, and borders are the exception, since at these locations Israel continues to monitor the Palestinians closely and to disseminate a series of norms through disciplinary practices that aim to teach those who wish to move the requirements of correct conduct. Israel, in other words, is no longer attempting to normalize the occupation by striving to shape the behavior of the Palestinian population; rather, it aims to shape and administer only the *moving subject*. Following the adoption of the separation principle, only those Palestinians who want to move within the OT or to leave the region are subjected to Israel's disciplinary practices and must, in order to become moving subjects, adopt a series of normative fiats. Palestinians who do not want any contact with Israel must remain within the confines of their refugee camp, village, town, or city.

THE SEPARATION BARRIER

In the midst of the second intifada, Israel introduced a new controlling apparatus.[46] On April 14, 2002, the Israeli cabinet decided to establish a permanent barrier in the West Bank, made up of a series of electronic fences, deep trenches, wide patrol roads, and, in certain places, nine-meter concrete slabs.[47] Although the barrier has been presented as a "temporary" security apparatus aimed at stopping suicide bombers, the Israeli government has constructed parts of the barrier deep inside the West Bank, using it as a political weapon to confiscate land and thus to contract Palestinian space. The barrier is being built east of as many Jewish settlements as possible to make it easier to annex them into Israel in the future. Its primary objective, as Azoulay and Ophir have convincingly claimed, is to extend and reproduce domination and reinscribe it in space.[48]

Palestinian land was confiscated in order to encircle Jewish settlement blocs from the east and in this way to incorporate them into Israel proper. The Ariel finger, for instance, penetrates 22 km into the West Bank, cutting inside 42 percent of the region's width (see map 6). The Ma'ale Adummim section will extend 14 km east across the most narrow section of the West Bank, thus cutting off all of the major traffic arteries between the northern and southern parts of the West Bank and, in effect, slicing the region in two.[49] Israel also built sixteen internal enclaves where Palestinian villages, towns, or cities are either totally surrounded by the barrier or surrounded on three sides. All in all, Israel has destroyed and confiscated thousands of dunams of fields and olive groves. The barrier has cut off farmers from their lands, patients from hospitals, and children from their schools. Thus, instead of separating Israelis from Palestinians, in many areas the barrier actually separates Palestinians from Palestinians.

Due to the enclaves' and the barrier's penetration into the West Bank, the planned route is more than twice the length of the Green Line—approximately 680 km long. And although the very essence and presence of the barrier is, as Weizman notes, the obvious, solid, material embodiment of state interests, the route should not be understood as the direct product of top-down government planning. Rather, the repeated modifications in the route's trajectory (indeed the route was changed several times, and in numerous cases a portion of the barrier was destroyed once an alternative route was adopted) are a result of a multiplicity of technical, legal, and political conflicts over issues of territory, demography, water, archaeology, and real estate, as well as over political issues relating to sovereignty, security, and identity. The route's course, in other words, is an effect of numerous developments on the ground and not a policy emanating from above.[50]

The barrier is the largest real estate project in Israel's history, and by the time it is complete, an estimated $3.5 billion will have been spent.[51] Although it influences practically every aspect of Palestinian life, its detrimental effects can be divided into two broad categories: it contravenes individual and collective rights while creating facts on the ground whose aim is to undercut the Palestinian state-building project. It is the paradigmatic example of the separation principle.

Once the construction is complete, about 12 percent of Palestinian land will be located between the barrier and the Green Line, not including large segments of land that may be confiscated if a barrier is erected in the Jordan Valley.[52] The appropriated territory includes some of the most fertile land in the West Bank and is currently home to about 27,250 Palestinians (excluding East Jerusalem). Life for these people has changed dramatically, as they now live on islands of sorts: entering and exiting their homes and plots of land has become a recurrent nightmare. There are gates between these villages and towns and the rest of the West Bank, yet these gates are often closed; when they are opened, a strict permit regime is imposed, making it impossible for many people who live in the area to pass. An additional 247,800 Palestinians reside in fifty-four communities east of the barrier that are completely or partially surrounded enclaves, which have one or two entrances through which the residents must pass in order to work their lands or travel to other parts of the West Bank.[53] In cities like Tulkarem and Qalqilya, where the barrier separates the metropolis from the neighboring villages, both urban and rural communities have been hard hit, since the fragmentation and isolation of the populations have undercut social support networks. The economic ramifications of the barrier have been serious, inflicting further suffering on a society already plagued by extreme poverty.

The barrier epitomizes the idea that physical forms of control have a life of their own and, through a series of effects, shape Palestinian comportment. The barrier has, for example, produced a whole bureaucratic apparatus that includes, among other things, a permit regime determining who can continue living in the areas closed by the wall as well as who can pass through the gates connecting between different parts of the West Bank. This permit regime not only determines who can attend schools, farm agricultural fields, or access medical institutions, using categories such as gender and age to discriminate among the Palestinians, but also determines which gate each person can pass through and at what time. People who were used to commuting to work are suddenly confined to their villages; women who had for years tended the olive groves can no longer reach their land; and teachers cannot reach schools located in adjacent villages. The barrier, in other words, creates a permit regime that helps shape the comportment of the people living in its vicinity, while slowly altering the social stratification of Palestinian society.

The barrier is a good example of a bio mode of power (in the sense of operating on the population as opposed to the individual), yet unlike biopower it is uninterested in life. This claim can be appreciated once one considers how it shapes the behavior of Israeli soldiers, most notably those who are positioned to guard it: the barrier transforms the soldiers into an effect of its own logic. Even though the military has been unwilling to publish its open-fire regulations, an array of incidents suggests that any suspect who approaches or touches the barrier can be "legitimately" shot.[54] Thus, the soldier standing guard on the panoptic tower or patrolling the barrier becomes, in a sense, an automatic weapon in the service of a concrete wall and a series of trenches and fences.

FROM GEOGRAPHY TO DEMOGRAPHY

By focusing on the violation of rights, however, one misses the overall objective of the reorganization of space. The fact that the barrier is not being built on the internationally recognized border underscores that its major objective is to redraw the border between Israel and the West Bank. The chosen route aims to mitigate the consequences of Israel's massive settlement project, whose goal has been to colonize the land without incorporating the occupied inhabitants into the Israeli demos. Ironically, though, as the settlement project deepened its hold on the OT, the very idea of Israel as a Jewish state, where Jews are the majority, has been undermined. Put differently, the fact that the majority of people living between the Jordan Valley and the Mediterranean Sea are not Jewish has underscored the inherent contradiction resulting from the separation between the dowry and the bride and has highlighted the difficulty of achieving the vision of a greater Israel while maintaining a Jewish state. The barrier should be considered both as an effect of this contradiction and as a new form of control that aims to overcome it.

Not unlike Israel's withdrawal from the Gaza Strip, the barrier aims to resolve the contradiction between Israel's geographic and demographic aspirations. For years the demographic "threat" was kept at bay by denying the occupied Palestinians Israeli citizenship and subjecting them to military rule. Israel created a colonial regime in the West Bank (and Gaza) in order to sustain the Jewish majority within its borders, installing a dual legal system within a single territory, one system for Jews, the other for Palestinians. But the contradictions arising from the Israeli system had by 2002 made it clear to many Israeli decision makers, even those on the far right, that the incongruence between Israel's geographic and demographic ambitions had led to a political juncture whereby it seemed that Israel would have to choose between one of two options: continue maintaining a colonial regime or, conversely, give up the idea of a Jewish state.

The barrier served as a third option. By annexing several parts of the West Bank, Israel aims to radically alter the region's demographic and geographic reality. Demographically, the barrier will surround about fifty-six Jewish settlements from the east, annexing the land that they now occupy, so that 171,000 of the West Bank's settlers will be incorporated into Israel's new borders and thus legitimized. The wall being built in East Jerusalem is meant to reinforce the 1967 annexation of this part of the city, and to further legitimize the 183,800 settlers living there. Thus, if the barrier does become the new border, it will solve the problem of about 87 percent of Israel's illegal settlers. The remaining 13 percent, or 52,500 settlers, will have to be evacuated, as Jewish settlers were forcibly evacuated from the Gaza Strip.[55] It is unlikely that Israel will use guns to expel the 27,250 Palestinians who are now living between the barrier and the Green Line. Rather, the barrier will "encourage" these communities to "voluntarily" move to its eastern side by destroying the infrastructure of their existence. This is already happening on an individual level, and, if nothing changes, one will likely see entire populations of villages and towns uprooted from their ancestral homes.[56]

Geographically and politically, the barrier does not resemble either one of the two traditional visions for peace: two national states side by side or one bi-national, secular polity.[57] Instead, its objective is to enlarge Israel's internationally recognized territory by annexing West Bank land, while creating self-governing enclaves for the Palestinians. Aside from the sixteen small enclaves mentioned above, the barrier's route cuts the Palestinian territory up into and at least two (north/south WB) and perhaps four larger enclaves (the north is divided into three parts, north of Ariel, south of Ariel, and Jericho). Taking the Gaza Strip into account, it becomes clear that the future Palestinian "state" to be will be made up of three if not five main regions. Each of these regions will be closed off almost completely from each other. Israel will continue to effectively control all of the borders, so that it will be able to implement a hermetic closure whenever it wishes and in this way continue controlling the legitimate means of movement.

What is new about the barrier is not the attempt to create closed enclaves in the OT, but the effort to transform these enclaves into quasi-independent entities that will ostensibly form a Palestinian state. The Gaza Strip provides a good indication of what will happen in the West Bank if Israel goes ahead and unilaterally withdraws from parts of the West Bank. Oren Yiftachel makes this point strikingly clear when he argues that Israel has entered a new phase in which it is restraining its expansionist impulse. Instead, it consolidates territorial gains by further Judaizing areas with a substantial Jewish presence, while ridding itself of the responsibility for the densely populated Palestinian areas and isolated Jewish settlements. Despite the important precedent of evacuating the Gaza settlements, the emerging political geography continues to be characterized by violent Jewish domination, strict separation, and ethnic inequality.[58]

OF FRONTIERS AND GHETTOS

James Ron's analysis of state violence helps explain why there has been a modification in the repertoires of violence, a suspension of the law, and an alteration in Israel's approach to the Palestinian inhabitants, but his model does not explain Israel's changing relation to Palestinian space. Ron, as mentioned in chapter 6, poses two spatial metaphors—ghettos and frontiers—suggesting that until the early 1990s the West Bank and Gaza Strip were Israel's ghettos, since they were densely institutionalized by Israel, were within its legal sphere of influence, and served as repositories for unwanted and marginalized populations. Lebanon, by contrast, was Israel's frontier, since it was not institutionalized by Israel and was distinguished from it by clear boundaries. The crucial point is that the different institutional settings determined the kind of violence Israel employed in each region. Whereas in its ghetto Israel used ethnic policing, mass incarceration, and harassment, at its frontiers it employed unruly, lethal violence.[59]

The thinning of Israeli institutions in the OT following Oslo and particularly after Israel's withdrawal from the Gaza Strip in August 2005 helps explain the unruly destruction of infrastructure and the adoption of remote and more lethal forms of violence. Ron also notes that with the institutional dilution comes the abdication of moral responsibility toward the population, a process that also manifested itself in the OT as Israel became indifferent to the management of the population and to the life of the inhabitants. The West Bank and the Gaza Strip—to an even greater degree—have indeed become Israel's Lebanon. This became patently clear in June 2006 when Israel bombed the electric grid in Gaza, thus cutting off seven hundred thousand people at once from electricity. It bombed all major traffic arteries connecting the northern part of the Gaza Strip with the south, and used

F-16 jets, Apache helicopters, and rocket launchers to continuously shell towns and villages; this attack killed scores of Palestinians, including many women and children. In the future, repertoires of violence of this kind will likely characterize Israel's assaults in the West Bank as well.

Even though Ron's insights are extremely important, the dichotomy that he poses between ghettos and frontiers cannot be directly applied to the OT. While Israel has in the past years substantially diluted its institutional presence in the territories, it has also placed hundreds of thousands of Palestinians in enclaves by surrounding the Gaza Strip and parts of the West Bank with fences and walls. There appears to be direct correlation between the de-institutionalization and the ghettoization of the two regions. The Gaza Strip, one of the most densely populated areas on earth, with four thousand people per square kilometer, has been transformed into one big prison.[60] So while Israel has withdrawn its troops from the Gaza Strip and dismantled the Jewish settlements, the Palestinians in this region are even further limited in terms of resources, mobility, and decision making, not least because they are held in a ghetto and have no control over their own borders—whether they involve land borders, air space, or access to the sea.

Gaza, it seems, will serve as the model for the West Bank. The methods of control Israel now uses are similar to the ones used on its frontier—they are more lethal, remote, and technologically sophisticated. Instead of deploying soldiers to patrol city streets, Israel now employs biometrics and surveillance aircraft backed up by F-16 fighter jets, Apache helicopters, and ground-to-ground missile launchers, and the rule of law has been, for the most part, suspended. Spatially, both regions have been transformed into hermetic ghettos, while institutionally they have been transformed into a frontier. This point is crucial because it underscores the unique form of control that Israel introduced in the OT following the adoption of the separation principle.

THE RISE OF HAMAS

The excesses and contradictions produced by Israel's controlling apparatuses and practices can also help explain the increasing popular support for Hamas. In 1995 public opinion polls showed Hamas with 10 percent support as opposed to Fatah's 55 percent, but by 2003, 21 percent supported Hamas, while Fatah's support had shrunk to 28 percent.[61] Hamas's gradual climb culminated in the organization's landslide victory in the democratic elections of January 25, 2006. An analysis of its ascendancy suggests that Hamas was empowered by Israel, a development that corroborates Susan Buck-Morss's theoretical claim concerning the "dialectic of power"—the notion that power produces its own vulnerability.[62] While such a claim might be obvious to some, in the literature on Hamas it has not been discussed.

Khaled Hroub, for example, contends that the organization's popularity stems from its being seen as the voice of Palestinian dignity and the symbol of the defense of Palestinian rights at a time of unprecedented hardship, humiliation, and despair, which have followed the historic concessions made by the PA. He underscores the relative success of Izzeddin al-Qassam, Hamas's military wing, in attacking Israeli targets, stating that this has also increased the organization's popularity, as has Hamas's reputation for clean conduct, modesty, and honesty, which have been pointedly contrasted with the conduct and corruption of many PA officials.[63] Shaul Mishal and Avraham Sela add that Hamas's success in winning over the masses has to do with its increasingly pragmatic approach, one characterized by support for the short-term objective of a Palestinian state in the West Bank and Gaza Strip, while still maintaining the long-term goal of establishing an Islamic state that would eventually replace Israel. They propose that "Hamas's decision-making processes have been markedly balanced, combining realistic considerations with traditional beliefs and arguments, emphasizing visionary goals but also immediate needs."[64] Most commentators stress that Hamas has also benefited from the extensive welfare services it offers to all Palestinians, regardless of their religious belief or political affiliation.[65]

While these insights undoubtedly help explain why Hamas has gained massive popular support in the OT, they all relate to Hamas as if it were some kind of free-floating actor from which a series of policies and actions originate. They do not address the structural effects of the occupation and how these effects have helped shape Hamas. The writers of a report on Hamas's social welfare activism conclude, for example, that the organization's positive image is significantly related to the efficiency of its social services, particularly when compared with the PA's weaknesses.[66] Taking into account both the scope of services Hamas offers and the sense of solidarity it provides, this conclusion is surely accurate, yet it substitutes the symptoms for the causes. The question is not whether Hamas's social welfare organizations have helped it garner popular support, but rather what the conditions were that shaped Hamas's practices and enabled it to become so popular.

In the previous chapter we saw how throughout the Oslo period Israel allowed the PA to fortify its security forces while generating an economic crisis and undermining the operation of Palestinian civil institutions. This situation further deteriorated after the intifada's eruption. According to the World Bank, following the outbreak of the intifada, the economic crisis in the West Bank and Gaza Strip "seriously compromised household welfare." If in 1999 per capita gross national income was $1,850, by 2003 it had fallen to $1,110. Thus, due to the various restrictions placed on the movement of people, labor, and goods, and on the transfer of revenues collected by the Israeli government on the PA's behalf, the Palestinians have experienced a contraction in real personal incomes of almost 40 percent — despite the more than doubling of annual donor disbursements in the same period. Using a $2.10 per day poverty line, an estimated 60 percent of the population was poor by December 2002, three times the amount documented on the eve of the intifada. The number of poor accordingly tripled, from 650,000 to 1.9 million, and the poor have gotten even poorer.[67] The economic and social calamity has produced new populations that need assistance just in order to sustain life. As one member of an Islamic charity stated, "[T]he novelty of this uprising is that it has engendered new types of need, which has increased the number of eligible beneficiaries and diversified the social groups requiring such assistance."[68] These new groups currently include landowners, shopkeepers, and those whose homes have been demolished by Israeli bulldozers; in other words, these new groups are not just the traditionally poor.[69]

The rapid decline in the standard of living has only served to deepen the de-legitimization of the Palestinian governing body, since by the end of 2002 many of the civil institutions were only partially functioning, and the services they were offering were less adequate than those offered by Israel in 1993. This is not surprising, considering that a decade after Israel created the PA to manage the Palestinian population, the fledgling governing body was undermined, thus producing an institutional vacuum in the OT.

The significant point is that these dire developments, and particularly the institutional vacuum Israel created, were transformed into an opportunity, and Hamas knew how to benefit from the situation. The movement's ascendancy is, in other words, not only due to its reaction to Israel's colonial project; it is also an effect of this project. Practically, the organization strengthened its policy of providing assistance on the basis of socioeconomic need rather than religious or political criteria, so that families in economic distress did not need to be Hamas members or even practicing Muslims in order to qualify for aid. As a chairman of an Islamic charity noted, "[T]he increase in poverty has vastly increased the pressure upon our organization, because we are receiving many more applications than before."[70] Hence, the claim that Hamas's popularity has resulted from its charity and welfare network conceals the fact that Israel has produced a situation where, on the one hand, there is desperate need for charity institutions, while, on the other hand, the state institutions cannot offer the required services.

The culminating effect of the second uprising has been devastating for the occupied inhabitants. A large percentage of Palestinians are now dependent on aid offered by international humanitarian organizations and Islamic charities, and this aid ensures that the ongoing crisis does not develop into a full-blown catastrophe. So if in 1994 the PA replaced Israel as the authority responsible for disciplining the population, following the eruption of the second intifada charity organizations took over many of the responsibilities for sustaining Palestinian life. If in the first decade of the occupation Israel aimed to manage the population by producing a certain kind of security, in the past decade it has controlled the population by producing insecurity. This insecurity has no doubt benefited Hamas, not only because of its ability to fill in the institutional vacuum, but also because of its ideological conviction. Simply put, within a context of widespread destruction and absolute uncertainty a worldview that accentuates the importance of faith, fate, and divine ordinance gains ground.[71]

Yet, it was not only the institutional vacuum and despondency of Palestinian society that enabled Hamas to win the day, but the specific kind of postmodern fundamentalism that the group had adopted.[72] Hamas's worldview and actions are shaped both by its opposition to modernity and colonialism as well as by its incorporation of certain elements integral to modernity. This postmodern fundamentalism combines its religious appeals with an unwavering attempt to intervene in the political system, mobilize the Palestinian inhabitants, and create a vibrant organization for assuming and retaining political power.[73] Thus, Hamas's critique of postcolonial Western domination and cultural imperialism is also tied to different modern phenomena, such as the expansion of higher education, urbanization, the emergence of vast markets for inexpensive Islamic books and newspapers, and the proliferation of religious radio and television programs.

Along similar lines, Hamas, like other Islamist movements, has been shaped through its interaction with globalization. The deconstruction of the universal pretensions of European civilization, Haldun Gülalp convincingly claims in a slightly different context, has led to a growing recognition that the West too is a provincial culture with its own hegemonic project. This recognition has allowed alternative visions of civilization to gain currency. Therefore it is no surprise that anti-Western Islamist themes that champion the periphery against the center found enthusiastic audiences among a new generation of students and other intellectuals who conceive religious culture not as a return to the past but as a site of social innovation.[74] Many of Hamas's leaders fit this description perfectly, as they are doctors, engineers, lawyers, and other professionals whose religious sense of justice is, in several respects, postnationalist and postsocialist, and represents an answer to modernity's unaccomplished promises. So, while they contest the absolute certainties and unfulfilled promises propagated by the West, they adopt many aspects of modernity, using them to increase their influence and garner popular support. Having said this, let me emphasize that Hamas aspires to establish a theocratic regime, one that is extremely oppressive toward women and several other segments of society. The successful consolidation of its control will be extremely tragic for all those who have fought for the establishment of a secular democracy in Palestine.

The sectarian clashes that erupted in 2006 between Hamas and Fatah as well as between different *hamulas* in the Gaza Strip have introduced a totally new dimension into the Israeli-Palestinian conflict. Most pundits have understood these latter clashes as either a struggle over who will control the Palestinian government and resources or as a local manifestation of a much broader international conflict between fundamentalist and secular forces in the Islamic world. While such interpretations no doubt capture some of the most important recent developments, they also obscure the central role that Israel and the United States have played in producing the internal Palestinian violence.

By wreaking havoc on the Palestinian economy and destroying the state institutions that had managed somehow to survive throughout the second intifada, the closure and economic sanctions imposed on the West Bank and Gaza Strip have helped precipitate the violent clashes among the factions. Indeed, the idea behind the economic sanctions, which both Israel and the United States have pressured other countries to enforce, is to shape the power relations within Palestinian society by adopting a scheme that, for clarity's sake, one could call the Somalia Plan.[1]

For months, the Palestinian Authority was unable to pay the salaries of its one hundred and sixty thousand employees. These workers provide the livelihood for more than one million people, almost a third of the population. Some seventy thousand of these unpaid employees work for one of the numerous security organizations, most of which are linked to political factions. Like their brethren who are employed by civil institutions, such as the education and health ministries, the security personnel are deeply frustrated and angry because they cannot feed their families. But unlike the civilian workers, they are armed. Under conditions of scarce resources and uncertainty, it is not surprising that a power struggle erupted among the armed Palestinians. Inadequate resources, economic sanctions, thousands of armed men in distress, and foreign support of certain factions are, after all, the ingredients from which warlordism, à la Somalia, is made.

The result is that Palestinian society, which for years struggled against social disintegration, has been divided. This is a tragic development, particularly considering that for two decades Israel deployed numerous forms of control informed by disciplinary power to engender and strengthen fragmentation within Palestinian society, but ultimately had failed to accomplish its objective. The failure was, I have claimed, due in large part to the unifying effect of Palestinian nationalism produced, *inter alia,* by the excesses and contradictions of the mechanisms of control as well as the occupied population's perseverance. The current divide characterizing Palestinian society does not, however, signify the disappearance of such contradictions or a lack of determination on behalf of the occupied inhabitants. Rather, it is a result of numerous processes and political circumstances, among which is the rise of Islamic fundamentalism. This fundamentalism, as I showed in the previous chapter, is intricately tied to the demise of certain kinds of disciplinary and bio modes of power and to the ascendancy of a sovereign power that does not hesitate to suspend the law as it attempts to control Palestinian society through the destruction of the infrastructure of existence.

Ironically, Israel's so-called success in fragmenting Palestinian society is inimical to its own interests. The rise of Islamic fundamentalism is only one part of the problem. One has to be extremely short-sighted not to see how the absence of a united Palestinian leadership will undermine all efforts to bring about local and regional peace. But even if the Palestinians overcome the internal feuds, the conflict with Israel still has to be resolved in order for any kind of peace agreement to emerge. According to the preceding analysis, the Israeli-Palestinian conflict can move ahead in one of two ways. On the one hand, the key to solving the conflict is by addressing the structural incongruities of the occupation, the most important of which is the distinction Israel has made between the Palestinians and their land. Once Israel relates to the two as one inseparable unit, a just and peaceful solution can evolve. If, on the other hand, Israel maintains the distinction between the people and their land, numerous contradictions will continue to emerge; the Palestinians will accordingly resist Israeli control.

Insofar as this is the case, the only tenable way to solve the conflict is by addressing the occupation's structural contradictions. Any attempt to reach or impose a solution to the conflict without reuniting the Palestinian people and their land and offering them full sovereignty over the land, including a monopoly over legitimate violence and the means of movement, will ultimately lead to more contradictions, and the cycle of violence will surely resume.

This diagram provides an overview of the structure of the civil branch of the West Bank's military government. Each department was directed by an Israeli officer, while almost all of the staff and employees were Palestinians.

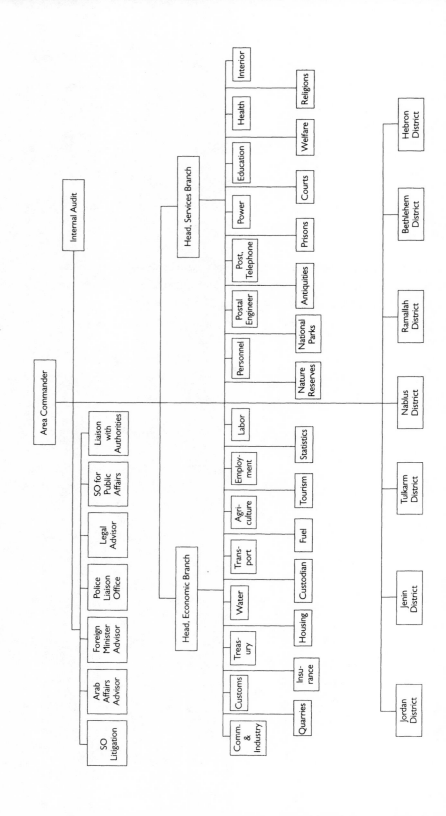

The following table lists West Bank settlements according to the year they were established. Numbers in parentheses indicate the order of establishment and correspond to map 2, page 126.

Year Established	Settlement	Year Established	Settlement
1967	Kefar Ezyon (1)	1973	Mekhora (18)
1968	Argaman (2)	1975	El'azar (19)
1968	Mehola (3)	1975	Ma'ale Adummim (20)
1968	Kalya (4)	1975	Ofra (21)
1969	Rosh Zurim (5)	1975	Peza'el (22)
1970	Allon Shevut (6)	1976	Netiv Hagedud (23)
1970	Mevo Horon (7)	1976	Ro'i (24)
1970	Gilgal (8)	1977	Almog (25)
1970	Yitav (9)	1977	Elqana (26)
1970	Ma'ale Efrayim (10)	1977	Bet El (27)
1970	Massu'a (11)	1977	Bet Horon (28)
1971	Hamra (12)	1977	Migdal Oz (29)
1971	Mizpe Shalem (13)	1977	Hallamish (30)
1972	Beqa'ot (14)	1977	Kokhav Hashahar (31)
1972	Har Gillo (15)	1977	Niran (32)
1972	Kiryat Arba (16)	1977	Sal'it (33)
1973	Gittit (17)	1977	Qedumim (34)

(continued)

Year Established	Settlement	Year Established	Settlement
1977	Rehan (35)	1981	Ateret (67)
1977	Rimmonim (36)	1981	Enav (68)
1977	Shaveshomeron (37)	1981	Pesagot (69)
1977	Teqoa (38)	1981	Shaqed (70)
1978	Ari'el (39)	1982	Eshkolot (71)
1978	Kefar Tappuah (40)	1982	Hermesh (72)
1978	Mevo Dotan (41)	1982	Newe Daniyyel (73)
1978	Mizpe Yeriho (42)	1982	Noqedim (74)
1978	Qarne Shomeron (43)	1982	No'omi (75)
1978	Tomer (44)	1982	Ale Zahav (76)
1979	Elon Moreh (45)	1982	Almon (77)
1979	Shadmot Mehola (46)	1982	Pene Hever (78)
1979	Kefar Adummim (47)	1982	Sa-Nur (79)
1979	Shilo (48)	1982	Telem (80)
1980	Efrata (49)	1983	Alfe Menashe (81)
1980	Bet Haarava (50)	1983	Asfar (82)
1980	Giv'on Hahadasha (51)	1983	Berakha (83)
1980	Wered Yeriho (52)	1983	Giv'at Ze'ev (84)
1980	Homesh (53)	1983	Migdalim (85)
1980	Hemdat (54)	1983	Gannim (86)
1980	Yafit (55)	1983	Dolev (87)
1980	Ma'ale Shomeron (56)	1983	Tene (88)
1981	Bet Arye (57)	1983	Yizhar (89)
1981	Barqan (58)	1983	Kaddim (90)
1981	Karmel (59)	1983	Ma'ale Levona (91)
1981	Hinnanit (60)	1983	Mezadot Yehuda (92)
1981	Yaqir (61)	1983	Suseya (93)
1981	Ma'on (62)	1983	Immanu'el (94)
1981	Ma'ale Mikhmas (63)	1983	Otni'el (95)
1981	Ma'ale Amos (64)	1983	Qiryat Netafim (96)
1981	Mattityahu (65)	1983	Sha'are Tiqwa (97)
1981	Nili (66)	1984	Adora (98)

(continued)

Year Established	Settlement	Year Established	Settlement
1984	Itamar (99)	1985	Shim'a (112)
1984	Geva Binyamin (100)	1986	Har Adar (113)
1984	Karme Zur (101)	1987	Nofim (114)
1984	Haggay (102)	1988	Na'ale (115)
1984	Nahali'el (103)	1989	Bat Ayin (116)
1984	Eli (104)	1989	Talmon (117)
1984	Pedu'el (105)	1989	Ofarim (118)
1985	Oranit (106)	1989	Zufim (119)
1985	Beitar Illit (107)	1990	Avne Hefez (120)
1985	Hashmona'im (108)	1991	Revava (121)
1985	Kokhav Ya'aqov (109)	1996	Modi'in Illit (122)
1985	Ez Efrayim (110)	1998	Kefar Haoranim (123)
1985	Qedar (111)	1999	Negohot (124)

SOURCE: Foundation for Middle East Peace. Available online at www.fmep.org.
NOTE: Four settlements were dismantled in August 2005.

NOTES

PREFACE

1. The numbers are taken from B'Tselem's website: www.btselem.org.

2. Associated Press, "U.N.: Iraq Civilian Deaths Hit a Record," CBS News, September 21, 2006. In addition to the 6,187 Palestinians who were killed by Israelis, fewer than 1,500 Palestinians were killed by other Palestinians. Consult www.btselem.org and www.iraqbodycount.org for up-to-date information.

3. In East Timor, for example, an estimated two hundred thousand people were killed out of a population of seven hundred thousand. See Mathew Jardine, *East Timor: Genocide in Paradise* (Tucson, AZ: Odonian Press, 1995).

4. Derek Gregory, *The Colonial Present: Afghanistan, Palestine, Iraq* (Oxford: Blackwell Publishing, 2004).

5. Benny Morris, *The Birth of the Palestinian Refugee Problem*, 2nd ed. (Cambridge: Cambridge University Press, 2003); Ilan Pappe, *The Ethnic Cleansing of Palestine* (Oxford: Oneworld, 2006).

6. Oren Yiftachel, *Ethnocracy: Land and Identity Politics in Israel/Palestine* (Philadelphia: University of Pennsylvania Press, 2006).

INTRODUCTION

Epigraph: Cited in Shlomo Gazit, *The Carrot and the Stick: Israel's Policy in Judea and Samaria, 1967–1969* (Washington, DC: B'nai Brith Books, 1995), 135. Levi Eshkol was Israel's prime minister at the time, and Golda Meir was the general secretary of the Mapai Party. See also Lev

Grinberg, "The Unwanted Bride: The Troubled Discourse of the Occupation's Resistance," *Theoria and Bikoret* 27 (Fall 2005): 187–96, in Hebrew.

1. Shlomo Gazit, *Trapped Fools: Thirty Years of Israeli Policy in the Territories* (London: Frank Cass, 2003), 162.

2. Shabtai Teveth, *The Cursed Blessing: The Story of Israel's Occupation of the West Bank* (London: Weidenfeld and Nicolson, 1970), 179.

3. State of Israel, Ministry of Defense, Unit for Coordination of Activities in the Territories, *Two Years of Military Government, 1967–1969: Figures on Civilian Activity in Judea, Samaria, the Gaza Strip and Northern Sinai* (Tel-Aviv: Ministry of Defense, May 1969), 39; Amnesty International, *Under the Rubble: House Demolition and Destruction of Land and Property* (London: Amnesty International, May 18, 2004). In the West Bank, Israel planted one million trees in 1968 (see Jewish National Fund archives file 31235/KKL5, letter dated March 28, 1969), and by 2002 it had uprooted literally hundreds of thousands of trees (see Amnesty International, *Under the Rubble*).

4. Among the important books that have analyzed these issues, see Noam Chomsky, *Fateful Triangle: The United States, Israel, and the Palestinians* (Boston: South End Press, 1999); Benny Morris, *Righteous Victims: A History of the Zionist-Arab Conflict, 1881–2001* (New York: Vintage 2001); Edward Said, *The Question of Palestine* (New York: Vintage, 1992); Avraham Sela, *The Decline of the Arab-Israeli Conflict: Middle East Politics and the Quest for Regional Order* (New York: State University of New York Press, 1997); Avi Shlaim, *The Iron Wall: Israel and the Arab World* (New York: W. W. Norton, 2001); Mark Tessler, *A History of the Israeli-Palestinian Conflict* (Bloomington, IN: Indiana University Press, 1994).

5. These studies include Geoffrey Aronson, *Creating Facts: Israel, Palestinians and the West Bank* (Washington, DC: Institute for Palestine Studies, 1987); Naseer Hasan Aruri, ed., *Occupation: Israel over Palestine* (London: Zed Books, 1984); Alan Dowty, *The Jewish State: A Century Later* (Berkeley and Los Angeles: University of California Press, 2001); Gershon Shafir and Yoav Peled, *The New Israel: Peacemaking and Liberalization* (Boulder, CO: Westview Press, 2001); Raja Shehadeh, *Occupier's Law: Israel and the West Bank* (Washington, DC: Institute for Palestine Studies, 1985); Raja Shehadeh and Jonathan Kuttab, *The West Bank and the Rule of Law* (Ramallah: International Commission of Lawyers, 1980); Idith Zertal and Akiva Eldar, *Lords of the Land: The Settlers and the State*

of Israel, 1967–2004 (Tel Aviv: Kinneret Zmora-Beitan, Dvir, 2004), in Hebrew.

6. For studies that have emphasized the agency of Palestinians, see Joost R. Hiltermann, *Behind the Intifada: Labor and Women's Movements in the Occupied Territories* (Princeton, NJ: Princeton University Press, 1991); Baruch Kimmerling and Joel S. Migdal, *The Palestinian People: A History* (Cambridge, MA: Harvard University Press, 2003); Zachary Lockman and Joel Beinin, eds., *Intifada: The Palestinian Uprising against Israeli Occupation* (Boston: South End Press, 1989); Julie Peteet, *Gender in Crisis: Women and the Palestinian Resistance Movement* (New York: Columbia University Press, 1991); Ze'ev Schiff and Ehud Ya'ari, *Intifada* (Tel-Aviv: Schoken Books, 1990), in Hebrew; Roane Carey ed., *The New Intifada: Resisting Israel's Apartheid* (London: Verso Books, 2001).

7. Timothy Mitchell, "The Limits of the State: Beyond Statist Approaches and Their Critics," *American Political Science Review* 85: 1 (1991): 77–96.

8. Michel Foucault, *Discipline and Punish* (New York: Vintage, 1979), and *The History of Sexuality*, vol. 1 (New York: Vintage, 1990).

9. Aronson's *Creating Facts* is an exception, but it was published in 1987, more than twenty years ago.

10. Although Fatah had been created a number of years earlier, and Palestinian refugees had been infiltrating into Israel since the 1948 War, the fact that Israel was now sole sovereign over Mandatory Palestine sharpened conflicting claims and rekindled the Palestinian struggle. See Kimmerling and Migdal, *Palestinian People*, 240–59.

11. Alan Dowty and Alvin S. Rubenstein, eds., *Arab Israeli Conflict: Perspectives* (New York: HarperCollins, 1990); Ian Black and Benny Morris, *Israel's Secret Wars: The Untold History of Israeli Intelligence* (London: Hamish Manilton, 1991), 206–35.

12. According to the theoretical framework employed here, these intentions were an effect of prior practices.

13. The annexation applied to the territory itself, whereas its inhabitants were given the option to become Israeli citizens, but in order to do so they had to relinquish their Jordanian citizenship. Only a small number complied. Nonetheless, all of the inhabitants were made permanent Jerusalem residents and could vote in municipal elections. See Eitan Felner, *A Policy of Discrimination, Land Expropriation, Planning and Building in East*

Jerusalem (Jerusalem: B'Tselem, 1995); Yael Stein, *The Quiet Deportation: Revocation of Residency of East Jerusalem Palestinians* (Jerusalem: HaMoked and B'Tselem, 1997).

14. Sasson Levi, "Local Government in the Administered Territories," in *Judea, Samaria and Gaza: Views on the Present and Future*, ed. Daniel J. Elazar (Washington: American Enterprise Institute for Public Policy and Research, 1982).

15. About one hundred thousand Muslim and a few Christian inhabitants became refugees, while Israel allowed only 5,875 Druze, 385 Alawis, and 300 Kuneitra residents, mostly Circassans, to stay. See W. W. Harris, "War and Settlement Change: the Golan Heights and the Jordan Rift, 1967–1977," in "Settlement and Conflict in the Mediterranean World," special issue, *Transactions of the Institute of British Geographers*, n.s. 3, no. 3 (1978): 309–30. Harris shows that a disproportionate number of inhabitants fled or were expelled during the 1967 War from two regions: the Golan Heights and the Jordan Valley. It appears that this was not coincidental and that Israel was interested in emptying both these regions of their populations in order to create a vacant buffer against Jordan and Syria.

16. Israel withdrew from the Sinai Peninsula following the 1979 Camp David peace agreement with Egypt.

17. See Michael Feige, *One Space, Two Places: Gush Emunim, Peace Now, and the Construction of Israeli Space* (Jerusalem: Hebrew University Magnes Press, 2002), 41, in Hebrew; Neve Gordon, "The Militarist and Messianic Ideologies," *Middle East Report*, July 2004, online edition.

18. On June 10, 1967, Israel also destroyed the entire Magharbia (north African) Quarter, which was located immediately in front of the Wailing Wall. It was home to thousands of people. See Eyal Weizman, *Hollow Land: Israel's Architecture of Occupation* (New York: Verso Books, 2007), 37–38.

19. For the demographic effects of the 1948 War, see Morris, *The Birth of the Palestinian Refugee Problem*. For the policy in the Jordan Valley, see Harris, "War and Settlement Change," and for the decision regarding the Latrun enclave, see Gazit, *Carrot and the Stick*, 45. An estimated seventy thousand Palestinians fled from the Jordan Valley during the war due to air bombardment of the villages and refugee camps, while the residents of four villages in the Latrun enclave were expelled from their homes, and the vil-

lages were bulldozed. In addition, Israel also annexed to its territory a strip of land parallel to the 1949 armistice line (i.e., the Green Line) along a few kilometers north and south of the Latrun area. This strip of land had been known as "no man's land," because from 1948 to 1967 it was not subject to the control of either the Israeli or Jordanian side. During the war, Israel expelled the residents of the villages of Imwas, Yalu, and Bayt Nuba and destroyed their homes. Over the years, Israel established four communities in this area, two in the OT and two on the border (Shilat, Lapid, Kfar Reuth, and Maccabim). See Yehezkel Lein, *Land Grab: Israel's Settlement Policy in the West Bank* (Jerusalem: B'Tselem, 2002), 12.

20. Gazit, *Carrot and the Stick,* 45.

21. There are numerous books underscoring this view. One prominent example is Benjamin Netanyahu, *A Place Among the Nations* (New York: Bantam, 1993).

22. Zertal and Eldar show how the Israeli government approved the confiscation of land immediately after the war in *Lords of the Land,* 13–81. See also Aronson, *Creating Facts,* 9–31.

23. Full annexation would mean the application of Israeli law to the land.

24. For a basic outline of the Allon plan, see Aronson, *Creating Facts,* 14–16, 31.

25. Ian Lustick, *Unsettled States, Disputed Lands* (New York: Cornell University Press, 1993), 32–37, 351–62.

26. Raja Shehadeh and Jonathan Kuttab, *The West Bank and the Rule of Law* (Ramallah: International Commission of Lawyers, 1980), 10. According to Teveth, the names were altered in March 1968 (*Cursed Blessing,* 258–59).

27. There is one interesting exception. The annual reports published by the Central Bureau of Statistics include a map that demarcates the West Bank and Gaza Strip (all the areas not formally annexed by Israel). See Yinon Cohen, "Sum Thing for Everyone: The Annual Abstract Put Out By the Central Bureau of Statistics Is Much Much More Than a Dry Collection of Statistics," *Ha'aretz,* November 29, 2002.

28. Nathan Brown, "Democracy, History, and the Contest over the Palestinian Curriculum," paper prepared for the Adam Institute, November, 2001. Available online at http://www.geocities.com/nathanbrown1/Adam_Institute_Palestinian_textbooks.htm.

29. Salim Tamari, "What the Uprising Means," in Lockman and Beinin, *Intifada,* 128.

30. The media played a central role in managing Israel's population. See Moti Neiger, Eyal Zandberg, and 'Assam Abu-Ra'iyeh, *Civil or Ethnic Media? An Evaluation of the Coverage of the October 2000 Violent Clashes between the Police and Israeli Arab Citizens* (Tel-Aviv: Keshev, 2000); Daniel Dor, *Newspapers Under the Influence* (Tel-Aviv: Babel, 2001), in Hebrew; and Neve Gordon, "Rationalising Extra-Judicial Executions: The Israeli Press and the Legitimization of Abuse," *International Journal of Human Rights* 8, no. 3 (Autumn 2004): 305–24.

31. Yitzhak Zaccai, *Judea, Samaria and the Gaza District, 1967–1987: Twenty Years of Civil Administration* (Jerusalem: Carta Books, 1987), 6–7.

32. Lustick, *Unsettled States,* 385–438.

33. Similar surveillance mechanisms were employed in Palestinian villages even before Israel's establishment; see Pappe, *The Ethnic Cleansing of Palestine,* 19–21.

34. Gilles Deleuze "Postscript on the Societies of Control," *October* (Winter 1992): 3–7.

35. For documentation of the contingency plans, including the so-called Granite Plan, regarding use of the Israeli military to establish a military government in the West Bank and Gaza Strip, see Gazit, *Carrot and the Stick,* 3–31. From 1956, the military actively discussed the prospect of occupying the West Bank, and slowly it became a common assumption that this might happen. Shlomo Ahronson, "Chief of Staff Yitzhak Rabin's Security Doctrine and the Road to the Six Day War," *Ha'aretz,* November 2, 2005, in Hebrew. In 1958, Chief of Staff Haim Laskov submitted a proposal to occupy the West Bank, but David Ben-Gurion did not approve it. See Moshe Zak, "The Shift in Ben-Gurion's Attitude toward the Kingdom of Jordan," *Israel Studies* 1, no. 2 (Fall 1996): 147–48.

36. Meir Shamgar, who was the military advocate general from 1961 to 1968, prepared the comprehensive *Manual for the Military Advocate in Military Government.* See Meir Shamgar, "Legal Concepts and Problems of the Israeli Military Government: The Initial Stage," in *Military Government in the Territories Administered by Israel, 1967–1980: The Legal Aspects,* ed. Meir Shamgar (Jerusalem: Harry Sacher Institute for Legislative Research and Comparative Law, 1982). For a short description of the semi-

nars, see David Ronen, *The Year of the Shabak* (Tel-Aviv: Ministry of Defence, 1989), 18, in Hebrew.

37. Between 1948 and 1966 the Palestinians who had remained in Israel and had become citizens were subjected to a military government. For a description of the controlling mechanisms used inside Israel proper, consult Ian Lustick, *Arabs in the Jewish State: Israel's Control of a National Minority* (Austin: University of Texas Press, 1980); and Elia Zureik, *The Palestinians in Israel: A Study in Internal Colonialism* (London: Routledge and Kegan Paul, 1979). In the second chapter I briefly discuss the major difference between the forms of control used in Israel proper and those used in the OT. Finally, both Sara Roy and Shabtai Teveth suggest that some of the controlling apparatuses were informed by Israel's brief occupation of the Gaza Strip in 1956. See Sara Roy, *The Gaza Strip: The Political Economy of De-development* (Washington, DC: Institute for Palestinian Studies, 1995); and Teveth, *Cursed Blessing,* 10–11.

38. Black and Morris, *Israel's Secret Wars,* 261–62. See also Felicia Langer, *With My Own Eyes: Israel and the Occupied Territories, 1967–1973* (London: Ithaca Press, 1975).

39. Only after the eruption of the second intifada in September 2000 did Israel stop deploying certain forms of control that had been used for some time.

40. See Foucault, *Discipline and Punish,* as well as Neve Gordon, "On Power and Visibility: An Arendtian Corrective of Foucault," *Human Studies* 25, no. 2 (2002): 125–45.

41. Foucault, *History of Sexuality,* 1: 88–97.

42. Mitchell, "The Limits of the State," 93.

43. Michel Foucault, *Society Must Be Defended* (New York: Penguin Books, 2003), 242–47.

44. Ibid., 246–47.

45. Carl Schmitt, *Political Theology: Four Chapters on the Concept of Sovereignty* (Chicago: University of Chicago Press, 2006). See also Michel Foucault, *Power/Knowledge,* ed., Colin Gordon (New York: Vintage, 1980).

46. Proclamation Two, June 7, 1967, Clause 3 (a). See Chief Military Command, *Orders and Proclamations, Judea and Samaria, 1968–1972* (Tel-Aviv: Israeli Defense Ministry, 1972), in Hebrew.

47. Employing some of Carl Schmitt's insights, Giorgio Agamben has turned the Foucauldian characterization of sovereign power on its head, suggesting that sovereignty is actually defined through the state of exception, namely, the power to withdraw and suspend the law. See Giorgio Agamben, *Homo Sacer: Sovereign Power and Bare Life* (Stanford, CA: Stanford University Press, 1998); and Georgio Agamben, *State of Exception* (Chicago: University of Chicago Press, 2005).

48. Michel Foucault, "Governmentality," in *Foucault Effect: Studies in Governmentality,* ed. Graham Burchell, Colin Gordon, and Peter Miller (London: Harvester Wheatsheaf, 1991), 87–104.

49. Thus, governing in modern societies is "undertaken by a multiplicity of authorities and agencies, employing a variety of techniques and forms of knowledge that seek to shape conduct by working through our desires, aspirations, interests and beliefs, for definite but shifting ends and with a diverse set of relatively unpredictable consequences, effects and outcomes" (Mitchell Dean, *Governmentality: Power and Rule in Modern Society* [Sage Publications, 1999]), 11.

50. Ibid., 19–20.

51. My analysis intimates, however, that we cannot make a rigid distinction among sovereign, disciplinary, and biopower. For instance, controlling apparatuses and practices operating by and through sovereign power retain a disciplinary component within them, while there is almost always a trace of sovereign violence within practices that operate by disciplining the inhabitants.

52. Despite the difficulty of sustaining the distinction among sovereign, disciplinary, and bio power, the emphasis of one mode of power and the de-emphasis of the other reflect important differences in the methods used to manage a population, and therefore the distinction is crucial. A politics of life is ultimately very different from a politics of death and must—necessarily—be maintained through forms of control operating in the service of disciplinary and biopower.

53. Over the years, schools, and particularly universities, were sites of Palestinian resistance, and Israel did not hesitate to shut down educational institutions for extended periods. See Sarah Graham-Brown, *Education, Repression, Liberation: Palestinians* (London: World University Service, 1984).

54. Meron Benvenisti and Shlomo Khayat, *The West Bank and Gaza*

Atlas (Jerusalem: Jerusalem Post, 1987), 112–13; Roy, *Gaza Strip,* 175–81; Lein, *Land Grab,* 18.

55. Schiff and Ya'ari, *Intifada,* 91.

56. I discuss the distinct modalities of control in the next chapter.

57. The term *structure* is not used here in its rigid, totalizing sense. The structure of the occupation is not external to the everyday reality in the West Bank and Gaza Strip, and is therefore tenuous, diverse, and changing. By highlighting a number of its components, however, I hope to uncover the way power has been organized in the territories while simultaneously showing that power creates its own vulnerabilities.

58. The notion of intentionality here and throughout the text is employed in the Foucauldian sense, whereby power relations are both "intentional and nonsubjective." They are a consequence of a series of aims, objectives, and calculations, but these cannot be traced to the decision of a free agent, particularly if the latter is identified with free consciousness. See Foucault, *History of Sexuality,* vol. 2: 94.

59. For instance, see Jonathan Kuttab and Raja Shehadeh, *Civil Administration in the Occupied West Bank: Analysis of Israeli Military Government Order No. 947* (Ramallah: Al-Haq, 1982).

60. Black and Morris, *Israel's Secret Wars,* 261–62.

61. State of Israel, *Two Years,* 10–11.

62. Meron Benvenisti, *Intimate Enemies: Jews and Arabs in a Shared Land* (Berkeley and Los Angeles: University of California Press, 1995). See also in this context Amira Hass, *Drinking the Sea at Gaza: Days and Nights in a Land under Siege* (New York: Metropolitan Books, 1996); Edward Said, *Peace and Its Discontents* (New York: Vintage, 1996); Graham Usher, *Dispatches from Palestine: The Rise and Fall of the Oslo Peace Process* (London: Pluto Press, 1999); Neve Gordon, "Outsourcing Violations: The Israeli Case," *Journal of Human Rights* 1, no. 3 (2002): 321–37.

63. Agamben, *Homo Sacer,* 81–86.

64. Amnon Straschnov, *Justice Under Fire* (Tel-Aviv: Yedioth Ahronoth Books, 1994), in Hebrew.

1. THE INFRASTRUCTURE OF CONTROL

Epigraph: Gazit, *Carrot and the Stick,* 51.

1. Mustafa Barghouthi and Ibrahim Diabes, *Infrastructure and Health*

Services in the West Bank: Guidelines for Health Care Planning (Ramallah: Health, Development, Information, and Policy Institute, 1993), xi.

2. Some two hundred thousand refugees fled to the Gaza Strip in 1948–49, whose original inhabitants numbered only eighty thousand. See Ibrahim Diabes and Mustafa Barghouthi, *Infrastructure and Health Services in the Gaza Strip: The Gaza Strip Primary Health Care Survey* (Ramallah: Health, Development, Information, and Policy Institute, 1996), 5.

3. To uncover the modalities of control, one has to deduce the underlying principle or logic that informs the operation of numerous controlling practices.

4. Adi Ophir discusses the ostensibly temporary nature of the occupation but does not conceptualize it as a modality of control. See Adi Ophir, "A Time of Occupation," in *The Other Israel,* ed. Roane Carey and Jonathan Shainin (New York: New Press, 2003), 51–67.

5. Weizman, *Hollow Land,* 57–86 (see intro., n. 18).

6. For a glimpse into the arbitrary nature of the bureaucratic apparatus, consult Hadaz Ziv, *The Bureaucracy of Occupation: The District Civil Liaison Offices* (Tel-Aviv: Machsom Watch and Physicians for Human Rights–Israel, 2004).

7. The research departments in the Bank of Israel, the Central Bureau of Statistics, as well as several other government ministries set up surveillance apparatuses and thus were also instrumental in the management of the population.

8. Gazit, *Carrot and the Stick,* 33.

9. Jordan had actually annexed the West Bank, but only England and Pakistan recognized the annexation. See Shamgar, "Legal Concepts and Problems," 35–36 (intro., n. 36).

10. Lisa Hajjar, *Courting Conflict: The Israeli Military Court System in the West Bank and Gaza* (Berkeley and Los Angeles: University of California Press, 2005), 56. For a detailed description of the construction of the legal doctrine in the OT as well as Shamgar's role, consult chapter 2. Not surprisingly, as Chief Justice Shamgar supported Israel's policy of suspending the Geneva Convention on every occasion, rights advocates petitioned against this policy in the High Court of Justice. Thus, one can gain a glimpse of how Israel's judiciary system supported the occupying power on all principal matters. See also David Kretzmer, *The Occupation of Justice:*

The Supreme Court of Israel and the Occupied Territories (Albany: State University of New York Press, 2002).

11. Shamgar, "Legal Concepts and Problems," 31–43.

12. Ibrahim Dakkak, "Back to Square One: A Study of the Reemergence of the Palestinian Identity in the West Bank, 1967–1980," in *Palestinians over the Green Line: Studies on the Relations between Palestinians on Both Sides of the 1949 Armistice Line Since 1967,* ed. Alexander Scholch (London: Ithaca Press, 1983), 67.

13. The Hague Convention also states that the occupying power will only be the temporary manager and beneficiary of land and other properties in the occupied territories, and is not permitted to create permanent "facts on the ground" that will remain in the area after the occupation.

14. In the Gaza Strip, Egyptian law and ordinances continued to be valid, while in the West Bank, Jordanian law and ordinances continued to be valid. The Jordanian and Egyptian laws were based on the laws of the British Mandate period. See Chief Military Command, *Orders and Proclamations, Judea and Samaria, 1968–1972* (Tel-Aviv: Israeli Defence Ministry, 1972), in Hebrew.

15. For a discussion of the military orders, see Kretzmer, *Occupation of Justice,* 27–29.

16. Many of these orders undercut international legal provisions that ensured the rights of occupied populations. See Raja Shedadah, *Occupier's Law: Israel and the West Bank* (Washington, DC: Institute for Palestine Studies, 1985).

17. Aronson, *Creating Facts,* 218 (intro., n. 5).

18. For an analysis of the Jordanian laws that Israel invoked and those that it changed to advance its political objectives, see Shehadeh and Kuttab, *West Bank and the Rule of Law,* 15–25 (intro., n. 26).

19. Israel, for example, was not the one to legalize house demolitions; demolitions were rendered legal by British Mandatory emergency regulations, and, according to the Hague Convention, it was Israel's obligation to apply the laws that existed in the area before it was occupied.

20. Hajjar, *Courting Conflict,* 132–54.

21. Raja Shehadeh, "The Changing Juridical Status of Palestinian Areas under Occupation," in *Occupation: Israel over Palestine,* ed. Naseer Hasan Aruri (London: Zed Books, 1984), 97.

22. Israeli law was imposed not only on Israelis resident in the OT, but also on Jews who moved to the settlements, even if they did not have Israeli citizenship. See Eyal Benvenisti, *Legal Dualism: The Absorption of the Occupied Territories into Israel* (Boulder, CO: Westview Press, 1990).

23. Hajjar, *Courting Conflict,* 35–36.

24. The September 2000 regulation banning Palestinians in the occupied regions from living with their spouses who are foreign residents is a case in point. It is presented as a temporary law, and yet it has been extended each year, so that in reality it has become permanent. A more recent example is the Nationality and Entry into Israel Law from 2003 that prohibits the granting of any residency or citizenship status to Palestinians from the OT who are married to Israeli citizens. It too is presented as a temporary law but extended each year.

25. State of Israel, Ministry of Defense, Unit for Coordination of Activities in the Territories, *Three Years of Military Government, 1967–1970: Figures on Civilian Activity in Judea, Samaria, the Gaza Strip and Northern Sinai* (Tel-Aviv: Ministry of Defense, 1970), 2.

26. Throughout the occupation, the Office of the Legal Advisor supported the bureaucratic institutions, while the operations performed by the military government were all subject to the supervision of the state comptroller, similar to those of all other government bodies. See State of Israel, *Two Years,* 1–3 (intro., n. 3).

27. *Summary of the Meetings Held by the General Directors to Discuss the Civilian Issues of the Areas Administered by the IDF,* vols. 1 and 2 (Tel-Aviv: Israel's Defense Ministry, 1967–71 and 1971–77), in Hebrew. See also State of Israel, *Two Years,* 1–3.

28. With the creation of the Civil Administration in 1981, the civil branches in the West Bank and Gaza Strip no longer had to report to the military governor and were from then on subordinate to the new governing body, which was under the direct command of the coordinator of activities in the territories. And yet, as mentioned, the coordinator of activities had to report to the military's chief of staff. The responsibility of the military governors, in turn, was diminished, and they were in charge solely of security in their regions.

29. Because of the nature of the organization, it is difficult to find information about the precise way it operated in the West Bank and Gaza Strip. In this part of the chapter I use the memoirs of three leading figures from

the GSS as well as a number of commentaries by military and intelligence historians. Some of the claims are based on personal experience through my work with Physicians for Human Rights Israel and the Gaza Team for Human Rights, where I had the opportunity to interview scores of Palestinians who had had some contact with the GSS. See Yaakov Perry, *Strike First* (Tel-Aviv: Keshet, 1999), in Hebrew; Carmi Gillon, *Shin-Beth between the Schisms* (Tel-Aviv: Yedioth Ahronoth Books and Chemed Books, 2000), in Hebrew; Yossi Melman and Dan Raviv, *The Imperfect Spies* (London: Sidgwick and Jackson, 1989); Black and Morris, *Israel's Secret Wars* (intro., n. 11); Ronen, *Year of the Shabak* (intro., n. 36).

30. Black and Morris, *Israel's Secret Wars,* 243.

31. Avigdor Feldman, "The Modern Inquisition State," in *Torture: Human Rights, Medical Ethics and the Case of Israel,* ed. Neve Gordon and Ruchama Marton (London: Zed Books, 1995), 85.

32. The GSS is mentioned in only four Israeli laws—the Protection of Privacy Law, the Phone Tap Law, the Criminal Procedures Regulations, and another law that concerns income and tax relief for GSS personnel—which grants it powers to invade privacy, tap telephones, and postpone meetings between a detainee and a lawyer for up to two weeks. These laws create a paradoxical situation, since the legislative branch has actually granted powers to a body that does not exist within the legal system. See Feldman, "Modern Inquisition State," 86.

33. Ibid., 86.

34. The law states, for example, that the GSS's role is to secure "the interests of national security," but since national security is not defined, the law actually bestows upon the GSS an almost unlimited amount of power. The GSS is supposed to frustrate and uproot "subversive" activities, which, like national security, are left undefined. One of the law's clauses orders a total blackout on the way the organization operates, while another clause stipulates the punishment for disclosing any information about the GSS. Moreover, the law provides for no external mechanism responsible for monitoring the organization's operations. So, although the GSS has been legalized, the law was formulated so as to ensure that the GSS will be able to operate in more or less the same way that it did before the legislation.

35. For a comprehensive discussion of the High Court of Justice and its role in the OT, see Kretzmer, *Occupation of Justice.*

36. Pierre Bourdieu, *In Other Words: Essays Towards a Reflexive Sociology* (Cambridge: Polity Press, 1990), 135.

37. Baruch Kimmerling, "Jurisdiction in an Immigrant-Settler Society: The Jewish and Democratic State," *Comparative Political Studies* 35, no. 10 (December 2002): 1130–31.

38. Kretzmer, *Occupation of Justice*, 3.

39. On June 7, for example, a military order (MO) was issued proclaiming that any military commander may halt work, impose curfews, close off an area, deny movement, restrict and regulate the usage of roads, and censor anything in the interests of security and order (MO 3). In such a situation, any person who wished to work, travel, or distribute information had to receive a permit. The Military Orders were published in Hebrew in two journals put out by the Israeli Defense Forces, one for the West Bank and the other for the Gaza Strip and North Sinai. See Israel Defense Forces, *Proclamations, Regulations, Rules, Orders, and Notices of IDF Command for the Gaza Strip and North Sinai,* 1968, in Hebrew; and Israel Defense Forces, *Proclamations, Regulations, Rules, Orders, and Notices of the IDF Command for Judea and Samaria,* 1968, in Hebrew. In 1967, 195 orders appeared, and approximately another hundred orders appeared in 1968. A list of many of the orders is available on the web at http://www.israellaw resourcecenter.org. These are subsequently cited as military orders (MO).

40. The fees one had to pay in order to obtain a permit were continuously raised over the years. Considering that almost every aspect of life needed a permit, the permit regime was also an important source of income for the occupying powers.

41. Military orders 25, 26, 229, 255, 88, and 65.

42. Roy, *Gaza Strip,* 230–31 (intro., n. 54).

43. Military orders 92, 375, 427, 602, 239, 47, 49, 96, 134, 544.

44. Military order 234.

45. Military orders 151, 200, 201, 202, 203, 204, 190, unnumbered MO December 1, 1969, unnumbered MO September 1, 1970, unnumbered MO November 30, 1968, unnumbered MO May 14, 1968.

46. Cited in Virgil Falloon, *Excessive Secrecy: Lack of Guidelines: A Report on the Military Censorship in the West Bank* (Ramallah: Al-Haq, 1986), 5.

47. Military order 379, which was published in April 1970, expanded military order 50 to include a provision that grants the "person responsible"

the power to confiscate any publication that does not have a permit. In August 1980, at the very end of the first period, military order 862 was issued, redefining the word *newspaper* to include "any publication," making it illegal to import and distribute any publication in the West Bank without a permit. See Falloon, *Excessive Secrecy,* 10–11.

48. Ibid., 7. For a discussion of Palestinian newspapers during the first years of occupation, see Daniel Rubenstein, "The Arab Newspapers in the Administered Territories," in *Journalists' Yearbook* (Tel-Aviv, 1975): 182–89, in Hebrew.

49. Michael Shashar, *The Seventh Day War: The Diary of the Military Government in Judea and Samaria, June–December 1967* (Tel-Aviv: Sifriat Poalim, 1997), 73, in Hebrew.

50. Military order 101.

51. Falloon, *Excessive Secrecy,* 12.

52. Ibid., 13. See also *Report of the Special Committee to Investigate Israeli Practices Affecting the Human Rights of the Population of the Occupied Territories* (New York: United Nations, 1982), 10/20/1982, A/37/486. These reports are published annually and are available on the web at http://domino.un.org/unispal.nsf.

53. For a partial list, consult military order 1079, October 14, 1983.

54. For example, one person whom Israel helped to maintain his status by allowing him to operate his business was Rashad Shawa, who also served as the mayor of Gaza for several years. See Ann M. Lesch, "Gaza: Forgotten Corner of Palestine," *Journal of Palestine Studies* 15, no. 1 (1985): 43–61.

55. Raphael Meron, *Economic Development in Judea-Samaria and the Gaza District: Economic Growth and Structural Change, 1970–1980* (Jerusalem: Bank of Israel Research Department, 1983), 18–25.

56. James Ron, *Frontiers and Ghettos: State Violence in Serbia and Israel* (Berkeley and Los Angeles: University of California Press, 2003), 132.

57. State of Israel, *Three Years,* 82–131. All numbers refer to the Gaza Strip during 1969 unless otherwise stated.

58. This was part of Dayan's strategic plan of control. See Weizman, *Hollow Land,* 93–94. According to Michael Shashar's diary, on September 10, 1967, Israel decided to confiscate 100,000 dunams (25,000 acres) in order to build five military bases in the West Bank. See Shashar, *Seventh Day War,* 175.

59. Foucault, *Discipline and Punish*, 187 (intro., n. 8).

60. The Israeli authorities usually refer to collaborators as *sayanim*, a Hebrew word that comes from the root "assist" or "abet." Palestinian collaborators can be divided into different groups according to their function. Most prominent are the informers, a category that includes people who infiltrate different Palestinian organizations as well as the "birds," or *asafir*, who relay information from political prisoners. Palestinian land brokers who sell property to Israelis are also considered collaborators by their copatriots, as are several other Palestinian functionaries who have served as intermediaries between the Israeli authorities and residents in need of certain services. This latter category has included several *mukhtars*, former policemen, members and heads of appointed municipal or village councils, workers in the tax and licensing system of the military government, and, in later years, the members of the Village Leagues. For a discussion of the use of *asafirs*, see Salim Tamari, "Eyeless in Judea: Israel's Strategy of Collaborators and Forgeries," *Middle East Report*, May–August 1990, 39–44. See also Hillel Cohen, *An Army of Shadows: Palestinian Collaborators in the Service of Zionism* (Jerusalem: Ivrit-Hebrew Publishing House, 2004), in Hebrew; and Hillel Cohen, *Good Arabs: The Israeli Security Services and the Israeli Arabs* (Jerusalem: Ivrit-Hebrew Publishing House, 2006), in Hebrew.

61. Yizhar Be'er and Saleh Abdel-Jawad, *Collaborators in the Occupied Territories: Human Rights Abuses and Violations* (Jerusalem: B'Tselem, 1994), 1; Perry, *Strike First*, 52.

62. The granting of requests for various permits directed to the Civil Administration is conditional upon the approval of the GSS, which is not obliged to substantiate its decisions nor to adhere to any criteria in its decision making. The interests of the GSS, such as recruitment of collaborators or pressuring families to turn wanted family members over to the authorities, displace the pertinent considerations and legitimate needs of those requesting services. See Be'er and Abdel-Jawad, *Collaborators in the Occupied Territories*, 12, 16; Perry, *Strike First*, 49; Yehezkel Lein, *Builders of Zion: Human Rights Violations of Palestinians from the Occupied Territories Working in Israel and the Settlements* (Jerusalem: B'Tselem, 1999), 27–33.

63. Be'er and Abdel-Jawad, *Collaborators in the Occupied Territories*, 16–22.

64. Black and Morris, *Israel's Secret Wars*, 248.

65. According to the *New York Times,* September 24, 1989, roughly eighteen intelligence agents worked in each village in the OT.

66. For the major functions of Palestinian collaborators inside Israel, see Cohen, *Good Arabs,* 153.

67. In order for Palestinian collaborators to become part of the controlling apparatus, they must be subjected to the technologies of the self. Collaborators must work on themselves in order to become elements of the occupation's web of control.

68. It is also important to keep in mind that violent measures did not necessarily rely on the permit regime or on surveillance, since Israel also used such measures as a deterrent and not only as a reaction to Palestinian defiance.

69. "There is no need for arms, physical violence, material constraints," Foucault asserts, "[j]ust a gaze. An inspecting gaze, a gaze which each individual under its weight will end by interiorizing to the point that he is his own overseer, each individual thus exercising this surveillance over, and against himself" (Foucault, *Power/Knowledge,* 155 [intro., n. 45]).

70. See, for example, Gazit, *Carrot and the Stick;* Meron Benvenisti, *The West Bank Data Project: A Survey of Israel's Policies* (Washington DC: American Enterprise Institute for Public Policy Research, 1984); Schiff and Ya'ari, *Intifada* (intro., n. 6); and Salim Tamari, "Israel's Search for a Native Pillar: The Village Leagues," in Aruri, *Occupation: Israel over Palestine,* 377–90.

71. Shlomo Gazit, Lecture, Tel-Aviv University, June 10, 2006.

2. "THE INVISIBLE OCCUPATION"

Epigraph: State of Israel, *Three Years,* 4 (see chap. 1, n. 25).

1. Black and Morris, *Israel's Secret Wars,* 239 (intro., n. 11).

2. Shlomo Gazit, Lecture, June 10, 2006, Tel-Aviv University.

3. State of Israel, *Three Years,* 4.

4. Gazit, *Trapped Fools,* 163 (intro., n. 1).

5. In 1968, for example, Israel employed 6,838 Palestinians in the civil institutions within the West Bank and Gaza as opposed to 349 Israeli civilian staff who worked in these institutions. In 1969, 8 Israelis were added to the civil branch's payroll and an additional 595 Palestinians. The civil branch allocated about 20 percent of its budget for agricultural devel-

opment, water systems, transportation, and communication; more than 50 percent was designated for social services, including health, education, religion, welfare, and employment, while the remainder was used for administrative, judicial, and police services (State of Israel, *Two Years,* 9 [intro., n. 3]).

6. Teveth, *Cursed Blessing,* 32 (intro., n. 2).

7. Schiff and Ya'ari claim that this was Moshe Dayan's explicit policy (*Intifada,* 42 [intro., n. 6]). Moreover, it often tried to set one mayor against the others, so that the Palestinian mayors would not unite. See Teveth, *Cursed Blessing,* 283–96.

8. Meron Benvenisti, *The West Bank Data Project: Survey of Israel's Policies, 1984 Report* (Washington, DC: American Enterprise Institute for Public Policy Research, 1984), 44–45. For a historical account of the relations between Zionist leaders and Jordan, consult Avi Shlaim, *The Politics of Partition: King Abdullah, the Zionists and Palestine, 1921–1951* (Oxford: Oxford University Press, 1990).

9. The informal power-sharing agreement between Israel and Jordan deepened after the 1970–71 showdown and expulsion of the PLO from Jordan and lasted until approximately 1978. In September 1970, King Hussein of Jordan decided to have a showdown with the PLO, which was undermining his authority. Armed conflict lasted until July 1971, ending with the expulsion of the PLO and thousands of Palestinians to Lebanon. See Benvenisti, *West Bank Data Project, 1984 Report,* 45.

10. Gazit, *Carrot and the Stick,* 176–80 (intro., epigraph note); Schiff and Ya'ari, *Intifada,* 42, in Hebrew.

11. Sara Roy contends that the objective of the open bridges policy was primarily economic, since Jordan was used as a trading outlet for the vast surplus of agricultural goods in the West Bank and Gaza Strip, while eliminating the possibility that Palestinian goods would flood the Israeli market and engender a decrease in prices. See Roy, *Gaza Strip,* 145 (intro., n. 37). See also B'Tselem, *Restrictions on Travel Abroad* (Jerusalem: B'Tselem, 1989); Association of Civil Rights in Israel, *Restrictions on the Right of Freedom of Movement in the Administered Territories* (Jerusalem: ACRI, 1989); Hamoked, *Restrictions on Travel Abroad for East Jerusalem and West Bank Palestinians* (Jerusalem: Hamoked, 1992).

12. Judah and Samaria Command, *Din VeHeshbon: The Administration's Fourteenth Year* (Jerusalem: IDF, 1981), in Hebrew; Civil Adminis-

tration of the Gaza Strip, *Din VeHeshbon: The Administration's Fifteenth Year* (Jerusalem: Ministry of Defence, 1982), in Hebrew.

13. Military order 101, August 27, 1967 (see chap. 1, n. 39).

14. Ronen, *Year of the Shabak,* 57 (intro., n. 36).

15. For documentation of many of the coercive measures used by Israel during this period, see the annual *Report of the Special Committee to Investigate Israeli Practices Affecting the Human Rights of the Population of the Occupied Territories,* 05/10/1971, A/8389; 09/10/1972, A/8828; 25/10/1973, A/9148; 04/11/1974, A/9817; 27/10/1975, A/10272; 01/10/1976, A/31/218; 27/10/1977, A/32/284; 13/11/1978, A/33/356; 13/11/1979, A/34/631; 06/10/1980, A/35/425 (see chap. 1, n. 52).

16. Gazit, *Carrot and the Stick,* 244–46.

17. The official reasons for deportations were spelled out by Colonel Joel Singer, the military's attorney general in the early 1980s, and appear in Joost R. Hiltermann, *Israel's Deportation Policy in the Occupied West Bank and Gaza* (Ramallah: Al-Haq, 1986), 66–69.

18. Ann M. Lesch, "Israeli Deportation of Palestinians from the West Bank and Gaza Strip, 1967–1978," *Journal of Palestine Studies* 8, no. 2 (Winter 1979): 101–31.

19. For an analysis of the deportation vis-à-vis international humanitarian law, see Hiltermann, *Israel's Deportation Policy,* 29–40.

20. The military government expelled, for example, eight Palestinian National Front leaders in December 1973, while Birzeit University's president together with four other people were deported in 1974, and the mayors of Halhul and Hebron in 1980. See Aruri, ed., *Occupation: Israel over Palestine,* 11, 19, 310 (chap. 1, n. 21). Also see *Report of the Special Committee,* October 5, 1971, A/8389.

21. Daphna Golan, *Detained Without Trial: Administrative Detention in the Occupied Territories Since the Beginning of the Intifada* (Jerusalem: B'Tselem, 1992), 22.

22. Another important strike was launched in 1967 by the West Bank lawyers. The Jordanian government paid the lawyers so long as they banned the Israeli legal system, and even though in 1971 a group of lawyers began appearing in the military courts, many continued striking until the late 1980s. See George Bisharat, *Palestinian Lawyers and Israeli Rule: Law and Disorder in the West Bank* (Austin: University of Texas, 1989).

23. Gazit, *Carrot and the Stick,* 246–48.

24. Ibid., 246–48; see also Hajjar, *Courting Conflict,* 171 (chap. 1, n. 10).

25. See *Report of the Special Working Group of Experts Established Under Resolution 6 (XXV) of the Commission on Human Rights,* E/CN.4/1016/Add.1, 11 February 1970, available online at http://domino.un.org/unispal .nsf; and *Report of the Special Committee,* October 5, 1970, A/8089. See also "Israel Tortures Arab Prisoners," *Sunday Times,* June 19, 1977. The reports cite the following practices: (1) suspension of the detainee by the hands and the simultaneous traction of his other members for hours at a time until he loses consciousness; (2) burns with cigarette stubs; (3) blows by rods on the genitals; (4) tying up and blindfolding for days (in one case for seven days); (5) bites by dogs; (6) electric shocks at the temples, the mouth, the chest and testicles.

26. Lesch, "Gaza: Forgotten Corner of Palestine," 43–61 (chap. 1, n. 54); Joan Mandell, "Gaza: Israel's Soweto," *Middle East Report* (October/December 1985), 10–11.

27. Roy, *Gaza Strip,* 105; Weizman, *Hollow Land,* 70 (intro., n. 18).

28. *Fedayeen* was the name of the Palestinian guerillas; it means "self-sacrifice" in Arabic. See Black and Morris, *Israel's Secret Wars,* 262.

29. Eyal Weizman (*Hollow Land,* 70) points out that as part of his counter-insurgency campaign in Gaza, Sharon wanted to sever the Strip from the Sinai Desert and thereby from the PLO guerrilla supply lines that supposedly traversed it. During the winter of 1971–72, Sharon ordered the destruction of the area south of Gaza, known as the Rafah Salient, which was settled by a five-thousand strong Bedouin tribe. He drew a line on the map where the encampment was located and ordered bulldozers to drive along it, carving a swath several dozen meters wide that ran over all obstacles in its path.

30. See table 1 in the preface for how the data was gathered.

31. Weizman, *Hollow Land,* 253.

32. Foucault, *History of Sexuality,* 1:86 (intro., n. 8).

33. Rashid Khalidi, *Palestinian Identity* (New York: Columbia University Press, 1998), 174. See also in this context Adnan Abu-Ghazaleh, "Arab Cultural Nationalism in Palestine During the British Mandate," *Journal of Palestine Studies* 1, no. 3. (Spring 1972): 37–63.

34. Khalidi, *Palestinian Identity,* 174; Graham-Brown, *Education, Repression, Liberation,* 66–67 (intro., n. 53).

35. State of Israel, *Two Years,* 13. In the West Bank, Israel inherited a total of 840 schools, 654 of them governmental, 95 private and 91 United Nations Relief and Work Agency (UNRWA) schools; while in Gaza it took over 78 governmental schools (118 operated before the war) and oversaw all the UNRWA schools. By 1980, the end of the first period of occupation, there were a total of 1,413 educational institutions, 498 of which were nongovernmental, thus indicating that the rate of increase during those years was much higher in the nongovernmental sector. See State of Israel, *Two Years,* 15, 43; Coordinator of Government Activities in Judea-Samaria, Gaza Strip District, Sinai, *A Fourteen-Year Survey, 1967–1981* (Tel-Aviv: Ministry of Defence, 1982), 19.

36. The books are listed in military order 107 from August 27, 1967, which states that "this lists 55 books which are banned from being taught in schools. These include Arabic language books, history, geography, sociology, and philosophy books."

37. As cited in Shashar, *Seventh Day War,* 220 (chap. 1, n. 49).

38. For more information about the disagreement between the Ministry of Education and Ministry of Defense, consult Teveth, *Cursed Blessing,* 178–88.

39. Following the introduction of Israeli textbooks in East Jerusalem, many parents opted to send their children to private schools. By 1979, the Ministry of Education allowed the government schools to revert to the Jordanian curriculum. See Graham-Brown, *Education, Repression, Liberation,* 70.

40. In the Gaza Strip, only 24 textbooks were approved out of the 160 used during Egypt's rule. See State of Israel, *Two Years,* 43; see also military order 107 from August 29, 1967.

41. "The books listed in military order 107 may now be used in schools in their new editions" (military order 183, December 4, 1967).

42. For an account of the strike from Israel's perspective as well as a detailed list of the different sanctions Israel used to stop it, see Gazit, *Carrot and the Stick,* 273–90. The unfolding events are significant in the context of our discussion of controlling technologies since they reveal how technologies informed by sovereign power are frequently needed to implement disciplinary forms of control.

43. Said Assaf, "Educational Destruction and Recovery in Palestine," in *Education: Destruction and Reconstruction in Disrupted Societies,* ed. S. Tawil (Geneva, Switzerland: UNESCO, 1997), 53.

44. Assaf, "Educational Destruction and Recovery in Palestine," 53.

45. Virgil Falloon, *Excessive Secrecy*, 10 (chap. 1, n. 46); Agustín Velloso de Santisteban, "Palestinian Education: A National Curriculum against All Odds," *International Journal of Educational Development* 22, no. 2 (March 2002): 145–54.

46. Benedict Anderson, *Imagined Communities: Reflections on the Origin and Spread of Nationalism* (London: Verso, 1991), 122.

47. Paulo Friere, *Pedagogy of the Oppressed* (London: Continuum International Publishing Group, 1995), 134. For an interesting discussion of how Palestinian citizens inside Israel were encouraged to mimic Jewish Israelis, see Catherine Rottenberg, "Dancing Arabs and Spaces of Desire," *Topia: Canadian Journal of Cultural Studies* 19 (Spring 2008), 109–26.

48. Teveth, *Cursed Blessing*, 331–32, 188; Daniel Rubenstein, "The Arab Newspapers in the Administered Territories," *Journalists' Yearbook: 43* (Tel-Aviv: Journalist Union, 1984), 102–4.

49. Assaf, "Educational Destruction and Recovery in Palestine," 52–53.

50. Graham-Brown, *Education, Repression, Liberation*, 77.

51. Dedi Zucker et al., *Report on Human Rights in the Areas Held by the IDF, 1979–1983* (Tel-Aviv: International Center for Peace in the Middle East, 1983), 57.

52. Assaf, "Educational Destruction and Recovery in Palestine," 53.

53. Graham-Brown, *Education, Repression, Liberation*, 73.

54. Nafez Nazzal and Leila Nazzal, "The Politicization of Palestinian Children: An Analysis of Nursery Rhymes," *Palestine–Israel Journal of Politics, Economics and Culture* 3, no. 1 (1996): 26–33; Velloso de Santisteban, "Palestinian Education," 149.

55. State of Israel, *Three Years*, 4.

56. State of Israel, *Two Years*, 11.

57. Ibid., 10–11.

58. It is important to stress that hundreds of thousands of nonfruit trees were planted as a way of guaranteeing that the Palestinians would not expand construction on their land. See Jewish National Fund archives, file 31235/KKL5, letter dated March 28, 1969. I want to thank Ariel Handel for alerting me to these files.

59. Central Bureau of Statistics, *Monthly Statistics of the Administered Territories* 1, no. 8.(August, 1971): 14–16.

60. Shmuel Fohorils, *The Development of Agriculture in the Administered Territories: Patterns of Economic Acceleration and Growth* (Tel-Aviv: Agriculture Ministry, 1976), 2–13, in Hebrew.

61. Roy, *Gaza Strip,* 222.

62. Central Bureau of Statistics, *National Accountability: Judea, Samaria and the Gaza Strip, 1968–1993,* publication 1012 (Tel-Aviv: Central Bureau of Statistics, 1996), 20, in Hebrew.

63. Michel Foucault, "Afterword: The Subject and Power," in *Michel Foucault: Beyond Structuralism and Hermeneutics,* ed. Hubert L. Dreyfus and Paul Rabinow (Chicago: University of Chicago Press, 1982), 208–26.

64. Roy, *The Gaza Strip,* 148.

65. Bank of Israel Research Department, *The Economy of the Administered Areas, 1969* (Jerusalem: Bank of Israel Research Department, 1971), and *The Economy of the Administered Areas, 1971* (Jerusalem: Bank of Israel Research Department, 1972); Uri Litvin, *The Economy of the Administered Areas, 1976–1977* (Jerusalem: Bank of Israel Research Department, 1980); Raphael Meron, *The Economy of the Administered Areas, 1977–1978* (Jerusalem: Bank of Israel Research Department, 1980); Raphael Meron, *Economic Development* (chap. 1, n. 55).

66. Gideon Weigert, *Training for a Brighter Future: The Story of Vocational Training in the West Bank and Gaza* (Jerusalem: Jerusalem Post Press, 1976), 1; Coordinator of Government Activities, *Fourteen-Year Survey,* 7.

67. State of Israel, *Two Years,* 13; Roy, *Gaza Strip,* 142.

68. Meron, *Economic Development,* 6.

69. Central Bureau of Statistics, *National Accountability,* 125.

70. United Nations, Report of the Secretary-General, *Development and International Economic Co-Operation: Living Conditions of the Palestinian People in the Occupied Arab Territories,* A/35/533, October 17, 1980.

71. Central Bureau of Statistics, *National Accountability,* 18.

72. Central Bureau of Statistics, *National Accountability,* 17. See also Arie Bergman, *Economic Growth in the Administered Territories, 1968–1972* (Jerusalem: Bank of Israel, 1974), in Hebrew; Yaacov Liphschitz, *Economic Development in the Administered Territories, 1967–1969* (Tel-Aviv, Ma'archot, 1970), in Hebrew.

73. Central Bureau of Statistics, *National Accountability,* 86, 105.

74. Ibid., 24.

75. Meron, *Economic Development,* 22.

76. Weigert, *Training for a Brighter Future*, 2.

77. Ibid., 8, 12, 17.

78. Mandell, "Gaza: Israel's Soweto," 11.

79. Aronson, *Creating Facts*, 24 (intro., n. 5).

80. Cited in Aronson, *Creating Facts*, 25.

3. OF HORSES AND RIDERS

Epigraph: Ministry of Defence, *Four Years of Military Administration, 1967–1971* (Tel-Aviv: Office of the Coordinator of Government Activities in the Administered Territories, 1971), 8.

1. Ironically, the incorporation of Palestinian workers into Israel was in some respects detrimental to the Israeli economy, since the availability of cheap labor allowed employers to refrain from investing in machinery, technology, and vocational upgrading, which, it may be argued, could have enhanced the productivity of the Israeli economy. See Shlomo Swirski, *The Price of Occupation: The Cost of the Occupation to Israeli Society* (Tel-Aviv: Adva Center, 2005), 16, 13.

2. Schiff and Ya'ari, *Intifada*, 91 (intro., n. 6).

3. Roy, *Gaza Strip*, 4, 128 (intro., n. 37).

4. According the Bank of Israel, average annual GNP growth in the West Bank and Gaza was 14 percent between 1970 and 1975, 7 percent between 1976 and 1980, and 0 percent 1981 and 1982. See Dan Zakai, *Economic Development in Judea-Samaria and the Gaza District, 1981–1982* (Jerusalem: Bank of Israel Research Department, 1985), 11.

5. Arie Arnon and Jimmy Weinblatt, "Sovereignty and Economic Development: The Case of Israel and Palestine," *Economic Journal* 111 (June 2001): 291–308.

6. Military orders 7 (June 8, 1967), 21 (June 18, 1967), 45 (July 9, 1967). See chap. 1, n. 39.

7. Laurence Harris, "Money and Finance with Undeveloped Banking in the Occupied Territories," in *The Palestinian Economy*, ed. George T. Abed (New York: Routledge, 1989), 191–222.

8. See, for example, MO 59 (July 1967: control of land); MO 92 (August 1967; control of water); MO 375 (February 1970; control of electricity). See also Benvenisti and Khayat, *West Bank and Gaza Atlas*, 112–13 (intro., n. 54); Roy, *Gaza Strip*, 175–81.

9. United Nations Conference on Trade and Development, *Palestinian External Trade under Israeli Occupation* (New York: United Nations, UNCTAD/RDP/SEU/1, 1989).

10. Bakir Abu Kishk, "Industrial Development and Policies in the West Bank and Gaza," in Abed, *Palestinian Economy*, 168.

11. Roy, *Gaza Strip*, 239.

12. Swirski, *Price of Occupation*, 15.

13. Roy, *Gaza Strip*, 238.

14. Mohammed K. Shadid, "Israeli Policy Towards Economic Development in the West Bank and Gaza," in Abed, *Palestinian Economy*, 125. For example, it introduced a 15 percent production tax on Palestinian manufacturers, which was not applied to Israeli manufacturers both inside the Green Line and in the OT, as well as a special tax on every Palestinian truck transporting produce to Jordan, averaging $2,000 per season until 1987, which, in the context of the OT, is a substantial financial burden and considerably decreased the profits from exports. See also Roy, *Gaza Strip*, 230–32.

15. Ibid., 237–42.

16. Osama A. Hamed and Radwan A. Shaban, "One-Sided Customs and Monetary Union: The Case of the West Bank and Gaza Strip under Israeli Occupation," in *The Economics of Middle East Peace: Views from the Region*, ed. Stanley Fischer, Dani Rodrik, and Elias Tuma (Cambridge, MA: MIT Press, 1993), 143.

17. Swirski, *Price of Occupation*, 11.

18. Shadid, "Israeli Policy Towards Economic Development," 124.

19. Arie Arnon, Israel Luski, Avia Spivak, and Jimmy Weinblat, *The Palestinian Economy* (New York: Brill, 1997), 19.

20. From 1967 to 1987, government investment accounted for close to 50 percent of gross capital formation in Israeli industry, but close to 0 percent in Gaza's industry (Roy, *Gaza Strip*, 241).

21. Arnon, et al., *Palestinian Economy*, 99. The trade deficit was covered by external remittances from Palestinians working in neighboring Arab states and wages earned by Palestinians working in Israel.

22. Roy, *Gaza Strip*, 245.

23. Ibid., 210, 217, 222.

24. Meron Benvenisti, *The West Bank Data Project, 1987 Report, Demographic, Economic, Legal, Social, and Political Developments in the West*

Bank (Washington, DC: American Enterprise Institute for Public Policy Research, 1987), 6.

25. Salim Tamari, "Building Other People's Homes: The Palestinian Peasant's Household and Work in Israel," *Journal of Palestine Studies* 11, no. 1 (Autumn 1981), 56.

26. Roy, *Gaza Strip*, 252.

27. Per capita consumption in the Gaza Strip rose from $379.8 in 1968 to $1,008.10 in 1987, and from $607.20 to $1,476.50 in the West Bank. See Arnon, et al., *Palestinian Economy*, 49.

28. Anita Shapira, *Futile Struggle: The Jewish Labor Controversy, 1929–1939* (Tel-Aviv: Tel-Aviv University Press and HaKibbutz Hameuchad, 1977); Gershon Shafir, *Land, Labor and the Origins of the Israeli Palestinian Conflict, 1882–1914* (Cambridge: Cambridge University Press, 1989); Sheila Ryan, "Israeli Economic Policy in the Occupied Areas: Foundations of a New Imperialism," *Middle East Report* no. 24 (January 1974): 3–24.

29. Emanuel Farjoun, "Palestinian Workers in Israel—A Reserve Army of Labor," *Khamsin* 7 (1980): 107–43; see especially 110–13.

30. Hiltermann, *Behind the Intifada*, 17–18 (intro., n. 6).

31. By 1988, the disparity had diminished but was still high, with Palestinian workers earning 35–50 percent less than Israelis (Swirski, *Price of Occupation*, 22).

32. Teveth, *Cursed Blessing*, 90–96 (intro., n. 2).

33. State of Israel, *Two Years*, 13 (intro., n. 3).

34. Ryan, "Israeli Economic Policy in the Occupied Areas," 13.

35. For more on the Allon Plan, see Benvenisti and Khayat, *West Bank and Gaza Atlas;* Aronson, *Creating Facts,* 14–16 (intro., n. 5); Sheila Ryan, "Plans to Regularize the Occupation," in Aruri, ed., *Occupation: Israel over Palestine,* 340 (chap. 1, n. 21).

36. Gazit, *Carrot and the Stick,* 222

37. Weigert, *Training for a Brighter Future,* 1 (chap. 2, n. 66).

38. Coordinator of Government Activities, *Fourteen-Year Survey,* 7 (chap. 2, n. 35).

39. Ryan, "Israeli Economic Policy in the Occupied Areas," 18.

40. State of Israel, *Two Years,* 42.

41. Weigert, *Training for a Brighter Future,* 12.

42. Ryan, "Israeli Economic Policy in the Occupied Areas," 13.

43. Central Bureau of Statistics, *National Accountability,* 125 (chap. 2, n. 62).

44. Lein, *Builders of Zion,* 8 (chap. 1, n. 62).

45. Ryan, "Israeli Economic Policy in the Occupied Areas," 13.

46. Central Bureau of Statistics, *National Accountability,* 86, 105.

47. Lev Grinberg, *HaHistadrut Meal Hakol* [The Histadrut above all] (Jerusalem: Nevo, 1993).

48. The Palestinian laborers also did not receive the same benefits granted to Israelis, such as bonuses for seniority, and were not incorporated into the Israeli social safety net, which offers Israeli citizens a variety of social security allowances. See Farjoun, "Palestinian Workers in Israel," 111–18.

49. Michael Mann, "The Dark Side of Democracy: The Modern Tradition of Ethnic and Political Cleansing," *New Left Review* 235 (May–June 1999): 18–45.

50. Lein, *Builders of Zion,* 27.

51. Birzeit, which had been a two-year college, became a university in 1972; Bethlehem University opened its gates in 1973; An-Najah was transformed from a college to a university in 1977, at around the same time Hebron University, which had been a college since 1971, became an accredited institution; and the Islamic University in Gaza opened in 1978.

52. Between 1975 and 1982, 102,000 Palestinians left the West Bank to find jobs in the Gulf States. See Maya Rosenfeld, *Confronting the Occupation* (Stanford, CA: Stanford University Press, 2004), 41. See also Hamed and Shaban, "One-Sided Customs and Monetary Union," 118; Ishac Diwan and Radwan A. Shaban, "Introduction and Background," in *Development under Adversity: The Palestinian Economy in Transition,* ed. Ishac Diwan and Radwan A. Shaban (Washington, DC: World Bank, 1999), 3–4.

53. Schiff and Ya'ari, *Intifada,* 91.

54. Tamari, "Building Other People's Homes," 33.

55. Joel S. Migdal, *Palestinian Society and Politics* (Princeton, NJ: Princeton University Press, 1980), 62.

56. On July 19, 1967, Israel organized a conference for the *mukhtars* in Nablus, where they were "warned that they would be punished if foreigners or terrorists would be found in their villages and if they distributed the communist party's paper *Al-Itihad.*" Each village *mukhtar* was paid 75

Israeli pounds a month, while the second *mukhtar* in the same village was paid 50. See Shashar, *Seventh Day War,* 105 and 161, respectively. See also MO 176, which authorizes the military commander to dismiss any *mukhtar.*

57. Central Bureau of Statistics, *National Accountability,* 135.

58. Migdal, *Palestinian Society and Politics,* 67.

59. Ryan, "Israeli Economic Policy in the Occupied Areas," 13.

60. "Israel Restructures West Bank Economy, Interview with A.R. Husseini," *Middle East Report* 60 (September 1977): 21–23.

61. Meron Benvenisti, *The West Bank Data Base Project, 1986 Report: Demographic, Economic, Legal, Social and Political Developments in the West Bank* (Boulder, CO: Westview Press, 1986), 10.

62. Ibid., 8–9.

63. Arnon and Weinblatt, "Sovereignty and Economic Development," 308.

64. For an analysis of this law, see chapter 4.

65. Yehezkel Lein, *Disputed Waters: Israel's Responsibility for the Water Shortage in the Occupied Territories* (Jerusalem: B'Tselem, 1998).

66. Benvenisti and Khayat, *West Bank and Gaza Atlas,* 45.

67. *Report of the Special Committee;* 10/20/1982, A/37/486 (chap. 1, n. 52).

68. *Ma'ariv,* February 9, 1973. Cited in Ryan, "Israeli Economic Policy in the Occupied Areas," 17.

69. Weizman, *Hollow Land,* 229 (intro., n. 18).

70. Cited in Weizman, *Hollow Land,* 230. Weizman adds that between 1972 and 1979 four new neighborhoods for refugees were constructed. They included Israeli-style dense housing schemes, simply replicating existing plans provided by the Israeli Ministry of Housing, constructed by Palestinian developers. The Israeli government took foreign visitors on tours to show the new housing schemes, claiming that they demonstrated their enlightened rule and attempts to solve the "refugee problem" by providing decent housing. In 1974 another approach for the resettlement of refugees was implemented: refugees were provided with plots of 250 square meters and with the means to build their own homes. Financial assistance was handed out on condition that refugees physically demolished their older homes in the camps. Methods used by Israeli occupation authorities to convince reluctant refugees included threats and random demolitions

within the camps as well as visits by Palestinian collaborators to refugee households. The PLO forbade refugees to accept these Israeli offers and killed some of those who did, as well as many of the Palestinian collaborators. The program failed to subdue Palestinian resistance, and some of the newly populated housing areas became themselves centers of resistance.

71. Ryan, "Israeli Economic Policy in the Occupied Areas," 17.

72. Hiltermann, *Behind the Intifada,* 33.

73. Tamari, "Building Other People's Homes," 60.

74. Hiltermann, *Behind the Intifada,* 8.

75. Ibid., 25.

76. Let me stress once again that my use of the term *intentional* does not presuppose a free agent or a statist approach, but a nonsubjective intentionality whereby the policies are a consequence of a series of aims, objectives, and calculations that do not originate in the decision of a free actor. The state is more a vehicle of articulation than the source of the policies.

77. Barghouthi and Diabes, *Infrastructure and Health Services in the West Bank,* xii–xvi (chap. 1, n. 1); Diabes and Barghouthi, *Infrastructure and Health Services in the Gaza Strip,* x–xv (chap. 1, n. 2).

78. Roy, *Gaza Strip,* 268.

79. Barghouthi and Diabes, *Infrastructure and Health Services in the West Bank,* xii–xvi; Diabes and Barghouthi, *Infrastructure and Health Services in the Gaza Strip,* x–xv. In Israel, the unrecognized Bedouin villages, which are home to some 75,000 Israeli citizens, do not have access to these basic services.

80. Roy, *Gaza Strip,* 276.

4. IDENTIFICATION TROUBLE

Epigraph: Coordinator of Government Operations in Judea-Samaria and the Gaza District, *Judea-Samaria and the Gaza District: A Sixteen-Year Survey, 1967–1983* (Tel-Aviv: Ministry of Defense, 1983).

1. Brigade General Yosef Lunz, who had served as the military governor of the West Bank, was appointed to be the first head of the Civil Administration in the Gaza Strip.

2. Menachem Milson, "How to Make Peace with the Palestinians," *Commentary* 71, no. 5 (1981), 31, 35.

3. Yehoshua Porath, *The Emergence of the Palestinian-Arab National*

Movement, 1918–1929 (London: Frank Cass, 1974); William B. Quandt, Fuad Jabber, and Ann Mosely Lesch, *The Politics of Palestinian Nationalism* (Berkeley and Los Angeles: University of California Press, 1973); Israel Gershoni and James Jankowski, eds., *Rethinking Nationalism in the Arab Middle East* (New York: Columbia University Press, 1997); Khalidi, *Palestinian Identity* (chap. 2, n. 33); and Cohen, *Army of Shadows* (chap. 1, n. 60).

4. Khalidi, *Palestinian Identity,* 173.

5. For an insider's exposition of the development of the national movement in the OT following the 1967 War, see Dakkak, "Back to Square One," 66 (chap. 1, n. 12).

6. Khalidi, *Palestinian Identity,* 178. The same claim is made in Issa Al-Shuaibi, "The Development of Palestinian Entity-Consciousness: Part 2," *Journal of Palestine Studies* 9, no. 2 (Winter 1980): 50–70.

7. Tom Segev, "Arabs More Than Arabs," *Ha'aretz,* June 8, 2005, in Hebrew.

8. Don Peretz, "Palestinian Social Stratification: The Political Implications," *Journal of Palestine Studies* 7, no. 1 (Autumn 1977): 48–74, 63.

9. Dakkak, "Back to Square One," 69.

10. See Moshe Ma'oz, *Palestinian Leadership on the West Bank: The Changing Role of the Arab Mayors under Jordan and Israel* (London: Frank Cass, 1984), 72.

11. The support of religious leaders in order to offset the nationalist drive was used by the security establishment also inside Israel in the 1950s and 1960s. See Cohen, *Good Arabs,* 98 (chap. 1, n. 60).

12. Schiff and Ya'ari, *Intifada,* 223–225 (intro., n. 6). For other attempts to create religious divisions, see Tamari, "Eyeless in Judea," 39–44 (chap. 1, n. 60).

13. Al-Shuaibi, "Palestinian Entity-Consciousness: Part 2," 58.

14. Ibid., 61.

15. Ibid., 62.

16. Cited in Ma'oz, *Palestinian Leadership on the West Bank,* 89.

17. Ibid., 64.

18. Al-Shuaibi, "Palestinian Entity-Consciousness: Part 2," 64–65.

19. For instance, MO 194, 236, 312, 394 (see chap. 1, n. 39).

20. Ma'oz, *Palestinian Leadership on the West Bank,* 80–81.

21. Levi, "Local Government in the Administered Territories," 110 (intro., n. 14).

22. Teveth, *Cursed Blessing*, 229, 287.

23. For a discussion of the legal aspects of the municipal elections, see Moshe Drori, "Local Government in Judea and Samaria," in Shamgar, *Military Government in the Territories Administered by Israel*, 237–84 (intro., n. 36).

24. The appointments were based on a 1934 British municipal law that gave the person in charge of the region the authority to appoint and dismiss the municipal council and the power to decide who could vote or be eligible for nomination. See Muhammad Al-Khaas, "Municipal Legal Structure in Gaza," in *A Palestinian Agenda for the West Bank and Gaza*, ed. Emile A. Nakhleh (Washington, DC: American Enterprise Institute for Public Policy Research, 1980), 103.

25. Al-Khaas, "Municipal Legal Structure in Gaza," 104.

26. Mandell, "Gaza: Israel's Soweto," 14 (chap. 2, n. 26).

27. Roy, *Gaza Strip*, 267.

28. Al-Shuaibi, "Palestinian Entity-Consciousness: Part 2," 60. Al-Shuaibi adds that Jordan also called on the West Bank inhabitants to boycott the elections because of its continued insistence that it was the legitimate sovereign of the region and represented its inhabitants. Accordingly it was no surprise that Jordan was against the election of a local leadership that might undermine its claims.

29. Gazit, *Trapped Fools*, 167–68 (intro., n. 1).

30. Drori, "Local Government in Judea and Samaria," 265.

31. The Jordanian municipality law grants the right to vote to every male born in the city registered as a resident of the city on the condition that he pay at least one dinar yearly in property or business tax. Someone who paid two hundred dinars in taxes could obtain for himself two hundred votes by recording the names of two hundred people in the voter registries as taxpayers. This is how the wealthy landowners secured their political power. See Levi, "Local Government in the Administered Territories," 106.

32. Ma'oz notes that although 50 percent of the elected council men were new, the election results did not create a qualitative change in the makeup of the municipal elites. Except for a number of mayors and council members who belonged to the intelligentsia and to the middle class, the

elected council members represented the large *hamulas* and the economic elites, not the workers' stratum whose recent financial gains from work in Israel were not yet translated into political power. There was a high correlation between socioeconomic status, expressed in landholding and business ownership, and political office. See Ma'oz, *Palestinian Leadership on the West Bank,* 105. See also Gazit, *Trapped Fools,* 179–82.

33. Lustick, *Arabs in the Jewish State,* 203 (intro., n. 37).

34. Ma'oz, *Palestinian Leadership on the West Bank,* 105.

35. Following two airplane hijackings carried out in early September 1970 by the PFLP, in which the planes were ordered to land on Jordanian soil, King Hussein imposed martial law in the country and ordered the Palestinian *fedayeen* to lay down their weapons. His decision to disarm the PLO derived from his sense that the PLO was trying take over the country. Ten days of clashes between the PLO and the Jordanian military ensued, with an estimated thirty-five hundred casualties on both sides. The incidents, referred to as Black September, ended with the PLO's forceful expulsion from Jordan.

36. Benvenisti, *West Bank Data Project, 1984 Report,* 45 (chap. 1, n. 70).

37. The PNF united the underground political organizations and leading figures who were considered nationalist personalities. See "Resistance in the Occupied Territories," *Journal of Palestine Studies* 3, no. 4 (Summer 1974): 164–66; and Issa Al-Shuaibi, "The Development of Palestinian Entity-Consciousness: Part 3," *Journal of Palestine Studies* 9, no. 3 (Spring, 1980): 99–124. For Israel's response to the demonstrations, see *Report of the Special Committee;* 04/11/1974, A/9817.

38. *Ma'ariv,* November 23, 1973, as cited in Al-Shuaibi, "Palestinian Entity-Consciousness: Part 3," 116.

39. The Arab summit took place on October 29, 1974; on November 13, Arafat gave his historic address to the United Nations. United Nations resolutions 3236 and 3237 of 22 November 1974 acknowledged the PLO as the representative of the Palestinian people and invited it to participate as an observer in the General Assembly and UN-sponsored international conferences.

40. Dakkak, "Back to Square One," 69.

41. Benvenisti, *West Bank Data Project, 1986 Report,* 25–29; Zertal and Eldar, *Lords of the Land,* 570 (intro., n. 5).

42. Hiltermann, *Behind the Intifada,* 6 (intro., n. 6).

43. Surely other social processes weakened the traditional elite, some of which began before Israel's occupation of the West Bank and Gaza. These include greater emphasis on the importance of education for both men and women, the impact of social displacement, and the need to make economic readjustments. See Peretz, "Palestinian Social Stratification."

44. Hiltermann, *Behind the Intifada*, 8.

45. Ma'oz, *Palestinian Leadership on the West Bank*, 134; Al-Shuaibi, "Palestinian Entity-Consciousness: Part 3," 122.

46. Gazit, *Trapped Fools*, 179–82.

47. Paradoxically, at this point the Israeli authorities were still less invasive in the OT than they had been in Israel during the military administration. Until 1966, the military administration determined the list of representatives from each *hamula* to the regional councils as well as the chairmen of the councils. See Lustick, *Arabs in the Jewish State*, 205.

48. Gazit, *Trapped Fools*, 179.

49. In two towns an agreed list was presented, and in a third elections had been held in 1974 and were not due to be held until later. See Drori, "Local Government in Judea and Samaria," 283.

50. Not long before the elections, Israel deported the mayors of Al-Bireh and Ramallah because they supported the PLO, and on March 28, 1976, two weeks before the elections, it deported two leading candidates from Hebron and Al-Bireh. See "Palestinian Resistance Threatens Israeli Occupation," *Middle East Report* no. 46, April 1976, 18–19.

51. Gazit, *Trapped Fools*, 182.

52. Ma'oz, *Palestinian Leadership on the West Bank*, 151, 139.

53. Ibid., 73.

54. For a list of events in the OT where Palestinians resisted the occupying power, see *Report of the Special Committee*, 05/10/1971, A/8389; 09/10/1972, A/8828; 25/10/1973, A/9148; 04/11/1974, A/9817; 27/10/1975, A/10272; 01/10/1976, A/31/218; 27/10/1977, A/32/284; 13/11/1978, A/33/356; 13/11/1979, A/34/631; 06/10/1980, A/35/425 (see chap. 1, n. 52).

55. Ma'oz, *Palestinian Leadership on the West Bank*, 155.

56. The members of the PNF had been persecuted in 1974–75, and the organization ceased to function for a while. After the Camp David Accords of 1977, it was revived and operated mainly underground against the accords and the occupation. See Ma'oz, *Palestinian Leadership on the West Bank*, 155.

57. In reaction to land confiscations, Palestinians from Halhoul blocked the highway from Jerusalem to Hebron on December 16, 1978, threw rocks at Israeli vehicles on February 2, 1979, and clashed with armed settlers and the Israeli military on March 15, 1979. In Nablus, strikes and protests were held at the end of January 1979, following the establishment of the Elon Moreh settlement.

58. Faced with a deadlock in the self-rule talks, President Sadat attempted to revive the negotiations in Aswan (January 1980) by dividing the advancement of Begin's autonomy initiative, first to Gaza and only later in the West Bank. See "Autonomy for the Gaza Strip," *Journal of Palestine Studies* 9, no. 3 (Spring 1980): 176–80.

59. The High Court lifted the restriction following an appeal.

60. Cited in Aronson, *Creating Facts,* 205 (intro., n. 5).

61. Although the Camp David Accords between Israel and Egypt were the basis for the peace agreement between the two countries, a relatively large portion of the accords was dedicated to resolving the Palestinian problem. The accords specify that there should be a transitional period not exceeding five years in which full autonomy will be given to the Palestinian inhabitants and the Israeli military government and its civilian administration will be withdrawn. Begin considered the autonomy to be the last stage and was unwilling to withdraw the military government or Civil Administration. For the wording of the accords and related correspondence, see http://www.jimmycarterlibrary.gov/.

62. Dayan defected from Labor after the 1977 electoral defeat and became foreign minister in Menachem Begin's Likud government.

63. Following the resignation of Defense Minister Ezer Weizman in May 1981 and before the appointment of Ariel Sharon, Chief of Staff Raphael Eitan seized the opportunity to alter the existing chain of command, compelling the coordinator of activities in the territories to report to him. See Benvenisti, *West Bank Data Project, 1984 Report,* 45.

64. Military order 947, November 8, 1981 (see chap. 1, n. 39).

65. Kuttab and Shehadeh, *Civil Administration in the Occupied West Bank,* 12 (intro., n. 59).

66. Ibid., 20, 9.

67. Tamari, "Israel's Search for a Native Pillar," 377–90 (chap. 1, n. 70).

68. Trudy Rubin, "Occupied Territories: Israel's 'Alternative Leadership' Plan," *Christian Science Monitor* August 28, 1981.

69. Ma'oz, *Palestinian Leadership on the West Bank*, 199.

70. Benvenisti, *West Bank Handbook: A Political Lexicon* (Boulder, CO: Westview Press, 1988), 118.

71. Yehuda Litani, "Leaders by Proxy," *Ha'aretz*, November 30, 1981, in Hebrew; Ma'oz, *Palestinian Leadership on the West Bank*, 199.

72. For instance, Ibrahim Dakkak, chairman of the West Bank Engineers' Union, Jiryis Khoury, chairman of the West Bank Lawyers' Union, and Abd Abu Diab, head of the Jerusalem District Electricity Company's Employees' Committee, were prevented from leaving the Jerusalem municipal area without prior authorization, and Hassan Bargouthi, general secretary of the Restaurant and Cafe Workers' Union, was informed that his town-arrest order had been extended for a period of six months. The editors of *Al Fajr* newspaper, who had been under house arrest for eighteen months, were not allowed to leave their towns of residence, Ramallah and El Bireh, while orders restricting the movement of Dr. Amin Al Khatib, chairman of the Charitable Societies, Faisal Husseini, director of the Arab Studies Centre, and Riyad Agha, president of the Islamic Institute, were also issued, to mention only a few of those whose movement was confined. See *Report of the Special Committee;* 10/20/1982, A/37/486.

73. For instance, at the funeral procession for eighteen-year-old Ibrahim Aly Darwish from Al-Bireh, who had been fatally shot in the abdomen during a protest, soldiers threw dozens of tear-gas grenades at the demonstrators, wounding a fifty-five-year-old woman. During a clash with demonstrators at the Dir Amar refugee camp northwest of Ramallah, Muhammed Hamad Dib (seventeen) was killed, and two others were seriously wounded. A thirteen-year-old boy, Bassam Mazoul Al Najar, was shot in the head during a demonstration south of Rafah, while in Jenin, Fadhi Kanouh (twenty-one), who had stabbed a border policeman, was shot at close range by another policeman. See *Report of the Special Committee;* 10/20/1982, A/37/486.

74. Security forces demolished the houses belonging to the families of Mahmoud Farhi Hasuna (eighteen) and Abram Abed Asibi (seventeen), suspected of participation in the stabbing of David Kopelsky in Hebron; the house of a third suspect, reportedly the instigator of the attack, was sealed. The Israeli military also demolished the houses of the Shumaly family in Beit Sahur because their son allegedly had thrown incendiary bottles, while four other houses were blown up in connection with the

same incidents in Beit Sahur. In Salfit and Qabalan two houses were destroyed because they had been built illegally, while the High Court of Justice ordered Hassan Khalil Al Abassi from Silwan to destroy his house because it had been constructed without a building license; failure to comply meant a fine of IL 25,000 and a one-and-a-half-year prison term. See *Report of the Special Committee;* 10/20/1982, A/37/486.

75. For a list of daily events from September 1, 1981, until July 25, 1982, see *Report of the Special Committee;* 10/20/1982, A/37/486.

76. Zucker, "Report on Human Rights," 58 (chap. 2, n. 51).

77. *Report of the Special Committee;* 10/20/1982, A/37/486.

78. In such a system, Milson maintained, "the most valuable prize for a public personality is access to those who hold central power. To deny this privilege is to undercut a leader's position within his constituency and to deprive him of his influence. If a notable or local politician cannot act as an intermediary between the central authority and his constituents (family, town or tribe) — a service absolutely crucial in that social and political structure — they will inevitably turn to somebody else." See Milson, "How to Make Peace," 31.

79. Salim Tamari, "In League with Zion: Israel's Search for a Native Pillar," *Journal of Palestine Studies* 12, no. 4 (Summer 1983): 41–56, 44; Litani, "Leaders by Proxy"; David Ronen underscores the close relationship between Hebron's Mayor Jabari and the GSS in *The Year of the Shabak,* 131–40 (intro., n. 36).

80. Cohen, *An Army of Shadows,* 22 (chap. 1, n. 60).

81. Litani, "Leaders by Proxy."

82. Salim Tamari cogently argues that the Leagues' creators displayed an astonishing ideological misconception of the relationship between town and village. The idea of mobilizing the dispossessed peasantry to rise against the privileged towns overlooked the radical changes in social structure that took place during the previous decades in the rural areas, the most significant of which was the complex integration of rural laborers into the Israeli workforce. With tens of thousands of villagers commuting each morning to work in Israel, a new stratum evolved whose standards of living, lifestyle, and political perceptions bore little resemblance to the situation prevailing in the 1920s when the first Zionist strategy towards Palestinian peasants was formulated. See Tamari, "In League with Zion," 44, 55.

83. Hiltermann, *Behind the Intifada,* 9.

84. Zucker, "Report on Human Rights," 89. In fiscal year 1983–84 the Leagues received 113 million shekels.

85. *Report of the Special Committee;* 10/20/1982, A/37/486.

86. Kuttab and Shehadeh, *Civil Administration in the Occupied West Bank,* 14.

87. Litani, "Leaders by Proxy."

88. Tamari, "In League with Zion," 46.

89. Zucker, "Report on Human Rights," 91–92.

90. Benvenisti, *West Bank Data Project, 1984 Report,* 44.

5. CIVILIAN CONTROL

Epigraph: Cited in Weizman, *Hollow Land,* 133 (intro., n. 18), and taken from Avi Mograbi (producer), *How I Learned to Overcome My Fear and Love Arik Sharon,* a documentary film, 1997.

1. Shashar, *Seventh Day War,* 47 (chap. 1, n. 49).

2. For the use of archaeology to advance Israel's claims to the land, see Nadia Abu El-Haj, *Facts on the Ground: Archaeological Practice and Territorial Self-Fashioning in Israeli Society* (Chicago: University of Chicago Press, 2002).

3. Gazit, *Trapped Fools,* 241–88 (intro., n. 1); Weizman, *Hollow Land,* 80–82.

4. Weizman, *Hollow Land,* 93.

5. For the status of settlements vis-à-vis international law, see Lein, *Land Grab,* 37–46 (intro., n. 19); Amnesty International, "Israel and the Occupied Territories: The Issue of Settlements Must Be Addressed According to International Law," 2003, available online at http://web.amnesty.org.

6. Weizman, *Hollow Land,* 95.

7. Rafi Segal and Eyal Weizman, *A Civilian Occupation: The Politics of Israeli Architecture* (London: Verso, 2003), 24.

8. The structure of the settlement was designed to provide defense against the potential attacks of local inhabitants who may have been disgruntled by the new neighbors and, in some cases, the appropriation of their land. The swiftness of the construction process was motivated by the Ottoman law, which guaranteed that the British Mandatory forces could not destroy the settlement after it was built. See Elisha Efrat, *Geography of Occupation: Judea, Samaria and the Gaza Strip* (Jerusalem: Carmel, 2002), 68–69.

9. Some of these methods were also used in the Gaza Strip.

10. Most of these mechanisms are discussed at length in Lein, *Land Grab,* 47–63.

11. See, for example, Article 46 of the Regulations Annexed to the Hague Convention on the Laws of War on Land, October 18, 1907.

12. Lein, *Land Grab,* 58–59.

13. Ibid., 52–53.

14. Weizman, *Hollow Land,* 46.

15. Lein, *Land Grab,* 61. The Jordanian law specifically states that the expropriation of land is permitted only when it is for a public purpose, so Israel has not used this law extensively to confiscate land intended for the establishment of settlements. An exception to this generalization is the case of Ma'ale Adummim, established in 1975 on an area of some thirty thousand dunams expropriated from Palestinians.

16. Benvenisti and Khayat, *West Bank and Gaza Atlas,* 60 (intro., n. 54).

17. Lein, *Land Grab,* 49. Among those established on this land were Matityahu, Neve Zuf, Rimonim, Shilo, Bet El, Kokhav Hashahar, Alon Shvut, El'azar, Efrat, Har Gilo, Migdal Oz, Gittit, Yitav, and Kiryat Arba.

18. Kretzmer, *Occupation of Justice,* 75–100 (chap. 1, n. 10).

19. Cited in Aronson, *Creating Facts,* 14 (intro., n. 5).

20. For the use of military bases for civilian settlements and a historical account of the NAHAL outposts, see Zertal and Eldar, *Lords of the Land,* 374–82 (intro., n. 5).

21. The justification for this settlement, which was the first one, is that prior to 1948 Jews lived in Kfar Etzion and were massacred by the Jordanian Legion.

22. Gazit, *Trapped Fools,* 251–54.

23. Cited in *Report of the Special Committee,* A/9148, 25 October 1973 (chap. 1, n. 52).

24. Consider the establishment of Ma'ale Adummim, the second largest settlement in the OT today and the first suburban settlement. On November 25, 1974, the *Jerusalem Post* reported that the government had decided to build an industrial center fourteen kilometers east of Jerusalem on the road to Jericho. On March 3, 1975, a group of Israelis tried to settle at the industrial center and were evacuated by the military. A month later the military government seized several thousand dunams of land located near

the industrial area, and on May 21 construction began at the site. On July 9, the military government expropriated an additional thirty thousand dunams of land, and on September 22, 1975, the *Jerusalem Post* reported that the government had given permission for sixty settlers to move into the newly established settlement Ma'ale Adummim. See *Report of the Special Committee*, A/10272, 27, October 1975.

25. David Newman, *Jewish Settlement in the West Bank: The Role of Gush Emunim* (Durham, England: Centre for Middle Eastern and Islamic Studies, 1982), 40–43.

26. It is presented as a watershed in Zertal and Eldar, *Lords of the Land*, 66–81; Newman, *Jewish Settlement in the West Bank*, 42–43.

27. On April 20, 1977, *Ha'aretz* reported on a decision by the Labor Government's Ministerial Committee on Settlements to allocate IL 225 million for the establishment of twenty-five new settlements, including seventeen in the occupied territories.

28. Gazit, *Trapped Fools*, 241. See also Zertal and Eldar, *Lords of the Land*, 376.

29. The data about Gaza is from 1983 and not 1980. Benvenisti and Khayat, *West Bank and Gaza Atlas*, 32, 62–63. Benvenisti, *West Bank Data Project, 1984 Report*, 21 (chap. 1, n. 70).

30. Eyal Weizman, *The Politics of Verticality*, chap. 7, published by Open Democracy at www.opendemocracy.net.

31. See military orders (MO) 92 and 498 (see chap. 1, n. 39).

32. The military orders required a permit for drilling, entailing a lengthy and complicated bureaucratic process. As B'Tselem points out, the vast majority of applications submitted during the occupation were denied, and the few that were granted were solely for domestic use. The number of wells in the territories rapidly declined, since permits for new wells were few and far apart (about thirteen wells from 1967 to 1996), while some of the existing wells ceased to function due to maintenance problems or because they had dried up. Also, in 1975, Israel set quotas for extracting water from existing wells and installed meters to enforce them. The quotas, as B'Tselem suggests, were inadequate to meet the population's needs. See Yehezkel Lein, *Thirsty for a Solution: The Water Crisis in the Occupied Territories and Its Resolution in the Final-Status Agreement* (Jerusalem: B'Tselem, 2000), 29.

33. Ibid., 29.

34. Weizman, *Politics of Verticality*, chap. 7.

35. Cited in Lein, *Land Grab,* 49–50. See HCJ 390/79, *Dweikat et al. v. Government of Israel et al., Piskei Din* 34 (1).

36. The essential elements of the Land Law were adopted first by British Mandate legislation and later by Jordanian legislation, and accordingly continued to apply at the time of the Israeli occupation in 1967. See Lein, *Land Grab,* 51–58.

37. Benvenisti and Khayat, *West Bank and Gaza Atlas,* 61. It is now known that about 30 percent of the land that was defined as state land following the Elon Moreh trial did not fit the criteria set by the Ottoman law, while 69 percent of the settlements were actually built on private Palestinian land that was never appropriated and made state property before the confiscations. Lecture given by Talia Sasson at Van Leer, March 17, 2006. See also Talia Sasson, *Sasson Report on Illegal Outposts* (report presented to the prime minister, Jerusalem, 2005), 81, in Hebrew (available online at http://www.fmep.org/reports/vol15/no2/05-sasson_report.html); Dror Etkes and Hagit Ofran, *Construction of Settlements upon Private Land* (Tel-Aviv: Peace Now, 2006).

38. Central Bureau of Statistics, *National Accountability,* 125 (chap. 2, n. 62).

39. Central Bureau of Statistics, *National Accountability,* 133. See also David Butterfield, Jad Isaac, Atif Kubursi, and Steven Spencer, "Impacts of Water and Export Market Restrictions on Palestinian Agriculture," paper prepared by McMaster University and Econometric Research Limited and the Applied Research Institute of Jerusalem, January, 2000 (available online at http://socserv.mcmaster.ca/kubursi/ebooks/water.htm).

40. Military order 25.

41. For a discussion of the World Zionist Organization's role in ensuring that the newly built settlements would be exclusively for Jews, see Lein, *Land Grab,* 21–22.

42. Ibid., 63.

43. Almost 50 percent of the West Bank's land and close to 40 percent of the land in the Gaza Strip had been appropriated. See Benvenisti and Khayat, *West Bank and Gaza Atlas,* 112–13; Roy, *Gaza Strip,* 175–81 (intro., n. 37).

44. Roy, *Gaza Strip,* 178–79.

45. Al-Haq, *Punishing a Nation: Human Rights Violations During the Palestinian Uprising, December 1987–December 1988* (Ramallah: Al-Haq, 1990), 114.

46. Weizman, *Hollow Land,* 57–86.

47. Ministry of Agriculture and the Settlement Division of the World Zionist Organization, *Master Plan for Settlement for Judea and Samaria, Development Plan for the Region for 1983–1986* (Jerusalem: Ministry of Agriculture, 1983), 27.

48. State Comptroller, *Annual Report 48* (Jerusalem: State Comptroller, 1998), 1032–33, in Hebrew, cited in Lein, *Land Grab,* 50.

49. Yehezkel Lein, *Forbidden Roads: The Discriminatory West Bank Road Regime* (Jerusalem: B'Tselem, 2004).

50. Lein, *Land Grab,* 116.

51. The municipal and regional boundaries of the local authorities were marked on maps signed by the military commander (consult MO 783 from March 1979 and MO 892 from March 1981). See Lein, *Land Grab,* 116. This includes the area of East Jerusalem that was annexed in 1967.

52. Ibid., 115–116

53. Ibid., 115.

54. Gush Emunim, *Master Plan for Settlement in Judea and Samaria* (Jerusalem: Gush Emunim, 1978), 15, in Hebrew.

55. Lein, *Land Grab,* 86.

56. Applications filed in the past by Palestinian residents to the Civil Administration (and still filed, in the case of Area C) for building on private land outside the area of these plans are almost always rejected. The reasons for the rejections are based both on the demarcation plans (the land is outside the plan area) and on the Mandatory outline plans (the area is zoned for agriculture or a nature reserve). For example, between 1996 and 1999, the Civil Administration issued just seventy-nine building permits. See Lein, *Land Grab,* 87; see also Yuval Ginbar, *Demolishing Peace: Israel's Policy of Mass Demolition of Palestinian Houses in the West Bank* (Jerusalem: B'Tselem, 1997).

57. Almost all the bypass roads run across privately owned Palestinian land, and Israel used two legal means to confiscate this land: "requisition for military needs" and "expropriation for public use." See Lein, *Forbidden Roads,* 6.

58. Jeff Halper, "The 94 Percent Solution: A Matrix of Control," *Middle East Report* 216 (Fall 2000): 14–19.

59. Ibid.

60. Lein, *Forbidden Roads,* 11–19.

61. Ibid., 3.

62. Ibid., 36.

63. Lein, *Land Grab*, 115.

64. Weizman, *Politics of Verticality*, chap. 5.

65. Ibid.

66. Segal and Weizman, *Civilian Occupation*, 85–86.

67. Ibid., 24.

68. Benvenisti, *West Bank Data Project, 1987 Report*, 59–61 (chap. 3, n. 24).

69. Segal and Weizman, *Civilian Occupation*, 24.

70. Yael Stein, *Tacit Consent: Israeli Policy on Law Enforcement toward Settlers in the Occupied Territories* (Jerusalem: B'Tselem, 2001), 2.

71. Aronson, *Creating Facts*, 198; Al-Haq, *Punishing a Nation*, 115; Benvenisti, *West Bank Data Project, 1984 Report*, 42. For documentation of literally hundreds of incidents of settler violence, consult the annual reports of the Special Committee to Investigate Israeli Practices Affecting the Human Rights of the Population of the Occupied Territories http://domino.un.org/unispal.nsf, as well as reports published by B'Tselem on the topic.

72. United Nations, "Economic and Social Repercussions of the Israeli Occupation on the Living Conditions of the Palestinian People in the Occupied Palestinian Territory, Including Jerusalem, and of the Arab Population in the Occupied Syrian Golan," A/57/63, E/2002/21 (New York: United Nations, May 17, 2002).

73. Benvenisti, *West Bank Data Project, 1987 Report*, 41.

74. Benvenisti, *Legal Dualism*, 16 (chap. 1, n. 22). Consult MO 432 and MO 817. In 1988, the Knesset empowered the government to impose its laws on the settlements in territorial terms, rather than merely on the settlers as individuals, as had been the case previously. In recent years, the Knesset has adopted several laws—relating to local authorities and elections for these authorities—that apply directly to the settlements. See Lein, *Land Grab*, 66.

75. Ron, *Frontiers and Ghettos*, 169 (chap. 1, n. 56); Stein, *Tacit Consent*, 28–30.

76. "Settlers: IDF Acting in Subdued Manner," YNET, 2 October 2000, in Hebrew; cited in Stein, *Tacit Consent*, 7.

77. For a description of the creation of settler militias, see also Ze'ev Schiff and Ehud Ya'ari, *Intifada*, 166 (intro., n. 6).

78. Ron, *Frontiers and Ghettos,* 169.

79. In the second intifada, however, non-incorporated militias reappeared on the scene.

80. Stein, *Tacit Consent,* 9–19; Ron Dudai, *Free Rein: Vigilante Settlers and Israel's Non-enforcement of the Law* (Jerusalem: B'Tselem, 2001), 2–18.

81. Stein, *Tacit Consent,* 20; Dudai, *Free Rein,* 2.

82. Stein, *Tacit Consent,* 3, 14; Dudai, *Free Rein,* 2.

83. Gadi Algazi and Azmi Badir, "Transfer's Real Nightmare," *Ha'aretz,* November 16, 2002.

84. Avi Issacharoff, "Report: 90% of Palestinian Complaints to Police 'Unsolved,'" *Ha'aretz,* September 10, 2006.

85. Dudai, *Free Rein,* 24.

86. Stein, *Tacit Consent,* 45.

87. It is crucial to keep in mind that this is not only a nationalist policy but also a racist one. Israeli law is imposed not only on Israelis resident in the Occupied Territories, but also on Jews who move to the settlements, even if they do not have Israeli citizenship. See Lein, *Land Grab,* 66.

88. Hajjar, *Courting Conflict,* 58 (chap. 1, n. 10).

89. Eitan Felner and Roley Rozen, *Law Enforcement on Israeli Civilians in the Occupied Territories* (Jerusalem: B'Tselem, 1994), 85–89.

90. Stein, *Tacit Consent,* 47–49.

91. Hiltermann, *Behind the Intifada,* 6 (intro., n. 6).

92. Ibid., 10.

6. THE INTIFADA

Epigraph: Yitzhak Zaccai, *Judea, Samaria and the Gaza District, 1967–1987: Twenty Years of Civil Administration* (Jerusalem: Carta Books, 1987), 7.

1. Literally, *intifada* means "shaking-off," but in this context it meant "popular uprising." See Schiff and Ya'ari, *Intifada,* 17–21 (intro., n. 6); Anita Vitullo, "Uprising in Gaza," in Lockman and Beinin, *Intifada,* 44–46 (intro., n. 6).

2. Vitullo, "Uprising in Gaza," 48.

3. For the mirage that Israel created, see Zaccai, *Judea, Samaria and the Gaza District, 1967–1987,* 6–7.

4. Straschnov, *Justice Under Fire,* 50 (intro., n. 64).

5. According to Al-Haq, during the three-year period 1984–86, Israel deported 37 Palestinians, held 168 in administrative detention, and demolished or sealed 107 homes. Cited in Benvenisti, *West Bank Data Project, 1987 Report,* 40 (chap. 3, n. 24).

6. Al-Haq, *Twenty Years of Israel Occupation of the West Bank and Gaza Strip,* 24–30 (Ramallah: Al-Haq, 1987); Benvenisti, *West Bank Data Project, 1987 Report,* 40.

7. Ian S. Lustick, "Writing the Intifada: Collective Action in the Occupied Territories," World Politics 45, no. 4 (July 1993): 560–94, 561.

8. Schiff and Ya'ari, *Intifada,* 87–95.

9. Lustick, "Writing the Intifada," 567.

10. Rashid Khalidi, "The Palestinian People: Twenty-Two Years After 1967," in Lockman and Beinin, *Intifada,* 113–26.

11. Benvenisti, *West Bank Data Project, 1987 Report,* 8.

12. Ibid., 12.

13. Schiff and Ya'ari, *Intifada,* 84.

14. Ibid., 82–83.

15. Hiltermann, *Behind the Intifada,* 37 (intro., n. 6).

16. Another example could be Israel's support of the Muslim Brotherhood in its struggle against the PLO. Israel, in other words, helped build the institutional apparatus that was later transformed into Hamas.

17. Shaul Mishal and Reuven Aharoni, *Stones Are Not All: The Intifada and the Communiqués* (Tel-Aviv: Hakibbutz Hameuchad, 1989), in Hebrew.

18. Amikam Nahmani, "The Intifada, 1987–1993: On the Symbol, Ritual and Myth in the National Struggle," *Alpayim* 29 (2005): 82, in Hebrew.

19. Schiff and Ya'ari, *Intifada,* 255.

20. Lockman and Beinin, *Intifada,* 361–63.

21. While the Islamic Jihad had been operating in the territories since the 1970s, Hamas was founded by Sheik Ahmad Yasin at the outbreak of the intifada. See Shaul Mishal and Reuben Aharoni, *Speaking Stones: Communiques from the Intifada Underground* (Syracuse, NY: Syracuse University Press, 1994).

22. For an example of a fake communiqué, see Lockman and Beinin, *Intifada,* 386.

23. Vitullo, "Uprising in Gaza," 48.

24. Schiff and Ya'ari, *Intifada,* 150.

25. Noga Kadman, *1987–1997: A Decade of Human Rights Violations* (Jerusalem: B'Tselem, 1998), 3–6. During the same period, 118 Israelis were killed by Palestinians.

26. James Ron, *A License to Kill: Israeli Undercover Operations Against "Wanted" and Masked Palestinians* (New York: Human Rights Watch, 1993).

27. Ron, *Frontiers and Ghettos,* 1–24 (chap. 1, n. 56).

28. Straschnov, *Justice Under Fire,* 50, 67. As a result of the high incarceration rate, thousands of Palestinian women became single mothers for extended periods and had to bear total responsibility for the family.

29. Kadman, *Human Rights Violations,* 9–10.

30. Israel initially wanted to use Hamas in order to undermine the nationalist political factions. After a year Israel realized that Hamas was not merely an Islamic organization but had a nationalist agenda, and therefore it too was outlawed.

31. Former Prime Minister Yitzchak Rabin used the word *shaken* rather than *tortured,* when he discussed the methods used by the GSS during interrogations. However, according to international covenants, to shake constitutes torture. See Kadman, *Human Rights Violations,* 13.

32. Neve Gordon, "Silent Reminders: The Purpose of Torture in Repressive Regimes," *Humanist,* March–April, 1997.

33. Kadman, *Human Rights Violations,* 18.

34. Ibid., 14.

35. Ibid., 19.

36. Lein, *Builders of Zion,* 9–10 (chap. 1, n. 62).

37. Yehezkel Lein, *One Big Prison: Freedom of Movement to and from the Gaza Strip on the Eve of the Disengagement Plan* (Jerusalem: B'Tselem, 2005), 57.

38. Lein, *Builders of Zion,* 27–33.

39. Ibid., 9–10.

40. Benvenisti *West Bank Data Project, 1987 Report,* 34–35.

41. Conclusions of the Sadan Committee, cited in Arnon and Weinblatt, "Sovereignty and Economic Development," 294 (chap. 3, n. 5).

42. Roy, *Gaza Strip,* 212–213

43. Helen Murray, *Barriers to Education: The Israeli Military Obstruction of Access to Schools and Universities in the West Bank and Gaza Strip* (Birzeit, West Bank: Birzeit University, 2004), 3.

44. Al-Haq, *Punishing a Nation*, 274 (chap. 5, n. 45).

45. Eleanor Shapiro, "A Bitter Pill—Health Care Cuts in the Territories," *Jerusalem Post*, February 1, 1989.

46. Fohorils, *Development of Agriculture*, 21–22 (chap. 2, n. 60).

47. Schiff and Ya'ari, *Intifada*, 28.

48. Cited in Schiff and Ya'ari, *Intifada*, 152.

49. Foucault, *History of Sexuality*, 1:86 (intro., n. 8).

50. See, respectively, Khalidi, "Palestinian People"; Tamari, "What the Uprising Means" (intro., n. 29). For an overview of several books written about the first intifada, see Lustick, "Writing the Intifada."

51. Schiff and Ya'ari, *Intifada*, 263.

52. Swirski, *Price of Occupation*, 16 (chap. 3, n. 1).

53. Neve Gordon and Nitza Berkovitch, "Human Rights Discourse in Domestic Settings: How Does It Emerge?" *Political Studies* 55, no. 1 (2007): 243–66.

54. Ze'ev Schiff and Ehud Ya'ari, *Intifada*, 167–68.

55. Aryeh Shalev, *The Intifada: Causes and Effects* (Boulder, CO: Westview Press, 1991), 3.

7. OUTSOURCING THE OCCUPATION

Epigraphs: Raja Shedadeh, *Strangers in the House: Coming of Age in Occupied Palestine* (New York: Penguin Books, 2003), 236; Glenn E. Robinson, "The Peace of the Powerful," in Carey, *The New Intifada*, 115 (intro., n. 6).

1. The term often used in this context is *proxy,* which the *Oxford Dictionary* defines as "A person appointed or authorized to act instead of another; an attorney, substitute, representative, agent." As I show below, *outsourcing* seems to be a more accurate term.

2. Benvenisti, *Intimate Enemies*; see also in this context Hass, *Drinking the Sea at Gaza;* Edward Said, *Peace and Its Discontents;* Usher, *Dispatches from Palestine;* Gordon "Outsourcing Violations" (all full citations appear in intro., n. 62).

3. Said, *The End of the Peace Process;* Chomsky, *The Fateful Triangle*

(intro., n. 4); Mouin Rabbani, "The Smorgasbord of Failure: Oslo and the Al Aqsa Intifada," in Carey, *New Intifada.*

4. Usher, *Dispatches from Palestine,* 9.

5. Cohen, *An Army of Shadows,* 22–28 (chap. 1, n. 60).

6. The SLA was created following Israel's invasion in 1978, in what Israel called Operation Litani.

7. Benvenisti, *West Bank Data Project, 1987 Report,* 47–49 (chap. 3, n. 24).

8. Cited in Noam Chomsky, *Powers and Prospects: Reflections on Human Nature and Social Order* (Boston: South End Press, 1996), 198.

9. The eight agreements in chronological order are: (1) Declaration of Principles on Interim Self-Government Arrangements (September 13, 1993); (2) the Paris Protocol on Economic Relations (April 29, 1994); (3) Agreement on the Gaza Strip and the Jericho Area (May 4, 1994); (4) Agreement on Preparatory Transfer of Powers and Responsibilities Between Israel and the PLO (August 29, 1994); (5) The Israeli-Palestinian Interim Agreement on the West Bank and the Gaza Strip (also known as Oslo II) (September 28, 1995); (6) Hebron Protocol (January 17, 1997); (7) The Wye River Memorandum (October 23, 1998); (8) The Sharem el-Sheikh Memorandum (September 4, 1999).

10. Declaration of Principles, Article 6, Article 8. See also Agreement on Preparatory Transfer of Powers and Responsibilities, August 29, 1994, particularly Annexes 1–6 (available online at www.palestinefacts.org).

11. Arnon and Weinblatt, "Sovereignty and Economic Development," 304 (chap. 3, n. 5).

12. Roy, *Gaza Strip,* 198 (intro., n. 37).

13. Rela Mazali, Noga Ofer, and Neve Gordon, *The Occupied Health Care System* (Tel-Aviv: Physicians for Human Rights, 1993).

14. Maskit Bendel, *The Disengagement Plan and Its Repercussions on the Right to Health in the Gaza Strip* (Tel-Aviv: Physicians for Human Rights, 2005), 58.

15. John Torpey, *The Invention of the Passport* (Cambridge: Cambridge University Press, 2000), 4.

16. In 1997, Hebron was divided into two parts: H1 under nominal control of the PA and the smaller H2 section under the control of the Israeli military. Area H2 is home to about thirty-five thousand Palestinians and five hundred Israeli settlers. The Old City and the Tomb of the Patriarchs

are also located in H2. Yellow Areas in the Gaza Strip are more or less equivalent to Area B in the West Bank and comprise 23 percent of the Strip, while White Areas are equivalent to Area A and comprise a little less than 10 percent of the Strip.

17. Geoffrey Aronson, "Recapitulating the Redeployments: The Israel-PLO 'Interim Agreements,'." Available online at http://www.palestine center.org/cpap/pubs/20000427ib.html. The Agreements were Wye I, II and III and Sharam I.

18. Lein, *Forbidden Roads,* 4 (chap. 5, n. 49).

19. Halper, "The 94 Percent Solution" (chap. 5, n. 58).

20. Jewish settlers could continue moving freely across the Green Line, while after Oslo a very small number of Palestinians received VIP cards and could travel even in times of closure.

21. The Palestinians did not oppose the construction of this fence because it was erected on the Green Line. See Lein, *One Big Prison,* 60 (chap. 6, n. 37).

22. The "normally" open and closed character of the border relates, of course, only to the occupied Palestinians; for Israelis, the Green Line continued to be permeable and in many respects invisible.

23. Annex 3, Article 4 of the Interim Agreement states that "in Area C, in the first phase of redeployment, powers and *responsibilities not related to territory,* as set out in Appendix 1, will be transferred to and assumed by the [Palestinian] Council in accordance with the provisions of that Appendix." This indicates that even though Israel had full authority over all matters in Area C, the PA took over responsibilities not related to territory.

24. Derek Gregory, *The Colonial Present: Afghanistan, Palestine, Iraq* (Oxford: Blackwell Publishing, 2004).

25. Kadman, *Human Rights Violations,* 10 (chap. 6, n. 25.

26. Ibid., 10–11.

27. Rema Hammami and Salim Tamari, "Anatomy of Another Rebellion," *Middle East Report* no. 217 (Winter 2000): 2–5.

28. Shir Hever, *The Economy Through the Eyes of Israeli Economists* (Jerusalem: Alternative Information Center, 2006).

29. In 1999 and 2000, years in which Israel did not impose any prolonged comprehensive closures, Palestinian GNP grew at around 4 percent a year. However, this growth did not "compensate for" the sharp decline that had occurred during the previous four years. See Sara Roy, "Decline

and Disfigurement: The Palestinian Economy after Oslo," in Carey, *New Intifada,* 91–110.

30. For a list of the attacks and the number of people killed, consult the Israeli Ministry of Foreign Affairs website: http://www.mfa.gov.il/MFA.

31. Lein, *Builders of Zion,* 9–10 (chap. 1, n. 62).

32. Usher, *Dispatches from Palestine, 97.*

33. B'Tselem, "The Palestinian Economy During the Period of the Oslo Accords: 1994–2000," available online at www.btselem.org

34. B'Tselem, "Palestinian Economy."

35. Kadman, *Human Rights Violations,* 19.

36. World Bank, *West Bank and Gaza Update,* report published by the World Bank Group, April 2006, 4.

37. Swirsky, *Price of Occupation,* 19 (chap. 3, n. 1).

38. Diwan and Shaban, *Development under Adversity,* 21 (chap. 3, n. 52).

39. Lein, *Forbidden Roads,* 3.

40. Cited in Usher, *Dispatches from Palestine, 73.*

41. Shlomo Shapiro, "The CIA as Middle East Broker," *Survival* 45, no. 2 (2003): 91–112; see also Shlomi Eldar, *Eyeless in Gaza* (Tel-Aviv: Yedioth Ahronoth Books, Sifrei Hemed, 2005), in Hebrew.

42. Usher, *Dispatches from Palestine, 67.*

43. Bassem Eid and Eitan Felner, *Neither Law Nor Justice: Extrajudicial Punishment, Abduction, Unlawful Arrest, Torture of Palestinian Residents of the West Bank by the Palestinian Preventive Security Service* (Jerusalem: B'Tselem, 1995), 33.

44. Wye Memorandum of October 23, 1998, Security Actions (Article 2, Clause 1a).

45. Yehezkel Lein and Renata Capella, *Cooperating Against Justice: Human Rights Violations by Israel and Palestine National Authority Following the Murders in Wadi Quelt* (Jerusalem: B'Tselem, 1999), 3.

46. Neve Gordon and Dani Filc, "Hamas and the Destruction of Risk Society, *Constellations* 12, no. 4 (2005): 548.

47. Gordon and Filc, "Hamas and the Destruction of Risk Society," 548.

48. Efraim Davidi, "Globalization and Economy in the Middle East," *Palestine-Israel Journal* 7 (2000): 33–38. The crucial point, though, is that even if the World Bank had not encouraged privatization and the PA had not

been infested with nepotism and corruption, it still could not have offered adequate services to the population because of the acute deficit in funds.

49. In the past seven years the West Bank's settler population has continued to grow, and in June 2007 it amounted to 267,000. But even this growth rate is lower than the one during the Oslo years.

50. Carey, *New Intifada*, 76.

51. Roy, "Decline and Disfigurement," 95.

52. Sasson, *Sasson Report on Illegal Outposts* (chap. 5, n. 37). See also Peace Now, "The West Bank—Facts and Figures—June 2006," online at http://www.peacenow.org.il.

53. Weizman, *Hollow Land*, 83–84 (intro., n. 18).

54. The separation between the functions of direct discipline and indirect control complicates, as Eyal Weizman points out, the narrative that presupposes the evolution of "disciplinary societies" to "control societies," and makes these two systems of domination coexistent as two components of a vertically layered sovereignty. See Deleuze, "Postscript on the Societies of Control," 3–7 (intro., n. 34); Weizman, *Hollow Land*, 145.

55. On the intentional production and maintenance of crises, see Ariella Azoulay and Adi Ophir, "The Monster's Tail," in *Against the Wall*, ed. Michael Sorkin (New York: New Press, 2005), 2–27.

8. THE SEPARATION PRINCIPLE

Epigraphs: Ehud Barak's slogan for the 1999 campaign for prime minister; John Torpey, *The Invention of the Passport*, 22.

1. See statistics at www.btselem.org. The numbers pertain to killings until September 15, 2006.

2. At the Camp David summit, Israel offered to establish a Palestinian state encompassing the Gaza Strip, 92 percent of the West Bank, and some parts of Arab East Jerusalem. In return, it proposed the annexation of Jewish neighborhoods (settlements) in East Jerusalem. Israel also asked for several security measures, including early warning stations in the West Bank and an Israeli presence at Palestinian border crossings. In addition, it would accept no more than a token return of Palestinian refugees under a family reunification program. The Israelis maintain that Palestinian leaders rejected Barak's offer and the diplomatic route to a peaceful settlement of the Arab-Israeli conflict. Instead, they tried to destroy Israel by pressing

throughout the Israeli-Palestinian talks for the return of millions of Palestinian refugees to Israel and by launching the second intifada, or uprising, in September 2000. See Jeremy Pressman, "Visions in Collision: What Happened at Camp David and Taba?" *International Security* 28, no. 2 (Fall 2003), 5–43.

3. According to Jeremy Pressman, despite Israeli contentions, Palestinian negotiators and much of the Palestinian nationalist movement favored a genuine two-state solution and did not seek to destroy Israel either by insisting on the right of return or through the second intifada. Pressman concludes that the Israeli belief that the Palestinians did not want to reach an agreement is based on five contentions that do not hold up when assessed in light of the evidence from 2000–01. "Israel's offer at the Camp David summit was not as generous or complete as Israeli and U.S. officials have claimed. The Palestinian Authority negotiated and made notable concessions on the final status issues. Many Palestinians favor a two-state solution, not the destruction of Israel. The second intifada was not a premeditated Palestinian Authority effort to destroy Israel. The Palestinian Authority recognized Israel's existential concerns about the Palestinian right of return and discussed policies to address those concerns" ("Visions in Collision," 7, 42). See also Clayton E. Swisher, *The Truth About Camp David: The Untold Story About the Collapse of the Middle East Peace Process* (New York: Nation Books, 2004).

4. Akiva Eldar, "Popular misconceptions," *Ha'aretz,* June 11, 2004, in Hebrew; see also Reuven Pedatzur, "More Than a Million Bullets," *Ha'aretz,* June 30, 2004, in Hebrew.

5. See statistics at www.btselem.org.

6. The colonial enterprise is, to be sure, a multifaceted and complex phenomenon that cannot be defined in one sentence or passage. For an analysis of different dimensions and types of the colonial project, see Timothy Mitchell, *Colonizing Egypt* (New York: Cambridge University Press, 1991); Partha Chatterjee, *The Nation and Its Fragments: Colonial and Post-Colonial Histories* (Princeton, NJ: Princeton University Press, 1993); Mahmood Mamdani, *Citizen and Subject: Contemporary Africa and the Legacy of Late Colonialism* (Princeton, NJ: Princeton University Press, 1996); and Shafir, *Land, Labor and the Origins of the Israeli Palestinian Conflict* (chap. 3, n. 28). Mamdani, for example, shows how different native populations (e.g., urban vs. rural sectors) were governed entirely differently.

7. Weizman adds that the "Israeli fantasy of separation seeks to create a defensible and homogeneous Israeli political space that will guarantee, if not protection from Palestinian attacks, a space of Jewish demographic majority and control" (*Hollow Land,* 178 [intro., n. 18]).

8. For a discussion about who actually shot Mohammed al-Dura, see James Fallows, "Who Shot Mohammed al-Dura," *Atlantic Monthly,* June 2003.

9. Amira Hass, "Don't Shoot Till You Can See They're Over the Age of 12," *Ha'aretz,* November 20, 2000.

10. Ron Dudai, *Trigger Happy Unjustified Shooting and Violation of the Open-Fire Regulations During the al-Aqsa Intifada* (Jerusalem: B'Tselem, 2002).

11. Ron, *A License to Kill* (chap. 6, n. 26).

12. B'Tselem, for example, documented the killing of 168 Palestinians during arrests in the West Bank between January 2004 and June 2006. At least 40 of those killed were civilians who were not connected in any way to the military operation, and another 54 were defined as "wanted" but were unarmed or otherwise *hors de combat* at the time they were shot and killed. None of these cases was investigated by the military police; consequently, none of the soldiers was charged with unlawful shooting or any other offense. See Ronen Shnayderman, *Take No Prisoners: The Fatal Shooting of Palestinians by Israeli Security Forces During "Arrest Operations"* (Jerusalem: B'Tselem, 2005).

13. Dudai, *Trigger Happy.*

14. The numbers are taken from B'Tselem's website: www.btselem.org.

15. After the terrorist attack at the Munich Olympics, Golda Meir authorized the Mossad to assassinate all those who were involved in the bloody assault on Israeli targets. See Gordon, "Rationalizing Extra-Judicial Executions," 314 (intro., n. 30).

16. Renata Capella and Michael Sfard, *The Assassination Policy of the State of Israel* (Jerusalem: Public Committee Against Torture in Israel, 2002).

17. David Kretzmer, "Targeted Killing of Suspected Terrorists: Extra-Judicial Executions or Legitimate Means of Defence?" *European Journal of International Law* 16, no. 2 (2005):171–212.

18. Weizman, *Hollow Land,* 239.

19. This is the point made by Weizman, first in *The Politics of Verticality* (chap. 5, n. 30) and later in *Hollow Land.*

20. Weizman, *Hollow Land,* 240.

21. Jessica Montell, "Operation Defensive Shield," *Tikkun Magazine,* July/August, 2002.

22. Peter Bouckaert, Miranda Sissons, and Johanna Bjorken, *Jenin: IDF Military Operations* (New York: Human Rights Watch, 2002), 4.

23. To be sure, Israel began altering the means of violence before Defensive Shield in a variety of ways, but the operation underscores the paradigmatic shift.

24. Montell, "Operation Defensive Shield."

25. Amira Hass, "The Real Disaster Is the Closure," *Ha'aretz,* May 21, 2002.

26. "Economic and Social Repercussions of the Israeli Occupation on the Living Conditions of the Palestinian People in the Occupied Palestinian Territory, Including Jerusalem, and of the Arab Population in the Occupied Syrian Golan," United Nations, A/57/63, E/2002/21 (New York: United Nations, 17 May 2002).

27. Another example of how the law has been suspended involves the massive destruction of Palestinian homes. During the first four years of the intifada, the Israeli military demolished more than twenty-five hundred Palestinian houses in the Gaza Strip. According to HRW, nearly two-thirds of these homes were in Rafah, a densely populated town and refugee camp located on the border with Egypt. As a result, sixteen thousand people—more than 10 percent of Rafah's population—lost their homes, most of them refugees who were dispossessed for a second or third time. To stop these demolitions, a few groups petitioned the Israeli High Court, which had consistently legitimized demolitions for decades but had developed a limited jurisprudence regarding the owner's right to be heard in advance of demolitions. During the second intifada, the High Court expanded the scope of the military's discretion to dispense with the right to a hearing. The Court ruled that the right to due process could be revoked in three instances: if destruction is absolutely necessary for military operations; if providing advance notice would endanger the lives of soldiers; and if providing advance notice would endanger the success of the demolition. Thus, even though before the uprising there were instances whereby demolitions could go ahead without a hearing, and although the hearing itself rarely stopped the demolition, according to HRW, the cumulative effect of the "three exceptions" rule has been "to give the military discretion to cir-

cumvent the already limited role of the Court and to avoid having to justify demolitions in the first place." Both the extrajudicial executions and the house demolitions accordingly indicate that in the OT the rule of law became superfluous. See Fred Abrahams, Marc Garlasco, and Darryl Li, *Razing Rafah: Mass Home Demolitions in the Gaza Strip* (New York: Human Rights Watch, 2004), 127–28; Kretzmer, *Occupation of Justice,* 145–64 (chap. 1, n. 10).

28. For Palestinian fatalities and soldier indictments, see www.btselem .org (the indictments appear only in Hebrew). See also Gideon Alon, "Military Prosecutor: 672 Investigations Were Opened During the Second Intifada," *Ha'aretz,* February 23, 2005, in Hebrew.

29. Straschnov, *Justice Under Fire,* 157 (intro., n. 65).

30. Schiff and Ya'ari, *Intifada,* 28 (intro., n. 6).

31. Yael Stein, *Human Shield: Use of Palestinian Civilians as Human Shields in Violation of High Court of Justice Order* (Jerusalem: B'Tselem, 2002).

32. For the High Court decision, see H.C. 3799/02, *Adalah, et. al. v. Yitzhak Eitan, Commander of the Israeli Army in the West Bank, et. al.* For the ongoing use of human shields, see "20 July 2006: Israeli Soldiers Use Civilians as Human Shields in Beit Hanun," at www.btselem.org.

33. Fohorils, *Development of Agriculture in the Administered Territories,* 22 (chap. 2, n. 60).

34. Meron, *Economic Development,* 22 (chap. 1, n. 55).

35. World Bank, "Supplemental Trust Fund Grant to the Second Emergency Services Support Project," Human Development Group, Middle East and North Africa Region, Report no. 27199–62, 2003. Research shows that "malnutrition is a contributing factor in nearly 60 percent of deaths in children for which infectious disease is an underlying cause" (Bahn Maharj, Bhandari Nita, and Bahl Rajiv, "Management of the Severely Malnourished Child: Perspective from Developing Countries," *British Medical Journal* 326 [2003]: 146). Per capita food consumption has declined by a quarter since 1998 (World Bank, "Emergency Services Support Project," 2).

36. Gro Harlem Brundtland, "Health Situation of Palestinian People Living in the Occupied Palestinian Territory," World Health Organization, 2002, available online at http://www.who.int/mediacentre/news/ statements/statement04/en/print.html.

37. Azoulay and Ophir, "The Monster's Tail," 2–27 (chap. 7, n. 55).

38. World Bank, *Twenty-Seven Months — Intifada, Closures and Palestinian Economic Crisis* (Jerusalem: World Bank, 2003), 1; see also Palestinian Red Crescent Society, "Curfew Tracking: June–July 2002," online at http://www.palestinercs.org/Presentation%20PowerPoint%20Curfew%20Tracking%20July%202002_files/frame.htm

39. World Bank, *Twenty-Seven Months,* 4.

40. Alice Rothchild, "Pitching In for Health on the West Bank," *Boston Globe,* March 6, 2004.

41. For a discussion of time and space in the territories and its impact on the Palestinian political scene, see Gordon and Filc, "Hamas and the Destruction of Risk Society" (chap. 7, n. 46).

42. Lein, *Forbidden Roads,* 2 (chap. 5, n. 49).

43. World Bank, *Twenty-Seven Months,* 3.

44. Lein, *One Big Prison,* 31 (chap. 6, n. 37); data compiled by the United Nations Office for the Coordination of Humanitarian Affairs (OCHA) and sent to the author.

45. Lein, *One Big Prison,* 57; data compiled by OCHA and sent to the author.

46. For an analysis of the separation barrier, including a description of its historical roots, see Neve Gordon, "The Barrier," in *Encyclopedia of the Israeli-Palestinian Conflict,* ed. Cheryl Rubenberg (Boulder, CO: Lynne Rienner, 2008).

47. United Nations Office for Coordination of Humanitarian Affairs (OCHA), *The Humanitarian Impact of the West Bank Barrier on Palestinian Communities* (Jerusalem: United Nations, 2005).

48. Azoulay and Ophir, "Monster's Tail, 21.

49. OCHA, *Humanitarian Impact of the West Bank Barrier,* 3–5. See also B'Tselem's website: http://www.btselem.org/english/Separation_Barrier/Statistics.asp (December 26, 2005), 3, 5, 34. In numerous areas, the barrier is used to appropriate the lands of nearby Palestinian villages so as to expand Jewish settlements. For example, the lands of the village Bilein are being used to build apartment complexes for the Jewish settlement Modiein Eilit.

50. Weizman, *Hollow Land,* 161–84; Meron Rapoport, "The Spirit of the Commander Prevails," *Ha'aretz,* May 21, 2007.

51. OCHA, *Humanitarian Impact of the West Bank Barrier,* 3–5. See also Yehezkel Lein and Alon Cohen-Lifshitz, *Under the Guise of Security:*

Routing the Separation Barrier to Enable the Expansion of Israel's Settlements in the West Bank (Jerusalem: B'Tselem and Bimkon, 2005).

52. "Israel Is Trying to Push Us Out of the Jordan Valley," *Jerusalem Post,* December 30, 2005.

53. OCHA, *Humanitarian Impact of the West Bank Barrier,* 3–5

54. In a letter to Prime Minister Ehud Olmert, dated June 6, 2006, a group of Israeli human rights organizations underscore the vagueness of Israel's open-fire regulation, pointing out that nine unarmed Palestinian civilians have been killed in close proximity to the barrier, of whom five were minors, and one an eight-year-old girl. See also Peter Hermann, "Shooting of Protester Sparks Debate in Israel," *Baltimore Sun,* December 29, 2003.

55. OCHA, *Humanitarian Impact of the West Bank Barrier.*

56. Yehezkel Lein, *Nu'man, East Jerusalem: Life under the Threat of Expulsion* (Jerusalem: B'Tselem, 2003).

57. Oren Yiftachel and Haim Yacobi, "Barriers, Walls and Dialectics: The Shaping of 'Creeping Apartheid' in Israel Palestine," in *Against the Wall,* ed. Michael Sorkin 138–58 (chap. 7, n. 55).

58. Yiftachel, *Ethnocracy,* 9 (preface, n. 6).

59. Ron, *Frontiers and Ghettos,* 15 (chap. 1, n. 56).

60. Lein, *One Big Prison,* 6. In comparison, the population density in Israel is 305 people per square kilometer.

61. Public opinion polls can be found online at Palestinian Center for Policy and Survey Research: www.pcpsr.org

62. Susan Buck-Morss, *Thinking Past Terror* (New York: Verso, 2003).

63. Hroub, Khaled, "Hamas After Shaykh Yasin and Rantisi," *Journal of Palestine Studies* 33, no. 4 (Summer 2004): 21–38.

64. Shaul Mishal and Avraham Sela, *The Palestinian Hamas: Vision, Violence and Coexistence* (New York: University of Columbia Press, 2000), 3.

65. See also Sara Roy, "Hamas and the Transformation(s) of Political Islam in Palestine," *Current History* 102 (2003): 13–20; International Crisis Group, "Islamic Social Welfare Activism in the Occupied Palestinian Territories: A Legitimate Target?" *Middle East Report* no. 13, 2 April 2003, online at http://www.crisisweb.org/home/index.cfm?id = 1662&l = 1. According to the International Crisis Group, Hamas devotes between 85 and 95 percent of its estimated US$70 million annual budget to an extensive social services network ("Islamic Social Welfare Activism," 13).

66. International Crisis Group, "Islamic Social Welfare Activism," 25.

67. In 1998, the average daily consumption of a poor person was equivalent to $1.47 per day; by 2003 it had slipped to $1.32. World Bank, "Emergency Services Support Project," 2–3; World Bank, "West Bank and Gaza Update," 3–4 (chap. 7, n. 36).

68. International Crisis Group, "Islamic Social Welfare Activism," 15.

69. Due to worsening conditions, the needs of the Palestinian population grew exponentially. Focusing on health, one finds that the population's well-being deteriorated both as a result of direct violence and of the general decline in living conditions. According to the Palestinian Red Crescent Society, six years of intifada left one out of every hundred, or more than thirty thousand Palestinians injured. Thus, the already dilapidated Palestinian health services had to cope with a massive influx of additional patients whose medical needs were directly related to the conflict. Simultaneously, the exponential growth in unemployment and poverty, the widespread and rampant destruction of infrastructure, as well as severe disruptions in water supply and problems with sanitation have had a significant and detrimental effect on the health of the occupied Palestinians and on their ability to purchase services. Moreover, the ongoing curtailment of movement along with the economic crisis and direct destruction of facilities have hindered access to health care services and reduced the number of services supplied. Consult http://www.palestinercs.org and Palestinian Central Bureau of Statistics, "Impact of the Israeli Measures on the Economic Conditions of Palestinian Households" (Ramallah: PCBS, April–June, 2004).

70. International Crisis Group, "Islamic Social Welfare Activism," 15.

71. This claim is explored in Gordon and Filc, "Hamas and the Destruction of Risk Society."

72. Although Hamas espouses a "grand narrative," and, in this sense, rejects a key postmodern edict, the organization is very critical of the Enlightenment project, "the assumption of universal progress based on reason," and the modern Promethean myth of humanity's mastery of its destiny and its capacity to resolve all of its problems. See Jeff Haynes, ed., *Religion, Globalization and Political Culture in the Third World* (Hampshire, U.K.: Macmillan Press, 1999), 248.

73. For a similar claim made in a different context, see Fred Halliday, "The Politics of Islam: A Second Look," *British Journal of Political Science* 25, no. 3 (1995): 399–417.

74. Haldun Gülalp, "Globalization and Political Islam: The Social Bases of Turkey's Welfare Party," *International Journal of Middle East Studies* 33, no. 3 (2001):433–48. See also in this context Faribah Adelkah, "Transformations of Mass Religious Culture in the Islamic Republic of Iran," in Haynes, *Religion, Globalization and Political Culture.*

EPILOGUE

1. Neve Gordon, "Uneasy Calm in Palestine," *Nation,* March 12, 2007.

INDEX

Page references in *italics* refer to figures and tables.

Al-Qaeda, xviii
Al Shaab (newspaper), 106
Al-Shuaibi, Issa, 97, 262n6, 263n28
Al-Zaro, Nadim, 52
Anderson, Benedict, 58–59
Ansar prison, 148
annexation vs. occupation of land,
    4–5, 6, 33, 57, 116, 235–36n13,
    237n23
appropriation of land. *See* confisca-
    tion of land
appropriation of water. *See* water
    appropriation policy
Arab-Israeli conflict. *See* Israeli-
    Palestinian conflict
Arabs: Arabic vs. Palestinian termi-
    nology, 60; Arabness, 95–96; killed
    during military occupations, *xvii,*
    xviii, 51–52, 54, 233n3, 233nn2–3;
    pan-Arabism, 60
Arafat, Yasser, 103, 167, 171, 184,
    264n39
arbitrary modality of control:
    excesses/contradictions and, 151;
    international law and, 27; labor
    force and, 82, 163, 184; legal system
    and, 29; permit regime and, 25, 34,
    39; settlements and, 25
archaeological sites, 115, 116, 213
areas A, B, and C, 177–78
areas H1 and H2, 177, 279–80n16
Argaman, 123, 229
Aronson, Geoffrey, 68
asafir (birds), use of term, 248n60
a-Sayegh, Abdel Hamid, 52
Assaf, Said, 60–61
assassination policy, 21, 202, 204,
    284n15
Assirah, 68
autonomy plan, 106, 107, 266nn58,61
Azoulay, Ariella, 208, 212

Balata refugee camp, 149
Bani Naim, 112
Bank of Israel's Research Depart-
    ment, 40, 41, 66, 242n7, 256n4
Barak, Ehud, 197, 282n2
barrier, separation, 3, 9, 168, 209, *210,*
    212–15
Bassam Shak'a, 106, 109
beatings policy, 156–57, 165, 166, 185,
    206
Bedouin villages, 252n29, 261n79
Begin, Menachem, 106, 107, 266n58
Beita, 68
Beitar Illit, 133, *135, 136,* 231
Beit Jalla, 105
Beit Sahur, 202, 267–68n74
Ben Eliezer, Binyamin, 93
Ben-Gurion, David, 238n35
Benvenisti, Meron, *xvii,* 49, 162
Bethlehem, 112, 113, 178, 202, 228
biopower: health field and, 9; labor
    force and, 90; legal system and, 13;
    for management of population,
    12–13; national identity movement
    and, 96; PA and, 191; permit regime
    and, 162; statist approach and, 12;
    transformation of occupation and,
    11–15, 19, 68, 240n52
Birzeit, 105
Birzeit University, 113, 164, 251n20,
    259n51
Block of the Faithful (Gush Emunim),
    124, 133
borders policy, xvi, 8–9, 82, 83, 161–
    63, 211–12. *See also* Green line, the
British Emergency Regulations, 36,
    52, 243n19
British Mandate period: demolition
    of houses policy during, 243n19;
    land held under, 4; laws during,
    243n14; local leaders appointed

civil administration period: appearance of termination of occupation, 108; autonomy plan and, 107; civil branch of, 107, 108, 244n28, 266n61; local leadership and, 20, 108–10, 109, 114, 115, 267n72; military branch of, 107–224n28, 266n61; Special Partial Outline Plans for West Bank, 136, 273n56

civil administration period (1981– 1987): coercive forms of control during, 110; collective punishments during, 110; colonial fantasy during, 147, 148; confiscation of land during, 108, 131; controlling apparatuses during, 107–8, 111, 266n63; elections during, 104; employees' salaries during, 186–87; first intifada and government in, 153–54; genealogy of control during, 18, 19–20; GSS's role during, 108; health field during, 190–91; knowledge regulations during, 109–10; labor force integration during, 81; leadership during, 93, 261n1; means of control during, 110–11; nongovernmental sector during, 153–54, 253n35; normalization of occupation during, 19–20, 50; Palestinians killed during, *xvii*, 54, 110; perpetuation of occupation during, 19; personal information database created during, 162; power modes used during, 50, 108–11, 115; protests/demonstrations during, 110, 267n73; security needs during, 21; settlements established during, 108, 131; social relations shaped during, 115, 268n82; travel permits during, 137; Village Leagues' role

during, 108, 111–14, 115, 170, 268nn78,82

civil employees, Palestinian, 30, 48, 49, 55, 173, 186–87, 249–50n5

civilian control mechanism. *See* management of population

closure policy, 163, 179, 180, 184–86, 188, 209, 280nn20,22, 289n69

coercive forms of control, 10, 11, 19, 33, 51–55, 110

collaborators, Palestinian: children as, 42; criminals as, 42–43; fragmentation of society and, 43; GSS recruitment of, 39, 161; independent Palestinian state and, 249n67; individual control, and recruitment of, 42–43; insecurity of individuals and, 43; legal system and, 43; modalities of control and, 43, 44, 161, 249n67; in OT, 43, 249n65; permit regime and, 39, 42; refugee camps and, 260–61n70; role of, 43, 249n65; self-rule and, 249n67; social hierarchies and, 43; types of, 248n60; Village Leagues, and seen as, 113

collective punishment: during civil administration period, 110; curfews as, 21, 30, 110, 156, 160, 203–4; demolition of houses as, 53, 54, 160, 205; fear of terrorists as justification for, 53

colonization principle: defined, 199, 283n6; education system and, 59; Islamic fundamentalism and, xviii, 221–22, 289n72; Israel's occupation and, 50, 51, 63, 167; military government period and, 50, 51; as operating force in OT, xix, 199– 200; resource extraction and, 9,

database, personal information, 40–41, 162

Dayan, Moshe: carrot and stick metaphor and, 45; Dayan Plan, 117; as foreign minister, 266n62; on functional compromise plan, 6, 107, 117; on governing OT, 46, 48, 247n58; intifada and, 250n7; on invisible occupation policy, 1, 49, 55, 250n7; Labor party defection of, 266n62; nonintervention policies of, 57, 106; open borders policy and, 163; on refugees and self-identity issue, 87–88; relocation program of, 87; on resistance, 106; on role of local leadership, 97, 101–2; settlement project of, 124

death of Palestinians. *See* Palestinians killed in OT

Declaration of Principles, 173, 279nn9–10

Defensive Shield military operation, 203–5

demolition of houses: during British Mandate period, 243n19; as coercive form of control, 10; as collective punishment, 53, 54, 160, 205; legal system and, 21, 29, 33, 243n19, 285–86n27; public information about, 166; sealed houses, 160, 267, 276n5; sovereign power and, 110, 267–68n74; statistics, 276n5; wall and tower (Homa ve-Migdal) ploy and, 119–20

demonstrations. *See* protests/demonstrations

deportation policy, 52–53, 160, 251n20, 276n5

detention, administrative, 28–29, 52–53, 54, 81, 149, 158, 276n5

DFLP (Democratic Front for the Liberation of Palestine), 158

Dheisa (refugee camp), 141

Din VeHeshbon ("Accountability") reports, 50–51

Dir Amar (refugee camp), 113, 267n73

Dir el-Balah, 99

disciplinary power: for control of individuals, 11–12, 19, 38, 61, 68, 206, 224, 240n52; individual prosperity and, 63, 68–69, 151; normalization of occupation using, 22, 151, 212; PA and, 172, 191; relocation program and, 79; restrictive policies overshadowed by, 70–71; transformation of occupation and, 50, 164, 206. *See also* labor force, Palestinian

dispossession mechanisms, 118, 119, 131, 146

Drobles Plan, 117

Dudin, Mustafa, 112, 114, 171

East Jerusalem: annexation of, 4–5, 57, 116, 235–36n13; censorship used in, 57, 58, 109, 253n39; citizenship in, 119, 235–36n13; legal system in, 109; Magharbia Quarter in, 236n18; partial integration in, 5; settlements near, 125; sovereignty in, 197

East Timor, xviii, 54, 233n3

economic field: bypass roads and, 132, 137; communal stagnation in, 71, 75, 91, 152, 256n4; disparity in prices of products and, 73; economic growth and, 74–75, 80; expansion in OT, 70; financial institutions and, 72; incomes and, 66; management of population in,

72, 76, 151–52; monetary regulations and, 72; and PA, limited control of, 172, 173, 174–75, 177, 223; poverty and, 19, 183, 187, 214, 220–21, 289n67; power modes and, 63, 68–69, 76; productivity and, 9; resistance and policies in, 150, 155, 166–67; standard of living and, 74–75, 80, 88, 151, 167; wages and, 80; water appropriation policy and, 128

economy, Palestinian: average annual GNP, 74, 75, 81, 183, 256n4, 280–81n29; closure policy and, 184–85; contradictions that engendered resistance in, 69, 92; control of, 71–76; development restrictions and, 74, 75, 83, 90–92, 118, 163, 175; empowered Palestinian nationalist movement, 22, 71, 92; excesses/contradictions and, 22, 71, 84, 92; export/import goods policies and, 74, 75, 257n21; GDP, 74, 75, 183, *184*; Gulf states employment opportunities and, 75, 163, 167, 184, 257n21; integration of labor force and, 66, 71–72, 75; investment and reinvestment in, 73, 74, 257n20; Israel's economy, and integration with, 62, 66, 71–72, 76, 256n1; lifestyle changes due to improvements in, 66–67, *67,* 68, 74–75, 82; local leadership and improved, 85, 259–60n56; management of population and, 188; markets in Israel and, 72, 73, 81, 83; means of control and, 70–71; movement restrictions and, 163, 185; New Deal-style projects and, 65, 77–79, 80; normalization of occupation through im-

provements in, 62–63, 71, 77, 78, 80, 88, 92; open bridges policy and, 250n11; outsourcing the occupation and, 183–87, *184*; Palestinian labor force and, 76–77; planting regulations, 72; political stability and, 71, 77, 78, 80, 85, 88; poverty and, 87; productivity and, 62, 63, 64–65, 68, 80; professionalization and, 83–84; reorientation of labor force away from agriculture and industry, 75, 130; resistance and restrictive measures on, 71; sanctions against, 223–24; sovereign power and, 68–71; student dropout rate and, 92; unemployment rates, 66, 77, 163, 185; violence and, 223–24; vocational courses, 65, 67–68, 77, 79–80

education system: artificial unity in Israel through, 59; bitterness and, 16, 84; censorship and, 57, 58, 253nn36,39; closing schools as form of punishment and, 62, 110, 164, 175; closure policy and, 186; Egyptian curriculum and, 56, 253n40; entry-permit regime and, 186; excesses/contradictions and, 16; fragmentation of society and, 61; infrastructure for, 91–92; Jordanian curriculum, 56, 57, 58, 253n39; knowledge regulations and, 38, 39, 55–62; management of population and, 59; Mandatory Palestine and, 55–56; national identity movement and, 56, 57, 59, 94; Palestinian history and, 56, 57, 58, 61, 173–74; for Palestinian population within Israel, 56, 57; politics and, 61–62; separation barrier and, 213, 214;

Fatah, 3, 53, 68, 219, 235n10

fedayeen, 103, 252n28, 264n35. *See also* Palestinian Liberation Organization

Feldman, Avigdor, 31–32, 245nn31,32

fencing policy, 3, 179–80, 280nn21–22. *See also* separation barrier

Food and Agriculture Organization of the United Nations, 208

forbidden road regime, 137

Foucault, Michel, 11, 65, 138–39, 241n58, 249n69

Fourth Geneva Convention, 26, 242–43n10

fragmentation of Palestinian society: closure policy and, 163; collaborators and, 43; education system and, 61; elections and, 102; excesses/contradictions and, 151, 153; forbidden road regime and, 137–38; GSS activities and, 39, 42, 161, 248n62; local and regional peace and, 224; management of population and, 88–89, 146; permit regime and, 39, 42, 161, 163, 248n62; separation barrier and, 214; settlements and, 146

Freij, Elias, 113

Freire, Paulo, 59

Frontiers and Ghettos (Ron), 157

fundamentalism, Islamic, xviii, 95, 221–22, 289n72

Gaza City, 65, 99

Gaza Strip, the: basic services in, 90; checkpoints in, 209; confiscation of land policy in, 120, 121, 131, 270n9, 272n43; economy of, 70; education system in, 56, 175, 253nn35,40, 259n51; fencing policy and, 179–80, 280nn21–22; GDP in, 74; government policy in, 4, 10, 24, 26, 243n14; health field and, 175; infrastructure conditions in, 90, 91; integration of labor force and, 6, 58, 66, 84, 87–88; intentions for, 4, 116; Israelis, and travel to, xvi; landscape of, 23; local leadership and, 99–100, 263n24; means of control in, 10, 239n37; movement restrictions in, xvi; municipal responsibilities in, 99–100; national identity movement in, 93; newspapers prohibited in, 109; 1971 military campaign in, 53, 82, 88, 252n29; during Oslo Accord period, 177, 279–80n16; Palestinians killed in, xviii; per capita consumption statistics for, 258n27; PLO activities in, 99; population statistics for, 23, 87, 131, 218, 242n2; poverty rate in, 87, 187, 220; refugee camps in, 87, 99, 242n2, 260–61n70; security road project, 78–79; settlements in, 125, 271n29; spatial control and, 177, 279–80n16; strikes by civilians in, 53–54; trade agreements between West Bank and, 185–86; tree policies and, 1–2, 64; *waqf* (religious trust) in, 95; White Areas, 177, 279–80n16; Yellow Areas, 177, 279–80n16

Gazit, Shlomo, 23, 46, 48, 70, 100, 125

genealogy of control, 16, 17–21

General Security Services: civil administration period and, 108; collaborators and, 39, 161; curfews under control of, 31; fragmentation of society and, 39, 42, 161; infrastructure of control and, 24, 31–32, 44; interrogations by, 159; legal system and, 31–32, 245n32; permit

lition of houses and, 267–68n74; Geneva Convention suspended by, 242–43n10; human shields and, 207; infrastructure of control and, 32–33, 44; judicial annexation of OT and, 33; knowledge regulations and, 266n59; morality of actions by Israel and, 33

Hiltermann, Joost, 76, 153

historical sites, 116, 140, 279–80n16

Hollow Land (Weizman), 252n29, 260–61n70

Homa ve-Migdal (wall and tower), 119–20, 127, 269n8

Homo sacer, 21, 205, 240n47

house demolitions. *See* demolition of houses

Hroub, Khaled, 219

human rights, 25, 34, 39, 143, 144, 167, 190, 243n16

Human Rights Watch (HRW), 203, 285–86n27

human shields, Palestinians used as, 21, 207

Husan, 135

identity, national. *See* national identity

identity cards, green, 160–61

incarceration policy, 158–59, 165, 277n28

independent Palestinian state: bypass roads and, 138; collaborators and, 249n67; contiguity of, 197; education system and, 59; first intifada period and, 20; functional compromise plan for, 6, 107, 117; Geneva Convention and, 26; geography/demography contradiction and, 4, 6, 16, 215–17, 235n10;

Greater Israel ideology vs., 5, 6, 115, 116, 124, 213, 215; infrastructure conditions and, 91; Palestinian rights and, 26; permit regime and, 138; power-sharing agreement between Israel and Jordan in West Bank and, 49–50, 170–71, 250n9; right of return and, 283n3; separation barrier and, 213; separation principle and, 216–17; spatial control and, 106, 107, 266nn58,61; surveillance apparatuses and, 249nn67,69; West Bank, and interests in, 96

individual, control of: closure policy and, 188; disciplinary power and, 11–12; education system and, 9; during first intifada period, 165–66; health field and, 9, 46; integration of labor force and, 9, 65, 81–84; lack of transparency in regulations and, 29; means of control used for, 3; permit regime and, 34, 35, 38, 161–62, 187–88; power modes and, 14; surveillance and, 42–43, 44, 249n69; torture policy and, 159; violence and, 157–58, 217–18

individual insecurity. *See* insecurity of individuals

individual prosperity: concealed communal stagnation, 71, 75, 91, 152, 256n4; disciplinary power and, 63, 68–69, 151; excesses/contradictions and, 22, 71; integration of labor force and, 9; national identity movement and, 22, 71; normalization of occupation and, 13; during second intifada period, 19 individuals: correct behavior of, 25, 38, 40, 80, 161; disregard for and loss of interest in lives of, 22, 166, 187–88, 196; and effects of integration into Israeli workforce, 81–84, 88–89; modes and modification of behavior, 3, 9, 29, 38–39, 82, 138, 158, 165; prosperity of, 9, 71, 91, 152; settlers as, 274n74; social relations shaped during occupation and, 4; usefulness of, 165, 174

industrial sector, 73–74, 75, 90, 130, 139, 179, 257n14

infrastructure conditions, 19, 90–91, 145–46. *See also* bypass roads

infrastructure of control: administration of OT and, 22, 23–24, 29–30; carrot and stick metaphor for, 44–47; GSS and, 24, 31–32, 44; High Court of Justice and, 32–33, 44; legal system and, 22, 26–29; MOs and, 246n39; Ottoman law and, 4, 27; permit regime and, 25, 33–40, 44; surveillance apparatuses and, 22, 33, 40–44, 242n7. *See also specific policies*

insecurity of individuals: collaborators and, 43; Hamas and, 221; legal system and, 29; management of population and, 21; permit regime and, 39, 161; during second intifada period, 21, 209

institutions for operations in OT: Egyptian, 4, 10, 24, 26, 243n14; financial, 72; Jordanian, 4, 10, 24, 49, 243n14, 263n31; judicial, 9–10, 13, 28; as means of control, 3; political, 2, 3, 169. *See also specific institutions; specific policies*

integration of labor force into Israel's economy: agricultural practices and, 85, 86; during civil administration period, 81; control of individual and, 9, 65, 81–84; economy of Palestinians and, 62, 66, 71–72, 75, 76, 256n1; individuals and, 9, 81–84, 88–89; Israel's economy and, 62, 66, 71–72, 75, 76, 256n1; local leadership and, 103–4, 111–12, 265n43, 268n82; management of population and, 81; during military government period, 48, 57–58, 60, 81; national identity movement and, 65, 68, 82, 103–4, 152; nonintegration vs., 86; partial, 48, 68, 82, 84, 152; resistance and, 71; social relations and, 81, 89, 115, 268n82; the Strip and, 6, 58, 66, 84, 87–88; West Bank and, 66, 84–87, 85

intentional acts vs. statist approach, 261n76

internal military government period (1948–1966), 48, 50

international aid, 21, 221

international law, 25, 26, 27, 32–33, 34, 52, 167, 243n16

intifada, use of term, 275n1

intifada period, first (1988–1993): border status during, 8, 161–63; communiqués issued during, 154, 155; confiscation of land during, 20; consequences of, 166–68; control of individuals during, 165–66; economic field during, 150, 155, 166–67; eruptions at beginning of, 147–48; excesses/contradictions during, 20, 22, 149, 150–54; genealogy of control during, 16; infrastructure conditions during, 90; iron fist policy during, 20, 156; Israelis killed during, 277n25;

47n47, 266n59; permit regime and, 34, 36–38, 246–47n47; population control measures and, 9, 38, 46; publications and, 37, 109
Kretzmer, David, 33

labor force, Palestinian: administrative detention and, 81; arbitrary modality of control and, 82, 163, 184; bitterness and, 12, 84, 89; confiscation of land and, 86; employer-employee relationship and, 83; entry-permit regime and, 184–85; excesses/contradictions and, 81, 90; history of, xvi; labor-intensive work for, 73, 75; management of population and, 82; normalization of occupation and, 82, 86; open borders policy and, 82, 83; recruitment of, 80, 81; restrictions on, 82, 83, 259n48; separation barrier and, 214; standard of living and, 82, 86, 88; statistics, 81; as temporary modality of control, 82; unregistered workers in, 81; wages and, 77, 80, 82, 258n31; work as privilege for, 83; work permits for, 82; Zionist policy and, 76, 268n82. *See also* integration of labor force
Labor Party government, 123, 124, 125, 271n27
Lahad, Antoine, 171
land confiscated by sovereign (*makhlul*), 129
land confiscation. *See* confiscation of land
Laskov, Haim, 238n35
Latrun enclave, 5–6, 236–37n19
lawyers' strike, 251n22
leadership, local. *See* local leadership

Lebanon, 170, 279n6
legal and bureaucratic mechanisms. *See* bureaucratic-legal mechanisms
legal system: settlements and, 28, 141, 244n22, 274n74
legal system in OT: annexation vs. occupation and, 4–5, 6, 33, 57, 116, 235–36n13, 237n23; assassination policy and, 202, 284n15; biopower and, 13; collaborators and, 43; contradictions in, 28–29; controlling apparatuses and, 28–29; East Jerusalem and, 109; erasure of the Green Line and, 144; ethnic policing and, 143–44, 275n87; forbidden road regime and, 137; infrastructure of control and, 22, 26–29; insecurity of individuals and, 29; investigations into Palestinians killed and, 204–5; Jews and, 120, 143–44, 175–76, 275n87; lack of transparency in, 25, 29; as means of control, 3, 29; during second intifada period, 21, 31, 202, 205–6; settlements and, 28, 141, 274n74; settlers' violence and, 143; sovereign power and, 14, 240n47; suspension of, 202, 205–6, 285–86n27; as temporary modality of control, 29, 244n24
Likud Party government, 106, 107, 125, 266n62
local leadership: during civil administration period, 108–10; contradictions informing occupation and, 98; deportation policy and, 52–53, 160, 251n20, 265n50, 276n5; invisible occupation and, 49, 97, 98, 113, 248n60; labor force integration and, 103–4, 111–12, 265n43,

31. *See also* settlements, Jewish; society, Palestinian; spatial control of OT

Mandatory Palestine, 4, 7, 8, 94, 235

Ma'oz, Moshe, 105, 263–64n32

Mapai Party, 1, 37

marriage restrictions, 160, 244n24

matrix of control, 179

means of control: defined, 3; education system as, 9; excesses/contradictions and, 3, 45; global processes and, 17; historical precedent for, 10–11, 238n35, 238–39n36, 239n37; judicial institutions as, 9–10; management of population and, 3; policies shaped by, 3–4, 92; protests/demonstrations shaped by, 92; relocation of Palestinians as, 78–79; resistance shaped by, 3–4; resources and, 9, 127–28; during second intifada period, 22; surveillance as, 9, 40, 238n33; through executive branch of state, 13; unemployment threat as, 77; variations in, 11. *See also* controlling apparatuses; *specific means of control*

media: knowledge regulations, 37, 106, 109, 246–47n47, 266n59; OT, and exposure in, 166, 167

Mehola, 123, 229

Meir, Golda, 1, 122

messianic ideology, 5, 6, 115, 116, 124, 140, 213, 215

Migdal, Joel, 85

militaristic ideology of Israel, 5, 116, 122–23, 125, 127, 131, 139–40, 270n17

military bases: confiscation of land policy and, 122; during military government period, 30, 53; outposts

and, 25, 193; spatial control and, 118, 179; as surveillance apparatuses, 42, 247n58; wall and tower ploy and, 120

military government period (1967–1980): civil branch of, 30, 227–28, *228*; civil employees during, 30, 48, 49, 55, 249–50n5; coercive forms of control during, 51–55; colonial principle and, 50, 51; deportations during, 52, 251n20; described, 19, 29–30, 265n47; economic growth during, 74–75, 80; education system during, 51, 55–62; forms of intervention during, 50; genealogy of control during, 18, 19; Israeli cabinet and, 30, 244n26; labor force integration during, 48, 57–58, 60, 81; management of population during, 30; national identity movement during, 51; normalization of occupation during, 19, 30; nutrition monitoring during, 165, 207–8; Palestinians killed during, *xvii,* 54; politics during, 51; power modes used during, 19, 50, 115; promotion of economic prosperity during, 19, 51, 62–69; punitive measures during, 30, 53–54, 252nn25,29; regional boundaries, 132–33, 273n51; security needs during, 30; standard of living during, 74–75, 80, 88; water appropriation during, 127, 271n32

military occupations, statistics on Arabs killed during worldwide, *xvii,* xviii, 51–52, 54, 233nn2–3. *See also specific countries*

military orders, 33–34, 246n39

militias, settlement, 141–43, 275n79

government period, 51; municipalities and, 104–5, 114, 265n49; 1973 October war and, 102; nongovernmental sector and, 153–54; normalization of occupation and, 13; pan-Arabism vs., 60; PLO and, 102–3, 115; power modes and, 96; productivity and, 68; racism and, 118, 143–44, 152, 217, 275n87; re-emergence of, 94–96, 102–4; repression by Israel, 88, 95; sanctions against local leadership and, 108; settlements and, 103, 146; Six-Day War and, 94–95; spatial control and, 95, 111–14; in the Strip, 93; teachers and, 61; unifying effect of, 224; Village Leagues and, 111–14; in West Bank, 26, 56–57, 59, 93–94, 96, 103, 146, 155, 166; Zionist policy and, 96. *See also* independent Palestinian state

Nationality and Entry into Israel Law, 244n24

neocolonial, 170. *See also* colonization principle

NGOs (nongovernmental) sector, 95, 153, 191, 253n35, 276n16. *See also specific nongovernmental organizations*

1948 War, xix–xx, 94

1949 Armistice Agreements. *See* Green Line, the

1973 October war, 82, 102

1967 Arab-Israeli War. *See* Six-Day War

Noar Halutzi Lohem (Fighting Pioneer Youth). *See* NAHAL

"no man's land," 236–37n19

noncoercive forms of control, 11, 50

non-interference policy, 50

non-presence policy, 50. *See also* invisible occupation policy

normalization of occupation: checkpoints and, 212; during civil administration period, 19–20, 50; control over resources and, 9, 127–28; disciplinary power and, 22, 151, 212; dispossession mechanisms and, 146; economic field and, 74–75, 80, 88, 151, 167; economy and, 62–63, 71, 77, 78, 80, 88, 92; education system used for, 8, 15, 240n53; during first intifada period, 153–54, 166; health field and, 9, 164; individual prosperity and, 13; labor force integration and, 82, 86; management of population and, 117, 118; during military government period, 50; national identity movement and, 13; during Oslo Accord period, 182; in OT, xvii, xix, 1, 3; power modes used for, 15, 22, 240n53; standard of living and, 74–75, 80, 88, 151, 167

nutrition monitoring, 165, 207–8

The Occupation of Justice (Kretzmer), 33

Occupied Territories, and occupation vs. annexation, 4–5, 6, 33, 57, 116, 235–36n13

October war (1973), 82, 102

Office of the Legal Advisor, 244n26

Old City, the, 279n16. *See also* East Jerusalem

open bridges policy, 50, 250n11

open-fire regulations, 157, 201–2, 215, 288n54

Operation Defensive Shield, 203–5

Operation Litani, 279n6

permit regime *(continued)*
  separation barrier and, 214; Shawa passports/exit permits, 99; social relations and, 34, 38; spatial control and, 34, 35–36, 39; as surveillance apparatuses, 39; as temporary modality of control, 34, 39; water well drilling and, 271n32; working-permit regime, 82–83, 160–61. *See also* entry-permit regime
Phone Tap Law, 245n32
physical edifices, 3, 204. *See also specific edifices*
place. *See* spatial control of OT
PLO. *See* Palestinian Liberation Organization
PNF. *See* Palestinian National Front
police-style measures, 53, 157
politics: education system and, 61–62; during military government period, 51; outsourcing the occupation and, 183–87, *184*; Palestinian economy and, 71, 77, 78, 80, 85, 88; permit regime and, 37–38, 39, 83, 247n54; PLO elite and, 169; political institutions, 2, 3, 169
politics of death policy, 88, 188, 207–8
Popular Front for the Liberation of Palestine (PFLP), 3, 53, 264n35
population control. *See* management of population
postmodern fundamentalism, 221–22, 289n72
poverty, 19, 87, 183, 187, 214, 220–21, 289n67
power modes: during civil administration period, 50, 108–11, 115; control of individual and, 14; economic field and, 63, 68–69, 76; education system and, 15, 240n53; excesses/contradictions and, 15–17;

first intifada period and, 21, 149–50; for governing OT, 2, 10, 11, 14–15, 45, 240n49; management of population and, 14, 145; during military government period, 19, 50, 115; in modern governing, 4, 14–15, 240nn49,51–53; national identity movement and, 96; normalization of occupation and, 9, 15, 22, 240n53; PA and, 172; permit regime and, 82–83; toleration of, 20. *See also specific types of power*
power-sharing agreement, 49–50, 170–71, 250n9
Pressman, Jeremy, 283n3
Proclamation Two, 13–14, 26–27, 29
prosperity, individual. *See* individual prosperity
Protection of Privacy Law, 245n32
protests/demonstrations: assassination of PLO leaders in West Bank and, 102; during civil administration period, 110, 267n73; civil disobedience activities, 53, 153, 155, 156; curfews, as punishments for, 58; during first intifada period, 147–48, 154–56; local leadership and, 105–6; police-style methods and, 157; rate of, 148–49, 276n5; in refugee camps, 87; sovereign power and, 115, 145; strikes by civilians and, 53, 57–58
publication regulations, 37, 109

Qabalan, 267–68n74
Qadi of Hebron, 106
Qalqilya, 178, 214
Qedumuim, 124, 229

Ra'anan Weitz Plan, 117
Rabat summit, 102, 264n39

separation principle *(continued)*
  fantasy element in, 200, 284n7;
  of frontiers and ghettos, 217–18;
  geography/demography contradiction and, 215–17; Hamas' rise and,
  218–22; politics of death, 88, 188,
  207–8; rule of law, 205–6; spatial
  control and, 208–12, *210*; transition
  to control using, 180, 196; violence
  and, 201–5

Settlement Master Plan for 1983–1986,
  132

settlements, Jewish: on areas controlled by, *134*; confiscation of land
  for, 122, 123, 270n17, 287n49; development restrictions and, 118; as
  dispossession mechanisms, 119, 131;
  established during civil administration period, 118, 131; established
  during Oslo Accord period, 192–
  94, *194, 195*; excesses/contradictions
  and, 15–16; as extra-governmental
  enterprise, 125, 243n13; extraterritorial status of, 28; fragmentation of
  society and, 146; Jordanian law
  and, 270n15; legal system and, 28,
  141, 244n22, 274n74; messianic
  ideology and, 123–24, 270n21,
  270–71n24; militaristic ideology
  and, 5, 116, 122–23, 125, 127, 131, 139–
  40, 270n17; militias, 141–43,
  275n79; national identity movement and, 103, 146; number of, 25;
  outposts and, 25; spatial control
  and, 146, 179; in the Strip, 125,
  271n29; as surveillance apparatuses,
  131; in West Bank, 103, 116–17,
  123–26, *126,* 146, *194,* 270n21

settlers: confrontations between
  government and, 117, 123, 124;

ethnic policing and, 118, 140–44;
  first intifada period and, 167–68; as
  individuals, 274n74; management
  of population and, 22, 131–32, *134,*
  140–43; messianic ideology and,
  140; militias and, 141–43; movement restrictions and, 132, 280n20;
  during Oslo Accords period, 193,
  194; patrols and, 139, 141, 142;
  policing role of, 194; relocation to
  OT and, 131, 139; surveillance and,
  42, 118, 138–39; violent activities of,
  106, 140–43, 144

Shabak. *See* General Security Services
Shabak Law, 31, 32, 245n34
Shamgar, Meir, 26, 27, 33, 238–39n36,
  242–43n10
Sharem el-Sheikh Memorandum,
  279n9
Sharon, Ariel, 1, 53, 88, 106, 197,
  252n29, 266n63
Sharon-Wachman Plan, 117
Shati refugee camp, 54
Shawa, Rashad, 99, 106, 109, 247n54
Shehadeh, Raja, 28, 169
Shin Bet. *See* General Security
  Services
Silwan, 267–68n74
Sinai Peninsula, xv, 4, 54, 123, 236n16
Six-Day War: areas occupied during,
  xii; geography/demography contra-
  diction and, 4, 235n10; the Green
  Line and, 7, 63, 70; intentions for
  land captured during, 4–5, 10,
  235n12, 236n15; international law
  and, 26; Israeli economy and,
  76–77; national identity move-
  ment and, 94–95
social control of population. *See*
  management of population

social welfare organizations, 173, 219–21, 288n65

society, Palestinian: economic sanctions and, 224; forbidden road regime and, 137–38; Islamic fundamentalism and, 222; means of control and, 3; social cleavages in West Bank, 85–86; social dependence on Israel and, 72; social relations and, 4, 34, 38, 43, 81, 89, 115, 268n82. *See also* fragmentation of Palestinian society

Somalia Plan, 223

South Lebanese Army, 170, 171, 279n6

sovereign power: carrot and stick metaphor and, 47; during civil administration period, 108–11; confiscation of land policy and, 131; demolition of houses and, 110, 267–68n74; described, 11; in East Jerusalem, 197; economy and, 68–71; education system and, 62; excesses/contradictions and, 150–51; first intifada period and, 158, 166, 170; invisible occupation policy and, 50, 55, 76; iron fist policy and, 20, 107, 156; Islamic fundamentalism and, 224; legal system and, 14, 240n47; Oslo Accord period and, 22, 180, 181; PA and, 192; politics of death and, 54; protests/demonstrations and, 115, 145; relocation program and, 79; transformation of Israel's occupation and, 11–15

space, control of. *See* spatial control of OT

spatial control of OT: controlling apparatuses and, 46, 117; education

system support for, 59; excesses/contradictions in, 22; Geneva Convention and, 26; ghettos/frontiers metaphor and, 157–58, 217–18; infrastructure conditions and, 91; matrix of control for, 179; messianic ideology support of, 116; militaristic ideology and, 5, 116, 131, 140; national identity movement and, 95, 111–14; outsourcing the occupation and, 172, 177–80, *178*; permit regime and, 34, 35–36, 39; place shaped in ongoing conflicts and, 4; power-sharing agreement and, 49–50, 170–71, 250n9; ruptured space and, xviii, 171, 180; during second intifada period, 208–12; self-rule and, 106, 107, 266nn58,61; separation barrier and, 212; separation principle and, 208–12, *210*; settlements and, 146, 179; verticality policy and, 127–28, 202–3, 282n54. *See also* management of population

Special Partial Outline Plans for West Bank, 136, 273n56

statist approach, 2–3, 12, 15, 16, 18, 45–46, 171, 261n76

steadfastness to land (*tsumud*), 154

strikes by civilians, 53, 57–58, 251n22. *See also* protests/demonstrations

Strip, the. *See* Gaza Strip

Supreme Court. *See* High Court of Justice

Surif, 113

surveillance apparatuses: bypass roads, 132; collaborators as, 42–43, 248n60; collection and analysis of data using, 40, 41; communication and, 41–42, 247n57; infrastructure

surveillance apparatuses *(continued)*
of control and, 22, 33, 40–44,
242n7; invisibility/visibilty of, 42,
247n58; management of population and, 138–39; military bases as,
42, 247n58; responsibility for lives
and, 41; self-rule and, 249nn67,69;
settlements as, 131; settlers as, 42,
118, 138–39; as temporary modality
of control, 41; violence and, 140–
43, 144, 249nn68–69

Tamari, Salim, 111, 182, 268n82
Tawil, Ibrahim, 109
teachers, 12, 30, 31, 49, 53, 56–57,
59–62, 164
teacher-training programs, 9, 61
Temple Mount/Harem al Sharif, 1,
197
temporary modality of control: controlling apparatuses as, 151; curfews
as, 24, 27; employment as, 82, 163;
legal system as, 29, 244n24; in OT,
7–9, 146; outposts as, 25, 193; permit regime as, 34; separation barrier as, 212
terrorists: collective punishment and,
53; extrajudicial executions and,
202, 284n15; GSS profiles for, 162;
incarceration of, 184, 185; mukhtar
policing for, 259–60n56; in Rafah,
xv; settlers as, 106; torture policy
and, 159
Teveth, Shabtai, 60, 239n37
ticking bomb scenario, 159
Tomb of the Patriarchs, the, 140,
279–80n16
Torpey, John, 177, 197
torture policy: during first intifada
period, 11, 158–59, 165, 277n31;

genealogy of control and, 21; High
Court of Justice and, 33; management of population and, 159; as
means of control, 11, 165; during
military government period, 32, 53,
252n25; of PA, 190; strikes by civilians and, 53, 252n25
tourist industry, 173, 183
traditional elite. *See* local leadership
transparency of regulations, lack of,
25, 29, 39, 116–19
tree policies, 1–2, 64, 234n3, 254n58
tsumud (steadfastness to land), 155
Tul-Karem, 67, 112, 178, 214, 228
two-state solution, 166, 283n3

Unified National Leadership of the
Palestinian Uprising, 154
Union of Palestinian Medical Relief
Committees, 209
United Arab Kingdom, 99
United Nations Economic and Social
Commission, 204
United Nations General Assembly,
103, 264n39
United Nations Relief and Work
Agency, 3, 56, 253n35
United Nations resolutions, 264n39
UNRWA. *See* United Nations Relief
and Work Agency
Unsettled States, Disputed Lands
(Lustick), 7
Usher, Graham, 189

verticality policy, 127–28, 202–3,
282n54
Village Leagues, 108, 111–14, 115, 170,
268nn78,82
village officials (*mukhtars*), 49, 97,
113, 248n60, 259–60n56. *See also*

collaborators, Palestinian; local leadership

violence/violent activities: economic sanctions due to, 223–24; during first intifada period, 148, 156–64; ghetto/frontier theory and, 157–58, 217–18; against Israeli citizens, xvii, 183, 198, 203, 212, 277n25; Israel's role in, 223; Israel's use of, 143, 156–60, 176, 179, 196, 198–99, 204; management of population and, 157–58, 225; means of control and, xviii–xix, xxi; permit regime and, 249n68; during second intifada period, xvi–xviii, *xvii,* 198–99, 204, 217; settlers and, 106, 140–43, 144

vocational courses, 9, 65, 67–68, 79–80

Wadi Fuchin, 135

wall and tower (Homa ve-Migdal) ploy, 119–20, 127, 269n8

waqf (religious trust), 95

water appropriation policy, 72, 85, 87, 127–31, *128,* 130, 271n32

Weber, Max, 140

Weizman, Eyal, 54, 87–88, 121, 138, 193, 213, 252n29, 260–61n70, 282n54

Weizman, Ezer, 105, 266n63

West Bank: agricultural production in, 85, 86; areas A, B, and C designations in, 177–78; areas H1 and H2, 177, 279–80n16; assassination of PLO leaders in, 102; basic services in, 90–91; bypass roads in, 193; checkpoints in, 209; citizenship in, 94; during civil administration period, 136, 273n56; civil branch of military government in, 227–28, *228;* confiscation of land policy in, 86, 103, 120, 121–27, *126,* 131, 272n43; controlling apparatuses and practices in, 4; de facto connection with, xx; education system in, 56, 57, 58, 253n35, 253n39; elections in, 100–105, 263nn28,31, 263–64n32, 265nn47,50; GDP, 74; infrastructure conditions in, 90–91; intentions for, 4, 6, 58, 78, 116, 236n15; Jordanian administrative institutions in, 4, 10, 24, 49, 101, 243n14, 263n31; labor force integration and, 66, 84–87, *85;* landscape of, 23; local leadership and, 96–99, 100, 104, 265n47; movement restrictions in, xvi, 132–33, *134,* 273n51; municipal boundaries, 132, *135,* 136, 273n51; national identity movement in, 26, 56–57, 59, 93–94, 96, 103, 146, 155, 166; newspapers prohibited in, 109; during Oslo Accord period, 177–78, *178,* 279–80n16; Palestinians killed in, xviii; peace in exchange for withdrawal from, 116–17; permit regime in, 209; population of, 23; power-sharing agreement between Israel and Jordan in, 49–50, 170–71, 250n9; regional boundaries, 132–33, *134,* 273n51; security road project in, 78; self-rule interests in, 96; separation barrier in, 212–15; settlements in, 103, 116–17, 123–26, *126,* 146, 192–94, *194, 195,* 229–31, 270n21, 282n49; social cleavages in, 85–86; spatial control and, 177–78, *178,* 279–80n16; status under Jordan, 26, 242n9; strikes by civilians

Text: 11/14 Adobe Garamond
Display: Adobe Garamond Gill Sans
Compositor: BookMatters, Berkeley
Indexer: J. Naomi Linzer
Illustrator: Bill Nelson